Queenship in Britain 1660—1837

GW00645443

Published by Manchester University Press
Oxford Road, Manchester M13 9NR, UK
and Room 400, 175 Fifth Avenue, New York, NY 10010, USA
www.manchesteruniversitypress.co.uk

Distributed exclusively in the USA by
Palgrave, 175 Fifth Avenue, New York NY 10010, USA

Distributed exclusively in Canada by
UBC Press, University of British Columbia, 2029 West Mall,
Vancouver, BC, Canada V6T 1Z2

British Library Cataloguing-in-Publication Data
A catalogue record for this book is available from the British Library

Library of Congress Cataloging-in-Publication Data
A catalog record for this book is available from the Library of Congress

ISBN 10: 0 7190 5770 1

ISBN 13: 978 07190 5770 0

First published 2002 by Manchester University Press

First digital, on-demand edition produced by Lightning Source 2010

MANCHESTER
UNIVERSITY PRESS

Queenship in Britain

1660—1837

✠

Royal patronage, court culture and dynastic politics

edited by Clarissa Campbell Orr

Manchester University Press

Manchester and New York

distributed exclusively in the USA by Palgrave

Contents

List of illustrations

List of contributors

Veronica Baker-Smith took her B.A. in History from the University of Wales, Cardiff. She is the author of *A Life of Anne of Hanover, Princess Royal* (Leiden, E. J. Brill, 1995), and is preparing a collective biography of the daughters of George II.

Andrew Barclay is currently a Research Fellow with the 1640–1660 Section of the History of Parliament Trust, working on those MPs who sat for East Anglian constituencies. The subject of his 1993 Cambridge Ph.D. thesis was the court of James II, and he has since published several articles on various aspects of the Restoration court. He is the Treasurer for the Society for Court Studies.

Robert O. Bucholz is an Associate Professor of History at Loyola University of Chicago, where he has taught since 1988. He is the author of *The Augustan Court: Queen Anne and the Decline of Court Culture* (Stanford, Stanford University Press, 1993) and the co-compiler, with Sir John Sainty, KCB, of *Officials of the Royal Household 1660–1837*, 2 vols (London, Institute of Historical Research, 1997–98). He is the project director of the Database of Court Officers 1660–1901, and is currently at work on the first scholarly survey of the history of the court during the long eighteenth century.

John L. Bullion is Professor of History at the University of Missouri-Columbia. He is the author of *A Great and Necessary Measure: George Grenville and the Genesis of the Stamp Act, 1763–1765* (Columbia, University of Missouri Press, 1982) and several articles on British politics and imperial policy during the 1750s and 1760s. He is presently completing a memoir of his family's connections with Lyndon B. Johnson and a collection of essays on George III, the Earl of Bute, and the American Revolution.

Clarissa Campbell Orr is a Senior Lecturer at Anglia Polytechnic University, Cambridge. She has edited two collections of essays for Manchester University Press, *Women in the Victorian Art World* (1995) and *Wollstonecraft's Daughters: Womanhood in England and France 1780–1920* (1996). She is developing a collection of essays on *Queenship in Europe: 1660–1815*. In addition to Queen Charlotte's cultural milieu, she has worked/is working on the Genevan educator Albertine Necker de Saussure, on the French educator Mme de Genlis, on Agnes and Eliza Strickland, the Victorian biographers of English queens, and on Mary Shelley as a biographer of French writers.

Edward Corp is Professor of British History at the University of Toulouse. He organised and curated the exhibition on 'La Cour des Stuarts à Saint-Germain-en-Laye aux temps de Louis XIV' (Musée des Antiquités Nationales) and co-edited the catalogue (1992). He has edited three collections of essays, *L'Autre Exil: les Jacobites en France au début du XVIIIe siècle* (Montpellier, Presses du Languedoc, 1993), *The Stuart Court in Exile and the Jacobites* (with Eveline Cruickshanks, London, Hambledon Press, 1995), and *Lord Burlington: The Man and his Politics* (Lewiston NY, Edwin Mellen Press, 1998). He is editing a volume of essays, *The King over the Water: Portraits of the Stuart Courts in Exile*, based on the exhibition he curated at the National Portrait Gallery, Edinburgh, in 2001; working on a comprehensive study of the Stuart court at Saint-Germain for Cambridge University Press; and planning a biography of Catherine of Braganza.

Christine Gerrard is a Fellow and Tutor in English at Lady Margaret Hall, Oxford. She is the author of *The Patriot Opposition to Walpole: Poetry, Politics, and National Myth* (Oxford, Oxford University Press, 1994), and co-editor of *Eighteenth Century Poetry: An Annotated Anthology* (Oxford, Blackwell, 1999). She has written widely on eighteenth-century poetry and is currently completing a study of the eighteenth-century author and entrepreneur Aaron Hill.

Richard King gained his doctorate from Stanford University in 1992. He is Assistant Professor of Music at the University of Maryland, editor of the Newsletter of the American Handel Society, and Associate Director of the Maryland Handel Festival. His work on eighteenth-century music in general and Handel in particular has been published in *Early Music, The Haendel Jahrbuch, Journal of the American Musicological Society, Journal of the Royal Musical Association, The Musical Quarterly* and the *Tijdschrift van de Vereniging voor Nederlandse Muziekgeschiedenis*. He is a contributor for the revised *New Grove Dictionary of Music*, and is editing Handel's opera *Alessandro* for the *Hallische Haendel-Ausgabe*.

Joanna Marschner is Assistant Curator for the Historic Royal Palaces. She undertook research in 1994–96 towards the restoration of the Queen's Apartments at Hampton Court Palace, and in 1995–98 for the re-presentation of the State Apartments and Royal Ceremonial Dress Collection at Kensington Palace. Her publications include *Splendour at Court: Dressing for Royal Occasions since 1700* (with Nigel Arch, London, Unwin Hyman, 1987); 'A Taste for the Orient: Queen Mary II and the Porcelain Collection at Kensington Palace', *Arts of Asia* (January–February 1992); 'Baths and Bathing at the Early Georgian Court', *Furniture History*, 31 (1995); and 'Queen Mary as Collector', in *Kensington Palace and the Porcelain of Queen Mary II* (London, Christie's, 1996). She is continuing her research on Queen Caroline's patronage of Anspach for a Ph.D.

A. W. Purdue is Senior Lecturer in History at the Open University. His publications include *The Second World War* (Basingstoke, Macmillan, 1999) and *Merchants and Gentry in North East England 1650–1830: The Carrs and the Ellisons* (Sunderland, University of Sunderland Press, 1999). He has co-authored, with J. M. Golby, *The Civilization of the Crowd: Popular Culture in England 1750–1900* (London, Batsford, 1984), *The Making of the Modern Christmas* (London, Batsford, 1986) and *The Monarchy and the British People* (London, Batsford, 1988).

Editor's acknowledgements

This book has had a lengthy gestation and has been brought into being with the assistance of many valued friends and colleagues, as well as the faith and patience of the editorial team at Manchester University Press, and the meticulous enthusiasm of Jane Raistrick, the copy-editor. The first spark of life was probably a conversation with Tessa Murdoch of the Victoria and Albert Museum, held suitably enough a stone's throw from St James's Palace on the terrace of Spencer House, during a conference on London town houses in 1993. Several papers emphasised the importance of women as patrons, yet this was always an incidental remark; none sought to address directly the issue of women's patronage. We decided to organise a day-school at the Victoria and Albert Museum on the theme of 'The Lady Patrons', which took place in 1994.

As the idea for a book on women's patronage matured, it was evident that one concentrating on royal patronage and royal womanhood would be useful. Perhaps the roots of this book go back even further than that summer conference to my many visits as a child to Windsor and to Brighton Pavilion, and to the formative environment of my four years at Claremont School, in the knowledge that Princess Charlotte had died giving birth in a room I knew as my upper fifth form room. (Hung with Victorian blue silk walls in a chinoiserie pattern, my friends will also realise it had a lasting impact on my taste in interior decoration.) But more immediately, the founding of the Society for Court Studies in 1996 happened at a most propitious time for this book. In 1998, with the chapters already commissioned, the Society asked me to convene the programme for their annual conference for 1999, on the theme of 'The Role of the Consort'. This was a wonderful context for most of the contributors to give a version of their chapters, and to discuss the interplay of themes. It was very rewarding to meet several of my contributors in person for the first time, and put a face to a voice or an email correspondent. It added to our enjoyment that the venue for the second day of the conference, dealing with the Hanoverian court, was Kew, a setting known to all the royal women discussed. Special thanks are due to the Society, particularly to Robert Oresko, Simon Thurley, Philip Mansel, David Starkey and Helen Payne.

All my contributors have been wonderful from start to finish, and have met or even anticipated their deadlines; how many editors can say that? Of a gallant team, honourable mention must go to John Bullion, Christine Gerrard and Veronica Baker-Smith, who came on board last and worked superbly to very tight timing. I was sorry to lose some potential contributors as other commitments took precedence, but delighted to make new friends who took the project to heart. My thanks go to Susan Jenkins, Elaine Chalus, Kim Reynolds and Brendan Simms, who were all early supporters of the book, and to Ruth Smith for putting me first in touch with Christine Gerrard, and then with Jane Clark and the Handel network, which brought in Richard King.

At work, my appreciation goes to John Pollard for his unstinting support of his colleagues' research; to Theo Sculte, Georgina Marshall and Glenn Jobson for technical assistance as emails with attachments whizzed to and fro over the Atlantic and down the road and needed to be translated into a form of life low enough for my antique computer to read; and to Rohan McWilliam for gallantly shouldering some of my administrative burdens in lieu of my being given sabbatical leave, which made the final editing possible alongside teaching. Generous financial assistance for the reproduction of illustrations and compiling of the index was also given from the slender research budget of the History Department at Anglia Polytechnic University, and is gratefully acknowledged.

Among the treasured friends who support my endeavours, I must single out for mention Helen and Charles Smart for accommodation during my visits to the Windsor Royal Archives, James Raven for his enthusiasm for the book and for help with visiting Stanton Harcourt, and Barbara Beard for her frequent hospitality in London. Renovating my house (fortunately when I was not yet residing in it) from attic to cellars started in parallel with the last months of the book project, and I thank my architect, Rosalind Bird, for keeping that on steady course with her terrific eye for detail, and Tim Saunders and his team for their careful craftsmanship in breathing new life into a neglected gem. If the architecture and finished quality of this book are in any way akin to their inspiring work, which coexisted so happily with time spent in front of the screen, the book will be well worth a reader's visit. And a special mention to Phil Cooper, too, for taking time out (suitably enough) from his work advising Diane Haigh and others on the structure of the Queen's House, Greenwich, to advise on how to brace the structure of my modest cottage and give me the confidence to go ahead with the job.

My house needed steel supports and similarly the preparation of this book, like all books perhaps, required nerves of steel at times. Ian and Felicia Gordon diverted the editor with supper and visits to the movies in the last six months of the project, while Jane Dickenson-Scott gave moral support at crucial moments. Nor could the composition of the introduction have taken place without the music of Sibelius to listen to, while Pushkin and Petrushka sat and purred approvingly on piles of paper, but tactfully kept their paws off the keyboard.

My mother, Sylvia Stephens Campbell, would have been so thrilled to see the completion of this particular book, and her vivid sense of living through historical time, and her delight in the homes and gardens of the past, were vital formative influences on me. I dedicate this book to her, as a celebration of her life well-lived.

Introduction

Court studies, gender and women's history, 1660–1837

Clarissa Campbell Orr

THE CHAPTERS in this book are pathbreaking attempts to unite court studies with women's history. They are pioneering for two reasons. First, most historians of women during the eighteenth century have focused on describing and understanding the lives of the majority of women, who were in the lower and middling social ranks. Second, there have been only a few studies of the British court in this period. This introduction will therefore endeavour to provide an outline of how to approach the question of the royal court of the later Stuarts and the Hanoverians, and the role of women, specifically royal women, within it. On the face of it, royal women represent an extreme case of 'relational' women, whose importance is determined by being the daughter, wife or mother of a royal man. But were women as 'incorporated' as this implies? Did their cultural patronage complement, contrast or conflict with that of their husbands? And even if they accepted that their chief role was to produce legitimate offspring and be as supportive of their husbands as possible, how did they actually accomplish what was a very complex task? As these chapters show, individual women managed a similar role very differently, depending on their education, personality, circumstance, and evolving relationship with the men in question. They both contended with and conformed to the roles expected of women in their own lifetimes, and subsequent historical assessment has been invariably filtered through the preconceptions and prejudices of historians.

Changing times: why 1660–1837?

The chronological boundaries of this book have been determined by the perspectives of court history and chime with current interdisciplinary exploration of British society and culture 'from Restoration to Reform'. Between 1660 and 1837 the British monarchy changed from being a composite monarchy ruling three kingdoms, typical of the dynastic unions of baroque Europe, to a parliamentary monarchy ruling over the United Kingdom of Great Britain.[1] The nature of the restored monarchy of 1660 and the degree to which it was 'absolute' or was intended by Charles II or later James II to become so have been variously interpreted, as has the significance of the 1688 Glorious Revolution. It established that monarchs could neither make nor unmake law without Parliament's consent: in this sense the monarchy became parliamentary rather than personal. But considerable executive initiative remained to a monarch, particularly in the sphere of patronage and appointments, and it was not until Victoria's reign that something like constitutional monarchy emerged. What is definite about the revolution of 1688 is the dynastic commitment to Protestantism, outlawing a monarch or a consort from being Roman Catholic. Monarchs in 1660 touched for the king's evil, and the outcome of the Glorious Revolution was interpreted in providential terms, but by 1837 the monarch was desacralised, and simply attempted to encourage philanthropy and to project an image of pious respectability characteristic of the middling ranks of society. Though Catholic Emancipation took place in 1828, the monarchy remained identified with Anglican Protestantism.[2]

Many historians use the term 'the long eighteenth century' to cover the period from the Restoration to the Reform Act of 1832, although not all would agree to this implied caesura in the middle of the seventeenth century. Nevertheless from the perspective of court history there is a logic to considering these particular starting and end dates. Whatever Charles II's monarchy was, it was not a personal monarchy in quite the way his father's and grandfather's had been. His reign showed that it would be less feasible for a monarch to manage for any length of time without Parliament, even if the ground rules for the monarch's relationship with Parliament were not yet clear, and both Charles and his brother aimed to control parliaments by 'packing' (i.e. influencing) them. After 1688 there was always an annual session of Parliament, which forced monarchs, extremely reluctantly in the case of William III, to continue developing the ground rules for working in conjunction with Parliament.

One of the principal factors that made Charles II's relationship with Parliament so difficult was the succession question: Catherine of Braganza's failure to produce an heir precipitated the politics of exclusion, that is the attempt to exclude Charles's openly Catholic brother, James, Duke of York, from the throne, and either force the King to divorce the childless Catherine and remarry, or legitimate one of his sons, the Protestant Duke of Monmouth. Thus, almost as soon as the monarchy was restored, its very nature became more problematic because for the first time a Stuart consort was infertile. These succession issues differentiate Charles's monarchy from the quasi-monarchy of Cromwell's Protectorate, and suggest that whatever the continuities between the interregnum and the return of kings in terms of the style and structure of government, 1660 is still a significant starting point for assessing the role of royal women.[3]

Why 1837? The obvious answer is the accession of Queen Victoria. But more significantly, during William IV's reign (1832–37) a decisive shift had taken place from parliamentary monarchy toward constitutional monarchy. The passage of the Reform Act in 1832 inaugurated a change in the nature of monarchy after which it became clear that the executive powers of a monarch in relation to Parliament were ever more limited. Here again the consort's role became important: not because, coincidentally like Catherine of Braganza, Queen Adelaide failed to provide heirs, but because she was seen as opposing this reform. The nature of her influence is here re-examined in Purdue's chapter on this much-neglected consort. However William IV's co-operation with his ministers over parliamentary reform, including his willingness to create enough peers to secure a majority in the Lords if necessary, marks a decisive shift toward constitutional monarchy. The Bedchamber crisis of 1839, when Queen Victoria refused to change her Whig Ladies in Waiting after her Whig ministry fell, shows that the new Queen did not accept a more limited, constitutional role easily. But it is indisputable that the 1832 Reform Act did alter the character of parliamentary politics and facilitate further changes: the two successive parliamentary reform acts of 1867 and 1884 were to create a masculine democratic parliamentary political culture, with women's enfranchisement delayed until 1919. The monarchy weathered both unpopularity and popularity as the political culture changed around it, with popular loyalism routing republican sentiment by the time of Victoria's Jubilees.

Even for post-Whig historians, then, the period 1660–1837 contains an important narrative about the structure of politics and the changing balance of power between monarchy and Parliament. All the consorts in this book had political parts to play. We should not, however, understand politics as narrowly focused on personalities (largely male), structures, and relationships at St James's, Whitehall and Westminster. As well as a narrative about the emergence of constitutional monarchy, this could also be characterised as a transition from a masculinised monarchy, where a king still acted as a warrior, even in Queen Anne's case, as an 'amazon', to a feminised role, suited to actual women as well as men, in which 'feminine' values associated with philanthropy moved to the forefront.[4] Yet the role of consorts (including the underrated George of Denmark, husband to Queen Anne) is barely mentioned in this narrative, except in connection with the development of the 'welfare' monarchy. As argued by Frank Prochaska, the later Hanoverians inaugurated the identification of the monarchy with the voluntary organisations of civil society, particularly its charitable enterprises, and so created a shift in the role of monarchy whereby it could stand above parliamentary conflict as the patron of good causes. In this perspective, Charlotte of Meckenburg-Strelitz and Adelaide of Saxe-Meiningen contributed substantially to this shift.[5] Aside from granting them their part in philanthropy, the role of the consort has not been given any sustained attention. Only the uncrowned Queen Caroline of Brunswick has received any recent re-consideration – and because of the wealth of recent discussion about her, she is excluded from this collection.

Even historians who accept this time-frame of Restoration to Reform disagree as to whether the British state, as distinct from the monarchy, was more like *ancien régime* continental monarchical realms, or can best be described in terms of its fiscal-military efficiency, strong parliamentary government, and similarity to the Dutch Republic.[6] Further, in its social composition, should eighteenth-century Britain be described primarily as the 'aristocratic century' of John Cannon (albeit one barely peopled by women in his and other accounts of aristocratic culture) or one typified by its 'polite and commercial' people, who are more commonly perceived, by historians emphasising this interpretation, as belonging to both sexes?[7] Royal women could either help or hinder the court's appeal to the political nation and the population at large; they were crucial in managing the elite through social functions and personal connections. They could help establish the character of the monarchy as haughty or accessible.

What exactly is court culture? How does it relate to the culture of the aristocracy at large? How does either royal or aristocratic patronage fit into a world of consumer society, with a hugely expanded market for books, magazines, prints and caricatures, for the visual and decorative arts and antiquities, and for the commercialised entertainment of theatres and pleasure gardens?[8] As this volume will demonstrate, royal patronage had a distinctive character, especially in art, architecture and music, even though it cannot be discussed in isolation from the trends developing in parallel among the aristocracy. For some queens – Mary of Modena, Mary II – it reinforced a programme they shared with their husbands. For other royal women – Catherine of Braganza, Anne of Hanover, Princess Royal – it helped define a distinct identity in competition with mistresses or siblings. A queen with the talent and education of Caroline Anspach could make a huge impact both as Princess of Wales and as Queen by a deliberate cultural programme which demonstrated how the Hanoverians were assimilating to British traditions. Her daughters had limited choices as husbands but were never passive dynastic pawns in the chess-board of international diplomacy. For conscientious consorts like Charlotte of Mecklenburg-Strelitz, scientific patronage opened up a private space in the midst of public duties. In the case of a queen regnant, Anne, and a queen mother, Augusta of Saxe-Gotha, they played their role so well that their very success has obscured their skill in imbibing the rules of royal womanhood, yet by contrast the case of Queen Adelaide shows that even a proverbially respectable consort could so misread the political game as to be accused of adultery.

The wider cultural shifts taking place in this period, to which court culture contributed and by which it was influenced, include the superseding of baroque culture by the Enlightenment, with its interest in rational inquiry and its critique of divine right as a basis for political authority, its increasing emphasis on the principle of religious toleration, and – though here again there is disagreement – a trend toward secularisation, or it least laicisation. The shift away from divine right monarchy was extremely vexed, and the disputed legitimacy of the Glorious Revolution challenged Anglican orthodoxy to redefine itself. Royal women who not only projected an atmosphere of piety and morality but were ready to identify themselves clearly with the Church of England could therefore help establish the dynastic changes. Queen Caroline's refusal to marry a Catholic Habsburg, her efforts to establish an English royal genealogy, and the pressure put on her daughter-in-law Augusta to renounce the Lutheran church, are significant contributions to stabilising the Hanoverians, who until the accession of 1760 could not be sure that Jacobitism had been successfully defeated, culturally and ideologically as well as politically and militarily.[9]

In architecture, the baroque was succeeded by Palladianism and then neo-classicism by way of diversions into rococo, chinoiserie and Gothic, and the creation of a distinctive style of landscape garden was to prove one of England's signal contributions to European culture. As patrons of architecture and garden design, the monarchy retained a significant role, though often building less than it wished. In the visual arts, both a Scottish and English native school developed, with special strengths in portraiture, whose stars such as Allan Ramsay, Thomas Gainsborough and Joshua Reynolds received royal commissions in the second half of the century, from both king and queen. Architects and artists, but not, yet, authors, performers and composers, were the recipients of knighthoods bestowed by the crown, which remained an important focus of artistic and architectural patronage. The period began with very little national 'cultural infrastructure'[10] other than the Royal Society, but at its end a Royal Academy, a Royal Society of Arts, a Royal Society of Authors and a Royal Literary Fund had all been founded, and there was a growing pride in the nation's compositional talent and its musical canon – especially in the works of Handel, teacher of George II's daughters and beneficiary of the patronage of the eldest, Anne, as Richard King's chapter demonstrates.[11]

Coexisting with these movements was the cult of sensibility and the religious revivalism of Methodism and Evangelicalism, while the British fight against France and the Napoleonic Wars saw Britain in the throes of a many-sided romanticism that included neo-chivalry and the sentimentalisation of the Scottish and Irish pasts of the Celtic kingdoms. All of these movements included loyalist sentiment to the principle of monarchy – romanticism was not exclusively republican – in which queens figured as important exemplars of womanhood.[12]

The question of the relationship of court culture to these wider cultural shifts has not yet been fully evaluated. Indisputably, there was a shift from the Restoration court, when royal patronage and social fashion were tightly connected, to the Hanoverian period, where court culture coexisted with and was sometimes eclipsed by the commercialisation of culture, and the court seemed dowdy rather than glamorous. But this editor would argue that the court has been dismissed too quickly, and that the ways in which it accommodated itself to new contexts of patronage in a commercial and more plural culture is itself an important and neglected question. Moreover, the long reign of George II is significantly under-examined; the five chapters here on the wife, daughters and daughters-in-law of this king should contribute significantly to a much-needed reassessment of the middle of the eighteenth century, which would bridge the decline in court culture first discerned by Robert Bucholz in his study of Anne's reign, and the emergent popularity of monarchy in the later reign of George III, surveyed by Marilyn Morris and Linda Colley.

Like that of monarchy, the existing political and cultural narrative is still only fitfully peopled by women, except in the case of women and writing, and women artists.[13] In exploring royal women's patronage of art, architecture, music, science, and patterns of collecting, this volume helps to reinscribe women into cultural history. It is historians of the changing economy and the world of work who have done most so far to integrate women into the picture and to examine the impact of gendered role prescriptions.[14] Studies of British womanhood have, with valuable exceptions, discussed below, tended to focus on women of middling or lower social rank;[15] aside from the attention given to Caroline of Brunswick, feminist historians have yet to revisit the royal family and are only just starting on the aristocracy.[16] Yet much is to be gained for women's history and feminist history by looking at women at the social apex, including their roles, representations and symbolic importance for other men and women. Royal women were at the centre of the 'celebrity culture' of this period. They could influence taste, fashion, social customs and moral values. And from Mary Astell to Mary Wollstonecraft, the early roots of English feminism can be found in critiques of court society. Some further clarification of terms and concepts deployed in this book is therefore in order, before discussing the relationship between court studies and women's history.

How British a monarchy?

The accession of James VI of Scotland to the throne of England and Ireland in 1603 created a personal union of three crowns under an Anglo-Scottish dynasty: a British monarchy insofar as the ruler ruled three kingdoms, but not yet a British state.[17] England and Ireland were now ruled by a Scotsman, whose mother Mary had been a French consort. James had wide international horizons and took an active interest in fostering the reunification of the Christian churches.[18] His wife Anne was a Danish princess who converted to Catholicism.[19] The marriage of their daughter Elizabeth to the Elector Palatine and the couple's ill-fated election to the Bohemian throne, which precipitated the Thirty Years War in central Europe, prompted English, Scottish and continental Protestants to look, ultimately in vain, to James as a leader. James hoped to be a mediator in the religious conflicts, and instead of military partisanship worked for alignment (and diplomatic influence over the Palatine problem) with either of the most important continental dynasties, both of which were Catholic: the Bourbons or the Habsburgs. As royal marriages were a tool of foreign policy, he planned his heir's marriage accordingly.

Instead of the first choice, the Spanish infanta, Charles I married Henrietta Maria, daughter of the Bourbon Henri IV.[20] But although the

Spanish match proved abortive, the future Charles I's visit to one of the greatest European courts in Madrid had a lasting impact on him. The fact that the Anglo-Scottish James could even attempt to marry his heir into either of the premier dynasties showed how much clout now accrued to the Stuarts – though the failure of that ambition showed that the Stuarts were not yet as significant as they wanted to be. The marriage was a fulfilment of suggestions made fifty years before for an Anglo-French alliance, centred on Elizabeth I and possible marriages with the sons of Catherine de Medici, the French Queen Mother. It was this French orientation, and all the religious and cultural associations it brought with it, which counteracted alternative ideas for a Spanish alliance. The choice of one particular foreign-born consort always needs to be understood as only one of a range of possible alternatives, with all of their differing political, cultural and religious consequences.

One of the persistent themes of this study of queenship is thus the contribution made by foreign-born queens to the cosmopolitanism of the British court and its Anglo-Scottish and Anglo-Hanoverian dynasties. All the Stuart monarchs and their consorts were familiar with courts outside Britain; French, Spanish, Flemish, Dutch and Italian influences were evident in court culture throughout the century. All the Hanoverians had German consorts, kept a sense of their German roots, and followed patterns of dynastic intermarriage established before they also acquired the British crown, which were sometimes in tension with this, as Baker-Smith's chapter on the marriage choices of George II's daughters amply demonstrates.

In an influential article heralding the theme of his book, *England's Troubles: Seventeenth-Century English Political Instability in European Context*,[21] Jonathan Scott urges historians to reconceptualise 'England's troubles' in the seventeenth century as a part of the European conflict over popery and arbitrary government commencing with the Thirty Years War (1618–48), with its English parallel in the breakdown of Charles I's government, continuing with the Exclusion Crisis (1679–83) and concluding with the Glorious Revolution (1688). While he might demur at attributing too much significance to the 1660 Restoration as a break within the century, one way to follow this counsel is to take into account the degree to which foreign, Catholic consorts contributed to the English anxiety that popery and absolutism were sweeping all before them. The first four Stuart consorts were all Catholic, and all controversial. As Edward Corp shows (Chapter 1), it was Catherine of Braganza's misfortune to marry into the monarchy at a time when anti-Catholic hysteria had never been more acute, while Mary of Modena's

Catholicism, demonstrated by Andrew Barclay to be relatively tolerant and consonant with Stuart tradition (Chapter 2), nevertheless helped to precipitate her deposition from the throne. Although the 1688 Glorious Revolution began the settlement of these vexed questions by insisting that monarchs and their spouses be Protestant, until the end of the War of Spanish Succession in 1713, when Louis XIV again accepted the Protestant character of the monarchy, and the defeat of the Jacobite rebellion of 1715, the settlement was precarious. Jacobitism attracted sympathisers up to the end of George II's reign.

The court culture of the early Stuarts with its international dimensions has been better studied than that of Charles II and James II. Some brief discussion of it is essential, since its Catholicism, personified by Henrietta Maria, Charles I's queen, prefigured the later Stuart panics against 'popery', while its cultural character became a benchmark for what royal patronage could achieve long after the Restoration. The myth of a halcyon reign of peace and harmony lingered even among Cromwell's supporters.[22] Charles I was the most important royal connoisseur before George IV: Joanna Marschner shows how Caroline of Anspach, wife of George II, worked hard to recover and redisplay what was left of his art collection, much of which had been dispersed by the Cromwellian regime (Chapter 4). Studies of this culture have also included some evaluation of the role of queens, which points the way forward for further enquiry into the nature of queenship.[23]

Erica Veevers, for example, has shown how Henrietta Maria, wife of Charles I and mother of Charles II and James II, brought with her a particularly French version of *préciosité*, or learned female intellectualism, which celebrated the ideal of the *honnête femme*.[24] This woman was the creator of social harmony, symbolised by both a loving marriage and the exercise of a wider circle of influence whose purpose was to reconcile disparate elements. Following this model, Henrietta's ideals of love drew on Renaissance Platonism, but unlike the witty and sophisticated woman of the salons, who perpetuated platonic traditions and was the object of an unconsummated adoration, the *honnête femme* had a less intellectual approach, idealising domestic harmony and the fulfilment of love within marriage. Married love was seen as an ennobling force that encouraged virtue at court, and within society, and led the soul to God. A gentle kind of feminism was a part of this outlook: women's essentially feminine qualities needed to be respected, their capacity for friendship and honour between themselves acknowledged, and their role as moral and intellectual beings, who were not exclusively preoccupied with sexual matters, recognised. As we shall see, subsequent consorts were associated in some degree with feminism, especially the kind that helped make intellectual interests acceptable in a woman.

There was also a Catholic dimension to Henrietta's ideals; indeed, as confessional allegiances were more significant than precise national origins throughout the seventeenth century, the religious dimension is of the essence. Henrietta Maria was a god-daughter of Pope Urban VIII and her marriage to Charles I was regarded by both the Papal and French courts as a means toward the conversion of Charles and of England. Henrietta had however been trained in the moderate school of Devout Humanism and her strategy was to be as tactful and conciliatory as possible. She and her advisers envisaged an accommodation between Anglicanism and this moderate Catholicism which would result in a religious culture midway between the extremes of militant Jesuits and doctrinaire Puritans. Veevers's study shows that Henrietta's courtly entertainments, both pastoral dramas and masques, projected these ideals of love, of feminism and of religion. It is a model of how exploration of the consort's cultural patronage, recreations and personal associations can lead directly to an improved understanding of the consort's role in the wider political, diplomatic and international context.[25]

The Restoration court did not start from scratch; it intended to suggest revival and continuity. Scott argues the Restoration generation was 'susceptible to nostalgia on the one hand and nightmares on the other', and that the anxieties generated by memories of the civil war predominated over the nostalgia.[26] But Charles II did not revive his father's full cultural programme; matters evolved in rather an *ad hoc* fashion; and financial straits soon led him to discontinue the revived Stuart practice of providing daily fare for all the court and its servants and later to curtail his ambitious building schemes. It was James rather than Charles who really got to grips with financing the royal household; Charles felt too great an obligation to please faithful Royalist exiles and loyal servants of his father to make substantial cuts.

The court culture of Charles II and James II is only now beginning to receive the consistent interdisciplinary attention that has been devoted to their parents and Stuart grandparents, or that Robert Bucholz has given to the last Stuart Queen Anne. The essays devoted to Charles II's court in Eveline Cruikshank's collection, *The Stuart Courts*, constitute a decisive step forward. In addition, biographies of the two kings discuss the court context in some respects, and an indispensable foundation from which such a proper assessment could properly emerge has been laid by Andrew Barclay's work on James II's court, followed by Robert Bucholz in his sketch of the reigns before Anne, and in his introduction to the prosopography of royal household officials compiled jointly with Sir John Sainty. Alan Marshall's primer appeared as this collection was going to press, and should prompt students to consider politics as a dynamic interplay between the royal court and Westminster, and to probe the world-view of court government.[27]

Thus the chapters here on Catherine of Braganza and Mary of Modena are important pioneering contributions towards a fuller exploration of Restoration court culture. Together with Frances Harris's biography of Sarah Churchill, Duchess of Marlborough, which sheds such a penetrating light on the nature of aristocratic and gentry women in relation to courtly politics, these chapters help to problematise and evaluate the role of royal women in the Restoration. Although Marshall does consider the role of the female politician, his remarks are mostly concentrated on the relationship between the royal mistress and political faction, or the family links which helped create aristocratic clienteles. This is welcome recognition for significant themes, but nevertheless he does not confront fully the additional fact that women had salaried positions in the royal household and that, effectively, court service enabled women to have public careers, as discussed below, in addition to deriving influence from their 'relational' character.[28]

Both chapters emphasise the cosmopolitan and confessional dimension to Catherine and Mary's role as queens. Catherine's advocacy of Italian music and art was, Edward Corp shows, a facet of her struggle to obtain a cultural identity that distinguished her and her circle from the humiliatingly fecund mistresses of her husband, the Duchesses of Cleveland and of Portsmouth, both of whom were Catholic and pro-French. Catherine thereby aligned herself with her young Italian sister-in-law. Naturally Catherine's household also enabled the English to further their understanding of Portuguese literature, history and customs, including the strange practice of drinking tea recreationally instead of medicinally, which came to be especially associated with female sociability. Andrew Barclay's chapter on Mary of Modena shows that although Catholic, her Catholicism was of the kind that accorded well with English royal Catholicism. But however moderate her faith was, she could not overcome the almost visceral fear of 'popery' which gripped the nation, intensified by the apparent triumph of Counter-Reformation monarchies in France and central Europe. Barclay's exploration of the Italian artists in court circles during her reign corrects the mistaken view of late Stuart court culture being mainly indebted to French exemplars. He also reminds us of the presence of various northern European artists. At the same time, he shows the continuum between royal and aristocratic patronage, a theme to which Campbell Orr's chapter on Queen Charlotte returns, and of the danger of exaggerating the royal court's role in patronage. In concluding that Mary was probably most successful as an exiled queen, he also makes a telling point about the cosmopolitanism of the British monarchy: that the Jacobite alternative court was always situated on the Continent – in Saint-Germain, near Paris, in Lorraine, and in Rome.[29]

After this sequence of foreign and Catholic consorts, Mary and Anne were welcomed as English and Protestant. Just as the queens consort Catherine and Mary were inevitably responsible for reinforcing popular prejudice against 'popery', so the queens regnant Mary II and Anne were crucial in establishing the Protestant character of the monarchy. Mary II gained popularity while still Princess of Orange for refusing her father's invitation to consider the merits of Catholicism, and for formulating her own theological arguments in reply to him, based on her personal reading.[30] But although safely Protestant, Mary II brought continental influences to bear in her patronage when she and her husband came to the throne, with her Dutch tastes in garden design, botany and architecture.

Her patronage and interests received extensive attention on the occasion of the tercentenary of the Glorious Revolution and therefore receive no separate treatment here. Her tastes derived from an international baroque style drawing strongly on French components, and looking back to the golden age of Caroline court culture. As Barclay suggests, it was William III who was the real francophile in artistic matters. The great grandson of Henri IV of France, through his mother, the Stuart princess Mary, and her mother, Henrietta Maria, he adopted Henri's emblem of Hercules, in contrast to his antagonist Louis XIV's identification with Apollo. Many of the superb craftsmen who worked for the royal couple at Hampton Court Palace and Kensington, such as Daniel Marot, Gerrit Jensen and Jean Tijou, were of Huguenot extraction. Their expulsion from France in 1685 had helped reinforce William of Orange's role as a Protestant champion, orchestrating an alliance against Louis XIV.[31]

Mary's patronage is therefore also part of the wider story of the Huguenots in Britain, who, as Barclay reminds us, had also been welcome to James II, who wanted toleration for dissenters in order to facilitate the reintegration of Catholics, too, into public life.[32] In addition, like

Catherine before her, Mary was a connoisseur of the luxury goods produced by seventeenth-century commercial expansion. Mary's role as a
collector of Chinese porcelain and other oriental decorative objects,
such as lacquer screens, imported by the Dutch, and the emulation she
inspired, has been described as 'her most outstanding contribution to
the artistic life of the nation'.[33]

Of the Stuarts, only Anne was less of a traveller, though her year at
Louis XIV's court as a small girl left her with lasting fluency in French.
But her strategy as a queen was to emphasise her Englishness. Her Danish husband Prince George has been wholly neglected, yet he was a
tactful consort who did not block the military eminence of John Churchill, Duke of Marlborough: a different male consort might have resented
another man supplying the masculine warrior role a reigning queen could
not sustain. George adapted to British life as a peer and naval officer,
and added weight to the Protestant alignment of the last Stuarts in his
patronage of Pietists from Halle for his Lutheran chapel at St James's.
Pietism, a strand within Lutheranism emphasising inward contemplation
and practical works, sat well with the emphasis within early eighteenth-
century Anglicanism on moral and humanitarian responsibilities rather
than doctrinal disputes. Thus Anne's consort did not seem intrusively
foreign.[34]

As Bucholz shows (Chapter 3), during a major continental war, her
identification with Englishness was one of Anne's greatest strengths,
along with her Protestantism, especially while rumours existed that
she was guilty of having her Catholic half-brother excluded from the
throne. Her reign also saw change in the nature of the British state: the
union with Scotland (1707) created the kingdom of Great Britain. It was
no longer a multiple monarchy formed from a union of crowns, but a
constitutional union. Moreover, since Anne's longest surviving child
died in 1701, her reign heralded further dynastic change which reinforced the cosmopolitanism of the British court. The Scottish Stuarts,
having anglicised themselves and excluded their Catholic branch, were
now succeeded by the Guelf Electors of Hanover.[35]

The sequence of chapters on Hanoverian queenship amply demonstrates that the eighteenth-century British court cannot adequately be
understood in isolation from the Continent.[36] Sophia of Hanover, the
matriarch of the Hanoverian line, granddaughter of James I, and daughter
of the exiled Elector of the Palatine and failed King of Bohemia, came
from a family whose marriage alliances on the Protestant side were with
other members of the House of Brunswick, with the Houses of Hesse, of
Orange (the Netherlands), of Hohernzollern (Prussia), and of Oldenburg

(Denmark). Her niece, Liselotte of the Palatinate, was married to Louis XIV's brother, Philippe I of Orléans, and their daughter was Duchess of Lorraine (then a French-speaking part of the Holy Roman Empire, with close links to the Habsburg Emperor). Liselotte's stepchildren by Philippe's first wife, Henrietta Anne, the sister of Charles II and James I, were Marie Luise, who became Queen of Spain, and Anne-Marie, Duchess then Queen of Savoy. Other Catholic Hanoverians were married into the House of Habsburg, and the Italian Houses of Este (Modena) and Gonzaga (Mantua). As to the rival Catholic Stuarts, James the Old Pretender, Queen Anne's half-brother, married Maria Clementina Sobieska, granddaughter of Jan Sobieski, King of Poland; one of Anne's aunts had married the Holy Roman Emperor Leopold I, and another the Elector of Bavaria. By 1714 Britain had a monarchy whose dynastic connections, if both Protestant and Catholic members are included, stretched throughout the courts of Europe, whose reach was not repeated until the reign of Queen Victoria.[37]

This interlinked dynastic network is especially relevant to the formative influences on Caroline of Anspach, wife of George II. As Joanna Marschner shows (Chapter 4), she was a scholar, collector and connoisseur in the Continental tradition as it evolved during the Renaissance. Her childhood and youth were spent at the court of Dresden in Saxony, with its fabulous wealth of treasures in the 'Green Vault', and in Berlin, where Sophie Charlotte, daughter of Sophia of Hanover and so George I's sister, was Queen. (The Hanover/Hohernzollern connection was repeated in the next generation when Sophia Dorothea of Hanover, sister of George II, was married to Frederick William I of Brandenberg Prussia.) Marschner shows how Caroline put what she had learned from the collecting practices of German princely courts, into creating an English pedigree for the monarchy which transcended recent dynastic adjustments.

Instead of thinking about a British monarchy, this book suggests that after 1714 we should think in terms of an Anglo-Hanoverian monarchy. But although, as Linda Colley has shown so eloquently, it was in the period 1707–1832 that a British state (as distinct from a British monarchy) developed following the formal union of England first with Scotland and then in 1800 with Ireland, the Hanoverians paid little attention to Scotland or Ireland in projecting their monarchical image.[38] (The sole exception was George IV and his coronation as King of Scotland, with ceremonies choreographed by Walter Scott.) However, the principality of Wales played a role in establishing the character of the 'reversionary interest', that is to say, the court of the heir to the

Anglo-Hanoverian monarch, who bore the title Prince of Wales.[39] Once queen, Caroline may have emphasised the monarchy's broadly *British* basis, but Christine Gerrard shows (Chapter 5) that before her accession, in her courting of popularity to distance herself and her husband from the court of George I, Caroline underlined her new identity as a Princess of *Wales*. The coincidence that her birthday happened to be St David's day, 1 March, was put to good use, although the identification with Welshness almost certainly never extended to an active interest in the welfare of the Welsh people. Augusta, Princess of Wales, also joined with her husband Frederick in courting the opposition, but she had to learn a lot more than Caroline about English and British ways: John Bullion shows (Chapter 8) that her mother had assumed the family her daughter was joining had retained an exclusively German identity and tongue.

Richard King's contribution (Chapter 6) underlines the international character of the Anglo-Hanoverians through an examination of the musical and artistic patronage of Anne, Princess Royal, eldest daughter of George II. Here is the reverse of a foreign queen consort's patronage enriching the Court of St James; instead we can see how a princess, reared in Hanover and England, the pupil of Handel, was able while Princess Royal to finance Italian opera in London, and then as a Dutch princess to use her dowry to enhance the little court at Leeuwarden, making it one of the premier musical centres of Europe. There were frequent exchanges between it and her cousin Frederick II, King of Brandenburg-Prussia, on musical matters, and touchingly Handel made it his base for his final visit to the Continent.

The cosmopolitan character of the monarchy continued into George III's reign, a period usually associated with a more British flavour, under a monarch who never went to Hanover. Nonetheless, the editor's chapter on Charlotte of Mecklenburg-Strelitz (Chapter 9) argues that she occupied a position as figurehead of a Christian Enlightenment, whose preoccupations were similar to Protestant centres in Germany, the Netherlands or Switzerland: to defend Christianity and ethics from the undermining influences of Deism and materialism. It also explores the complex relationship she and several of her courtiers and court intellectuals had with that scourge of courtly artificiality, and darling of the French grand salonières, Jean-Jacques Rousseau.

Finally A. W. Purdue (Chapter 10) shows how Adelaide of Saxe-Meiningen brought with her not so much the cultural preoccupations of her native principality, but its liberal piety and its political nightmares. Unlike Britain, her homeland had been occupied and mediatised by Napoleon; a true child of legitimist, Restoration Europe, Adelaide genuinely feared that the boisterous crowds in London and Westminster who represented the voice of the 'nation out of doors', i.e. outside the Houses of Parliament, presaged a revolution, and that her fate could resemble Marie Antoinette's. The same crowd imagined that in her alleged hostility to the Reform Act, she would induce William to use his possession of Hanover as a base for counter-revolution. Although Adelaide's *gemütlich* style adapted well to early nineteenth-century notions of respectability, her political attitudes did not.

Europe was now becoming a collection of nation-states; the larger German principalities, including Hanover, together with Belgium and Holland were raised to monarchical status.[40] Although the Habsburgs remained exemplars of a pre-Revolutionary world of multiple monarchies and dynastic unions, the trend was toward national unification and self-determination. The Anglo-Hanoverian character of the British monarchy was changing; with the accession of Queen Victoria, and her marriage to her cousin, Albert of Saxe-Coburg Gotha, the practice of a German consort continued, but the dynastic link with Hanover was broken, since the Salic Law prohibited female inheritance there. The account of an Anglo-Hanoverian monarchy in this volume therefore fittingly concludes with William and Adelaide.[41]

Queens, multiple roles and dynastic politics

Whether a queen was marrying in the quasi-absolutist political culture of Charles II and James II or the emergent parliamentary monarchy of Hanoverian Britain, she had to learn to become English or British. She became a figure represented in the literary and visual culture of the age, as well as an actress on the political stage. Many of the contributors show how much was demanded, often of very young women with little or no formal education or experience of the world, once they married into the British monarchy. To succeed, they had to be able to adapt quickly, to learn a new language both literally and metaphorically. They had to be discreet and tactful, and to adjust to a marriage partner not of their choice, in many cases to men many years their senior with either a marriage or a succession of mistresses behind them. If they were lucky, the mistresses would all be in the past and not the present tense, and their husbands would not pass on any sexually transmitted diseases to them. To ensure their sexual purity as fit mothers of the heir, they had to be virgins, so this arranged marriage was also the first sexual experience of their lives. They sometimes had to contend with parents-in-law who were also the ruling king and queen. As well as learning to be wives, they were also expected to be mothers as soon as possible. Should they survive their husbands before their sons were of age, they might have to act as regents. Whatever they did, they would be under constant scrutiny from the multiple groupings within the court itself, from Parliament, which determined their financial settlements and their powers if they were appointed regents, and from the press of the day, whose curiosity was every bit as prurient and scandal-mongering as ours, and whose caricaturists were permitted – or got away with – a degree of sexual innuendo and scatological humour our own supposedly more tolerant age finds unacceptable. These multiple roles could produce impossibly difficult conflicts; striking a wrong note could risk alienating the one person they needed most as an ally, their husband. Their success or failure in their allotted roles could make a real difference to the politics of dynastic continuance. Yet many of these young women coped extraordinarily well with these exigencies. The learning curve was steep, but they usually surmounted it. Nevertheless their personal adroitness, adaptability and intelligence were consistently underestimated at the time, and subsequently by historians. Many of the chapters in this book break new ground in offering a reassessment.

One queen needing new and sensitive reassessment is Catherine of Braganza, whose adaptation to life in the Restoration court of Charles II was probably the most gruelling faced by any of the queens in this book. She was aged twenty-four at her marriage, and her early effort to prevent her rival, Charles's established mistress Lady Castlemaine, being appointed to her household was thwarted by her new husband in no uncertain terms. Yet Catherine managed to attract his respect and affection, helped by the fact that in one of her attempts to fulfil her royal duty to give birth, she nearly died, which strengthened his allegiance.[42] Her failure to provide a child was her greatest disadvantage, and as we have seen created the opportunity for the politics of exclusion, with such crucial reverberations for crown–parliamentary relationships. Yet Charles II refused to bow to pressure to divorce his wife: at the purely personal level, his sense of family was too strong. The dynastic mindset could work in favour of even a childless wife. But the heart of the issue was how the Restoration was to be made politically intelligible: whose interpretation of it, ideologically and practically, was to triumph – the King's or his opponents and critics?[43]

By the second half of the reign, the pattern of court life resembled, it has been argued, that of Charles's cousin, Louis XIV: a king, a consort, and, in effect, a *maîtresse en titre*, Louise de Kéroualle, Duchess of

Portsmouth, who was not just a sexual partner of the King's, but also a key agent of influence between the French and British courts.[44] Edward Corp recognises that although Catherine never ceased to find her husband's behaviour wounding, after 1670 her position improved. Not only did she establish her own cultural identity, she even encouraged a dalliance between Charles and Mary of Modena's aunt, Hortense Mancini, to counteract the pro-French role of the Duchess of Portsmouth. But it was as a dowager that Catherine really came into her own, helping to establish the legitimacy of James II's baby boy, yet also recognising William III, thus making no obstacle to the 1688 dynastic revolution. She finished her life as the able and respected Regent for her ailing brother, King Pedro of Portugal. As Agnes Strickland observed in her 1845 biography, 'Who would have ventured to calculate, after all the blighted hopes, the bitter disappointments and mortifications which had darkened the meridian horizon of Catherine of Braganza's existence, that the evening of her days would be cloudless and serene, and her sunset glorious?'[45]

As the bride of a forty-year-old man, Mary of Modena was literally young enough to be the future James II's daughter; on her marriage in 1673, she became at fifteen the stepmother of James's two daughters by his first marriage, Mary and Anne, who were then aged thirteen and eleven. Like Catherine she had to contend with her husband's infidelities, while her failure to produce a surviving child effectively made her the dynastic rival of these two stepdaughters, the heiresses apparent. The warmth of her relationship with Mary, who became Princess of Orange in 1677, may be gauged by the affectionate nickname of 'lemon' she then gave her, but she was never on such cordial terms with Anne. Paradoxically, as Andrew Barclay shows, in 1688, by producing a male heir, Mary's biological success as a queen precipitated the timing of the intervention into British politics of her stepdaughter's husband, William of Orange, also her nephew by marriage. Her legitimate son was branded an imposter, and William was able to use the rationale of protecting his wife's and his own rights in the Protestant succession as part of his strategy to create an alliance against Louis XIV. The 1688 Revolution, though often discussed chiefly in terms of its impact on the relationship of monarchy and Parliament, was mainly a dynastic revolution, replacing the older Stuart branch of the family with the younger one, and permanently barring Mary of Modena's legitimately born children from the throne. Exile was the price she paid for successful motherhood, instead of the honour normally accorded to a queen's achievement of her main function: producing a male heir. In 1688, the conspicuous support for William displayed not only by Mary but by two other royal women – Princess Anne and the Dowager Queen Catherine – ensured the success of this dynastic and family revolution; acclaim in Parliament followed but did not create William's claim to the throne, which he based on his hereditary rights. Of course the political and military reality of William's intervention was his need to secure the English as allies against Louis XIV.[46]

Even more conspicuously than these two wives, the intimate family relationships of Mary Stuart, Mary II, were fraught with political significance, as daughter, wife and sister. Moreover, like her aunt Catherine of Braganza, she failed in the most crucial role of being a mother.

But before William's intervention in British politics, Mary had had to decide whether to be deferential or co-equal with William; her dynastic claim to the British throne was stronger than his, but she made it clear she would not be a real co-ruler. Though a queen regnant, she functioned more as a consort. This wifely deference accorded well with emergent ideals of domestic womanhood. Yet as Regent in William's absences, Mary surprised contemporaries with her political talent and her powers of decision. When admirers sought for an image that crystallised her ability to switch roles between deferential wife and publicly able queen, they could only compare her to a man: to Cincinnatus, the Roman general who aided his country in an emergency but then retired into private life. Loyalists to the Catholic Stuarts were quick to castigate 'lemon' as an unnatural daughter for colluding with her father's deposition; she was likened to the Roman figure of Tullia, who had colluded with her husband to murder her father.[47]

It was Mary's charm and social talents that were crucial in helping to establish English loyalty to the new regime at a time of political transition, when the first outlines of parliamentary monarchy were emerging, just as Queen Adelaide would help William IV establish an even more limited, constitutional character to the British monarchy, despite the turbulence of the Reform Act years. But in making choices between loyalty to her husband and respect for her father, Mary faced the prospect that in Ireland an army led by her husband might be responsible for her father's death, or vice versa. It was only when she learnt that her father had colluded in assassination schemes against her husband that she felt guiltless about her wifely loyalty. All Mary's personal relationships were thus highly politicised, including those with her sister.[48]

Anne also had the charge of being an unnatural daughter levelled at her; and her ability to bear children made her and her offspring the rival in succession to her infertile sister, notwithstanding the poor survival rate of these children. She was an assiduous protector of her succession rights and for most of William's reign had an uneasy relationship with her brother-in-law. Yet her claim to the throne rested on the convenient myth that her stepmother's son was smuggled into the birth chamber in a warming pan: a rumour she may have helped to initiate. Critics believed she had slandered her stepmother to oust her half-brother, and Jacobites fondly hoped that guilt would induce her to alter the succession act in his favour. There is little need to underline the poignancy of her career as a mother.[49]

The dynastic politics of the Anglo-Hanoverians were only marginally less complex than this late Stuart sequence of political and religious family divisions and dynastic disinheritances. As Christine Gerrard shows, the repeated scenario of kingly fathers at war with the Princes of Wales told heavily on the Princesses Caroline and Augusta. These conflicts extended even to the settings and surroundings of their confinement while pregnant. When their labour began, both of them were forced to leave their father-in-law's residence and give birth in a dynastic space controlled by their husbands, against the dictates of medical prudence, etiquette and law – an heir to the throne was legally the ward of the ruler.

Through Gerrard's analysis we can appreciate how adroitly Caroline of Anspach juggled several roles: wife, political confidante, connoisseur, and mother. As Princess of Wales, the normality of her life with George Augustus contrasted favourably with George I's household in Britain, which included his half-sister from his father's second, morganatic marriage, and his own morganatic wife, yet to many people it was far from clear who these women were and they were both popularly supposed to be mistresses.[50] Yet for all the strength of Caroline's relationship to George II and his devotion to her, she had to tolerate mistresses in England and Hanover. Henrietta Howard, arguably the most important of these, was no rival to her in political intelligence but had a distinctive role as a patron of culture.[51] As a mother, Caroline had to endure an extraordinarily hostile relationship with her eldest son. Frederick had to be left behind in Hanover to represent the family's electoral interests when her father-in-law became King George I and took his son and daughter-in-law to Britain with him. This helped to produce an estrangement between mother and son which was never healed, and perpetuated the Hanoverian family tradition of toxic hostility between kings and their heirs. Like Augusta of Saxe-Gotha later, Caroline endeavoured to sustain a cordial relationship with her father-in-law in spite of her husband's difficult relationship with him.

Bullion's closely observed analysis of Augusta shows how shrewdly she assessed the possibilities and challenges of her position, and reveals how consistently her contemporaries and generations of historians have underestimated her. She helped play the role of *ingénue* wife, in contrast to her worldly mother-in-law and her husband's vulgar companions, but knew that she needed to keep in good favour with her father-in-law even when her husband was at odds with him. This foresight was never more vindicated than when she was widowed and in need of control over her children, legally George II's wards. She achieved this with astonishing skill and resolution, and even risked her reputation for chastity in her desire to provide her son and heir with a mentor. Though never a crowned queen, she was a formidable mother to a king, and George III cautioned his young bride Charlotte of Mecklenburg-Strelitz to beware of her influence.

Queen Caroline had already borne half of her children when she moved to England in 1714: Frederick (1707–51), Anne (1709–59), Amelia (1711–86) and Caroline (1713–59). Her first child born in England, George William, was short-lived (1717–18), but William (1721–65), Mary (1723–72) and Louisa (1724–51) all lived to adulthood. It was inevitable, as Baker-Smith's chapter shows, that dynastic marriages for the princesses would follow the Hanoverian family precedents of links to the leading Protestant powers: Prussia, the Netherlands, Hesse or Denmark. Yet as the children of a king-elector, their choices became narrower since their grander status unfitted them for some of the princely German courts which might otherwise have had princes of marriageable age. Anne of Hanover, the Princess Royal, was first destined for her cousin Frederick II of Prussia, which would have been the third generation of Hanoverian/Hohernzollern marriages. Subsequently he was considered suitable for Amelia, who wore his picture for the rest of her life. Anne had to be contented with a less prestigious match with the Prince of Orange, who was not yet the elected Stadtholder of all seven United Provinces, but only the hereditary Prince of three of them. She became one of many Princesses of Orange who were effective regents for their sons, being given, exceptionally, the title of Princess Gouvernante.[52] Well-equipped by their cultured mother to be royal brides, both Anne and Louisa went 'native', adapting thoroughly to their new families and being less effective than had been hoped at representing British interests. Tools of diplomacy these daughters may have been, but they were not automata. Like Catherine of Braganza, the French protégée who nevertheless opposed the French faction at court, Anne of Orange realised she had to follow her own political agenda and discriminate between her father's and her husband's interests.

Veronica Baker-Smith and Richard King both show that for a king's daughters, their marriage choices were limited, but that marriage could seem a better option than dependency on a disliked brother. The unwed Caroline and Amelia became extreme examples of the 'surplus woman' as the Hohernzollerns too had produced more eligible royal princesses than the marriage market could sustain. And lest we conclude that princesses were exceptionally disadvantaged as royal women at a time when their aristocratic contemporaries were exercising increasing freedom of choice over their partners, Baker-Smith shows how the Duke of Cumberland, brother to Anne, Amelia, Louisa, Caroline and Mary, managed to escape an undesired marriage through Walpole's adroit advice. The unsuitable marriages of his nephews prompted George III in 1773 to legislate that *all* royal marriages had to have Privy Council permission, to prevent unions with commoners or Catholics. (Flouting this, in marrying Mrs Fitzherbert, George Prince of Wales transgressed both prohibitions.)[53]

If three of George II's daughters were able to profit from the needs of diplomacy in obtaining husbands, this was less true for George III's daughters. George could deploy his second son Frederick to repeat a Hanover/Hohernzollern alliance (he married Frederica of Prussia), while the need to have a Scandinavian ally was cemented by the marriage of his hapless sister Caroline Matilda to her cousin the schizophrenic Christian VII. Another sister, Augusta, was married into the House of Brunswick, closely connected to the Hanoverians, and this was the family which provided Caroline as Princess of Wales to the future George IV. Her daughter Charlotte in turn nearly perpetuated the connection with the House of Orange: Anne's grandson, the future King William II, was considered as a husband for her. Continental war by 1793 gave the eldest daughter of George III a chance to escape because of the usefulness of securing an ally to protect Hanover; she married into the House of Württemberg, which had links to the Danish and Russian royal dynasties and aspired to electoral status. But Britain's isolation from the Continent during the Revolutionary and Napoleonic Wars, as well as their status as princesses of a superpower, were both factors hindering the marriages of her other five sisters. There seemed no burning necessity to marry the princesses for dynastic reasons, so their parents' preference for keeping them at home was indulged at their expense.[54]

George III and Queen Charlotte were probably the most fortunately matched arranged dynastic partners since Charles I and Henrietta Maria. Charlotte had absolutely no rivals in the shape of mistresses, though she did have the usual Hanoverian disharmony between kings and their eldest sons to contend with. This was exacerbated when her husband's illnesses in 1788 pitted her as a rival to the possible regency of the son and heir. During the actual regency starting in 1811, she was in charge of the King's household and person, while the Prince of Wales acted as head of state. Although she kept out of matters of state, she had to help smooth appearances for the royal family after the disastrous débâcle of her son's failed marriage to Caroline of Brunswick, and largely supervised the education of her granddaughter Princess Charlotte, her only legitimate grandchild to be born during her lifetime. Although Queen Charlotte was a paragon of domestic rectitude, all her sons but one lived with mistresses or unofficial wives. When her son Ernest of Cumberland married her niece Frederica, who was twice divorced, she was constrained not to receive her in case it gave a chance to the discredited Caroline of Brunswick to claim the right to be received as well.[55]

Charlotte's daughter-in-law Adelaide, as Bill Purduc shows, tactfully acknowledged the ten FitzClarences and her husband's sentiments toward his former long-time companion, the actress Dorothy Jordan. Her modest demeanour helped confer much-needed respectability on the royal family. But all of these personal family travails and embarrassments for Charlotte and her daughters-in-law did not have quite the dynastic political significance of the early Hanoverian wives' role in the reversionary interest. Carlton House had no official consort to help George, Prince of Wales, rally the Whigs in opposition to his father's ministries or to argue for advantageous terms for a regency in 1788–89; it fell to political aristocrats like Georgiana, Duchess of Devonshire, to help cement the opposition, socially and politically.[56] However, Caroline of Brunswick's cause was advocated in turn by Whigs and Tories to embarrass any incumbent ministry.[57] But the threat of the rival Stuart family did not exacerbate family politics as it had done for the later Stuarts and the first two Georges. In an act of dynastic closure, George IV commissioned the monument in Rome to the last Stuart, Henry, Cardinal Duke of York, and obtained Stuart papers for the Royal Archives.[58]

Adelaide's failure to bear healthy children was a great *personal* sorrow to her, but unlike Catherine of Braganza's parallel misfortune, it had no *dynastic* significance. With the Dukes of Cumberland, Kent and Cambridge all marrying respectably and fathering children after the death of Princess Charlotte of Wales, heiress apparent, there was no threat to the Hanoverian succession. They also foreclosed the possibility that someone would suggest that one of William IV's ten bastards should be legitimated; there would be no effort resembling the attempts to secure the Duke of Monmouth's rights in Charles II's reign. As the heiress to the British throne, Princess Victoria, born to the Duke and Duchess of Kent, weeks before her cousin the Duke of Cambridge, benefited from the fact that British law and custom permitted female sovereignty and that the examples of Mary and still more of Anne showed how successful it could be. When she married her cousin Albert, her mother the Duchess of Kent (Albert's aunt) assured him that the British people liked reigning queens.[59] However, it was this female succession in Britain which had dynastic repercussions for Hanover, where the Duke of Cumberland as George III's eldest surviving son took precedence over his niece.

Royal women and court culture, 1660–1837

A court is both an institution and a place; it is constituted by various sets of personnel, and governed by its own ethos. In Robert Bucholz's words, it is an intangible entity that involves people from the top to the bottom of society and requires to be understood holistically.[60] A few remarks are in order about the nature of courts and court culture in Britain during the 'long eighteenth century'.

Some historians define the court quite narrowly. To the Tudor doyen of court studies, David Starkey, writing in 1987, the early modern English court should be seen predominantly as Royal Bedchamber, Privy Chamber, the Council Chamber, and, leading between them, the Privy Gallery, concentrated in close proximity within Whitehall Palace, together with the fifty or so individuals with access to these rooms.[61] Historians such as Malcolm Smuts and Robert Bucholz in contrast would argue that the court must also be understood in terms of a larger cultural geography, one that links the court at Whitehall or St James's with the London metropolis. Smuts, in his work on the early Stuarts, argues that cultural activity relating to the court must include in its farthest reach the studios of court artists and the galleries of their aristocratic, courtier patrons. Since royal life had public and ceremonial aspects – coronations, attending chapel or divine service at Westminster Abbey, holding regular drawing rooms, and so on – then our idea of court culture must extend beyond the concentrated core of rooms of Starkey's seminal definition. Most court historians would now concur with the view that court culture is polycentric, with multiple royal and aristocratic 'foyers of patronage'.[62]

Above all, the concept of access to the monarch's person must be considered. The period under discussion is usually described in terms of a process in which the balance of power weighed more and more in Parliament's favour, diminishing the role of the court. Consequently, the historiography has been weighted toward Westminster politics. Nonetheless the crown, and the person of the monarch, remained central. The monarch was still the fount of honours and the apex of all the patronage networks in Whitehall, Westminster, the Church, Law, Army and Navy. Being near the monarch, or near to those who were, was essential for the ambitious. Members of aristocratic or gentry families might move fluidly between a post in the royal household to a position as a minister of state or a stint as a diplomat; their wives, mothers and daughters helped to cement a family's political position, often by holding household positions with the consort's household. There is an enormous amount to be done to review the relations between the Hanoverians and their elite and to bring to light a more balanced view of the court's role, even if it certainly competed as a centre of fashion and social achievement with the aristocratic town houses of the metropolis and its locales – theatre, opera, pleasure gardens – of commercialised leisure.

When in London the monarch lived in proximity to the Houses of Parliament at Westminster, to the Inns of Court, and to the town houses of the aristocracy, which spread westwards throughout the eighteenth century. The court was the centre of both politics and high society, and sometimes though not always of high fashion. 'Going to court' might mean attending a drawing room to be presented to the monarch, or only going to Westminster to seek the favour of individuals closer to the monarch. At the opposite reach to this approximate access is the question of private, royal retreat. A monarch like Charles II might be ostensibly accessible walking across Horse Guards Parade, but equally the place where real influence could be exercised, and not only by the mistress in question, was in her apartments over a game of cards with a few close advisers, or visiting diplomats.[63]

The chapters in this book accept a wide definition of court culture: one that embraces the royal household, together with its public and private poles, within its concentration in the heart of the main palace, or its rural retreats. They examine its circles of sociability, especially through networks of common intellectual or artistic interests, and its connections to an aristocracy maintaining metropolitan and local power bases. Secondly, the book underlines the polycentricity of courts in its chapters on princesses of Wales as well as queen consorts. There are nearly always several courts in existence at any one time, insofar as there are often several royal households, each with their officials: Treasurers, Masters of the Horse, and so on. The King has one household, the Queen a second, the heir, once of age, a third. In the reign of Charles II, the household of his brother, James, Duke of York, the heir presumptive, was an important second focus. Princess Anne had her own household once married, throughout the reigns of her uncle, father and brother-in-law. The Dowager Queen Catherine of Braganza, Charles II's widow, lived in England until 1692.

Once queen, Anne rejected all suggestion that either Sophia of Hanover or the next heir, George, be allowed to reside in England, providing visible evidence of the reversionary interest (and reminding her, she said, of her coffin). After the Hanoverians succeeded, however, the pattern began of a reversionary court of the Prince of Wales centred on Leicester House, Kew, or Carlton House. There were also the separate households of George II's son and daughters, some of whom lived on into their nephew George III's reign, and the latter's unruly brothers, in addition to his unruly sons. Baker-Smith contrasts the way Princesses Caroline and Amelia deported themselves during their father's reign, and Bullion shows that their sister-in-law Augusta, Princess of Wales, genuinely feared that the Duke of Cumberland (second son of George II) might usurp her son should the King die before his majority.

The court's physical setting

Since courts need a physical setting, architectural historians, cultural geographers and historical topographers have much to say about court culture. At the Restoration, the main palace was Whitehall, the largest royal palace in Europe. Charles's plans to build a new palace at Whitehall to designs first by Jebb and then Wren were frustrated when money was needed to rebuild London after the 1666 Fire; financial shortages similarly prevented the completion of a new palace at Winchester. Instead he had to refurbish various parts of Whitehall, and at Windsor commissioned some of the most extravagant baroque interior decorative schemes England has ever possessed, now sadly lost.

Once a king married, he had to provide a suitable set of apartments for his queen as well as a dower house. Until Mary II gave Greenwich Palace over to the navy veterans, the Queen's House designed by Inigo Jones was given to the consort, or Somerset House. Catherine of Braganza had a modernised suite of rooms at Whitehall, dating from the Tudor period. There were also apartments for the two most important mistresses: first Barbara, Lady Castlemaine, and then Louise, Duchess of

Portsmouth. Despite the King's dislike of London, Ronald Hutton has concluded that the untidy mix of rooms at Whitehall, its combination of large formal halls, chambers and privy rooms together with numerous corridors and small rooms, 'was admirably suited to Charles' style of kingship, at once very open and very devious'. He also had a 'sequence of rural retreats', at Newmarket and Winchester.[64]

One of the first decisions James II made was to abandon the plans for Winchester and to concentrate on Whitehall. His main project, a lavish chapel for Catholic worship, only added to his unpopularity. He commissioned new apartments for Mary of Modena, but they were completed and used by her stepdaughter Mary when she became co-monarch at the Glorious Revolution of 1688. Ten years later the palace was largely destroyed by fire, but William and Mary had in any case preferred their new, fairly modest palace at Kensington, and the altered sections of Hampton Court. William not only found the riverside location of Whitehall aggravated his asthma, he disliked its easy accessibility; J. R. Jones has suggested that, assuming Mary would outlive him, he thought she would find it easier to reside at Hampton Court, where she would be less plagued by visitors and supplicants.[65] Nonetheless dynastic prestige demanded that a new Whitehall be built if money allowed, and Wren again designed a magnificent modern palace. But neither this design nor Anne's commissioned plans from Talman were implemented. Bucholz however argues here that this apparent failure to leave behind a lasting architectural legacy is a monument to Anne's prudence and good judgement, in the context of the changing constitutional and political climate.

The Hanoverians adjusted to a kingdom with no impressive modern seat, such as the monarchs of France, Denmark, Sweden, Spain, Portugal and numerous German princes possessed. Even the impecunious Habsburgs were able to build Schonbrunn just a few miles from the old Hofburg during the course of the century. But both George I and George II may have had little objection to this lack of splendour in Britain. There was a new palace at Herrenhausen in the Electorate to enjoy; George I disliked public display, and adapted to St James's, which also symbolised the continuity of the monarchy back to Tudor times,[66] while George II and Caroline used William and Mary's grand new suite of rooms at Hampton Court. Instead the important political geography of the Hanoverians was the contrast between the King's home and that of his sons at Leicester House.

Joanna Marschner shows how Caroline's activities as a collector and connoisseur took place in Kensington, Hampton Court and the private retreat of Richmond. Bullion demonstrates the importance of Kew to Frederick and Augusta as a domain to display their domestic virtues. To politicians and court wits, decoding the meaning of conversations and gestures at Kew was as important as were the activities of the Soviet Politburo to Cold War Kremlinologists. Frederick and Augusta also began the creation of Kew as a landscape and botanical garden. Under Augusta's later patronage, William Chambers's built a sequence of buildings – a mosque, a pagoda, a triumphal arch and so on – as princely lessons in world architecture for the future George III. But Chambers's plans for a grand palace there to accommodate George's expanding family were never implemented. It seems fitting, for a monarchy whose political strength rested on tax-efficiency and public credit, that the great public building of George III's reign was not a home for the royal family but John Soane's complex of buildings for the Bank of England, commissioned by the Prime Minister, Pitt the Younger. Grand plans to create an imperial city-scape for London after the Battle of Waterloo, including a new palace, were suggested by Soane, not the monarch.[67]

George III rehabilitated the old castle at Windsor, not entirely to Charlotte's comfort; in reaction to the semi-public life the royal family led there she bought Frogmore as her private retreat. Her official residence was the newly purchased Queen's House, formerly Buckingham House. Unlike their Hanoverian predecessors, George and Charlotte stayed with or visited some of their courtier families at their rural seats, and in the latter half of the reign patronised the seaside resort of Weymouth. The homes of various members of the royal family along the Thames valley (Kew and Richmond; two successive Dukes of Cumberland in Windsor Great Park; the Duke of York at Oatlands; the young Princess Charlotte of Wales at Claremont) made it a significant site of royal cultural geography.[68]

George IV was the greatest royal Maecenas since Charles I, but as he barely lived with Caroline of Brunswick, his marriage gave him no excuse to create a lavish architectural setting for her. What a palace he might have commissioned had he been a happier royal groom! As Prince of Wales, his clandestine marriage to Mrs Fitzherbert prompted the purchase of a villa in Brighton, which eventually metamorphosed into the luxuriously extravagant oriental Pavilion. He pulled down his father's incomplete, Gothic palace at Kew, and embellished Windsor, cancelling some of George III's plans and removing entirely Charles II's lavish baroque interiors.[69] His sybaritic tastes were increasingly out of kilter with the dominant values of 'respectability' upheld by influential sections of the elite and the middling classes, and the fact that Adelaide did not occasion any lavish building or redecoration schemes reflected the modest style of monarchy she and William IV projected.

Cultural programmes and the court's ethos

The term 'court culture' can also indicate the deliberate cultural programme of a court, expressed through a variety of media in addition to the architectural and decorative setting: through the visual arts, especially portraiture and history painting; through theatre, opera, and music, both sacred and secular; and in conjunction with various branches of literature and learning, including the work of poets laureate and historiographers royal. To foster the cultivation of the right artistic standards as a vehicle for the symbolically charged programmes of meaning the arts were intended to convey, princely courts in the Renaissance founded academies of art or letters. The arts convey spiritual and moral values as well as aesthetic ones, and court culture also plays a role in establishing the dominant ethos of a court. Are the values most prominently on display martial or pacific? Is the court a by-word for piety and probity, or for licentious dissipation? How does the court prescribe physical decorum, gesture, body language, table manners?

Renaissance courtesy manuals such as Castiglione's *Book of the Courtier* and Della Porta's *Galatea* outlined the role of the court as a civilising influence. Twentieth-century court historiography in turn has been immensely influenced by Norbert Elias's studies of the court as a civilising process, although most historians would now want substantial modifications to their views. Royal women often function as the gatekeepers of morality, measured by whom they will receive in person and whom they will exclude. Etiquette becomes a form of moral policing.[70]

During the Renaissance, courts in Italy and France often developed such programmes of culture and manners in accordance with neoplatonic philosophy – as glimpsed above in brief reference to Henrietta Maria's French tastes. The aim was to project, through the rituals, entertainments and social fashions, an earthly resemblance of the world of enduring, Platonic, ideal reality. Even though in retrospect the court of Charles I and Henrietta Maria seemed a golden age of court culture, and the benchmark for the Restoration's attempts to recreate the court, the early Stuart court never produced an entirely coherent programme, and the degree to which Charles I and Henrietta's masques project 'Platonic politics' remains a matter of controversy.[71] It is important to note that monarchs and their consorts were not the only active patrons; they were surrounded by peers and financiers, many with more disposable income than the crown, who could collect art, pioneer new styles of building, or patronise poets. Moreover, British monarchs were slow to found academies of art or learn to help regulate taste or sponsor scholarship. Francis Bacon's *Novum Organon* outlined a programme of scientific collaboration, complete with libraries, laboratories, and zoological gardens, that a monarch should inaugurate, but the Royal Society, founded by Charles II, was a pale reflection of this intended programme, and owed as much to aristocratic and clerical amateurism as it did to any royal scheme of scientific sponsorship.[72] Andrew Barclay emphasises that late Stuart royal patronage already coexisted with an embryonic commercial art market. It was not until George III's reign that Britain acquired a Royal Academy of Arts, founded in 1768.

Had British monarchs wanted to instigate a more coherent cultural programme, on the model of Louis XIV's regulatory policy of royal academies of art, letters, science and inscriptions (i.e. ancient history), they had a vehicle for this in the Lord Chamberlain's department of the royal household. The Lord Chamberlain organised royal ceremonial and regulated the protocol of diplomatic and foreign visits. His department also supervised the Master of the Revels, responsible for dramatic performances until this was reorganised in 1737 with new arrangements for licensing the public stage, superintended the Chapel Royal and its officials, including its musicisans, and made appointments such as Poet Laureate and Painter in Ordinary to the King. A consort's household had its own Lord Chamberlain with parallel roles and responsibilities. But few monarchs between 1660 and 1837 achieved a systematic promulgation of the royal image and court culture.[73]

Edward Corp's chapter suggests that a proper account of Charles II's court culture would have to understand its cultural interests in terms of its political factions – which is another way of talking about its foreign influences. As to the moral tone of the Restoration court, Catherine of Braganza was able to make little headway against its prevailing licentiousness. Although lacking a systematic cultural programme, however, Charles II's reign saw one crucial development: what one might call the commercialisation of the court theatre. The plays, operas and masques of Charles I had had a restricted court audience and the protagonists of the latter were mainly the courtiers themselves, including the King and Queen. At the same time there were also commercial theatre companies operating under royal licence and aristocratic patronage. What was new about Charles II's reign was that although he had a theatre installed in Whitehall there were no exclusive performances of entertainments; the players were all from the different commercial theatre companies. Unlike the continental courts, the British court had no exclusive court theatre. This continued under the Hanoverians, who simply commanded performances at the public theatres. Effectively the court came to the city, not the other way round. But as Bullion shows so persuasively, theatricality and role-playing were essential elements of Hanoverian court culture, and the personalities of the day must be construed as consciously aware of these roles.

However, Charles II's dalliances with actresses, and his court's habit of 'slumming it' at popular entertainments, had compromised the dignity of the monarch, although like any baroque king worth his salt Charles was also capable of acting the part of monarch in royal ceremonial such as touching for the king's evil – so playing his part in the theatre of monarchy.[74] As Andrew Barclay shows, Mary of Modena's Italian patronage had its roots in her role at her brother-in-law's court, but was not unique to her. Rather, it was coterminous with aristocratic patronage at large. Her brief reign, though symbolically important for women writers (a theme resumed below), gave her little opportunity to exercise decisive cultural influence. Her husband James's main cultural programme – the creation of a Catholic chapel and support for Catholic publishing and open debate – was precisely what contributed to his unpopularity and downfall.

Aware of the need to project the legitimacy of their rule, William and Mary embarked on an extensive cultural programme, whose continental influences have already been explored. Simon Thurley's forthcoming work on the Stuart royal palaces will further explore Mary's role as an architectural patron. Although architecture, garden design and interior decoration represent the bulk of their joint and individual achievements, music continued to be important. Mary's death in 1694 prompted the culminating masterpiece of an English composer, Purcell, who, as Corp and Barclay show, had gained much early inspiration from the Italian music encouraged by Catherine and Mary of Modena. It was also the occasion for the last great public royal funeral until this century. In her well-informed interest in botany, Mary set a precedent followed later by Caroline, Augusta Princess of Wales and Charlotte.[75]

In determining the ethos of the court, Bucholz has emphasised that Mary was decisively urged by William to eschew the sleazy tastes of her uncle's and father's court, especially in its theatre-going. Mary's patronage of good causes such as the new seaman's hospital at Greenwich and her support for the Societies for the Reformation of Manners therefore inaugurated the British court's attempt to mix aristocratic style and bourgeois propriety. Caroline and Augusta were both aware of the usefulness of projecting the same moral ethos, and the latter succeeded in giving the heir to the throne an unusually virtuous upbringing which he never repudiated. Despite the dissolute ways of their sons, George III and Charlotte helped foster royal popularity by their family orientation. George III consciously harked back to the moral reform impulses of Mary II and Anne when in 1788 he issued a proclamation against vice. This identification of monarchy with middle-class morality, now ever more influential than in the late Stuart period, culminated in Queen Adelaide's success, explored by Purdue's chapter, in toning down the naval uncouthness of William IV and in her relentless charities, but at the price of making the court synonymous with boredom.[76]

Bucholz's exemplary study of Queen Anne's court stands out as an oasis in court studies between the sketchy treatment of the Restoration court and the almost entire neglect of all the Hanoverians. In this collection he offers a major reassessment of the image and reality of her reputation and achievements. Beattie's pioneering study of George I's court is admired for its solid scholarship on the royal household, but now seems deficient in its treatment of social and cultural dimensions. The most neglected chapter in the reasssessment of English court culture is probably the reign of George II: the chapters here on his consort, daughters and daughters-in-law indicate what a rewarding enterprise this will be. Marschner's and King's chapters especially indicate how important the court still was in terms of cultural patronage. If anyone had a cultural programme, it was Caroline; following her example, her daughter Anne was supremely capable of creating her own cultural role when still Princess Royal and then stamping Dutch life with her personality and interests.[77]

The court culture of George III and Queen Charlotte is also an underexplored arena, except in relation to their architectural and artistic patronage. The chapter on Queen Charlotte as a patron of the Christian Enlightenment touches only on a few aspects of this role, which she shared with her husband. Had George's Chapel to Revealed Religion been finished and preserved, and his plan to found a chivalric Order of Minerva to commemorate achievement in the arts implemented, there would be more visible material and institutional manifestations of their religious, artistic, scientific and intellectual preoccupations.

Court studies, gender and women's history

From all that has been said above it will be apparent that if a proper account of court culture is to be given, it must be inclusive of women.

The fact that relatively little research has yet been done of the British court from 1660 to 1837 provides a wonderful opportunity to integrate women into the picture from the outset. This concluding section will try to indicate how the connection between court studies, gender and women's history might be made.[78]

In his stimulating reappraisal of past and future directions for court history, John Adamson has urged historians to remember that courts were not centred exclusively on the monarch, but were polycentric; other centres included the consort, the mistress, the heir, or the favourite. All the essays in his collection on early modern courts c. 1500–1750 demonstrate the importance of a consort, queen mother, daughter, daughter-in-law or mistress in establishing or modifying the nature of the court. Yet in his reconceptualisation of court studies, Adamson himself stops short of calling for an exploration of the role of gender, and a delineation of the constructions of masculinity, femininity and alternative sexualities promoted by the codes of courtly life.

Ultimately the goal must be to deploy the concept of gender, rather than to concentrate solely on a critical and historical account of women's position within court society, because it is grounded in the observable reality that both masculinity and femininity are socially and culturally constructed.[79] Furthermore, the Renaissance court was the matrix in which important reformulations of masculinity and femininity emerged, as well as a seminal influence on creating the court society of sixteenth-century monarchies, which in turn were crucial in forming *ancien régime* society. The medieval, unlettered feudal warrior was transformed by the new codes of civility enunciated in books like Castiglione's *The Courtier* into the gentlemanly courtier, still skilled in the arts of war, but also a connoisseur of beauty in the visual arts, of elegance in the world of letters, who sought moral instruction from the civilisation of antiquity, or from neo-chivalry, and who studied and collected the curiosities of nature. The arts of conversation, of polite sociability, and of refined love, were considered to be essentially the domain of women. At the same time – and this was one of the lessons of the classical moralists, which reinforced elements of misogyny within the Christian tradition – the sexual power of women, and of attractive young men, was feared for the way it could subvert hierarchies of gender and social rank. The royal mistress, the royal favourite and the royal confessor alike presented the problem of making the prince's power accountable and transparent. In this world, women were therefore both idealised and demonised. The theatrical nature of power in the Renaissance and baroque courts of Europe, which required a larger than life projection of kingly and queenly images, could only contribute to the construction of powerful symbolic images of manhood and womanhood.

In the particular circumstances of seventeenth-century France, the salon and its culture styles emerged as a critique of the competitive and sometimes boorish manners of the royal court. The *salonière*'s role of raising standards of civility and providing a setting for cultural discourse began increasingly to be interwoven with the social fashions of court society. We glimpsed above how Henrietta Maria brought new definitions of the *honnête homme* and *femme* into the Caroline court. Historians have traced the way this salon tradition was disseminated to a wider audience and shaped new ideals of politeness, which were further adapted to the new urban culture of coffee houses, reading clubs, learned societies, and other manifestations of eighteenth-century sociability, in Britain. Britain's advanced commercial economy meant that this ideal of urbane politeness was both the preserve of the aristocratic town house and of the commercialised leisure facilities of public pleasure gardens or assembly rooms.[80]

Women's history has been dominated – one might say, dogged – by the contrasting binaries of the public/private sphere. As ever more sophisticated and constructive critiques of the idea of a gendered public/private sphere have been provided, the concept of sociability has become one of the most useful clarifications of the conceptual muddle. Lawrence Klein, John Brewer and Michèle Cohen have shown how the concept of conversation – the practice of heterosocial discourse on matters germane to polite society such as standards of taste – gave an important role to women.[81] A pioneering attempt to relate the study of women and cultural conversation to the Georgian court is Julius Bryant's portrait of Henrietta Howard, reluctant mistress to George II, as a 'Woman of Reason'. Isobel Grundy's biography of Lady Mary Wortley Montagu is an illuminating case study of an exceptionally important figure; and Susan Whyman's examination of the Verneys is a model of how the category of gender can illuminate the nature of both masculinity and femininity.[82] But so far, the concept of sociability and, to use Erica Veevers's term, of social fashion has not been systematically applied to the British court, which in any case is usually sidelined in discussions of the character of eighteenth-century culture. Yet as Gerrard and Bullion show, Caroline of Anspach and Augusta of Saxe-Gotha were both instrumental in creating styles of sociability which linked the court and the reversionary interest to the aristocratic elite. Bullion's chapter demonstrates how much we need to understand the codes of conversation, etiquette and propriety – in other words, the nature of sociability in the Georgian court – in order to construe what Augusta was really about. Jupp's suggestive essay which underlined how much women controlled aristocratic sociability c. 1782–1832 set an agenda for the later Hanoverian period that awaits full implementation.[83]

The concept of sociability, then, is one way of integrating court studies with gender and women's history. Another way to clarify the debate on the public/private sphere is to reconsider what the public sphere really meant. Its primary meaning was the world of public office.[84] The monarch, his/her consort, and their children were the central public figures. Their households gave employment to people of varying social rank, from the lowest to the highest. Because of the way state positions grew out of household appointments, the monarch's ministers were both part of the royal entourage and possessors of public office. A glance at even a handful of leading male public figures in the court of George III and Queen Charlotte underlines the fluidity of public office holding, which the concentration on the history of Parliament has tended to obscure. An English peer of the realm had a permanent institutional base in the House of Lords; but if he wanted high office, he needed to be personally acceptable to his sovereign. A public career might move between a royal household position such as Master of the Horse, a diplomatic posting, and a cabinet position. Biographies of Charles II, James II and William III and some of the leading political figures and bureaucrats of the era have shed light on crown–elite relations, but we need to know a lot more about how Hanoverian sovereigns managed theirs. This cannot be accomplished so long as the dominant historical paradigm remains the Namierite concentration on Westminster careers, rather than on the interplay between Westminster and Whitehall, St James's or Windsor, and this paradigm is only beginning to shift.

Two issues then follow from this: the place of women in a world of public office holding; and the nature of the aristocratic culture of Britain, which is the broader context of such office holding. Crucially, the one place where women of the right social status could have salaried public positions was at court. Here they were Maids of Honour, Ladies in Waiting, Mistress of the Robes and so forth.[85] Often a wife and husband were both given positions respectively in the King's and Queen's household.[86] Even where a wife had no salaried role, if her husband was in the royal household she could influence appointments. There are therefore generations of women with public careers who would merit consistent study. Such study would, moreover, need to take place within a concept of a political culture where family and dynastic interests within aristocratic and gentry families were paramount. To accomplish this, historians must be willing to look vertically into successive generations, horizontally across marriage networks, and inclusively at both sexes. This task is not helped by the gender blindness of most studies of the British aristocracy, which mostly concentrate on men, virtually implying that the aristocracy and gentry reproduced by parthenogenesis.[87] The few examples given in the chapter on Queen Charlotte suggest for instance that George III's vexed relationship with ministries headed by the 3rd Duke of Portland looks different when his wife's close friendship with Portland's mother and sister are factored in. Some excellent studies point the way forward, including biographies of figures like the ambitious dynast Sarah Churchill, Duchess of Marlborough, and the celebrity politician Georgiana, Duchess of Devonshire. Essays by Elaine Chalus have also been seminal in this reconceptualisation of politics, demonstrating the role of women in the whole electoral process and as political advisers, while K. D. Reynolds has analysed Victorian aristocratic women, including the hidden political role of the royal Ladies in Waiting.[88]

Clarifications of the public sphere along these lines would not only throw into sharper relief the presence of both sexes in public life, albeit on different terms, they would also help refocus what is meant by the private sphere. A man who chose not to pursue a career in statesmanship, or for various reasons had to give one up, would be described as being a private gentleman, or leading a private life. In the case of wealthy peers such as the Earls of Harcourt discussed in the chapter on Queen Charlotte, this private life does not mean a life of domesticity, in the sense of domestic management. This remained a female role. It *did* mean giving up ambitions to shine at the apex of political society, and concentrating on local issues and responsibilities, perhaps as a magistrate, perhaps by sponsoring philanthropy, perhaps by setting an example of attending public worship, all of which were often combined with a life of connoisseurship or science.[89] And even if domestic management was seen as primarily a female task, women of high social status were public figures too. Their marriages, lyings in and deaths were matters of public comment; their tombs dominated parish churches; their social entertainments included 'public days' at the family seat; their sexual or sartorial indiscretions (like those of their male partners) were the subject of salacious gossip. If their husbands were away from the family seat for any reason, they substituted as 'deputy wife' or head of the household.[90]

Malcolm Smuts has argued that a concept of private retirement was integral to court life as it developed in Elizabethan and early Stuart

Britain; it was the necessary polar opposite to the life of ambition and fickle fortune. The ideal retreat of the Horatian farm removed from the corruptions of public life was a classical motif that had powerful resonance in real lives.[91] It was constantly re-stated in different idioms, throughout the Augustan period. For late Georgians one of the most compelling voices idealising rural virtue was that of Rousseau; another was the call to virtue articulated by Wilberforce, Hannah More and other Evangelicals. Both were influential at Queen Charlotte's court.

This ideal of private retirement was one which had greater meaning for *men*, who might have to choose between public and private options, or have the latter forced on them, and who risked the loss of fortune and reputation if they made mistakes in public office. One of the classical heroes most admired for his retirement was the Roman general Cincinnatus, who was persuaded to leave his farm only for the public good. As we have seen, it was applied to Mary II in her role as Regent, and she attracted praise for graciously resuming her subordinate role as co-ruler without administrative responsibility whenever her husband returned to Great Britain.[92] But women who scorned either the life of shared ambition with their husbands, or the whirligig of fashion, could also profess devotion to the rural seat, to their gardens, and to their humble beneficiaries. However, historians who discuss women's allegedly exclusive identification with the private sphere need to follow Amanda Vickery's case study where she explores the variety of meanings 'private' and 'public' have for an interconnected set of gentry families. When the home is a place of entertainment for tenants or tradesfolk, is it a public or a private place?[93] By the same token, if a landowning magistrate acts in his function as JP in a room such as the estate office in his house, he is performing a public role in his home.

What Gerrard's, Bullion's and Campbell Orr's chapters suggest, however, is that for a queen consort or princess of Wales it was much more difficult to establish a *truly* private retreat. Caroline of Anspach and Augusta both assisted their husbands in juxtaposing a life of domestic felicity and private retirement at Richmond or Kew to the monarch's court at St James's, but this was a strategy with an important public, political meaning. The identification of George III and Queen Charlotte with domestic virtue meant that even their evening walks at Windsor became a public display of private life; the Queen therefore acquired Frogmore as an even more exclusively private domain.

The issue of motherhood and domesticity is another connecting link between court studies and women's history, which literary historians are now beginning to explore. One of the dominating narratives of motherhood in this period is 'the rise of domestic woman': that is to say, a new emphasis on women not simply as child-bearers, but as child-rearers.[94] This narrative concentrates on women of the middling sort. As they became increasingly free of shared responsibility in the family enterprise, the argument goes, moralists and conduct writers urged them to concentrate on their duties as mothers, and to avoid a self-indulgent use of their leisure. Some historians have seen this emphasis on motherhood as a route toward empowerment as much as confinement: if women can argue that to be good mothers, they require education, then they are equipping themselves for a powerful role as the primary socialisers of the young generation. By the end of the eighteenth century, probably the most influential exponent of this ideal of domestic education was Maria Edgeworth, who outlined how both men and women of the gentry or prosperous bourgeoisie could be involved in the home-based education of their children. Teaching emerged as a suitable profession for the unmarried or the widowed; for women living from literary earnings, the literary persona of maternal educator was often adopted.[95] As guardians of the moral conscience of the family, women also emerged into public life, campaigning on such issues as the emancipation of slaves, or cheap bread for the poor, and extended their domestic responsibility into the neighbourhood and parish as philanthropists.[96]

Although this is an account of 'bourgeois' motherhood, this style of motherhood was not confined to the bourgeoisie. Schneid Lewis showed how the more child-centred type of parenting was adopted by some aristocrats even while others continued a distant relationship within their children; Stella Tillyard's study of the Lennox women shows how two of them, Emily and Sarah, successively embody different styles of mothering in their successive marriages.[97] To complete these accounts, styles of royal motherhood need to be included, for a queen or princess could function as a powerful maternal icon. An obvious example is how Caroline of Anspach's inoculation of her children against smallpox made the practice acceptable in England. Both Toni Bowers and Carole Barash have shown how Queen Anne's biological failure as a mother contrasted poignantly with her construction in literature as a domestic woman. In this book Gerrard shows how Caroline successfully projected herself in a multiplicity of roles, including that of mother. After her death, as Bullion points out, George II's poor relationship with his heir and his attachment with the Duchess of Yarmouth enabled Frederick and Augusta to show off their superior style of parenting. With the two last Hanoverian consorts, Charlotte and Adelaide, we see a continuing identification of queens, motherhood and philanthropy. Queen Charlotte, a prolific mother, who took a great interest in the education of her daughters, founded a maternity hospital and patronised another for fallen women; the childless Adelaide was one of the greatest charitable sponsors.[98]

The pressure on women to be morally serious mothers was supposed to encourage women to give up the dissipations of fashionable society – opera, theatre, balls, masquerades, card-games, gambling, gossip, and conspicuous consumption. In the expanding economy of eighteenth-century Britain, women were supposedly in greater need than men of guidance on how to spend their time and how to use their spending power in a tasteful rather than vulgar manner. In this context, who could be a more powerful influence on consumer habits and tastes than royal women? Richard King shows how Anne, Princess Royal, as an investor in Italian opera in London, was one of the figures who helped create the entertainment industry of Hanoverian London. Catherine of Braganza and Mary II were both importers of colonial luxuries, with the former responsible for introducing a habit that became peculiarly associated with women and gossip: the recreational drinking of tea. Caroline of Anspach visited the warehouses of East India Company merchants; Augusta of Saxe-Gotha promoted a 'Buy British' policy and courted the Bristol merchants. Under the aegis of Josiah Wedgwood's skilful marketing strategy, female royalty became another commodity in consumer society, with a range of china similar to Queen Charlotte's being branded as 'Queensware'.[99]

Literature was to become another commodity which benefited from queenly connotations. Prior to the full development of the literary market, Carole Barash argues how significant it was for women in the Restoration to establish their identity as authors through their association with royal literary culture. She emphasises the precedent set by Henrietta Maria's culture of *préciosité* in introducing the figure of the heroic woman: 'The French salons represented an ideal community in which the queen and the woman writer participated equally'. This link between royalty, women and learning was perpetuated with Mary of Modena, who brought with her the continental ideal of the female community in a conventual setting. Barash argues that for the writers Anne Killigrew and especially the convert Jane Barker, 'the queen's symbolic presence was crucial in justifying [their] creative endeavours'. Although Queen Anne's symbolic and biological role as a mother were at variance with each other, prior to her accession the Protestant princess was co-opted into the Amazonian tradition, and continued to be figured in this heroic mode as well. Barash also points out that after Mary II's death and before Anne's accession (1694–1702), several works appeared discussing the condition of women, including Mary Astell's *Serious Proposal to the Ladies*, Part II of which was dedicated to Queen Anne. During her reign, female poets who looked to the image of a female sovereign to give them poetic authority included Mary Lady Chudleigh, Sarah Egerton, Catherine Trotter and Anne Finch.[100]

Astell has been dubbed England's first feminist. Her *Serious Proposal* (1697) advocated the ideal of a Protestant nunnery, where women could reside before or instead of marriage, and devote themselves to learning and piety. In a virulently anti-Catholic Britain, Queen Anne, even had she been sympathetic, was unable to found an institution with such 'popish' connotations. However, Queen Charlotte, who had been canoness of an Imperial Protestant nunnery before her marriage, thought of her Frogmore retreat which she shared with her five unmarried daughters as a kind of nunnery, and she patronised a charity for officers' widows modelled on Astell's idea. As well as helping women to identify with scientific pursuits, Charlotte was also something of a figurehead for the Bluestockings, most obviously Frances Burney, but also Mrs Montagu, Elizabeth Carter and Hannah More. The dedication of a book to Queen Charlotte was also a helpful marketing ploy, used by writers such as Helen Maria Williams to launch themselves in the literary marketplace, as well as by established bestsellers such as the children's writer Sarah Trimmer.[101]

Queen Charlotte, who created a library of over 4,500 volumes, had a precursor as bibliophile in Caroline of Anspach, who was famously learned. But unlike the former's unmarried daughters, neither Princess Amelia nor Princess Caroline used their singleness to pursue a life of Bluestocking seriousness. We cannot know how much psychic pain was behind Caroline's hypochondria: she seems a forerunner of the languishing 'surplus woman' of the Victorian age, worn out after a morning arranging the flowers. When Amelia argued the case for the single life, had she read or heard of any of the early eighteenth-century feminist argument? Unlike their aristocratic contemporaries who were winning more freedom of choice in their marriage partners, royal princesses had less leeway and still had their marriages arranged.

Astell's *Reflections Upon Marriage* was prompted by the marital travails of Olympe Mancini, who was briefly a part of the court circle of her niece, Mary of Modena, and of the latter's sister-in-law, Catherine of Braganza.[102] If Astell is the first feminist, then that feminism has a court context. There are many sources of eighteenth-century 'feminism';

a consistent strand, from Astell to Hannah More, is an essentially Christian critique of worldliness, urging women to embrace rationality and moral seriousness, yet to accept the socially unequal ordering of society and the divine foundations of authority. The republican feminism of Mary Wollstonecraft with its hostility to the 'pestiferous purple' was a significant but distinctly minority view. At the end of our period, feminism and popular radicalism found a royal figurehead in the wrongs of the uncrowned consort of George IV, Caroline of Brunswick, combining a discourse of natural rights with neo-chivalry.

By contrast to this language of rights and wrongs, Linda Colley has suggested that the way women were able to claim the high moral ground of patriotism and moral reform in the early nineteenth century owed something to the confidence inspired by the prospect of female succession: first of George IV's daughter Princess Charlotte, and then, after her untimely death in 1817 had united the nation in mourning a favourite surrogate daughter, of Princess Victoria of Kent, born in 1819. Historians of feminism therefore need to consider how royal women became representative figures for women, and what contribution they made to popular loyalism.[103]

As these examples of popular sympathy indicate, another link between court studies and women's history is in the study of print culture, especially of prints and caricatures. A king's marriage represents what literary theorists, borrowing from anthropologists, have designated a liminal or transitional event. It represents an actual and a symbolic reordering of the social hierarchy in which the king's need for a wife in order to produce a legitimate heir is also a reminder of his mortality, and of the possibility of introducing foreign claims to sovereignty into his territories. Abby Zanger has studied the marriage of Louis XIV with Maria Theresa of Austria through the 'nuptial fictions' the event generated: the prints, pamphlets, theatrical and pyrotechnic celebrations and literary accounts. Some of this literary and visual material is used in this volume to show how consorts were perceived.[104] Andrew Barclay's chapter on Mary of Modena demonstrates how a queen could be as demonised as she was extravagantly admired. Christine Gerrard's chapter draws on these nuptial fictions to discuss the varying public perceptions of Queen Caroline. It was the common fate of entirely virtuous women like Augusta, Princess of Wales, and Adelaide of Saxe-Meiningen to be accused of adultery if their friendships with men had unpopular political overtones, as Bullion and Purdue both show. The rambunctious, no-holds-barred press of the later eighteenth century published simultaneously the scatological cartoons of a Richard Newton or a Cruikshank as well as engravings of royal portraiture by Ramsay, Reynolds or Gainsborough. Royalty could never have a uniform public image: a queen like Charlotte could be extolled for her domestic virtues or scolded for meanness.[105]

Royal women are perhaps the clearest examples of the contradictory representations of women within the western tradition. As this volume shows, although they have often been the subject matter of popular biography, serious historiography has either neglected them altogether as an extreme example of the incorporated wife, or viewed them through misleading filters representing the contemporary attitudes or political prejudices of the age writing the history. Thus, a fairer assessment of Queen Anne, as provided here by Robert Bucholz, is two hundred years overdue. Medieval historians have made great headway in studying queens and queenship. The subject now needs to be included by early modern and modern historians as part of the full gamut of women's experience in their past. This inclusion should also prompt us to consider more even-handedly the meaning of gender in court society, and in the wider arena of British life.

Notes

I would like to thank Robert Bucholz, John Bullion, Andew Hanham and Jonathan Scott for commenting on successive drafts of this chapter; its remaining shortcomings are entirely my responsibility.

1 Mark Greengrass, ed., *Conquest and Coalescence*, London, Arnold, 1991.

2 M. C. Jacob, *The Newtonians and the English Revolution 1689–1720*, Hassocks, Sussex, Harvester Press, 1976; James R. Jacob, *Robert Boyle and the English Revolution: A Study in Social and Intellectual Change*, New York, Franklin, 1977; W. M. Jacob, *Lay People and Religion in the Early Eighteenth Century*, Cambridge, Cambridge University Press, 1996; Frank Prochaska, *Royal Bounty: The Making of a Welfare Monarchy*, New Haven, Yale University Press, 1995.

3 On the Cromwellian regime and its quasi-monarchical character see Roy Sherwood, *Oliver Cromwell, King in All But Name*, Stroud, Sutton, 1997, and idem, *The Court of Oliver Cromwell*, Cambridge, Willingham, 1977. John Adamson, 'The Kingdoms of England and Great Britain: The Tudor and Stuart Courts' in idem, *The Princely Courts of Europe, 1500–1750*, London, Weidenfeld and Nicolson, 1999, ignoring the role of consorts and their bearing on the succession, stresses the continuity rather than the contrast between the Cromwellian and Restoration regimes. The succession anxieties of this period, with their confessional dimension, echo similar problems in Elizabeth I's reign: see Patrick Collinson, 'The Elizabethan Exclusion Crisis', *Proceedings of the British Academy*, 84 (1994), pp. 51–92. I am indebted to Jonathan Scott for this reference.

4 David Cannadine, 'How Should We Write the History of the Modern British Monarchy?', paper given to the Society for Court Studies seminar, London, 9 June 1999;

Walter Arnstein, 'Victoria as Warrior Queen', paper given to 67th Anglo-American Conference of Historians, 'Monarchies', Institute of Historical Research, 3 July 1998.

5 Prochaska, *Royal Bounty*.

6 Representatives of these opposing interpretations include J. C. D. Clark, *English Society, 1688–1832*, Cambridge, Cambridge University Press, 1986, and Nicholas Henshall, *The Myth of Absolutism*, London, Longman 1992, versus John Brewer, *The Sinews of Power: War, Money and the English State 1688–1783*, London, Unwin Hyman, 1989 and Jonathan Scott, *England's Troubles: Seventeenth-Century English Political Instability in European Context*, Cambridge, Cambridge University Press, 2000; see also John Miller, ed., *Absolutism in Seventeenth-Century Europe*, London, Macmillan, 1990.

7 John Cannon, *Aristocratic Century: The Peerage of Eighteenth-Century England*, Cambridge, Cambridge University Press, 1984; idem, 'The British Nobility, 1660–1800', in H. M. Scott, ed., *The European Nobilities in the Seventeenth and Eighteenth Centuries, Vol. 1, Western Europe*, London, Longman, 1995; M. L. Bush, *The English Aristocracy: A Comparative Synthesis*, Manchester, Manchester University Press, 1984; J. V. Beckett, *The Aristocracy in England 1660–1914*, Oxford, Oxford University Press, 1986; Paul Langford, *A Polite and Commercial People: England 1727–1783*, Oxford, Oxford University Press, 1989; Roy Porter, *English Society in the Eighteenth Century*, Harmondsworth, Penguin, 1982; Robert B. Shoemaker, *Gender in English Society 1650–1850: The Emergence of Separate Spheres?*, London, Longman, 1998.

8 For a recent synthesis of these cultural developments, see John Brewer, *The Pleasures of the Imagination: English Culture in the Eighteenth Century*, London, HarperCollins, 1997; also Dustin H. Griffin, *Literary Patronage in England 1650–1800*, Cambridge, Cambridge University Press, 1996; Michael Foss, *The Age of Patronage: The Arts and Society 1660–1750*, New York, Cornell University Press, 1971; David H. Solkin *Painting for Money: The Visual Arts and the Public Sphere in Eighteenth-Century England*, New Haven, Yale University Press, 1985; Marcia Pointon, *Hanging the Head: Portraiture and Social Formation in Eighteenth-Century England*, New Haven, Yale University Press, 1993.

9 Joseph M. Levine, *Between the Ancients and the Moderns: Baroque Culture in Restoration England*, New Haven, Yale University Press, 1999; A. M. Wilson, 'The Enlightenment Came First to England', in Stephen B. Baxter, ed., *England's Rise to Greatness, 1660–1763*, Berkeley and London, University of California Press, 1783; Roy Porter, 'The Enlightenment in England', in Roy Porter and Mikuláš Teich, eds, *The Enlightenment in National Context*, Cambridge, Cambridge University Press, 1981; Jacob, *Lay People and Religion*; Jeremy Gregory, 'Anglicanism and the Arts: Religion, Culture and Politics in the Eighteenth Century' in Jeremy Black and Jeremy Gregory, eds, *Politics and Society in Britain 1669–1800*, Manchester, Manchester University Press, 1991; Norman Sykes, *Church and State in England in the Eighteenth Century*, Cambridge, Cambridge University Press, 1934; Justin A. Champion, *The Pillars of Priestcraft Shaken: The Church of England and its Enemies 1660–1730*, Cambridge, Cambridge University Press, 1982; J. G. A. Pocock, *Barbarism and Religion, Vol. 1, The Enlightenments of Edward Gibbon, 1737–1764*, Cambridge, Cambridge University Press, 1999. The large literature on Jacobitism includes Paul Monod, *Jacobitism and the English People*, Cambridge, Cambridge University Press, 1989, and Eveline Cruickshanks, ed., *Ideology and Jacobitism: Aspects of Jacobitism 1689–1759*, Edinburgh, John Donald, 1982.

10 I borrow this useful phrase to denote royal sponsorship of academies and cultural programmes together with the building of palaces and townscapes, especially in capital cities, from John Gagliardo, *Germany in the Old Regime 1600–1790*, London, Longman, 1991.

11 William Weber, *The Rise of the Musical Classics in Eighteenth-Century England: A Study in Canon, Ritual and Ideology*, Oxford, Clarendon Press, 1992.

12 Representative discussions on sensibility include G. Barker-Benfield, *The Cult of Sensibility: Sex and Society in Eighteenth-Century Britain*, Chicago, University of Chicago Press, 1992; on Methodism and Evangelicalism, M. Jaeger, *Before Victoria*, London, Chatto and Windus, 1956; A. D. Gilbert, *Religion and Society in Industrial England: Church, Chapel and Social Change 1740–1914*, London, Longman, 1976; on Romanticism, Marilyn Butler, *Romantics, Rebels and Reactionaries: English Literature and its Background 1760–1830*, Oxford, Oxford University Press, 1981.

13 On women and literature, the many studies include Janet Todd, *The Sign of Angellica: Women, Writing and Fiction 1660–1800*, London, Virago, 1989; Toni Bowers, *The Politics of Motherhood: British Writing and Culture 1680–1780*, Cambridge, Cambridge University Press, 1996; Carol Barash, *English Women's Poetry, 1649–1714: Politics, Community, and Linguistic Authority*, Oxford, Clarendon Press, 1996; Nancy Armstrong, *Desire and Domestic Fiction: A Political History of the Novel*, New York, Oxford University Press, 1989; Jane Spencer, *The Rise of the Woman Novelist from Aphra Behn to Jane Austen*, Oxford, Basil Blackwell, 1986; Cheryl Turner, *Living by the Pen: Women Writers in the Eighteenth Century*, London, Routledge, 1992. Women artists have received attention from e.g. Marcia Pointon, *Strategies for Showing*, Oxford, Clarendon Press, 1997; Wendy Wassyng Raworth, ed., *Angelica Kaufmann, A Continental Artist in Georgian England*, London, Reaktion Books, 1992.

14 For example, Bridget Hill, *Women, Work and Sexual Politics in Eighteenth-Century England*, Oxford, Blackwell Books, 1989; Jane Rendall, *Women in an Industrializing Society: England 1750–1880*, Oxford, Blackwell Books, 1989.

15 For example, in addition to note 14 above, L. Davidoff and C. Hall, *Family Fortunes: Men and Women of the English Middle Class, 1780–1850*, London, Hutchinson, 1987; Margaret Hunt, *The Middling Sort: Commerce, Gender and Family in England, 1680–1780*, Berkeley CA and London, University of California Press, 1996; a pioneering study of the gentry is Amanda Vickery, *The Gentleman's Daughter: Women's Lives in Georgian England*, New Haven, Yale University Press, 1998. Hannah Barker and Elaine Chalus, eds, *Gender in Eighteenth-Century England: Roles, Representations and Responsibilities*, London, Longman, 1997, provide a superb overview of work on women in the eighteenth century, as well as including essays on women of high social rank.

16 See references in note 88 below.

17 I am grateful to Jonathan Scott for conversations on this point. See also John Reeve, 'Britain or Europe? The Context of Early Modern English History: Political and Cultural, Economic and Social, Naval and Military', in Glyn Burgess, ed., *The New British History*, London, I. B. Tauris, 1999.

18 W. B. Patterson, *James VI and I and the Reunion of Christendom*, Cambridge, Cambridge University Press, 1997.

19 Leeds Barroll, 'The Court of the First Stuart Queen', in Linda Levy Peck, ed., *The Mental World of the Jacobean Court*, Cambridge, Cambridge University Press, 1991.

20 R. Malcolm Smuts, *Court Culture and the Origins of a Royalist Tradition in Early Stuart England*, Pittsburgh, University of Pennsylvania Press, 1987.

21 Scott, *England's Troubles*; idem 'England's Troubles 1603–1702', in R. Malcolm Smuts, ed., *The Stuart Court and Europe*, Cambridge, Cambridge University Press, 1996.

22 Smuts, *Court Culture*.

23 Barroll, 'The Court of the First Stuart Queen'; Caroline Hibbard, 'The Role of a Queen Consort: The Household and Court of Henrietta Maria, 1625–1642', in Ronald G. Asch and Adolf M. Birke, eds, *Princes, Patronage, and the Nobility: The Court at the Beginning of the Modern Age*, London, German Historical Institute, and Oxford, Oxford University Press, 1991.

24 Erica Veevers, *Images of Love and Religion: Henrietta Maria and Court Entertainments*, Cambridge, Cambridge University Press, 1989.

25 As Veevers points out, Henrietta's cultural activity was by no means original, but drew on elements espoused by Catherine de Medici as consort to Henri II of France, and continued by Catherine's descendant, Marie de Medici, Henrietta's mother, who herself resided at the English court between 1638 and 1641.

26 Scott, 'England's Troubles', p. 26

27 See Eveline Cruikshanks, ed., *The Stuart Courts*, Stroud, Sutton Publishing, 2000, especially Neil Cuddy, 'Reinventing a Monarchy: The Changing Structure and Political Function of the Stuart Court, 1603–88', Andrew Barclay, 'Charles II's Failed Restoration: Administrative Reform Below Stairs, 1660–4' and Gerald Aylmer, 'Patronage at the Court of Charles II'. I am grateful to Eveline Cruikshanks for advance information on this publication. See also R. O. Bucholz and J. C. Sainty, *Officials of the Royal Household 1660–1837*, 2 vols, London, University of London, Institute of Historical Research, 1997, Introduction by R. O. Bucholz; idem, *The Augustan Court: Queen Anne and the Decline of Court Culture*, Stanford, Stanford University Press, 1993; Smuts, *Court Culture*, pp. 285–92; Adamson, 'The Tudor and Stuart Court'; Alan Marshall, *The Age of Faction: Court Politics, 1660–1702*, Manchester, Manchester University Press, 1999. Biographies of Charles II and James II also discuss the court context and the role of the consort to some degree: Ronald Hutton, *Charles II: King of England, Scotland, and Ireland*, Oxford, Clarendon Press, 1989; John Miller, *Charles II*, London, Weidenfeld and Nicolson, 1991; idem, *James II: A Study in Kingship*, Hove, Wayland, 1989; idem, *Bourbon and Stuart: Kings and Kingship in France and England in the Seventeenth Century*, London, George Philip and Son Limited, 1987. Of course historians of literature and the theatre are far in advance of court historians in exploring Restoration court culture. I am grateful to Andrew Barclay for discussing the later Stuart court with me.

28 Frances Harris, *A Passion for Government: The Life of Sarah, Duchess of Marlborough*, Oxford, Clarendon Press, 1991; see also note 85.

29 Edward Gregg, 'Monarchs without a Crown', in R. Oresko, G. C. Gibbs and H. M. Scott, eds, *Royal and Republican Sovereignty in Early Modern Europe c. 1450–1650*, Cambridge, Cambridge University Press, 1997; Edward Corp, 'The Jacobite Court at St Germain-en-Laye: Etiquette and the Use of the Royal Apartments', in Cruikshanks, ed., *The Stuart Courts*; Eveline Cruikshanks and Edward Corp, eds, *The Stuart Court in Exile and the Jacobites*, London and Rio Grande OH, Hambledon Press, 1995.

30 Lois G. Schwoerer, 'The Queen as Regent and Patron', in Robert P. Maccubin and Martha Hamilton-Phillips, eds, *The Age of William III and Mary II: Power,*

Politics and Patronage 1688–1702, Williamsburg VA, College of William and Mary, 1989.

31 Discussions of Mary's tastes and patronage include Schwoerer, 'The Queen', John Harris, 'The Architecture of the Williamite Court', John Dixon Hunt, 'The Anglo-Dutch Garden', W. T. Stean, 'Horticulture and Botany', and Charles Saumarez Smith, 'Decorative Arts', in Maccubin and Hamilton-Phillips, eds, *The Age*; J. R. Jones, 'The Building Works and Court Style of William and Mary', John Dixon Hunt, '"Netherlandish Hesperides": Garden Art in the Period of William and Mary 1650–1702' and 'D. O. Wijnando, '*Hortus Curiaci*: The Gardens of Orange and their Place in Late 17th C. Botany and Horticulture', in John Dixon Hunt and Erik de Jong, eds, *The Anglo-Dutch Garden in the Age of William and Mary*, special issue, *Journal of Garden History*, 8: 2–3 (1998); Gervase Jackson-Stops, 'The Court Style in Britain' and John Dixon-Hunt, 'The Lion in the Garden', in Renier Baarsen, Philip M. Johnston, Gervase Jackson-Stops and Elaine Evans Dee, eds, *Courts and Colonies: The William and Mary Style in Holland, England and America*, Washington and London, University of Washington Press, 1988; David Jacques and Arend Jan van der Horst, eds, *The Gardens of William and Mary*, London, Christopher Helm, 1988; and Uta Janssens-Knorsh, 'From Het Loo to Hampton Court: William and Mary's Dutch Gardens and their Influence in English Gardening', in Paul Hoftijzer and C. C. Barfoot, eds, *Fabrics and Fabrications: The Myth and Making of William and Mary*, Amsterdam, Editions Rodopi B. V., 1990. On William's francophile inclinations, Stephen B. Baxter, 'William III as Hercules: The Political Implications of Court Culture', in Lois G. Schwoerer, ed., *The Revolution of 1688–9: Changing Perspectives*, Cambridge, Cambridge University Press, 1992. Equestrian portraits and statues of William echo those of Charles I: Jane Roberts, ed., *The King's Head: Charles I, King and Martyr*, London, Royal Collection, 1999.

32 Irene Scouloudi, ed., *The Huguenots in Britain and their French Background 1550–1800*, Basingstoke, Macmillan, 1987.

33 Joanna Marschner, 'Queen Mary II as a Collector', in Mark Hinton and Oliver Impey, eds, *Kensington Palace and the Porcelain of Queen Mary II*, London, Christies, 1998, p. 49.

34 I am grateful to Francis Harris for the first point about George as tactful consort, and to Robert Bucholz for information on George and Halle Pietism; his colleague at Loyola University Chicago, Hanns Gross, is making a study of Halle Pietism. See also Jacobs, *Lay People and Religion*, p. 98.

35 Scotland regained its Parliament in 1999, the year these essays were completed. Within six months it was beginning to discuss a revision of the Act of Succession which would permit the royal family to marry Catholics without forfeiting their succession rights – the fate of two current members of the family, Prince Michael of Kent and the Earl of St Andrews, both married to (divorced) Catholics – on the grounds that a modern egalitarian society no longer finds the prejudice against Catholicism permissible. Royal Catholic brides are still problematic 250 years after the chequered experiences of Catherine of Braganza and Mary of Modena. It is an open question whether changing this part of the Revolution Settlement will begin to unravel the rest of it, especially as the House of Lords now excludes all but ninety-two hereditary peers as a result of 1999 legislation.

36 This reinforces the perspectives currently being followed by historians of Germany, who are now researching more thoroughly the nature of the union between Hanover and Great Britain. See, for example, Heide N. Rohloff, ed., *Grossbritannien und Hannover: Die Zeit der Personallunion 1714–1837*, Frankfurt Main, R. G. Fischer Verlag, 1989.

37 Jonathan Israel, 'The Courts of the House of Orange, *c.* 1580–1795', in Adamson, ed., *The Princely Courts*, includes a helpful discussion of the Orange–Stuart–Hohernzollern links. The Hohernzollern consorts will be discussed by Thomas Biskup in Clarissa Campbell Orr, ed., *Queenship in Europe 1660–1815*, Cambridge, Cambridge University Press, forthcoming 2004. See also Maria Kroll, *Sophia, Electress of Hanover*, London, Victor Gollancz, 1973; Elborg Forster, trans. and ed., *A Woman's Life in the Court of the Sun King: Letters of Liselotte von der Pfalz, Elisabeth Charlotte, Duchesse d'Orléans, 1652–1722*, London, Johns Hopkins Press, 1984. I owe the comparison to Queen Victoria to conversations with Joanna Marschner. Edward Corp, 'English Royalty in Exile: Maintaining Continuity in France after 1689', in François Laroque and Franck Lessay, eds, *Figures de la royauté en Angleterre de Shakespeare à la Glorieuse Révolution*, Paris, Presses de la Sorbonne Nouvelle, 1999, points out that the Stuart–Sobieska marriage also represents a failure to secure a royal rather than a princely bride.

38 Linda Colley, *Britons: Forging the Nation 1707–1837*, New Haven, Yale University Press, 1990.

39 For the cultural patronage of Princes of Wales, see ex. cat., *Princes as Patrons: The Art Collections of the Princes of Wales from the Renaissance to the Present Day*, London, Merrell Holbertson, 1998.

40 These new German monarchies included the Duchy of Württemburg, where Queen Charlotte's daughter Charlotte, Princess Royal, had become consort in 1797. The duchy was made into a monarchy by Napoleon. When the new queen addressed her mother as a fellow queen, this was completely unacceptable to a monarchy braced to oppose 'Corporal Napoleon'. Dorothy Stuart, *The Daughters of George III*, London, Macmillan, 1939.

41 However, it has been asserted that the royal family continued to feel German, even after the First World War: Edward VIII supposedly always spoke German to his mother, born Princess Mary of Teck. The present Prince Consort, Philip Duke of Edinburgh, is descended from that branch of the Hohenzollern family which took over the throne of Greece once it achieved independence from Turkey.

42 Hutton, *Charles II*, p. 204

43 Hutton also observes how much Charles II's foreign policy toward the Netherlands and France was conditioned by 'two of his strongest instincts, for royalty and for family'. The former was ruled by his nephew and the latter by his cousin.

44 Nancy Klein Maguire, 'The Duchess of Portsmouth: English Royal Consort and French Politician, 1670–85', in Smuts, ed., *The Stuart Court and Europe*; Sonia Wynne, 'The Mistresses of Charles II and Restoration Court Politics', in Cruikshanks, ed., *The Stuart Court*; Marshall, *The Age of Faction*, pp. 49–54 and 91–125. Hutton, *Charles II*, Miller, *Charles II*, and Antonia Fraser, *Charles II*, London, Weidenfeld and Nicolson, 1980, all discuss unsensationally the King's relations with all his mistresses. Robert Bucholz, in his review of Smuts, ed., *The Stuart Court and Europe*,

argues that the Duchess of Portsmouth's influence, though widely asserted, remains unproven: *Seventeenth Century News*, LVI (1998), pp. 113–15.

45 Agnes Strickland, *Lives of the Queens of England*, VIII, London, Henry Colburn, 1845, p. 475.

46 Robert Beddard, 'The Unexpected Whig Revolution of 1688', in Robert Beddard, ed., *The Revolutions of 1688*, Oxford, Clarendon Press, 1991; Rachel Weil, 'The Politics of Legitimacy: Women and the Warming-Pan Scandal', in Schwoerer, ed., *The Revolution of 1688–9*; Henri and Barbara van der Zee, *1688: Revolution in the Family*, London, Viking, 1988; Jonathan Israel, ed., *The Anglo-Dutch Moment*, Cambridge, Cambridge University Press, 1991.

47 Schwoerer, 'Images of Queen Mary II', *Renaissance Quarterly*, 42 (1989), pp. 217–24; Melinda Zook, 'The Propogation of Queen Mary II', in Louise Olga Fradenburg, ed., *Women and Sovereignty*, Edinburgh, Edinburgh University Press, 1992.

48 See Schwoerer, 'Images'; Zook, 'Propagation'; van der Zee, *1688*; Beddard, 'The Unexpected Whig Revolution'; Speck, 'William – and Mary?', in Schwoerer, ed., *The Revolution of 1688–9*; Schwoerer, 'The Queen'.

49 Weil, 'The Politics of Succession'; Edward Gregg, *Queen Anne*, London, RKP, 1980.

50 Ragnhild Hatton, *George I, Elector and King*, London, Thames and Hudson, 1978.

51 Julius Bryant, *Henrietta Howard, Woman of Reason*, London, English Heritage, 1988.

52 For princesses of the House of Orange, see H. H. Rowen, *The Princes of Orange*, Cambridge, Cambridge University Press, 1988; for Anne of Orange, see Veronica Baker-Smith, *A Life of Anne of Hanover, Princess Royal*, Leiden, E. J. Brill, 1995.

53 Nancy Mitford, *Frederick the Great*, Harmondsworth, Penguin, 1973, shows how the Protestant North European marriage market in this generation was overstocked not only by the six Hanoverians but also by Frederick's nine siblings and the fourteen siblings of his wife, Elizabeth-Christina of Brunswick. For the Duke of Cumberland, see Rex Whitworth, *William Augustus, Duke of Cumberland*, London, Leo Cooper, 1992. I am indebted to Andrew Hanham for this reference.

54 Elizabeth eventually married Frederick, Landgrave of Hesse-Hoburg, a relatively minor prince from a collateral branch of the Hesse family with a distinguished war record in Tsarist service, and Mary married her cousin William of Gloucester. Stuart, *Daughters of George III*.

55 As suggested by Anthony Bird, *The Damnable Duke of Cumberland*, London, Barrie and Rockcliff, 1960.

56 Amanda Foreman, *Georgiana, Duchess of Devonshire*, London, HarperCollins, 1998.

57 Flora Fraser, *The Unruly Queen*, London, Macmillan, 1996.

58 Gregg, 'Monarchs', in Oresko *et al.*, *Royal and Republican Sovereignty*.

59 Colley, *Britons*.

60 Ronald G. Asch, 'Introduction: Court and Household from the Fifteenth to the Seventeenth Centuries', in Asch and Birke, *Prince, Patronage, and the Nobility*; Bucholz, *The Augustan Court*, ch. 1; Bucholz and Sainty, *Officials of the Royal Household*, Introduction; Marshall, *Age of Faction*, Part I.

61 Starkey, ed., *The English Court*, Introduction, and 'Intimacy and Innovation: The Rise of the Privy Chamber'.

62 Adamson, ed., *The Princely Courts*, passim, but especially Olivier Chaline, 'The Kingdoms of France and Navarre: The Valois and Bourbon Courts *c.* 1515–1750'.

63 Hutton, *Charles II*; I am grateful to Andrew Barclay for discussing this with me. See also Brian Weiser, 'Access and Petitioning during the Reign of Charles II', in Cruikshanks, ed., *The Stuart Courts*.

64 Hutton, *Charles II*, pp. 104, 420. For Whitehall, Simon Thurley, *The Lost Palace of Whitehall*, ex. cat., London, Historic Royal Palaces and RIBA, 1998; idem, *Whitehall Palace: An Architectural History of the Royal Apartments, 1240–1648*, New Haven, Yale University Press in association with Historic Royal Palaces, 1999; and idem, 'A Country Seat Fit for a King: Charles II, Greenwich and Winchester', in Cruikshanks, ed., *The Stuart Courts*.

65 Jones, 'The Building Works and Court Style'.

66 Hatton, *George I*; John M. Beattie, *The English Court in the Reign of George I*, Cambridge, Cambridge University Press, 1967.

67 John Harris and Michael Snodin, eds, *Sir William Chambers: Architect to George III*, New Haven, Yale University Press, 1996; Margaret Richardson and Mary Anne Stevenson, eds, *John Soane, Architect: Master of Space and Light*, London, Royal Academy of Arts, 1999.

68 Roger Fulford, *Royal Dukes*, London, Collins, 1973; Jane Roberts, *Royal Landscape: The Gardens and Parks of Windsor*, New Haven, Yale University Press, 1997; Whitworth, *William Augustus*. William Augustus Duke of Cumberland's landscaping at Windsor was philanthropic as well as aesthetic in intent as it employed ex-soldiers from the 1740–48 campaigns.

69 Dana Arnold, ed., *'Squanderous and Lavish Profusion': George IV, his Image and Patronage of the Arts*, London, Georgian Group, 1995.

70 Norbert Elias, *The Civilising Process*, 2 vols, Oxford, Basil Blackwell, 1982; idem, *The Court Society*, Oxford, Basil Blackwell, 1983; for critiques, see Jeroen Duindam, *Myths of Power: Norbert Elias and the Early Modern European Court*, Amsterdam, Amsterdam University Press, 1995: Adamson, ed., *The Princely Courts*, passim. Cf. Susan Whyman's observations of how women controlled etiquette and thereby influenced the functioning of familial and social networks in an ambitious landed/mercantile family, the Verneys, *Sociability and Power in Late Stuart England: The Cultural Worlds of the Verneys 1660–1720*, Oxford, Oxford University Press, 1999, pp. 87–109.

71 Smuts, *Court Culture*, pp. 253–76.

72 Charles Webster, *The Great Instauration: Science, Medicine and Reform, 1626–1660*, London, Duckworth, 1975.

73 See Ragnhild Hatton, 'At the Court of the Sun King', in A. G. Dickens, ed., *The Courts of Europe: Politics, Patronage and Royalty, 1400–1800*, London, Thames and Hudson, 1977; Peter Burke, *The Fabrication of Louis XIV*, New Haven, Yale University Press, 1992; Bucholz and Sainty, *Officials of the Royal Household 1660–1837*.

74 Hutton, *Charles II*; Adamson, 'The Tudor and Stuart Court'; Bucholz, *The Augustan Court*; Marshall, *Age of Faction*; Lorraine Madway, '"The Most Conspicuous Solemnity": The Coronation of Charles II', in Cruikshanks, ed., *The Stuart Courts*.

75 Speck, 'William – and Mary?'; Paul S. Fritz, 'From "Public" to "Private": The Royal Funerals in England, 1500–1830', in J. Whaley, ed., *Mirrors of Morality: Studies in the Social History of Death*, London, Europa, 1981, and idem, 'The Trade in Death: The Royal Funerals in England, 1685–1830', *Eighteenth Century Studies*, 15 (1982), pp. 291–316; Cornelis W. Schonveld, '"How Lov'd She Liv'd, and How Lamented Fell":

Congreve and Prior on the Death of Queen Mary, and their Dutch Translator Willem Sewel', in Hoftijzer and Barfoot, eds, *Fabrics and Fabrication*.

76 Bucholz, *The Augustan Court*, Introduction; Parke Rouse, 'Their Majesties' Royal College in Virginia', in Maccubin and Hamilton-Phillips, eds, *The Age of William and Mary*; Jacob, *Lay People and Religion*; Marilyn Morris, *The British Monarchy and the French Revolution*, New Haven, Yale University Press, 1998; Linda Colley, 'The Apotheosis of George III: Loyalty, Royalty and the British Nation 1760–1820', *Past and Present*, 102 (1984), pp. 94–129.

77 Queen Caroline's interventions in ecclesiastical patronage are explored by Stephen Taylor, 'Queen Caroline and the Church of England', in Stephen Taylor, Richard Connors and Clyve Jones, eds, *Hanoverian Britain and Empire: Essays in Memory of Philip Lawson*, Woodbridge, Boydell Press, 1999. The cultural dimension to opposition politics in the reign of George II, centred on Frederick Prince of Wales, has been explored by Christine Gerrard, *The Patriot Opposition to Walpole: Politics, Poetry, and National Myth, 1725–1742*, Oxford, Oxford University Press, 1994.

78 Adamson, ed., *The Princely Courts*, Introduction.

79 Joan Scott, 'Gender: A Useful Category of Historical Analysis', *American Historical Review*, 91: 5 (1986), pp. 1053–75.

80 The study of masculinities *c.* 1660–1837 is in its infancy; but see Tim Hitchcock and Michèle Cohen, *English Masculinities 1660–1800*, London, Longman, 1999; Cohen, *Fashioning Masculinity*, London, Routledge, 1996; Barker and Chalus, eds, *Gender in Eighteenth-Century England*; Barker-Benfield, *The Culture of Sensibility*; and on the growth of politeness, Dena Goodman, *The Republic of Letters: A Cultural History of the French Enlightenment*, Ithaca NY, Cornell University Press, 1994, and Lawrence E. Klein, *Shaftesbury and the Culture of Politeness*, Cambridge, Cambridge University Press, 1994.

81 Klein, 'Gender, Conversation and the Public Sphere in Early Eighteenth-Century England', in J. Still and M. Worton, eds, *Textuality and Sexuality*, Manchester, Manchester University Press, 1993; idem, 'Gender and the Public/Private Distinction in the Eighteenth Century', *Eighteenth Century Studies*, 29 (1995), pp. 97–109; John Brewer, 'This, That and the Other: Public, Social and Private in the Seventeenth and Eighteenth Centuries', in Dario Castiglione and Lesley Sharpe, eds, *Shifting the Boundaries*, Exeter, University of Exeter Press, 1995; Amanda Vickery, 'Golden Age to Separate Spheres? A Review of the Categories and Chronology of English Women's History', *Historical Journal*, 36 (1993), pp. 383–414; Shoemaker, *Gender in English Society*.

82 Bryant, *Henrietta Howard*; Isobel Grundy, *Lady Mary Wortley Montagu, Comet of the Enlightenment*, Oxford, Clarendon Press, 1999; Whyman, *Sociability and Power*.

83 John Brewer, *Pleasures*, is the most recent historian to dismiss the importance of the eighteenth-century court. P. J. Jupp, 'The Roles of Royal and Aristocratic Women in British Politics *c.* 1782–1832', in Mary O'Dowd and Sabine Wichert, eds, *Chattel, Servant or Citizen: Women's Status in Church, State and Society, Historical Studies*, XIX (1995), pp. 103–113.

84 Dena Goodman, 'Public Sphere and Private Life: Toward a Synthesis of Current Historiographical Approaches to the Old Régime', *History and Theory*, 31 (1992),

pp. 1–20; Clarissa Campbell Orr, ed., *Women in the Victorian Art World*, Manchester, Manchester University Press, 1995, Introduction.

85 Harris, *A Passion for Government*; idem, '"The Honourable Sisterhood": Queen Anne's Maids of Honour', *British Library Journal*, 19: 2 (1993), pp. 181–198; Anne Somerset, *Ladies in Waiting: From the Tudors to the Present Day*, London, Weidenfeld and Nicolson, 1984.

86 As demonstrated by Barroll, 'The Court', with reference to the household of Queen Anne of Denmark, consort to James I.

87 Unfortunately this is the problem with studies by Cannon, Bush and Beckett, note 7 above. Judith Schneid Lewis, *In the Family Way: Childbearing in the British Aristocracy 1760–1860*, New Brunswick, Rutgers University Press, 1986, demonstrates that the aristocracy did in fact reproduce in the usual way.

88 Harris, *A Passion for Government*; Foreman, *Georgiana*; Elaine Chalus, 'That Epidemical Madness', in Barker and Chalus, *Gender in Eighteenth-Century England*, and idem, '"My Minerva at My Elbow": The Political Roles of Women in Eighteenth-Century England', in Taylor *et al.*, *Hanoverian Britain and Empire*; K. D. Reynolds, *Aristocratic Women and Political Society in Victorian Britain*, Oxford, Clarendon Press, 1998, esp. ch. 6; Jupp, 'The Roles of Royal and Aristocratic Women'; K. von Steinem, 'The Discovery of Women in Eighteenth Century Political Life', in B. Kanner, ed., *The Women of England from Anglo-Saxon Times to the Present: Interpretative Bibliographic Essays*, London, Mansell, 1980.

89 An illuminating case study is Peter D. Brown, 'Bute in Retirement', in Karl Schweizer, ed., *Lord Bute: Essays in Reinterpretation*, Leicester, Leicester University Press, 1988.

90 Smuts, *Court Culture*; Maren-Softe Røstvig, *The Happy Man*, 2 vols, 2nd edn, Oslo, Universitetsforlaget, 1971.

91 Schneid Lewis, *In the Family Way*; Cindy McCreery, 'Keeping Up with the Bon Ton: The Tête-a-Tête Series in the Town and Country Magazine', in Barker and Chalus, eds, *Gender in Eighteenth-Century England*.

92 Schwoerer, 'The Queen'; idem, 'The Images of Mary II'; Speck, 'William – and Mary?'.

93 Vickery, *The Gentleman's Daughter*.

94 Armstrong, *Desire and Domestic Fiction*; Bowers, *The Politics of Motherhood*.

95 Alice Browne, *The Eighteenth-Century Feminist Mind*, Brighton, Harvester Press, 1987; Jane Rendall, *The Origins of Modern Feminism: Women in Britain, France and America, 1780–1860*, London, Macmillan, 1985; Anne Shteir, *Cultivating Women, Cultivating Science: Flora's Daughters and Botany in England*, Baltimore, Johns Hopkins Press, 1996.

96 Vickery, 'Golden Age to Separate Spheres'; Alex Tyrrell, '"Women's Mission" and Pressure-Group Politics in Britain, 1825–1860', *Bulletin of the John Rylands University Library*, 63 (1980), pp. 194–230; Claire Midgley, *Women Against Slavery*, London, Routledge, 1992; Jane Rendall, ed., *Equal or Different? Women's Politics 1800–1914*, Oxford, Basil Blackwell, 1987; Linda Colley, *Britons*, ch. 7; Ruth Watts, *Gender, Power, and the Unitarians in England 1760–1860*, London, Longman, 1998.

97 Kathryn Shevelow, *Women and Print Culture: The Construction of Femininity in the Early Periodical*, London, Routledge, 1989; Schneid Lewis, *In the Family Way*; Stella Tillyard, *Aristocrats*, London, Chatto and Windus, 1994.

98 Barash, *English Women's Poetry*; Bowers, *The Politics of Motherhood*; Olwen Hedley, *Queen Charlotte*, London, John Murray, 1975; Prochaska, *Royal Bounty*.

99 B. Kowaleski-Wallace, 'Tea, Gender and Domesticity in Eighteenth-Century Eng-
land', *Studies in Eighteenth-Century Culture*, 23 (1993), pp. 131–45; idem, 'Women,
China and Consumer Culture', *Eighteenth Century Studies*, 29 (1995–96), pp. 153–67;
Neil McKendrick, in J. H. Plumb, Neil McKendrick and John Brewer, eds, *The Birth
of Consumer Society: The Commercialization of Eighteenth-Century England*, London,
Hutchinson, 1983, pp. 109–12.

100 Barash, *English Women's Poetry*, pp. 37, 152.

101 Hedley, *Queen Charlotte*; Alice Drayton Greenwood, *Lives of the Hanoverian Queens
of England*, 2 vols, London, G. Bell & Sons Ltd, 1911. I hope to address Queen
Charlotte's importance for literary women in a further article. Helen Maria Williams
is better known as a Paris-based journalist reporting on the French Revolution, but
her first book, a collection of poetry (1786), was dedicated to the Queen. Sarah
Trimmer's famous 'Story of the Robins' in her *Fabulous Histories* (1786) was dedicated to Princess Sophia, her *Sacred History* (1788) and *Economy of Charity* (1801
edn) to Queen Charlotte, and her *Companion to the Book of Common Prayer* (1801)
to Charlotte, Princess Royal. Trimmer's father, John Joshua Kirby, was from 1761
Clerk to the Works at Kew and had taught architectural drawing to George III when
Prince of Wales.

102 Ruth Perry, *The Celebrated Mary Astell, An Early English Feminist*, Chicago, Univer-
sity of Chicago Press, 1986; Schwoerer, 'Women and the Glorious Revolution' *Albion*,
18: 2 (1986), pp. 195–218; Weil, 'The Politics'. On Queen Caroline, Thomas Laquer,
'The Queen Caroline Affair: Politics as Art in the Reign of George IV', *Journal of
Modern History*, 54 (1982), pp. 417–66; Alice Clark, *The Struggle for the Breeches:
Gender and the Making of the English Working Class*, London, Rivers Oram Press,
1995, and Clark, 'Queen Caroline and the Sexual Politics of Popular Culture in
London, 1820', *Representations*, 31 (1990), pp. 47–68; Dorothy Thompson, 'Queen
Victoria, the Monarchy and Gender', in her *Outsiders: Class, Gender and Nation*,
London, Verso, 1993; D. Wahrman, '"Middle-Class" Domesticity Goes Public: Gen-
der, Class and Politics from Queen Caroline to Queen Victoria', *Journal of British
Studies*, 32 (1993), pp. 396–432; Tamara Hunt, 'Morality and Monarchy in the Queen
Caroline Affair', *Albion*, 23 (1991), pp. 697–722; J. Fulcher, 'The Loyalist Response
to the Queen Caroline Agitation', *Journal of British Studies*, 34 (1995), pp. 481–502;
E. A. Smith, *A Queen on Trial: The Affair of Queen Caroline*, Stroud, Alan Sutton
Publishing, 1994; Mark Girouard, *The Return to Camelot: Chivalry and the English
Gentleman*, New Haven, Yale University Press, 1981.

103 Colley, *Britons*, ch. 7.

104 Abby E. Zanger, *Scenes from the Marriage of Louis XIV: Nuptial Fictions and the
Making of Absolutist Power*, Stanford, Stanford University Press, 1997, p. 7.

105 Diana Donald, *The Age of Caricature: Satirical Prints in the Reign of George III*, New
Haven, Yale University Press, 1996; Marcia Pointon 'Maternal Paragon or Luxurious
Consumer: Queen Charlotte in Portraiture and Caricature', paper given to 'The
Role of the Consort' conference of the Society for Court Studies, London and Kew,
16–18 September 1999; David Alexander, *Richard Newton and English Caricature in
the 1790s*; Manchester, Whitworth Gallery and University of Manchester, in association with Manchester University Press, 1998.

Queen Anne presenting the plans of Blenheim to Military Merit
by Godfrey Kneller, 1708: the Whig view

Queen Anne by Antonio Verrio, *c.* 1703: the Tory view

Anne of Orange and Hanover, self-portrait, c. 1740

The Family of Frederick, Prince of Wales by George Knapton, 1751

✠ III *and* IV ✠

Panel from the Mary Moser room at Frogmore House, mid-1790s

✠ V ✠

I

Catherine of Braganza and cultural politics

Edward Corp

C ATHERINE OF BRAGANZA was the only queen consort of England
between the sixteenth and the nineteenth centuries who failed in
her primary function of providing an heir to the throne. This was the
most important single fact which determined the course of her life in
England between 1662, when she first arrived to marry Charles II, and
1692, when she left the country for good to return to Lisbon.[1]

As a foreign, Catholic princess she shared some of the difficulties
already encountered in the seventeenth century by Anne of Denmark
and Henrietta Maria of France.[2] But these difficulties were greater for
Catherine than they had been for her predecessors. Her husband was
notorious for his infidelities and for the extent of his marital insensitiv-
ity.[3] Her upbringing had not prepared her for the exceptional licentiousness of the Restoration court. Her thirty years in England coincided
with an extraordinary and unparalleled outburst of anti-Catholic feeling. And she came from a parvenu dynasty, still trying to establish itself
in a far-away and vulnerable country, which could provide her with
little diplomatic support. Against this background, her failure to produce an heir was to have major political consequences.

Catherine was frequently disregarded by her contemporaries, and
she has perhaps also been underestimated by many historians.[4] It took
her a little time to adjust to her new circumstances, but the fact is that
she managed remarkably well. She did not and could not overcome the
problems she faced, but her natural dignity and attractive fun-loving personality enabled her to maintain her position and survive some of the
most difficult situations faced by any English queen consort. When she
eventually returned to her homeland she did so with honour. In 1704,
eleven years after her return, she was appointed Regent of Portugal and
she was still in charge of the government when she died at the end of 1705.

One of the first and most influential accounts that we have of the
court of Charles II was published only eight years after Catherine's

death. Contained in the *Mémoires de la vie du comte de Grammont*, it was written in exile at Saint-Germain-en-Laye by Anthony Hamilton, nearly half a century after the events it describes.[5] Referring to her arrival in 1662, Hamilton commented that 'the new queen gave but little additional brilliance to the court, either in her person or in her retinue'.[6] This was not entirely fair. The Queen actually conformed to a different ideal of femininity, with her olive-tinted Portuguese skin and a hair style and formal court costume that were not at all fashionable in the England (or France) of the early 1660s (FIGURE 1).[7] She might not have been beautiful, but she *was* both young and pretty. Her retinue consisted of older women, whom Hamilton (and subsequent historians) chose to describe as 'frights' or 'monsters' in order to contrast them

1 *Catherine of Braganza* by Dirk Stoop, 1661

with the various English beauties 'who shone at court'. For Hamilton, therefore, the Queen 'was far from appearing with splendour in the charming court where she came to reign'. The most significant part of his account, however, is his admission that 'in the end she was pretty successful'.[8] This laconic remark is intriguing. In what ways, and by when, was she successful?

It cannot have been during the 1660s. This was the period when Charles II's attentions were focused on Barbara Palmer, Countess of Castlemaine (later Duchess of Cleveland), who gave birth to five of the King's illegitimate children between 1661 and 1665. Shortly after their mariage in 1662 Charles II ordered most of Catherine's Portuguese attendants to leave the country and he then forced her to accept Lady Castlemaine as one of her Ladies of the Bedchamber. It was a profound humiliation which, as Catherine wrote, will 'expose me to the contempt of the world',[9] and which she had to endure until 1670. Catherine also had to put up with the King's passion for Frances Stuart, who resisted him and married the Duke of Richmond. The Queen did everything she could to please, on one occasion ordering three of her Catholic chaplains to 'dance country dances in her bedchamber' to amuse the King.[10] But her ultimate failure was sexual and beyond her control. She did not attract the King and she could not give him children. Her first miscarriage was in October 1663 and another followed in February 1666.[11] In May 1668 Charles II wrote that 'my wife miscarried this morning, and though I am troubled at it, yett I am glad that 'tis evident she was with childe, which I will not deny to you; till now, I did feare she was not capable of'.[12] In June 1669, when Catherine was thirty years old, he added that 'my wife, after all our hopes, has miscarried againe'.[13]

It was only natural that Catherine's main aim during the 1660s was to establish herself at the English court by providing her husband with an heir. That would at least have enhanced her position and given her hopes of longer-term influence. By 1670 it was clear that she had failed and that she would have to find an alternative outlet for her ambitions at court. The opportunity came her way in 1670–71, when she began to place herself at the head of a faction which could oppose the influence of the reigning mistress. The ground she chose was not politics, where her influence would be minimal, but cultural patronage, where her position was likely to be much stronger.

So long as Charles II had had a single mistress who was both English and Protestant, Catherine had been at a disadvantage. She, a Portuguese Catholic, could never compete at Whitehall with Lady Castlemaine, even when the latter decided to become a Catholic to please the King.[14] But the situation began to change at the end of the 1660s when the latter's influence declined and the King began to turn to other and less important mistresses. Actresses like Moll Davis (who bore Charles a daughter in 1665), or Nell Gwyn (who bore him two sons in 1670 and 1671), were not serious rivals. Nor was Winifred Wells, one of Catherine's own Maids of Honour, who also became a royal mistress. But by weakening the position of Lady Castlemaine they helped enhance the relative status of the Queen. When the King took a French Catholic mistress, Catherine was at last able to confront a rival who was both a foreigner and a genuine Papist. The woman was the 21-year-old Louise de Kéroualle, and it was perhaps because she seemed more easy to control that both the English Secretary of State and the French ambassador could assure her 'that the Queen wished her to submit' to the King.[15]

There was another factor which helped Catherine at this important moment. Throughout the 1660s Charles II's political and family loyalties had primarily been given to his sister Henriette, duchesse d'Orléans. French influence at Whitehall had therefore tended to be supreme. The death of the duchesse in the summer of 1670, shortly after the signature of the secret Treaty of Dover, opened up new possibilities, as the French faction at the English court no longer had the formidable backing of the King's own sister. Louise de Kéroualle, who had previously been a Maid of Honour to the duchesse d'Orléans, was brought over to Whitehall to be a Maid of Honour to Queen Catherine and she quickly became the King's new mistress. The Queen then put herself forward as the patron of Italian culture in opposition to the French culture represented by Louise, created Duchess of Portsmouth in 1673.

In the early 1670s Catherine was also helped by a growth of Catholicism at court. Her sister-in-law, the Duchess of York (née Anne Hyde), died a Catholic in 1671. Two years later the Duke of York publicly revealed that he too had converted to Catholicism. As the King's younger brother, the Duke had remained the heir presumptive thanks to Catherine's failure to have a child. When, in the autumn of 1673, he took as his second wife an Italian princess, Mary of Modena, a pro-Italian cultural and dynastic faction came into being which the Queen could use to oppose the French influence of the Duchess of Portsmouth. This was a dramatic change from the isolation which Catherine had experienced in the days of Lady Castlemaine.

In the years that followed, Catherine and the new Duchess of York used cultural patronage to enhance their influence at court. In 1675 they even imported Hortense Mancini, duchesse Mazarin, in the hope of supplanting the Duchess of Portsmouth as the King's mistress. Hortense, like Mary of Modena's mother, was a niece of Cardinal Mazarin, and thus one of the 'Mazarinettes'. As the estranged wife of a French duke she could supply the King with his desire for things French, but her Italian family background, and the fact that she had previously lived in Turin, made her an ideal ally for the Italian faction. Charles thought 'she was the finest woman he had ever met'[16] and she quickly became his mistress.

These factional manoeuvrings improved Catherine's position at court but, as one of the King's biographers has observed, 'that is not to say that she was happy'.[17] It was humiliating to have to play one mistress off against another in this way. The behaviour of the Duchess of Portsmouth, however, testifies to Catherine's relative success in carving out an independent factional role at court. The Duchess supported exclusion during the great crisis of 1679–81, and thus earned the permanent enmity of the future James II,[18] and in May 1684 she tried to take revenge 'by insinuating herself among Catherine's maids and waiting upon the Queen at dinner'. Catherine could not cope with such tactics and 'she broke down and wept in public',[19] but perhaps the most significant part of the story is the need that the Duchess felt to behave in that way.

The improvement in Catherine's position after 1670 was reflected in the way she organised her household. During the 1660s her bedchamber had included English ladies only, because her Portuguese attendants had been sent home. Under the Groom of the Stole (the Countess of Suffolk), there had been five Ladies of the Bedchamber,[20] four Dressers or Bedchamber Women and six Maids of Honour.[21] The only Portuguese lady of any importance who had remained with the Queen was the Countess of Penalva, the sister of the ambassador (Francisco de Melo), but she had had no salaried position and merely received a pension as a personal friend. Catherine now abolished the post of Lady of the Bedchamber, to avoid a repetition of the appointment of Lady Castlemaine, and unofficially placed her bedchamber under the control of the Countess of Penalva. Although she retained Lady Suffolk as her Lady of the Robes and Groom of the Stole, the relative status of the two ladies was reflected in their remuneration. Lady Suffolk's salary was £300 per annum, but the Countess of Penalva's pension was £960.[22] To replace the Ladies of the Bedchamber, Catherine increased the number of her Dressers to eight in 1671 and later to ten by 1677, twelve by 1682 and fifteen by 1684.[23] A new post of Keeper of the Sweet Coffers was created, to assume one of the responsibilities of the former ladies, and a governess, called the Mother of the Maids, was appointed to supervise them and shield them from the King. By reducing the social status of her bedchamber servants, the Queen was thus able to establish a more dominant position in the most private room of her apartment. During the 1670s she was able to appoint another Portuguese lady to assist the Countess of Penalva, as well as four Portuguese Dressers. One of the latter was described as the Queen's favourite, and they all received much higher salaries.[24]

No comparable changes were needed in the other departments of the Queen's household, although the operation of the 1673 Test Act, particularly during the Exclusion Crisis, resulted in a reduction of the numbers of servants employed in her Privy, Presence and Great Chambers. Of more significance was the fact that Catherine now had more control over the appointment of the members of her Council. Her Lord Chamberlain after 1667 was Viscount Cornbury, the eldest son of the Earl of Clarendon who had advocated and negotiated her marriage in 1660–62, and thus the brother of the 1st Duchess of York. When he later became the 2nd Earl she made him her Treasurer and appointed the Earl of Ossory in his place. Her private secretary from 1662 to 1692 was Sir Richard Bellings, one of the only four men who were privy to and actually signed the secret Treaty of Dover. It seems almost certain that Catherine knew about the contents of the Treaty,[25] and this would help explain the improvement in her position after 1670, if Charles II was willing to confide in her as a Catholic now that Lady Castlemaine had lost her influence. It would also explain why Charles was never prepared to agree to a divorce. It seems indeed that the relations between Charles and Catherine became much more stable once it was clear that the Queen would have no children and that the throne would pass to the Duke of York. One of the other three men who signed the secret Treaty of Dover was the Earl of Arlington, and it is noticeable that the Queen strengthened her household by appointing him to be her Lord Steward and the Countess of Arlington to be her Groom of the Stole.

Queen Catherine attached considerable importance to maintaining her own financial independence. The 'Establishment of (her) ordinary wages, fees, allowances and pensions' has survived for 1671–72, the year after she reorganised her bedchamber.[26] This shows that of her annual income of £40,000 she kept £27,042, or 67.6 per cent, for herself and spent £12,958, or 32.4 per cent, on salaries and pensions.[27] Of the latter figure £2,127, or 16.4 per cent, was spent on pensions and £466, or 3.6 per cent, on the salaries of the officers of her revenue. The distribution of the remaining money provides an accurate indication of

Catherine's priorities. The chapel received £5,680, or 43.8 per cent, whereas all the rest of the household combined received £4,683, or 36.2 per cent. Her apartment was a public world where most of her servants, even in the bedchamber, were English. Her chapel was the private world to which she could retire and where the majority of her servants were Portuguese.[28]

The Queen's chapel at St James's Palace was originally placed under the direction of her Grand Almoner, the Abbé d'Aubigny, replaced in 1665 by Father (later Cardinal) Philip Howard, the brother of the Duke of Norfolk. There was also a Dean (until 1670), a Portuguese confessor, four almoners and four preachers. In addition the Queen employed eleven Portuguese Franciscan friars (known as Arabados, of the Order of St Peter of Alcantara) and six English Benedictine monks. There seems to have been a conscious decision to maintain the Anglo-Portuguese character of the chapel, as half of the almoners and preachers were English and half were Portuguese.[29]

This balance was upset during the 1670s. After the death of Queen Henrietta Maria in 1667, Catherine of Braganza was given the use of Somerset House, and she transferred the six Benedictines to the chapel there in 1671. Then in March 1675, two years after the passing of the first Test Act, all English-born priests were expelled from the court.[30] As Father Howard had already fled to Bornhem in Flanders the previous year, the result of this was that the priestly establishment of Catherine's chapel, with only two almoners and two preachers, became exclusively Portuguese.[31] It was even necessary to employ additional Portuguese monks to replace the English Benedictines at Somerset House.[32]

Meanwhile the music of the chapel was taken over by Italians. The documentary evidence concerning the Queen's musicians is incomplete, but we know that during the 1660s the organist of the chapel was Matthew Locke, and that he was supported on the violin by Francis Bridges. There was also a Master in charge of four boy sopranos.[33] Catherine brought with her a Portuguese singer named Timotheo de Faria, who had a great reputation in Portugal, but he unfortunately lost his voice after arriving in England,[34] so she increasingly employed Italians to support her Portuguese priests. Pepys, who disliked the music when the Queen's chapel was reopened in 1662, felt that by Christmas 1667 it was 'very good endeed'.[35] In April 1668 Catherine appointed Giovanni Sebenico (who had previously worked at St Mark's in Venice) to be the Master of the Italian music of her chapel.[36] The Italians and the Portuguese, presumably with the Queen's approval, then marginalised Locke as much as they could: they 'did not approve of his manner of play, but [insisted that they] must be attended by more polite hands'. This meant that while Sebenico 'used the great organ', Locke 'had a chamber organ by, on which he performed with them the same services'.[37] When Sebenico left England in 1673 he was replaced by Giovanni Battista Draghi,[38] who provided Catherine with Italian music of a quality to rival anything that the French faction could offer. Unfortunately we know nothing of the Italian musicians employed in the Queen's chapel by Draghi, except that they included Cornelio Galli from Lucca: one source says they were 'as well Italians as Portugueses'.[39] It was these musicians whose performances influenced the young Henry Purcell when he composed his first set of trio sonatas and published them in 1683 as 'a just imitation of the most famed Italian masters'.

Catherine did not introduce Italian music to England – Charles II had already imported a group of Italians in 1660[40] – but her achievement was to patronise the Italians so thoroughly that she succeeded in identifying herself with the music that they offered. This can be illustrated from the diary of Samuel Pepys. When he heard Italian music in 1667 it was at the house of the Queen's Chancellor, Lord Brouncker. He noted that Thomas Killigrew, whose brother was the Queen's Vice-Chamberlain, was planning to mount an opera by Draghi.[41] In 1668 he recorded that at Whitehall 'the Italians came in a large barge under the leads, before the Queen's drawing-room, and so the Queen and ladies went out and heard it for almost an hour; and endeed it was very good'.[42] The Queen's patronage was successful, for whereas musical taste in London during the 1660s had been mainly French, by the 1670s it had become for the most part Italian.[43] According to John Evelyn, the first Italian opera in England was put on in January 1674, during the marriage celebrations of the Duke of York and Mary of Modena,[44] though it was followed a few weeks later by a French opera composed by Robert Cambert.[45] Two years later, when the duchesse Mazarin threatened to supplant the Duchess of Portsmouth, the latter employed Cambert and a group of French singers and musicians to introduce extracts from the first four operas by Lully in order to counter the Italian influence of the Queen.[46]

In her choice of portrait painters Catherine made a similar attempt to create an independent cultural identity. During the 1660s she was content to be painted by Sir Peter Lely, along with the other ladies of the court.[47] By the 1670s, however, Catherine had stopped sitting to Lely, a Protestant, and patronised instead the Catholic Jacob Huysmans, who, since 1664, had succeeded in giving her a magnificent new image. Instead of the youthful and pretty figure which was captured by Lely,

Huysmans represented the Queen as a mature and sensuous beauty, clothed in ever more ravishing satin dresses with a very low corsage and tucker. In his portraits we see how Catherine grew in confidence and chose a more statuesque appearance. We also see that her curled foretop and falling ringlets gradually gave way to the new hair style of the 1670s.[48] Her two most famous portraits by Huysmans are the early ones of 1664 which show her as a shepherdess (FIGURE 2, now at Windsor Castle)

2 *Catherine of Braganza as a Shepherdess* by Jacob Huysmans, 1664

and as St Catherine (FIGURE 3).[49] In both she wears a satin dress, though
the portrait as St Catherine is the only one in which she is shown without her pearl necklace. It clearly identified the Queen with her namesake who converted the pagans to true Christianity (as Catherine did in
her chapel), but who was nevertheless cruelly mistreated by the Roman
Emperor (as Catherine had been by the King). It was engraved and
thereby achieved a wide circulation.[50]

3 *Catherine of Braganza as St Catherine* after Jacob Huysmans, *c.* 1664

Catherine does not seem to have patronised Wright, Verelst, Riley or Wissing, and is not among the ten sovereigns said to have been painted by Kneller.[51] She did, however, patronise the Italian Catholic Benedetto Gennari, who arrived in England in 1674. Gennari was a nephew of Guercino and had made a reputation in Bologna as both a portraitist and a painter of decorative works. His arrival was timely as Catherine was able to use him to strengthen her position as the champion of Italian cultural styles. The Duchess of Portsmouth responded by patronising the French portraitist Henri Gascars, who also arrived in 1674.[52]

Like most painters Gennari worked for a variety of patrons, but he was mainly employed by Catherine of Braganza, and then by the King and the Duke and Duchess of York.[53] In 1674 Catherine commissioned from Gennari a portrait of herself which she sent to her family in Portugal,[54] and she then employed him to decorate the Queen's chapel at St James's Palace which had been recently expanded by Wren with a new apse at the east end. In the years that followed Gennari continued to decorate Catherine's chapels at both St James's and Somerset House. Prompted by his work for Catherine, Charles II employed Gennari to decorate his new apartment at Windsor, so that the Italian produced sacred works for the Queen and profane ones for the King.[55] The members of Catherine's household and chapel also employed him to produce both sacred works and portraits. Catherine's favourite, Donna Francesca de Vasconcellos, commissioned three works, including her own portrait,[56] and Emanuel Dias, the Treasurer of the chapel, commissioned five.[57] Other works were produced for Giovanni Battista Draghi, Cornelio Galli and one of the Portuguese priests.[58] It was also Gennari who produced the last two portraits of Catherine herself, one in 1678 to be sent to Modena and another in 1684 for the Countess of Arlington.[59]

Gennari's work for the Duke and Duchess of York and the interplay between his royal and aristocratic patrons are discussed by Andrew Barclay in the next chapter. However, we may note here that, in addition to Catherine's own servants and those of the King, Gennari's patrons included people of widely differing political opinions. He worked for the leading ministers such as Lord Danby, the 2nd Earl of Sunderland and the Duke of Lauderdale,[60] but there were other aristocrats, particularly the 3rd Earl of Devonshire and his son-in-law, the 5th Earl of Exeter, who gave him commissions.[61] Later on, he was even employed to paint religious pictures by the Whig 4th Earl (later 1st Duke) of Devonshire for his new house at Chatsworth.[62] Other patrons included the Duke of Monmouth and the exclusionist Ralph Montagu, later the 1st Duke of Montagu, who was then rebuilding part of Boughton House in the French style.[63] Montagu had previously been Catherine's Master of the Horse and Charles II's ambassador to France, but he had become a leading opponent of the court when he commissioned five pictures from Gennari. The Queen's patronage of Gennari needs to be seen as part of a wider picture of aristocratic patronage of Italian artists. But from the Queen's point of view, her commissions of Gennari and others had an added dimension to them.

If the Queen could not compete with the royal mistresses in the King's bed, she was at least a match for them as regards cultural patronage. She did not succeed in ousting her rivals: there was always room at the English court for both French and Italian styles. But by substituting cultural for sexual politics Catherine found an alternative method of attracting the attention of her husband and countering the influence of the favourite mistresses at court. Her achievement might have been of only relative importance, but for a queen who had no children, and who came from a peripheral dynasty with few links with the other royal and princely families of western Europe, and whose marriage had been sponsored by the French court as a counter-weight to Spanish influence, it was considerable. Gascars withdrew to the Continent in 1677, just as the Duchess of Portsmouth's French singers already had the previous year. Gennari and Draghi remained. Although it is customary and probably correct to discount Catherine of Braganza's influence with Charles II as regards political matters, it is surely a mistake to do so in cultural matters as well.

There is another important way in which Catherine played a major role in creating the cosmopolitan nature of the English court, which might otherwise have been a cultural extension of the French court of Saint-Germain-en-Laye. The commercial clauses of her marriage treaty included free trading rights for English ships in Brazil and the Portuguese East Indies, as well as the cession of the port of Bombay which soon became the foundation of the wealth of the East India Company. Her own apartment at Whitehall was embellished with the cane chairs, lacquer cabinets and porcelain which she brought with her from Portugal, and she taught the ladies and women of her household to drink tea not as a medicine, but 'solely for pleasure'.[64] Catherine also popularised the painted Indian cottons, known as calicoes, which were used after the 1660s to make clothes, bedcovers and wall hangings.[65] In her book entitled *Richer than Spices*, and subtitled 'How a Royal Bride's Dowry Introduced Cane, Lacquer, Cottons, Tea, and Porcelain to England, and so Revolutionised Taste, Manners, Craftsmanship, and History in both

England and America', Gertrude Thomas wrote that 'hundreds of Portuguese artisans . . . followed her to England [and] brought to the . . . English a fascinating amalgamation of designs, materials, and customs divergent in origin, yet oddly blended together through generations of use in Portugal. In England, this foreign influence shaped the turn of a chair leg, popularized the use of woven cane, made fashionable a cup of tea, and further dramatically enriched English living in countless unexpected ways.'[66]

Starting in the apartment of the Queen, these novelties rapidly spread to the rest of the court and then to society as a whole. In April 1673 John Evelyn visited one of Catherine's Dressers (Lady Tuke) in her own London residence and found 'vases, cabinets, and other so rich furniture as I have seldom seen; to this excess of superfluity were we now arrived, and that not only at Court, but almost universally'.[67]

Catherine's household was also a place where the Portuguese language could be acquired. The translator John Stevens was the son of a Page of the Queen's Bedchamber 'attending at the Backstairs', who served her for thirty years 'since her first landing' in England.[68] John Stevens's brother Richard served the Queen in the same capacity in England for over twenty years and remained with her when she returned to Portugal.[69] John Stevens lived in Lisbon with his brother from 1693 to 1695 and translated the important works of Manuel de Faria y Sousa (1590–1649), *Asia Portugueza* (1666–75) and *Europa Portugueza* (1667), both of which had been published posthumously soon after Catherine's arrival in England. These histories of the Portuguese nation were published in English in 1695 and 1698, the former dedicated to Queen Catherine.[70] They explained to the educated English public the achievements of the Portuguese people with whom they now regularly traded. They also helped pave the way for the important Anglo-Portuguese commercial treaty (the Methuen Treaty) of 1703, which consolidated the growing English taste for the Portuguese wines which had been imported from the upper Douro since the 1660s.

It was one of the Queen's priests, Father Huddlestone, who gave Charles II his last rites when he declared himself a Catholic on his death bed in 1685. Thereafter she ceased to have any useful role in England. Being a queen dowager (the first since 1547) was very different from being a queen mother. She withdrew to Somerset House with a reduced household, and prepared to return to Portugal. She did, however, have one more dynastic duty to perform. She was present at the birth of the Prince of Wales in June 1688 and agreed to be godmother at his baptism in October. She also testified before the Privy Council a week later that the Prince really was the legitimate son of the Queen, thus lending the prestige of her name and rank to the continuance of the Stuart dynasty.[71] Indeed she and James II had always been allied in wanting to preserve the legitimate hereditary succession, rejecting the idea of divorce as much as exclusion or the legitimisation of bastards. Nevertheless, political realism prompted her to visit the invading Prince William on his arrival in London in December 1688, and thus give countenance to the 'Glorious Revolution'. Perhaps this was because William was the leader of a coalition opposing Louis XIV. In any case she had no powerful basis from which she could have opposed William's evident success in winning over the English elite, and her desire was to leave for Portugal as soon as possible. Making difficulties for William and Mary would only have hindered this.[72]

When Catherine finally left England in April 1692 James II and Mary of Modena had been deposed and were living in exile with their son at Saint-Germain-en-Laye.[73] Despite her anti-French feelings, she crossed the Channel from Margate to Dieppe,[74] having been granted a safe passage in time of war, and made her way to Rouen, where she stayed at the Convent of English Poor Clares, and where she assured the nuns that Charles II really had died a Catholic.[75] From there she travelled to Pontoise to be met by her godson Prince James, now three years old.[76] For political reasons she was unable to stay at Saint-Germain, even though James II was not there at the time, so she slept instead at Poissy and then Saint-Denis,[77] but she did visit Mary of Modena, who was eight months pregnant, at the end of May.[78] She had left her collection of paintings at Somerset House, which still belonged to her, so she commissioned Benedetto Gennari, who was living at Saint-Germain, to produce for her a painting of the Virgin Mary which she could take with her to Portugal.[79] She was spared any obligation to visit Versailles, because her old enemy Louis XIV was at the siege of Namur, and she deliberately avoided any contact with the French royal family. She then proceeded slowly on a journey lasting six months through France and Spain, eventually reaching Lisbon in January 1693.[80]

Catherine took with her from England a large retinue of 103 servants.[81] All her Portuguese attendants and priests went with her but so too did many of her English servants, such as Sir Richard Bellings, Lady Tuke and Richard Stevens. In particular she was accompanied by the servants who attended in her bedchamber,[82] a reversal of the situation of 1662 when she had arrived in England with her Portuguese attendants.[83] Her closest advisers in Portugal included Thomas Sandys (Gentleman Usher of her Privy Chamber) and John Cary (her Equerry).[84]

Catherine had more political influence in Portugal than she had ever had in England, particularly when she eventually became Regent, and she used it to advocate an anti-French foreign policy. This contributed to the Anglo-Portuguese Methuen Alliance of 1703.[85] However, it conflicted with her desire to see the restoration of the exiled, legitimate Catholic Stuarts to the English thrones. 'When James II died Catherine sincerely mourned him, and Somerset House was hung with black by her orders, and all her servants there commanded to wear mourning for a year.'[86] But James II and his son had been obliged to turn to France for support, and Catherine told her physician in December 1705 that 'when she was in England . . . she had never been a promoter of the French interest . . . ; on the contrary, she was grieved to think that the French fashion [sic] in her brother's Court would do England ill offices in Portugal' after her death.[87] The anti-French feelings that Catherine developed in England were thus stronger than the dynastic and religious links that she maintained with the family of her deposed brother-in-law.

Catherine of Braganza had more influence on English public life than most queens consort. It was her failure to produce an heir which resulted in one of the most significant crises in the nation's history, from the Exclusion Crisis to the Glorious Revolution and beyond. But she did also have a more positive influence. It was her hostility to the French faction at court which made her encourage a preference for Italian music and painting while she was in England, and which eventually contributed so decisively to the course of English foreign policy when she was Regent of Portugal during the War of the Spanish Succession. Her opposition to the French interest, and the fact that it was her thirty years in England which saw a revolution in English taste regarding design, costume and interior furnishings, meant that Catherine made a significant contribution to the development of the cosmopolitan character of the English court in the late seventeenth century.

Notes

1 There is no modern biography of the Queen. The best account of her life remains Lilias Campbell Davidson, *Catherine of Braganza, Infanta of Portugal and Queen-Consort of England* (London, John Murray, 1908).
2 When Catherine arrived in 1662 she spoke neither English nor French and had to speak to Charles II in Spanish (Davidson, *Catherine of Braganza*, p. 117). She could speak to no one else. Not until 1664 was she able to make progress with speaking English, though her understanding remained difficult (p. 205).
3 Of the many available biographies, I have found Ronald Hutton, *Charles II* (Oxford, Clarendon Press, 1989) the most useful.

4 The unfavourable comments in *The Life of Edward, Earl of Clarendon . . . Written by Himself* (1759) were analysed and discredited by Davidson, but have remained influential.

5 Eveline Cruickshanks and Edward Corp (eds), *The Stuart Court in Exile and the Jacobites* (London, Hambledon Press, 1995), p. xix.

6 Anthony Hamilton, *Memoirs of the Count of Grammont*, trans. Horace Walpole (London, Swan Sonnenschein, 1911 edition), pp. 122–3.

7 Davidson, *Catherine of Braganza*, p. 97: 'her complexion was a clear and beautiful olive, with an excellent colour . . . she was slight in figure, and perfectly made'. The portrait by Dirk Stoop (National Portrait Gallery, 2563) shows her as she was when she arrived, wearing a dress with a wide Portuguese farthingale.

8 Hamilton, *Memoirs*, p. 124.

9 Davidson, *Catherine of Braganza*, p. 135. For the return of the attendants to Portugal, see pp. 139 and 164. Catherine's Portuguese attendants did not all leave. The most important one who remained was Donna Maria, Countess of Penalva, the sister of the Portuguese ambassador to the English court.

10 *My Dearest Minette: Letters between Charles II and his Sister, the Duchesse d'Orléans*, ed. Ruth Norrington (London, Peter Owen, 1996), p. 63, 9 February 1663.

11 Davidson, *Catherine of Braganza*, p. 198 and pp. 218–19.

12 *My Dearest Minette*, p. 151, 7 May 1668.

13 *Ibid.*, p. 182, 7 June 1669. See also the King's letter to his sister of 24 May 1669, in *The Letters of Charles II*, ed. Arthur Bryant (London, Cassell, 1935), pp. 235–6.

14 Lady Castlemaine openly converted to Catholicism in 1663 (Davidson, *Catherine of Braganza*, p. 164).

15 Hutton, *Charles II*, p. 280.

16 *Ibid.*, p. 336.

17 *Ibid.*, p. 335. The suggestion was made by Davidson, *Catherine of Braganza*, p. 361, concerning the period after the Exclusion Crisis.

18 At Saint-Germain-en-Laye in 1692 James II warned his son against the Duchess: 'beware of such kind of cattel, they never consider but themselves' (Royal Library, Windsor Castle, RCiN 1006012, 'For My Son the Prince of Wales', pp. 55–6).

19 Hutton, *Charles II*, p. 417.

20 Edward Chamberlayne, *Angliae Notitia: or the Present State of England*, 1669 edition, 'The Court of the Queen Consort of England', pp. 300–4. The Ladies of the Bedchamber in 1669 were the Duchess of Buckingham and the Countesses of Castlemaine, Bath, Marischal and Falmouth.

21 The Dressers in 1669 were Lady Scroop, Lady Fraser, Lady Killigrew and Mrs La Guard; the Maids of Honour included Miss Cary, Miss Boynton, Miss Wells and Miss Price.

22 Queen Catherine's 'Establishment of ordinary wages, fees, allowances and pensions', 1671–72, in *Registers of the Catholic Chapels Royal and of the Portuguese Embassy Chapel, 1662–1829; I: Marriages*, Catholic Record Society vol. 38 (London, 1941), pp. xxix–xxxii.

23 Queen Catherine's 'Establishment of ordinary wages, fees, allowances and pensions', 1677–78, in Davidson, *Catherine of Braganza*, pp. 309–13; 'The Queen's Court' in *Angliae Notitia*, 1682 edition, pp. 223–8, and 1684 edition, pp. 221–6. Davidson does

not mention the fact that the post of Lady of the Bedchamber had been abolished and wrongly describes the Dressers as Ladies of the Bedchamber. Her comment that the Duchess of Portsmouth became one of the Queen's Ladies of the Bedchamber in 1673, and was one of the only nine ladies allowed to remain in the Queen's household after the Test Act, seems to be misleading (see pp. 282, 293 and 332).

24 The Portuguese lady was Donna Anna de Quintana. The four Portuguese Dressers were the latter's daughters Donna Armada and Donna Maria, and the two daughters of the Count of Castelmelhor, Donna Louisa and Donna Francesca de Vasconcellos. (Castelmelhor was a Portuguese nobleman living in exile in London, sometimes mistakenly described as the Portuguese ambassador.) They are shown separately in the Queen's household list for 1677–78, but were not included in any of the published lists until 1684. Benedetto Gennari described Donna Francesca de Vasconcellos as 'portughese favorita della Regina Catterina' (Prisco Bagni, *Benedetto Gennari e la Bottega del Guercino*, Bologna, Nuova Alfa Editoriale, 1986, pp. 157–8). The only other Dresser who was not English was Henrietta Desbordes, who had previously worked for the duchesse d'Orléans. The only Maid of Honour who was not English was Louise de Kéroualle.

25 See also Davidson, *Catherine of Braganza*, p. 254.

26 See note 22.

27 These figures need to be qualified, because for many years Catherine was cheated of a large part of her income (Davidson, *Catherine of Braganza*, pp. 159, 187–8, 207). Her position improved after 1667 when the dower formerly enjoyed by Queen Henrietta Maria reverted to her (p. 291). As late as 1681, when her income was meant to be £41,000, she was still only receiving £38,0000. Of this sum she spent £18,695 on salaries and pensions (the figures are taken from Davidson pp. 394–5, which quotes a 'View of Revenues and Expenses' for 1681, but have been corrected and rounded off).

28 The authority on the Queen's Chapel is David Baldwin, who kindly allowed me to read the paper he delivered on 'The Benedictine Community at the Queen's Chapel, St James's Palace' during the conference to mark the centenary of Ealing Abbey. The Queen's Anglican attendants were expected to accompany her to mass. (See *The Diary of Samuel Pepys*, ed. Robert Latham and William Matthews, 12 vols, London, G. Bell & Sons, 1970–77), III, p. 202, 21 September 1662, and V, p. 183, 24 June 1664).

29 The English almoners were Bishop Richard Russell and Father Patrick Maginn; the English preachers included Dr Thomas Godden.

30 See note 28. An exception was made for Father Huddleston, one of the Benedictines.

31 See note 28. The Benedictines were allowed to return in 1685.

32 Davidson, *Catherine of Braganza*, p. 311 (see note 23), which gives the Queen's establishment for 1677–78.

33 The Queen's musicians are shown in the list of her household for 1671–72 (see note 22, p. xxxi). The master in charge of the boys was Clement Roche.

34 *Ibid.* For details concerning Faria, see the Queen's letter of 1687 to Peter II of Portugal, quoted in Davidson, *Catherine of Braganza*, pp. 407–8. Neither Bridges, Roche nor Faria is included in Andrew Ashbee and David Lasocki, *A Biographical Dictionary of*

English Court Musicians, 1485–1714, 2 vol (Aldershot, Ashgate, 1998). In 1662, according to John Evelyn, 'the Queen's Portugal music' consisted of 'pipes, harp and very ill voices', a reference to Faria among others (*The Diary of John Evelyn*, ed. William Bray, 2 vols, 1907 edition, revised 1952, I, p. 371, 9 June 1662). After her return to Lisbon, her musicians included 'one harpist, one player on the violin, one player on the guittar and one organist' (Davidson, *Catherine of Braganza*, p. 497).

35 Pepys, *Diary*, III, p. 202, 21 September 1662; VII, p. 87, 1 April 1666; VIII, pp. 588–9, 24 December 1667. See also IX, pp. 319–20, 27 September 1668.

36 Ashbee and Lasocki, *Biographical Dictionary*, pp. 992–3.

37 *Ibid.*, pp. 734–5. The great organ was half way down the south side of the chapel. This arrangement apparently continued until Locke's death in 1677.

38 *Ibid.*, pp. 359–61. Draghi remained in the service of Queen Catherine and did not become, as suggested by Ashbee and Lasocki, the organist in the new Catholic Chapel of James II in 1686. (That was Giovanni Battista Casale. Both men, like Jean-Baptiste de Lully, were referred to as 'Mr Baptiste'.)

39 *Ibid.*, p. 453; *Angliae Notitia*, 1682 edition, p. 223. By 1677 the number of boys employed in the Queen's Chapel had risen from four to five (see note 23).

40 Margaret Mabbett, 'Italian Musicians in Restoration England (1660–90)', *Music and Letters*, 67 (1986), p. 237.

41 Pepys, *Diary*, VIII, p. 54, 12 February 1667.

42 Pepys, *Diary*, IX, p. 32, 28 September 1668.

43 Mabbett, 'Italian Musicians', pp. 240–1.

44 Evelyn, *Diavy*, II, p. 93, 5 January 1674.

45 John Buttrey, 'New Light on Robert Cambert in London, and his "Ballet et Musique"', *Early Music*, May 1995, pp. 199–220, at p. 210.

46 *Ibid.*, p. 205. Catherine had a French dancing master, Jérome Gehors, whom she appointed Groom of the Privy Chamber. She gave the same position to Francesco Corbetta, the guitarist (Ashbee and Lasocki, *Biographical Dictionary*, pp. 303 and 487–8).

47 There is a full-length state portrait (Royal Hospital, London), and a seated three-quarter length (Governor's Palace, Williamsburg, Virginia) which was engraved several times. In both of them the Queen is shown wearing an ermine-lined cloak over her costume, with the crown placed beside her. Another shows her in a less formal seated pose, but still with the pearl necklace and drop-pearl earrings which can be seen in nearly all her portraits (private collection in Portugal). There is also the celebrated miniature by Samuel Cooper (Royal Collection) which, like the earlier portrait by Stoop (see note 7), was engraved. The portrait of Catherine at Versailles (MV. 3590) seems to be a copy after these two engravings.

48 There are three in private collections, one of which is in Lisbon, and one of which was exhibited in 'The Royal House of Stuart' exhibition at the New Gallery, London, in 1889, catalogue no. 109. The one in the National Portrait Gallery (NPG. 597) is a reduced version of a three-quarter length seated portrait at the Fundaçao Madeiros de Almeida in Lisbon. (I am very grateful to Katharine Gibson for helping me to locate the portraits of the Queen.)

49 Collection of the Earl of Verulam. This original version measures 81″ × 50″, but there is also a smaller copy by Huysmans, measuring 49″ × 39″, which was painted for Lord Clifford (*Royal House of Stuart* catalogue, no. 120 and no. 108).

50 It was engraved by W. Sherwin and by R. Tompson.

51 *Royal House of Stuart* catalogue, no. 110. She was, however, painted by Lely's assistant, John Baptist Gaspars. His full-length state portrait of Catherine is at Oxburgh, where it used to be identified as showing Mary of Modena. (I am very grateful to Alastair Laing for helping me to re-identify this portrait.)

52 Ironically, Gennari had worked in Paris from 1672 to 1674 and the first pictures he produced in England were portraits of the Duchess and her son (Bagni, *Gennari*, p. 147).

53 'Nota autografa di Benedetto Gennari dei quadri eseguiti a Londra dal 1674 al 1688', in Bagni, *Gennari*, pp. 147–61. For Gennari's commissions from Mary of Modena, see the chapter by Andrew Barclay.

54 It was a full-length portrait of the Queen 'sedendo alla riva del mare che in atto malenconico sospira la partenza di Lisbona sua patria che dall'altra riva del mare in lontananza si vede' (Bagni, *Gennari*, p. 147, no. 3, lost).

55 The King also employed the Italian Antonio Verrio, who had been brought to England in 1672 by the Queen's Master of the Horse (Ralph Montagu). See the chapter by Andrew Barclay in this volume.

56 Bagni, *Gennari*, pp. 157–8, nos 93, 97, 104 (all lost).

57 *Ibid.*, pp. 149–61, nos 26, 51, 52, 101, 137 (all lost).

58 *Ibid.*, pp. 149–56, nos 23, 75, 84, 88 (all lost).

59 Reproduced in *ibid.*, p. 84 (Government Art Collection) and p. 98 (Goodwood House). These were the last portraits known to have been painted in England. Others were produced in Portugal after 1693 by Domingos Vieira.

60 *Ibid.*, pp. 149–53, nos 21, 27, 47, 48 (lost).

61 *Ibid.*, pp. 154–5, nos 72, 73, 74, 76 (lost), 77 (lost), 105.

62 *Ibid.*, p. 161, nos 135, 136.

63 *Ibid.*, pp. 151–3, nos 40 (lost), 41, 46, 49, 53, 59 (lost).

64 Gertrude Z. Thomas, *Richer than Spices* (New York, Alfred A. Knopf, 1965), p. 95. Catherine's apartment contrasted with those of Charles II's mistresses, who furnished theirs in the French style. In her bedchamber 'she had a curiously inlaid cabinet of ebony, mother-of-pearl, ivory and silver' (Davidson, *Catherine of Braganza*, p. 211).

65 Thomas, *Richer than Spices*, chapter 4, particularly pp. 46–8.

66 *Ibid.*, p. 31.

67 Evelyn, *Diary*, II, p. 86, 17 April 1673.

68 Martin Murphy, 'A Jacobite Antiquary in Grub Street: Captain John Stevens (*c.* 1662–1726)', *Recusant History*, 24: 4, (October 1999), pp. 437–54.

69 His father and brother were both called Richard Stevens. They are shown in the list of Queen Catherine's establishment for 1671–72 (see note 22) and that of her court in the 1692 edition of *Angliae Notitia*, pp. 176–81. The servants of Queen Catherine who accompanied her to Portugal in 1692 are shown in *Calendar of State Papers, Domestic*, William and Mary, 1691–92 (London, HMSO, 1900), pp. 208–9.

70 *Asia Portugueza* had actually been originally written in Spanish, not Portuguese (Murphy, 'Jacobite Antiquary', p. 449).

71 Davidson, *Catherine of Braganza*, p. 421.

72 Catherine also sent her Vice-Chamberlain to attend William of Orange on 14 December, four days before the Prince arrived in London (Robert Beddard, *A Kingdom without a King*, Oxford, Phaidon, 1988, p. 101).

73 Catherine's departure was delayed from 1685 to 1688 for several reasons: she had to persuade her brother to receive her back; she had a law suit against her Treasurer, Lord Clarendon; she then fell ill and could not travel. She was still in England when the Glorious Revolution took place, after which she met with obstruction from both William III and Louis XIV. Of the latter Catherine wrote that he 'has twice denied me leave . . . to pass on to my own country' (Davidson, *Catherine of Braganza*, p. 443).

74 Philippe de Courcillon, Marquis de Dangeau, *Journal*, ed. Soulié and Dussieux, 19 vols (Paris, 1854–60), IV, p. 75, 13 May 1692; Davidson, *Catherine of Braganza*, p. 473.

75 Ann M. C. Forster, 'The Chronicles of the English Poor Clares of Rouen: I', *Recusant History*, 18: 1 (May 1986), p. 97.

76 British Library, Add. MSS 10118, p. 516, Benet Weldon's 'Life of James II'.

77 Louis-François du Bouchet, Marquis de Sourches, *Mémoires*, ed. Comte de Cornac, 13 vols (Paris, 1882–93), IV, p. 38, 25 May 1692; Dangeau, *Journal*, IV, p. 84, 27 May 1692.

78 British Library Add. MSS 10118, p. 516; Dangeau, *Journal*, IV, p. 84, 27 May 1692. Catherine was accompanied by Lady Tuke, whose brothers Ralph and Dominic Sheldon were both members of the court at Saint-Germain. She was also accompanied by the Dowager Countess of Fingall, whose nephew Lord Clancarty was a Gentleman of the Bedchamber at Saint-Germain.

79 Bagni, *Gennari*, p. 164, no. 26, 'un ovato con dentro una Vergine che con le mani giunte riguarda a il cielo e questo mi fu ordinato dalla Regina Vedova Cattarina per portarlo in Portugallo' (lost).

80 Davidson, *Catherine of Braganza*, pp. 474–6; Dangeau, *Journal*, IV, pp. 195, 198, 227. She reached Moulins on 2 June and Avignon by 28 September, and crossed the frontier into Spain on 7 November.

81 *Calendar of State Papers, Domestic*, 1691–92, pp. 208–9.

82 The others were her cooks and the people employed in her chapel and stables. Some 39 were members of her household, 32 were specially recruited, and the rest were the servants of her servants. For Bellings (not in *CSPD* list) and his correspondence with his wife in England, see Davidson, *Catherine of Braganza*, p. 478. The most important ladies with the Queen were Lady Fingall and her daughter, Lady Emily Plunkett, both of whom remained in Portugal until 1700 (p. 481).

83 Thomas, *Richer than Spices*, p. 147. Because the ladies at the Portuguese court still wore farthingales, the King of Portugal asked Catherine to start wearing one again. She was reluctant, so the Portuguese ladies petitioned her to ask the King to allow them to stop. The King agreed (Davidson, *Catherine of Braganza*, p. 478).

84 *Inventario dos bens da Rainha da Gra-Bretanha, D. Catarina de Bragança*, ed. Virginia Rau (Coimbra, Biblioteca da Universidade, 1947), pp. 15–16. For Catherine's high opinion of Sandys, see her letter of 1688 to Peter II (Davidson, *Catherine of Braganza*, pp. 417–18). For the English servants still with Catherine when she died in 1705, see Davidson pp. 494–7. They included James Martin, who performed in her chapel.

85 Davidson, *Catherine of Braganza*, p. 482, for Catherine's support of the Methuen Treaty.

86 *Ibid.*, p. 482. The inventory of her posessions, drawn up in 1706 after her death (note 81), indicates where her loyalties lay. It includes an oval portrait of her godson, the Prince of Wales, and another of his sister Louise-Marie, the baby that Mary of Modena was carrying when Catherine visited her at Saint-Germain: 'retratos redondos . . . do Principe de Gales e de sua Jrmaa' (p. 83). The paintings were probably by François de Troy.

87 *Ibid.*, p. 488.

2

Mary Beatrice of Modena:
the 'Second Bless'd of Woman-kind'?

Andrew Barclay

M ARIA BEATRICE, wife of James II and VII, was finally able to fulfil her main purpose in life when, on 10 June 1688, she provided her husband with a male heir. All political calculations were transformed the moment a jubilant James announced to the throng of witnesses crowded around her bed that the baby was a boy. The ambition with which she had comforted herself throughout her fourteen years at this strange, foreign court in a land of heretics – that one day she would produce a son who would found a line of Catholic kings under whose guidance Britain might return to the fold of orthodoxy – seemed at last to have come to pass. It was unfortunate that everyone else assumed the same.

To those who welcomed this birth (and many did), it was viewed either as evidence of the intercession of St Winifrid, to whose supposedly miraculous well in Flintshire the King had gone on pilgrimage the previous autumn, or as an advertisement for the attractions of the fashionable spa town of Bath in whose waters the Queen had bathed just ten months before. The King's supporters made sure that the birth was greeted with all the acclaim expected for the birth of a Prince of Wales. The Catholic courtiers, hitherto rather apologetic, were suddenly filled with confidence. The extreme response, in terms of scale if not in its sycophancy, was that of the Secretary of State for Scotland, the Earl of Melfort. No one was more anxious to demonstrate his loyalty than this recent convert to Rome and the large marble monument which he erected at Bath is the perfect symbol of this brief moment of Catholic triumphalism (FIGURE 4). The monument he commissioned for the Cross Bath consisted of a canopy formed by three Composite columns and a dome surmounted by a cross and the Crown of Thorns. The decoration included the royal arms, the Drummond arms and three putti holding aloft the regalia. Its centrepiece beneath the canopy was a

4 *View of the Cross Bath at Bath with the defaced Melfort monument commemorating the conception of the Prince of Wales,* engraving, 1739

representation of the descent of the Holy Spirit – an audacious conceit suggesting a comparison between the Queen's pregnancy and the Virgin Birth. The inscription was somewhat more circumspect, attributing the conception to the spirits which infused the waters. The corporation of Bath would order the removal of some of the more offensive details in December 1688, but the monument seems otherwise to have survived unscathed until it was defaced at the time of the 1715 Rebellion and it was not until later in the eighteenth century that it was dismantled.[1] This was not a unique use of the descent of Holy Spirit to symbolise this event, for the Queen had given birth on Trinity Sunday and the Poet

Laureate, John Dryden (another Catholic convert), was therefore able to declare,

> Last solemn Sabbath saw the Church attend,
> The Paraclete in fiery pomp descend;
> But when his wondrous octave roll'd again,
> He brought a royal infant in his train:
> So great a blessing to so good a king,
> None but th'Eternal Comforter could bring.[2]

If these particular displays of loyalty seem close to blasphemy, they were hardly more so than other works produced to celebrate the Queen's pregnancy or her son's birth, such as the verse anthem, *Behold, I bring you glad tidings*, which the Protestant composer, Henry Purcell, had set for the Christmas Day service in the Protestant Chapel Royal the previous December.[3] All things considered, the court's supporters would have been better advised to have played down the idea of the pregnancy as an indication of divine favour, although it must be remembered that, given the limited conventions of seventeenth-century panegyric, there were few other ways in which a royal birth could be presented.

There is no need to invoke St Winifrid, the waters of Bath or subterfuge as an explanation for this latest development. Mary Beatrice's gynaecological history was not in the least unusual. She was a 29-year-old woman who, in fourteen years of marriage, had been pregnant eight times. She had had a miscarriage as recently as 1684 and the gap between her pregnancies in 1677 and 1682 had been longer. (One also wonders whether she and James had been sleeping less often with each other during those periods when James's affair with Catherine Sedley placed strains on their relationship.) These simple observations did not prevent the emergence of the allegations that the baby was a changeling, smuggled in at the last moment by means of a warming pan, or that he was the product of an affair between the Queen and one of the Catholic priests at court, usually identified as either James's Clerk of the Closet, Edward Petre, or the papal nuncio, Count d'Adda. These rumours were widely believed to be one of the major factors contributing to James's overthrow later that year. The two conflicting views of Mary Beatrice – that she was a model wife and mother who had blessed the monarchy with its rightful heir, or that she was a wicked bigot who had tried to defraud the kingdom into tyranny – were fixed by these events.

In fact, no royal birth in English history was better documented. A special session of the Privy Council was held on 22 October 1688 to hear evidence from those courtiers who had been present and these statements were then published.[4] This was precisely why so many people had been allowed to attend the birth in the first place. James was doing no more than making use of the precautions which had long been thought sufficient as a guard against allegations of this sort. It must be conceded that there is some truth in the argument that these proceedings did little more than to give the rumours the widest possible publicity. That however may be to overstate James's aim. Asking the senior members of his court, whether Catholic or Protestant, to swear to the authenticity of the birth bound them to support his son's claim to the succession. This was a shrewd move, bearing in mind that, if the rumours were really to be taken seriously, the status of the Prince of Wales was likely to become one of the key points in the negotiated settlement which most hoped would be the outcome of the imminent invasion by the Prince of Orange. Not the least reason why the Convention Parliament never pursued its promised investigation into the birth was that all the possible witnesses had already given sworn statements supporting James's case. How far all the bad publicity made a real difference also remains debatable. The sexual antics of Charles II had made sure that the most lurid claims of royal scandal were now a familiar feature on the margins of English journalism and there was no way in which the humorous possibilities of these latest events were going to be ignored. The one doubt is whether such satire might have proved as ineffectual as most examples of the genre had it not been backed up by William's invasion force. As Rachel Weil has made clear, all sides were in the end convinced by what they wanted to hear.[5]

Politics and religion

Now, as then, it is this controversy surrounding the birth of the Prince of Wales which defines the reputation of his mother. Today no serious historian believes that James Francis Edward Stuart was anything other than the legitimate offspring of James and Mary Beatrice. The 'warming pan' theory is recalled by historians only with embarrassment. This change has had a profound, if usually unacknowledged, influence on how Mary Beatrice has come to be viewed. A sense that she had been unfairly traduced has led several generations of historians to soften the harsh judgements which had so often been delivered against her role in the failure of James's kingship. For this, much credit must go to Agnes Strickland, whose biography of her, published in her *Lives of the Queens of England* as long ago as the 1840s, still has a strong claim to be the best study of her life.[6] As one might expect, the few authors who have produced full-scale biographies since then, most notably Marie Hallé *alias* Martin Haile, Mary Hopkirk and Carola Oman, have treated their subject sympathetically and have done so very much by following the lines already laid down by Strickland.[7] Ultimately all these biographies attempt to rehabilitate Mary Beatrice by the simple means of denying that she played any significant part in the politics of the reign. Thus, whoever it was who was to blame for misguiding James, it was not his wife. This was an interpretation which fitted all too easily into the conventions of old-fashioned biographies of royal women. If anything, this is the same approach which has been half-heartedly adopted by academic historians of the reign. Writing as he did in Strickland's wake, Lord Macaulay failed to develop a thought-through analysis of Mary Beatrice's precise role, with the surprising result that she was reduced to a bit player in his vast and overcrowded narrative.[8] Had Macaulay given her greater prominence, there would have been more in his *History* for his successors to develop or react against. Those successors have therefore usually rejected the worst elements in the myth of the Queen recklessly nagging James on to destruction, while retaining the assumption that what influence she did have was probably counterproductive. The prevailing image is of Mary Beatrice as an innocent whose limited outlook merely reinforced the flawed advice James was receiving from his clique of (male) Catholic advisers. Unflattering though it is, this interpretation seems to be thought a fairer alternative to set against the black legend of the warming pan conspiracy. It is now James's Catholicism, far more than that of his wife, which is assumed to have been the main problem.

This may be correct. Rediscovering Mary Beatrice's hidden contribution to her husband's political programme would be the obvious response to the current reassessment of the influence of elite women close to the centres of political power. It might even be thought that she took such influence for granted, having grown up at a court at which her mother ruled as Regent. However, to do so in this case would be to risk misreading the particular relationship between James and his second wife. Just because some royal women played a decisive political role does not mean that Mary Beatrice did so too. From the outset she was hampered by the fact that she married James aged only fifteen and that he was twenty-five years her senior. As with most men remarrying at the age of forty, James was already set in his ways and it seems never to have occurred to him that his young Duchess might seek a political role. Edward Colman, the secretary appointed in 1673 to manage her affairs (such as they were), had been very much his man and it was for the

Duke, not the Duchess, that Colman was acting when he conducted the secret intrigues which brought him to grief in 1678.[9] On succeeding as King in 1685, James retained all the advantages. His knowledge of the inner workings of government was as great as that of any of his ministers and he was only too willing to master the paperwork they placed before him. This was also one royal husband who had seen more of the world than his foreign-born wife. James is unlikely to have thought it necessary that she be consulted regularly on matters of state. Godolphin was appointed by James as her Lord Chamberlain in order to sideline him.

This does not mean that Mary Beatrice was isolated. A number of the leading Catholic courtiers saw advantages in cultivating her. The Earl of Sunderland, who used his position as Secretary of State to entrench himself as the King's leading minister, certainly did so, possibly more as a precaution against her potential interference than as a means of direct influence over her husband.[10] Melfort adopted the same tactic, as did the Lord Deputy of Ireland, the Earl of Tyrconnel, perhaps because they both felt they lacked a secure power base in England. In Tyrconnel's case, it may have helped that his wife was one of the Queen's Ladies of the Bedchamber. Sunderland, Melfort and Tyrconnel were, of course, the most zealous of all James's ministers who were equally determined to push through the King's policies whatever the opposition. This did not make them a 'Queen's party'. If anything, the three of them saw themselves as rivals, each trying to monopolise the King's favour by outbidding the others in their support for his policies. For Melfort, who had not converted until 1685, and Sunderland, who delayed his conversion until after the birth of the Prince of Wales, it was particularly important that, by associating with the Queen and the Catholics around her, they helped reinforce the idea that they could be relied upon. Cultivating the Queen could sometimes be just another way of impressing the King.

James would later claim that Mary Beatrice had advised him against promoting his Jesuit confidant, Edward Petre, to the Privy Council, arguing that 'it would give great Scandal not only to Protestantism but to thinking Catholics and even to the Societie [of Jesus] it self'.[11] If so, James disregarded her advice and went ahead with Petre's appointment, which then gave rise to just the sort of criticism she had warned against. The rudimentary state of the Catholic hierarchy also made it difficult for Mary Beatrice to interfere in ecclesiastical patronage, which was one area of policy in which a consort with strong religious views often meddled. James's procurement of a cardinal's hat for her uncle, Rinaldo d'Este, had no direct implications for domestic policy, other than to make it easier for Innocent XI to refuse the same honour to Petre and to confirm James's distrust of the senior English cleric at the papal court, Cardinal Howard. Mary seems not to have shared that distrust. When James removed the title of Cardinal Protector from Howard and gave it to Cardinal d'Este, her secretary, John Carryll, probably wrote to Howard to offer him her commiserations. He insisted that she had not wanted the change and that she had disassociated herself from it.[12] Caryll may just have been trying to soften the blow, but he had hitherto been Howard's trusted secretary, only recently transferring himself to the Queen's service, and so is unlikely to have set out to mislead him. Caryll had brought with him from the papal court a healthy grasp of political pragmatism, which may have coloured the Queen's thinking. Mary Beatrice's influence over her husband could be weakest when it seemed most obvious.

There was only one occasion on which Mary Beatrice undoubtedly intervened in court politics with decisive results. That occurred in January 1686 when she made it clear to James that he must banish his mistress, her former Maid of Honour, Catherine Sedley, whom he had only recently raised to the peerage as Countess of Dorchester. This had considerable ramifications, not least because the group of Protestant courtiers centred around the Lord Treasurer, the Earl of Rochester, had encouraged James to continue this affair in the hope that they could use Dorchester (a Protestant) as their ally. The Queen's protests galvanised the King's priests, led by Bonaventure Gifford, into action. James now found himself cornered by his own hypocrisy. Determined to draw a line under the brother's dissolute example, he had begun the reign by making a point of sending Sedley away from court. He could therefore hardly deny it when Giffard and others accused him of relapsing into sin. Dorchester's temporary banishment to Ireland was without question a victory for the Queen and a crucial setback for Rochester. Here was a clear instance in which the Queen and the priests combined forces in opposition to the Protestant ministers and won. Whether Mary Beatrice grasped the full implications is more doubtful, for her role was little more than that of the aggrieved wife. It was others, such as Sunderland, who exploited the outcome, and James felt able to resume the affair once the fuss had died down.[13]

In this particular case, Mary Beatrice can be seen apparently defending the cause of Catholic orthodoxy against her husband's back-sliding. That she saw her principal role as Queen as acting as James's orthodox conscience is plausible enough. Her whole upbringing had been intended to instil in her an acceptance of the Catholic Church at its most unimaginative. This was very different from James's basic position, which started from an acceptance of the principle of religious toleration. What would have seemed heresy in Modena – that other religions should be allowed to worship freely – had long been accepted by many English Catholics as the only sane response to decades of persecution. This was the all-important issue and, significantly, it was not the one which gave rise to the fault lines among the Catholics at court. Although one can speak of Catholic moderates and Catholic hardliners, the existence of a Catholic faction determined to repudiate this central plank of James's policies has never been pinned down. Perhaps only Tyrconnel in Ireland (which, as always, was a special case) was seriously thinking in such terms. If Mary Beatrice and her Italian priests were indeed troubled by such doctrinal permissiveness, they would have found themselves with few potential allies. That she seems to have looked with most favour on Sunderland, the shameless egomaniac who had no principles whatsoever, might be thought a sign of desperation. In fact, Sunderland's whole strategy was to encourage James to push ahead regardless with what he wanted to do anyway and, in backing him, she may well have thought she was doing no more than giving her husband her full support.

James had set out with a clear idea of what he wanted to do and he was not a man to be easily dissuaded. Any advice Mary Beatrice dared offer him may have been intended to satisfy her own conscience, so that she could feel that she had at least done her duty to God and the Church, without any expectation that James would listen. She was probably resigned to the fact that her views were going to be ignored. It would therefore have been perfectly possible for her to withdraw into personal piety, leaving it to her husband to wrestle with the challenge of how best to promote the political cause of Catholicism.

One reason why Mary Beatrice's faith has seemed so enigmatic is because it was so conventional. At heart she remained the good Catholic girl who had wanted to retreat from the world to the simple certainties of a convent. When young she had hoped to enter the Order of the Visitation and, had she been allowed to get her own way at the time, she would have preferred to have done so rather than marry James.[14] Just how important that break was is revealed by her continuing devotion to St François de Sales (1567–1622), the Bishop of Geneva who had helped St Jane de Chantal found that order. It is by considering this that we can perhaps come closest to understanding the real nature of her faith. It is clear that she retained the sense that her duty to her family had had to take precedence over her vocation. On her journey to England in 1673 she had made a point of paying her respects to de Sales's heart at Lyon, as if to acknowledge that she would not forget the commitment she had been prevented from making.[15] Nor did she forget. One of the two paintings she commissioned from Benedetto Gennari for her private oratory at St James's in 1682 depicted de Sales.[16] As Queen she would write to the Pope on behalf of the Convent of the Visitation at Modena supporting their request that the Catholic Church's commemoration of de Sales be promoted to a double feast.[17] It also seems quite possible that the Prince of Wales was given the middle name of Francis partly in honour of his uncle, Francesco II of Modena, and partly in memory of de Sales.[18] In 1693 she would present an image of her new-born daughter, Princess Louise, to the shrine at de Sales's tomb at Annecy.[19] As is well known, the long periods, increasing as the years passed, in which she took refuge from the court at Saint-Germain in the Convent of the Visitation of St Mary at Chaillot on the outskirts of Paris were to be an important feature of the years of exile.[20] It might even be thought something of a surprise that in 1706, after her son reached his majority, she did not fulfil her earlier ambition by taking the vows as a nun of the order. Their chapel was certainly the obvious place to bury her when she died in 1718.

By coincidence, the Catholic members of the Stuart family had their own reasons to remember de Sales. This link was older, dating back to 1619, when de Sales had attended the wedding of Marie Christine, daughter of Henri IV, to the future Duke of Savoy, Vitterio Amedeo I. The future saint was said on that occasion to have predicted that the bride's sister, the young Henrietta Maria, would go on to greater things than Marie Christine.[21] It was, in part, because of this that in later life Henrietta Maria had established the convent at Chaillot. Henrietta Maria had also begun the tradition of royal burial in its chapel, for her heart had been buried there in 1669, and, in due course, that of her second son would be placed alongside it. Chaillot thus came to rival St Edmund's or the Scots College in Paris as the mausoleum of the dynasty in exile. That Mary Beatrice was also devoted to de Sales seems to have reinforced for James the example already set by his mother. James is known to have owned a set of the Parisian edition of the saint's collected works and he was evidently familiar with specific passages of his *Introduction à la vie dévote*, a book which the royal printer, Henry Hills, republished in a new English edition in 1686.[22] De Sales's feast day was marked at court in 1686 with a sermon by Philip Ellis in the presence of the King and Queen.[23] Later generations of the Stuarts also kept up this association

Guercino's nephew. Half a century before, Charles I had failed to attract Guercino to England. With Gennari's arrival in London in 1674, the British court at least gained the satisfaction of being able to commission second-rate imitations of the master. Gennari's obvious limitations as a painter seem not to have held him back. The large and fashionable practice he established in London was almost entirely due to the kudos which rubbed off onto him from his late uncle's reputation. He was literally Guercino's heir. It was probably through him that collectors such as Sir Peter Lely and the Earl of Devonshire acquired examples of Guercino's drawings, and, as paintings by Guercino were still a rarity in England, this was one of the first ways in which collectors in Britain came into direct contact with the work of the greatest Bolognese painter since the Carracci.[35]

From the outset of his time in London Gennari resisted strict specialisation, becoming known equally for his portraits, his paintings on classical themes, and his religious works. His classical paintings, usually dominated by semi-nude female figures, had proved particularly popular. Between about 1676 and 1681 Charles II had bought seven of them for his private apartments, most notably a set of four commissioned in 1677 for the Eating Room at Windsor.[36] James had also ordered a couple of such works, together with several family portraits.[37] Gennari had also built up a near-monopoly at court in Catholic devotional images. This market was larger than might be supposed. The number of altarpieces and other religious paintings ordered by Queen Catherine and her Catholic servants was enough to provide him with a steady source of income.[38] Moreover, since Lely's death in 1680, it was difficult to say who had been the most fashionable portrait painter at court – Gennari, Wissing or Kneller.

This patronage of Gennari by the Stuart court could be regarded as a continuation of earlier patronage of Guercino by the Este. As a native of nearby Cento, Guercino had cultivated strong links with the ducal court at Modena, and Mary Beatrice's grandfather, Francesco I, had been one of Guercino's most important early patrons. To the Modenese, Guercino and the Gennari had been very much local artists.[39] It also seems most unlikely that Gennari would have chosen to base himself at the British court in 1674 had the Duke of York not married the sister of the Duke of Modena the year before. So what part had Mary Beatrice played in Gennari's career in England? The answer to that, at least initially, seems to have been surprisingly little. The works she ordered from him while Duchess of York were few in number – a *Mary Magdalen* for her bedchamber at Windsor in about 1677 and the two altarpieces, a

5 *The Holy Family* by Benedetto Gennari, 1682

Holy Family (FIGURE 5) and the *St François de Sales*, for her private oratory at St James's in 1682.[40] The purpose behind these commissions was probably devotional rather than aesthetic. Others (including, as we have seen, Charles II and Queen Catherine) had so far proved to be at least as important in their support for Gennari as she had.

It was not until she became Queen that Mary Beatrice really emerged as one of Gennari's leading patrons. A series of new altarpieces were commissioned by her for the Queen's Chapel, which temporarily formed the focus of the religious life of the court while the King's new Catholic chapel at Whitehall was under construction. The first of those altarpieces, *The Holy Family*, survives and is large enough to suggest that it was placed above the high altar; it may well be the painting shown in that position in the engraving of the interior of the Queen's Chapel at about this time. A second altarpiece showing the Crucifixion soon followed. On Easter Day 1687 this was replaced by a painting of the Resurrection, also by Gennari, who had meanwhile supplied a *Saint James*, an obvious choice of subject, for one of the side altars.[41] However, even these commissions were overshadowed by James's decision to award to Gennari the contract for the altarpieces for the new Whitehall chapel, which, for Gennari, proved to be the opportunity of a lifetime. Overall, there seems to be little sense in which it had been the backing of Mary Beatrice which had proved to be crucial to her compatriot's success.

The point can also be made that there were just as many foreign artists and musicians at James's court who were neither Italian nor French. Gennari may have supplied the altarpieces for the Whitehall chapel, but it was two sculptors from Holland and Flanders, Grinling Gibbons and Arnold Quellin, who created the vast baroque reredos into which they were set. The other foreign musician imported by James to join Fede in composing music for that chapel, Gottfried Finger, was originally from Olmütz in Moravia. Willem Wissing, who, until his death in 1687, secured all the key portrait commissions from James (FIGURE 6), was Dutch, as was Simon Verelst. Jacob Huysmans was originally from Antwerp, while Kneller was a native of Lübeck. Although he never benefited from any of James's patronage, John de Medina, a Flemish painter of Spanish extraction, arrived in London in about 1686 clearly hoping that he would.[42] What this does is to underline that the British court in the 1680s was a rather cosmopolitan place. Were the Italians any more privileged than these other foreigners?

What may have made a difference was not Mary Beatrice herself but rather the presence of other Italians within her household. By the 1680s the number of such Italians was small, being limited to her priests, a couple of Women of the Bedchamber, Peregrina Turine and Isabella Waldegrave, and her Surveyor of the Robes, Francesco Riva.[43] However it is reasonable to assume that these Italians formed a tight-knit group. The Ronchi family were an obvious presence, including not only several of the priests but also Isabella Waldegrave, who had married Mary Beatrice's physician, William Waldegrave, in 1681. In Gennari's case, it seems suggestive that he was closely related to Riva, for his brother, Cesare, was married to Riva's sister, Francesca.[44] What is not clear is whether it was Riva who helped Gennari's career, or the other way round. That William Waldegrave, Isabella Waldegrave, Giacomo Ronchi, Treasurer of the Queen's Chapel, and Marco Antonio Galli, her Jesuit

6 *Queen Mary Beatrice* by William Wissing, c. 1682

confessor, all bought paintings from Gennari might be thought further evidence hinting at mutual friendships within this group.[45] Carol Barash has noted that it was these Italians who helped introduce the court to a wider range of literary works from the Continent.[46] Although mere specu- lation, it does seem plausible to suppose that the other Italians at court would have gravitated towards this Modenese clique, whether or not they thought that Mary Beatrice might take an interest in their careers. Draghi certainly knew Waldegrave well enough to borrow money from him.[47] There was, over and above this, the mutual bond created by the fact that they were all Catholics, which, even at James's court, placed them in a minority.

Success however depended on the widest possible connections. Verrio's career is a case in point. Although originally from Lecce in southern Italy, he had spent time in France and it was from there that he had been brought to London by Ralph Montagu in 1672, the year before James married Mary Beatrice. It was the commissions he then received from Montagu and from the Earl of Arlington which had made his reputation in England. As Montagu was the Master of the Great Wardrobe and Arlington the Lord Chamberlain, his advancement into royal service was a natural next step. Once James became King, Verrio was already well established as the leading decorative painter on whose services he could call. There is no sign here that he had benefited from the backing of an Italian connection around the Yorks and, if anything, this shows how it was the influence of a number of well-placed courtiers, rather than the King and his family, which moulded the tastes of the Restoration court.

It should not in any case be assumed that the court had a monopoly over the development of taste. Royal patronage was never enough. Even Verrio accepted private commissions while in royal service (Christ's Hospital and Burghley), while Draghi composed for the theatre. It is moreover in the 1680s that the first signs of an organised London art market have been detected, and, as it developed, that market would become a wholly commercial phenomenon, only tenuously connected with the court.[48] As it was, it cannot be said that the marked preference for Italian art among those in Britain collecting or commissioning paintings during the final decades of the seventeenth century was noticeably associated with a circle around Mary Beatrice or indeed with court circles at all – the best known and best documented cases of collectors of Italian art in this period are the 5th Earl of Exeter and Sir Thomas Isham, neither of whom had obvious links with the court.[49] Whig grandees, such as Devonshire, who were out of favour with the King were just as likely to be buying Italian paintings as Tories with court offices. In all this, any possible contribution on the part of Mary Beatrice begins to look less than crucial. Her artistic patronage, if hardly negligible, was neither trend-setting nor even particularly distinctive.

It was Aphra Behn who, confidently anticipating the birth of the Prince of Wales in 1688, hailed Mary Beatrice as the 'Second Bless'd of Womankind'.[50] Although that blessing quickly turned out to be a disaster, making such tributes seem hollow, the language used by Behn and others celebrating the birth of the Prince of Wales was conventional enough. The Virgin Mary as a model for queenship was a commonplace even in

Protestant England.[51] This was also an archetype with which Mary Beatrice herself would have been entirely comfortable. If such an elevated conception of queenship seemed to impose impossible expectations, it must be acknowledged that, in reality, a queen consort's duties were limited and observers were usually (but not always) easily pleased. Mary Beatrice's time as Queen should have given her the opportunity to flourish. She was young, charming, reasonably good-looking, could speak English better than many foreign consorts, was supportive of her husband, and, as it turned, still fertile. Given that James himself was so obviously a Catholic, her religion was not quite the central problem for him that that of Henrietta Maria and Catherine of Braganza had been for his father and his brother – James's critics did not need him to be married to Mary Beatrice for them to convince themselves that he was pursuing a pro-Catholic agenda. On the other hand, so far as Mary Beatrice's own reputation was concerned, her religion was indeed the central problem. The public images imposed on her were almost entirely the products of pre-existing prejudices, either favourable or, more obviously, derogatory. Her personal qualities had little to do with it. As she found to her cost, queenship in this period was never something created only by the queen herself. To those who encountered her at first hand, however, impressions do seem to have been favourable, if sometimes superficial, and helped to provide a useful contrast to James's rather austere personality. She was the best advertisement that English Catholicism had had since the 1630s. A case can be made for saying that she did, on balance, assist her husband's cause, but only if that judgement is confined to the very narrow limits of the court. It is no paradox that she would be more obviously successful as a queen once her husband's realms had dwindled to little more than the even smaller court at Saint-Germain.

Notes

1 T. Guidott, *De Thermis Britannicis Tractatus* (London, 1691), plate opp. p. 208; *The Journeys of Celia Fiennes*, ed. C. Morris (London, 1947), pp. 236–7; W. Stukeley, *Itinerarium Curiosum* (London, 1724), p. 140; J. Wood, *A Description of Bath*, 2 vols (2nd edn, London, 1765, reprinted in facsimile in one vol., Bath, 1969), II, pp. 259–62; *Post-Reformation Catholicism in Bath*, ed. J. A. Williams (Catholic Record Society, LXV–LXVI, 1975–76), I, p. 43; J. Manco, 'The Cross Bath', *Bath History*, 2 (1988), pp. 63–6.

2 *Poems on Affairs of State IV*, ed. G. M. Crump (New Haven and London, 1968), p. 245, lines 19–24. See also *The Works of Aphra Behn*, ed. J. Todd (London, 1992–95), I, p. 297, lines 15–22.

3 *The Works of Henry Purcell* (Purcell Society, 1878–1965), XXVIII, pp. 1–27.

4 Public Record Office, London, C 212/7, mm. 5–19, declarations concerning the birth of the Prince of Wales, 1688; printed as *The Several Declarations, Together with the Several Depositions made in Council on Monday, the 22nd of October, 1688* [London, 1688]. See also British Library, Additional MS 26657, testimony of Margaret Dawson on birth of the Prince of Wales.

5 R. J. Weil, 'The Politics of Legitimacy: Women and the Warming-Pan Scandal', in L. G. Schwoerer (ed.), *The Revolution of 1688–1689* (Cambridge, 1992).

6 A. Strickland, *Lives of the Queens of England*, 8 vols (2nd edn, London, 1851–52, reprinted in facsimile, 1972), VI.

7 M. Haile, *Queen Mary of Modena* (London, 1905); M. Hopkirk, *Queen over the Water* (London, 1953); C. Oman, *Mary of Modena* (London, 1962).

8 Lord Macaulay, *The History of England*, 5 vols (London, 1849–61).

9 A. Barclay, 'The Rise of Edward Colman', *Historical Journal*, 42 (1999), pp. 109–31.

10 J. P. Kenyon, *Robert Spencer, Earl of Sunderland 1641–1702* (London, 1958, reprinted Aldershot, 1992), chs 4–6.

11 *The Life of James the Second*, ed. J. S. Clarke, 2 vols (London, 1816), II, p. 77.

12 British Library, Additional MS 28226, fo. 80: [John Caryll] to [Cardinal Howard], [c.Dec.1687] (draft).

13 Historical Manuscripts Commission, *The Manuscripts of His Grace the Duke of Rutland, preserved at Belvoir Castle*, 4 vols (London, HMSO, 1888–1905), *12th Rep.* app. v., II, p. 103; *The Diary of John Evelyn*, ed. E. S. de Beer, 6 vols (Oxford, 1955), IV, pp. 496–7; *The Ellis Correspondence*, ed. G. A. Ellis, 2 vols (London, 1829), I, pp. 32, 35, 38, 42; *Memoirs of Sir John Reresby*, ed. A. Browning (Glasgow, 1936, rev. edn, London, 1991), pp. 409–10; G. Burnet, *History of his Own Time*, 6 vols (Oxford, 1833), III, pp. 120–1, 245; *Calendar of State Papers, Domestic 1686–7* (HMSO, 1964), p. 253; P. Cooke, 'Letter from a Lady of Quality to King James II', *Gentleman's Magazine*, 72 (1802), part ii, p. 919.

14 R. Halstead [pseud. 2nd Earl of Peterborough and R. Hands], *Succinct Genealogies* (London, 1685), p. 427.

15 Oman, *Mary of Modena*, p. 26.

16 P. Bagni, *Benedetto Gennari e la bottega del Guercino* (Bologna, 1986), pp. 155 (no. 82), 156 (no. 96).

17 *Les Deniers Stuarts à Saint-Germain en Laye*, ed. Marquise Campana de Cavelli, 2 vols (Paris, 1871), II, p. 104.

18 This seems more plausible than Agnes Strickland's suggestion that he was named after St Francis Xavier. Strickland, *Lives of the Queens*, VI, p. 243.

19 Historical Manuscripts Commission, *Calendar of the Stuart Papers belonging to His Majesty the King, preserved at Windsor Castle*, 7 vols (London, HMSO, 1902–23), I, p. 80.

20 *Stuart Papers relating chiefly to Queen Mary of Modena*, ed. F. Madan, 2 vols (London, Rexburghe Club, 1889).

21 C. Oman, *Henrietta Maria* (London, 1936, reprinted 1976), p. 215.

22 M. Caillet, 'Scotland in the Antiquarian Collection of the Library of the Irish College in Paris', *Innes Review*, 43 (1992), p. 49; 'Letters of James the Second to the Abbot of La Trappe', ed. 1st Lord Acton, *Miscellanies of the Philobiblon Society*, 14 (1872–76), part 7, p. 9.

23 P. Ellis, *The Fifth Sermon Preach'd before the King and Queen* (London, 1686).

24 *Stuart Papers*, II, p. 479; J. de Chantal, *St Francis de Sales*, ed. E. Stopp (London, 1967), p. 107n.

25 W. C. Marceau, 'Recusant Translations of Saint Frances de Sales', *Downside Review*, 114 (1996), pp. 221–33; E. H. Plumptre, *The Life of Thomas Ken, D.D. Bishop of Bath and Wells* (London, 1888), I, p. 265n. The sermon referred to is printed in *The Prose Works of the Right Reverand Thomas Ken*, ed. W. Bonham [1889], pp. 75–91.

26 A. Killigrew, *Poems* (London, 1986, reprinted in facsimile, Gainesville FL, 1967); *The Poems of Anne Countess of Winchilsea*, ed. M. Reynolds (Chicago University, decennial publications, 2nd ser. v. 1903); *The Wellesley Manuscript Poems of Anne Countess of Winchilsea*, ed. J. M. E. D'Alessandro (Florence, 1988); C. Barash, *English Women's Poetry, 1649–1714* (Oxford, 1996), pp. 152–74.

27 See K. Gibson, '"Too resplendent bright for subjects' eyes": The Decoration of St George's Hall, Windsor, for Charles II', *Apollo*, 158 (May 1998), pp. 30–40, for a refreshingly subtle view on this point.

28 J. Lionnet, 'Innocenzo Fede et la musique à la cour des Jacobites à Saint-Germain-en-Laye', *Revue de la Bibliothèque Nationale*, 46 (Hiver 1992), pp. 14–18.

29 P. Holman, *Four and Twenty Fiddlers* (Oxford, 1993, new edn, 1995), pp. 425–30.

30 E. Corp, 'The Musical Manuscripts of "Copiste Z": David Nairne, François Couperin, and the Stuart Court at Saint-Germain-en-Laye', *Revue de Musicologie*, 84 (1998), pp. 56–8.

31 Evelyn, *Diary*, IV, pp. 537, 547.

32 J. Munby, 'Signor Verrio and Monsieur Beaumont, Gardeners to James II', *Journal of the British Archaeological Association*, 149 (1996), pp. 55–71.

33 *The Life and Times of Anthony Wood*, ed. A. Clark, 5 vols (Oxford Historical Society, 1891–1900), III, p. 239.

34 Bagni, *Gennari*. I wish to thank Tabitha Barber for discussions about Gennari's career in England. The views expressed here are my own.

35 D. Mahon and N. Turner, *The Drawings of Guercino in the Collection of Her Majesty the Queen at Windsor Castle* (Cambridge, 1989), pp. xvii–xviii; F. Russell, 'Guercino and England', in M. Helston, T. Henry and F. Russell, *Guercino in Britain* (London, 1991); M. Jaffé, *Old Master Drawings from Chatsworth* (London, British Museum, 1993), pp. 12, 73.

36 Bagni, *Gennari*, pp. 74 (no. 37), 78–81 (nos 41–4), 90 (no. 53), 148 (no. 14), 149 (no. 24), 150–1 (nos 35–8), 154 (no. 66); M. Levey, *The Later Italian Pictures in the Collection of Her Majesty the Queen* (London, 1964, 2nd edn, Cambridge, 1991), pp. 86–8 (nos 492–7), pls. 144–7, 150–1.

37 Bagni, *Gennari*, pp. 54 (plate), 69 (no. 32), 72 (no. 35), 147 (no. 5), 148–9 (nos 17–19), 153 (no. 62); Levey, *Later Italian Pictures*, p. 86 (no. 491), pl. 139.

38 See p. 63 above.

39 *L'arte degli Estensi – La pittura del Seicento e del Settecento a Modena e Reggio* (Modena, 1986), pp. 178–82, 186–91; J. Southern, *Power and Display in the Seventeenth Century* (Cambridge, 1988), pp. 20, 26–7, 29, 32–3, 36–7, 60, 63, 66, 69, 145–9.

40 Bagni, *Gennari*, pp. 62 (plate), 97 (no. 60), 150 (no. 28), 155 (nos 81–2).

41 Bagni, *Gennari*, pp. 100–1 (no. 63), 158–60 (nos 103, 114, 118, 125). The engraving of the Queen's Chapel is reproduced in H. M. Colvin (ed.), *The History of the King's Works*, 6 vols (HMSO, 1963–82), V, pl. 28.

42 R. K. Marshall, *John de Medina 1659–1710* (Edinburgh, National Galleries of Scotland, 1988).

43 No full list of Mary Beatrice's household as Queen survives. However, see British Library, Althorp papers D1, household establishment of the Duke of York, 1682; Althorp papers D2, household establishment of the Duke of York, [c. 1685]; Bodleian Library, Oxford, MS Rawlinson C 987, household papers of Mary of Modena; E. Chamberlayne, *Angliae Notitia* (16th edn, London, 1687), part i, pp. 199–205. An official list of the positions within her household without names can be found in Public Record Office, LR 8/418, accounts of Robert Werden, Treasurer and Receiver-General to Queen Mary, 1687–88.

44 Campana de Cavelli, *Les Derniers Stuarts*, II, pp. 21–3; E. T. Corp and J. Sanson, *La Cour des Stuarts à Saint-Germain-en-Laye au temps de Louis XIV* (Paris, Réunion de Musées Nationaux, 1992), pp. 185–6.

45 Bagni, *Gennari*, pp. 154 (nos 69, 70), 155 (no. 75), 156 (nos 84, 87, 88), 158 (nos 108, 110, 113).

46 Barash, *English Women's Poetry*, p. 149.

47 Cambridge County Record Office, Cambridge, R.51.17.31, memo. book of William Waldegrave, 1679–85, unfol.

48 I. Pears, *The Discovery of Painting* (New Haven and London, 1988, 2nd edn, 1991).

49 H. Brigstocke and J. Somerville, *Italian Paintings from Burghley House* (Alexandria VA, 1995); G. Burdon, 'Sir Thomas Isham, an English Collector in Rome in 1677–8', *Italian Studies*, 15 (1960), pp. 1–25.

50 Behn, *Works*, I, p. 295, line 33.

51 See for example, C. Hibbard, 'Translating Royalty: Henrietta Maria and the Transition from Princess to Queen', *The Court Historian*, 5 (2000), pp. 22, 28.

3

Queen Anne: victim of her virtues?

Robert O. Bucholz

O F ALL THE WOMEN who ever ruled in Britain, surely Queen Anne has received the most equivocal press.[1] The popular views of her female predecessors and successors are all fairly clear and consistent, if not always accurate, nuanced or fair: Mary I as a cruel religious bigot, Mary Queen of Scots as a capricious but glamorous tragic heroine, Elizabeth I as an unattainable but popular mistress of Renaissance *realpolitik*, and Victoria as a respectable matron and constitutional monarch. In every case, the achievements and failures of the reign have generally been associated with, even attributed, either directly or indirectly, to the virtues and defects of the individual ruler's personality. Indeed, the two success stories in the above list became national symbols while they lived and lent their names to their times after they died. In every case, the current scholarly orthodoxy has, despite occasional dissent, advanced surprisingly little from the popular view.

Queen Anne is a different case entirely. Her reign presents historians and the general public with an apparent paradox: a woman of seemingly ordinary virtues and minor vices who presided over an age of phenomenal military, diplomatic, economic and cultural success. While Anne wore the crown the British nation strode on to the European stage and began to assume a position of leadership which it would retain, for good or ill, for two centuries. Historians and their readers have generally mediated this apparent disjunction of what is, for other reigns, offered as cause and effect by simply removing the Queen from the equation. The achievements of her reign were those of her subjects, accomplished not because of, perhaps not quite in spite of, but certainly independent of the stolid presence on the throne of the last Stuart. In the words of Justin McCarthy, 'When we speak of the age of Queen Anne we cannot possibly associate the greatness of the era with any genius of inspiration coming from the woman whose name it bears'. Or, as Beatrice Curtis Brown argues in her lugubriously entitled *Alas,*

Queen Anne: 'Anne as a historical pivot does not exist'.[2] Not only did the Queen fail to give her name to the age (the term 'Augustan' seems to express a wish for someone else), but she and her reign are often omitted from the roll call of the Stuarts entirely.[3] And yet it was very largely during this reign that so many of the controversies engendered or faced by the descendants of James I – constitutional, political, religious, diplomatic – were settled, once and for all. It was under Anne that seventeenth-century debates about the succession; the respective roles of the monarch and Parliament; the established religion and toleration; and Britain's place in Europe were resolved, thanks to the continued durability of the Revolution Settlement, the victory in the War of the Spanish Succession and, at Anne's death, the triumph of the Hanoverian succession.

The case against the Queen's character and abilities – and, therefore, her importance to these developments – is summed up nicely in a current popular (and, it must be said, generally judicious) survey of English history written primarily for the American market:

> Princess Anne, daughter of James II, ascended the throne in 1702. She was 37 years old, exceedingly fat, red and spotted in complexion, and wracked by gout. She had to be carried to her coronation. She was slow-witted, uninformed, obstinate, and narrow-minded; yet also pious, sensible, good-natured, and kind. She bore fifteen children and buried them all. She loved the Church and those who defended it, but had no interest in art, music, plays, or books. Her one hobby was eating; her husband's drinking. This ordinary woman, whom the laws of hereditary monarchy raised to the throne, helped shape events during these years in two ways: first, by naming the Earl of Marlborough in 1702 to command her troops, and secondly by dismissing him from that command in 1711. By the first act she brought England unparalleled military victories; by the second she brought peace to her kingdom.[4]

Faint praise indeed! This dismissive view of Anne has, in fact, been the dominant one since the eighteenth century. And yet, even the most careless reader cannot possibly miss the logical difficulty at the heart of the passage. On the one hand, Anne was clearly unfit, by her constitution, intelligence, temperament, education, experience – and even, apparently, her appearance – to rule. And yet, this 'ordinary woman . . . helped shape' the fate of her people (and of Europe in general) by two actions which 'brought England unparalleled military victories' and 'peace to her kingdom' – a positive joint outcome heretofore notably absent in this or any other text's account of Anne's Tudor and Stuart predecessors!

As we shall see, the interpretation offered above was not necessarily that of the Queen's subjects or contemporaries. It has always had its critics, from Anne's own day to the authoritative biography, published in 1980, by Edward Gregg – to which the present chapter will owe a great deal.[5] The following pages will seek to trace the evolution of these conflicting views of Anne and her reign. Along the way, they will offer a rebuttal to some of the charges made above while placing others in context. In particular, this chapter will seek to explain why the negative interpretation offered above proved to be so seductive for so long. It will argue that the view of Anne as a dull and overweight *housfrau* may not fit the facts exactly, but it does fit quite nicely with a raft of long-standing prejudices about the public and private roles of women in general. Anne's virtues were those of the good housewife. She lacked entirely the supposedly 'masculine' attributes usually, but narrowly, sought in our rulers. In other words, far more than, say, Elizabeth I, Anne fulfilled contemporary expectations for women almost perfectly – and so doomed for her own and for future generations the serious appraisal of her abilities as Queen. She became, as James Ralph wrote, 'the Bubble of her Virtues'.[6]

The Queen's contemporary image

The Lady Anne, daughter of James, Duke of York, and Anne, *née* Hyde, Duchess of York, was born on 6 February 1665. She spent her early years in the royal nursery at Richmond Palace, safely out of the public eye – and away from the possibly pernicious influence of the Restoration court. Given the young Princess's sheltered upbringing and quiet personality, it is not surprising that her earliest portrayals in public discourse were unspecific. Anne's first significant public exposure came as a result of her marriage to Prince George of Denmark in 1683. Almost certainly because the young lady was such an unknown quantity in the early 1680s, her image in the celebratory verse produced for the wedding is stereotypical. That is, she is praised for her modesty, her virginity and her innocence – admittedly, rare and refreshing qualities at the Restoration court.[7] Subsequently, Anne's high moral standards with regard to chastity and matrimony would become legendary, figuring frequently in contemporary panegyric. Even her most dismissive later critics admit that 'Her private character was irreproachable'.[8] However, as we shall see, even such positive attributes could be turned to the disadvantage of her reputation – in this case with the charge that she was a prude.[9]

In 1683 there was also praise for the Princess's 'Affability, Benignity, and a constant Charity'. This reputation was, perhaps, unearned as yet, but these qualities were also soon to be among her more famous attributes.[10] Somewhat more surprisingly, given the long passage quoted at the beginning of this chapter, she is also praised for her beauty: she is the conqueror of the conqueror, a reference to Prince George's considerable military reputation as a young man.[11] Perhaps most remarkably, Anne's chastity and marital devotion are offered in contrast to and atonement for the late political/religious imbroglios of the Popish Plot, Exclusion Crisis and their aftermath. Thus, according to John Adams:

> 'Tis She, the spotless She who can alone
> For Englands late Ingratitude attone,
> Who ev'n in Hell could such respect create,
> She was exempted from the Publick Fate. [12]

Complimentary as these expressions may be, they also represent the first strokes of the pen in what would prove to be a more dismissive picture of Anne's abilities. In the absence of some ringing achievement or sign of individual temperament on her part, it is her new husband's military prowess which is praised. Anne's one achievement so far, her atonement for the nation's sins of faction and disorder through her personal and marital virtue, is essentially passive and private. The 'spotless She' is so because she has not entered the arena. Here, the fact that Anne was raised as a typical seventeenth-century upper-class woman has produced typical seventeenth-century expectations of that gender: to preserve her spotlessness, she has nothing to do – but to do nothing.

The reign of James II and its conclusion in the Revolution of 1688–89 redefined politics, political careers and reputations – and so it was for Anne. The Princess's maintenance of her Anglicanism in the face of strong paternal pressure and her subsequent flight from the court at the height of the Revolution made of her household a centre of Anglican loyalties and of its mistress, in some eyes, a Protestant heroine, if not exactly a saint or martyr.[13] But, like so much of the Revolution, these actions were open to less complimentary interpretations. In abandoning her unfortunate father, she provided his defenders with an opportunity to compare her and her sister, Mary, to Tullia, famous in Roman history for betraying her father.[14] Some of the satirical poetry of the day also pursues another, more recurrent theme of Anne's subsequent image: that the idea to flee Whitehall on the night of 25–26 November 1688 was not original to her, but the result of persuasion by favourites, in this case her former tutor, Henry Compton, Bishop of London, and her

Groom of the Stole, Sarah, Lady Churchill.[15] Subsequently, in the 1690s, Sarah was portrayed by Williamite loyalists as the Machiavellian evil genius who persuaded Anne to remain loyal to her and her husband, the Earl of Marlborough, despite the suspicion of the latter's Jacobite associations and the resultant disfavour with the King and Queen.[16] The implication was that the Churchills could make the Princess act against her own interests and those of the nation, if they so chose. This charge would be a mainstay of criticism from both sides of the political fence and it has continued to loom large in the popular view of Anne down to our own day.

Anne's accession as Queen in 1702 made it much more difficult for pamphleteers and satirists to criticise her. In any case, she was never subjected to the kind of gross abuse that Charles II and James II had taken. She virtually disappears from satirical verse and her portrayal in sermons is almost always complimentary. That delivered by John Sharp, Archbishop of York, at her coronation set much of the tone of subsequent such portrayals during her reign. She is offered as English (a reference to her own first speech to Parliament on 11 March 1702 in which she claimed that her heart was 'entirely English'); a second Elizabeth; a pious daughter of the Church; the 'nursing mother' of her people; and the staunch defender of the peace of Europe against the depredations of Louis XIV.[17] Each of these themes would be replayed again and again during her reign, but each would also be sufficiently complex or problematic to provide grist for less complimentary views of the Queen than Sharp's, some of them Tory, some Whig.

On the surface, the new Queen's piety would seem to be the least problematic of these themes. Anglican sermonisers, in particular, praised Anne repeatedly for the sincerity of her private devotions and the conduct of her private life; her loyalty to the Church in time of trouble; her Proclamation encouraging virtue and discouraging vice; and, later, her 1704 donation to the clergy of the proceeds of First Fruits and Tenths (known as 'Queen Anne's Bounty') and her support for the 1710 Act for Building Fifty Churches in London.[18] Some went so far as to attribute the military successes of her reign to God's favour for his loyal royal daughter.[19] But even this apparently positive theme had damaging implications in some eyes for Anne's present and posthumous reputation. After all, her piety and love for the Church were specifically and, often, ostentatiously Anglican. Her promise, at the close of her first session of Parliament in May 1702, to 'countenance those who have the truest zeal' to support the Church of England[20] could not have been very encouraging to her Dissenting subjects (just as her assertion of an

'English heart' in her first speech to that body did nothing for her people of Irish, Scottish or Welsh descent). Anne's support of the early Bills against Occasional Conformity and later acceptance of the Schism Act could only have rendered her an enemy to an important segment of her subjects, regardless of how she may have seen the matter. Their fears, and resultant antipathy to the Queen, are well conveyed in a sermon commemorating her death, many years after that event, during the Hanoverian-Whig ascendancy:

> it was too well known to be concealed, that she was, by the instigation of evil counsellors, upon the brink of yielding up, at once, all that had been obtained with so much blood and treasure. Our toleration was broke in upon, our Liberty lay wounded and gasping at the feet of the Queen, and she was just lifting up her arm to give it the last and fatal wound; when on that very day, that the iniquitous act was to take place, God appeared for us, in the most remarkable and distinguishing manner; took away the Princesse, who had been so far seduced, as to seek our ruine; and introduced, as King William's legacy, the illustrious house of Hanover.

While Anne was popular with most of her people, that feeling was apparently not universal: 'O that glorious first of August! that signal day, which ought never to be forgotten! . . . Then were our mouths filled with laughter, and our tongues with singing.'[21] In fact, Queen Anne made no overt moves to rescind the Toleration and was never comfortable with High Church firebrands like Atterbury or Sacheverell, or even Swift. Rather, her failure to run those of tender consciences to ground disgusted many High Tory and Church adherents who had hoped to come into the promised land at her accession.[22] While some gave her credit for her grudging toleration,[23] others saw it as wooly or weakminded. On the other hand, her loyalty to the established Church and antipathy to the interests of Dissenters put off her more freethinking subjects, like the Duchess of Marlborough, and it has not played well with modern historians.[24] It has made her seem intolerant, overly conservative and, perhaps, unreflective.

The idea that Anne was the 'nursing mother' of her people seems to have been especially popular. It is to be found not only in contemporary sermons but also in addresses and petitions to the throne.[25] In it was implied many of the Queen's most attractive qualities and, thus, an explanation for the personal popularity which the generality of her subjects seem to have accorded her for most of the reign.[26] There was, first, her reputation for having a sweet and gracious disposition.[27] There was, too, her concern for her subjects' welfare and her personal charity. At her death, John Smith referred to 'those Pensions, and Private Alms, which She was continually bestowing in so bountiful a Manner, till there seem'd to be little more left for Her to give'. Indeed, Anne kept a pensions list made extensive not by the names of the powerful, but by innumerable widows, orphans and poor people whose personal connection to the crown was often tenuous.[28] According to Smith, this bounty was paid for at the expense of a magnificent court and state. While the frugality of Anne's court, in fact, owed more to the expense of the war and parliamentary hostility to courtly extravagance, there is no doubt that she shared her father's aversion to courtly extravagance and passion for good husbandry. She reduced household expenditures and corruption to, arguably, their lowest point between 1688 and 1760. However, even to this there was a countervailing cost to the prestige of the crown, for, in the words of Bishop Burnet, she 'laid down the splendour of a court too much'.[29]

In fact, Anne's pursuit of economy and her willingness to abide a reduction in her 'state' were consistent with a reputation for respecting the constitution and a reluctance to push the prerogative to its limit which stood in stark contrast to that of previous Stuart occupants of the throne. Again, Smith has written:

> So far from exerting Her Prerogative to the Stretch, . . . she hardly ever made use on't, unless to pardon and reprieve; So far from invading the Publick Rights of the Community, or breaking in upon the cry'd up Liberty and Property of the Subject, that to appease the Turbulency of the Factious and Seditious, and unite the Divided Interests and Affections of all, She seem'd rather inclin'd to give up Her own.[30]

Contemporaries recognised Anne's reign as being relatively free from the kind of constitutional strife or politically motivated violence which had characterised those of her immediate predecessors. Almost uniquely among both Tudor and Stuart reigns, there were no political beheadings and but one such hanging, for William Gregg's treason in 1708. Even in the latter, open and shut case, the Queen was said to have shown sympathy for the condemned man.[31] In comparison to the machinations which took place around the state trials of Thomas More, the Regicides or the Fenwick Affair, the Sacheverell trial looks very civilised indeed. As a result, commentators frequently remarked on the Queen's reputation for gentleness, mercy and clemency. According to Francis Atterbury she 'rules a Willing People, not by the Terror of Rods and Axes, but with the Indulgent Tenderness of a Common parent'.[32] Anne's apparent lack of vindictiveness was also consistent with her avowed desire to 'be Queen of all her subjects, . . . [who] would have all the parties and distinctions of former reigns ended and buried in hers' – that is, to pursue political moderation and refuse to embrace wholeheartedly the programme or personnel of either political party.[33]

And yet, even the Queen's thrift, mercy and moderation may be seen as 'Tenderness to a Fault'.[34] At best, they amount to a sort of negative achievement. Once again she appears passive, more famous for her omissions than her accomplishments, for her qualities than for what she did with them. Indeed, her obsession with household probity seems only to confirm the notion that women belonged in a separate, domestic sphere; while her qualities of frugality, charity, marital fidelity, mercy and moderation, etc. are traditional housewifely virtues, hardly calculated to impress historians who for most of the nineteenth and twentieth centuries have taken as their theme the rise of the modern nation-state at the hands of rapacious and dynamic Renaissance princes or baroque monarchs.[35]

Anne's role as Queen during the War of the Spanish Succession is even more problematic in this regard. As a woman in the first decade of the eighteenth century, convention dictated that she could not lead her armies in combat: 'Her Majesty was no Amazon, it was not expected that she should ride her self in the Head of her Troops'.[36] She was, therefore, prevented from achieving her reputation in the traditional arena in which so many of her predecessors had achieved theirs: she could not prove herself on the field of battle. Even the initial decision to go to war was not hers; it was recognised as a continuation of William III's policies.[37]

> In William's Steps sedately she proceeds,
> William's a Patern to immortal Deeds.
>
> And cou'd she but as well the Camp supply,
> The World the sooner wou'd their grief lay by;
> But there the Fatal Breach is made so wide,
> That Loss can never be —— supply'd.

The poet's fatalism notwithstanding, that breach would have to be filled by a subordinate male. The Queen's attempt to have her husband named Commander-in-Chief of the allied forces failed miserably, but her selection of John Churchill, Earl of Marlborough as her Captain-General produced only minor controversy at the time, and has been viewed, even by her critics, as an excellent choice since. While Marlborough had proved competent in previous commands, the string of military victories which he achieved for Anne, including Blenheim,

Ramillies, Oudenarde, Malplaquet and Bouchain, seems to have astounded everyone, at home and abroad. But 'the Pious Queen' had not won these victories; they had merely been accomplished in her name.[38] Marlborough's success captured the popular imagination in ways that Anne's serene immobility could not do. While a systematic survey is probably impossible, it seems clear that the Duke of Marlborough was the subject of far more panegyrics than his royal mistress.[39] Contemporary poets and preachers saw the difficulty. Sometimes they were unable to solve it: Matthew Prior's *Ode to the Queen* spends but four pages on its ostensible subject, devoting most of its length to the exploits of her Captain-General. Anne is portrayed as 'The Woman Chief', the 'Master of the War', who nevertheless must view it from Olympian height:

> In calm Heav'n, and a serener Air
> Sublime, the Queen shall on the Summet stand,
> From Danger far, as far remov'd from Fear,
> And pointing down to Earth her dread Command.[40]

Similarly, Daniel Defoe failed consistently to find a way to celebrate Anne's role in a way which served to render her other than a passive bystander or well-wisher: 'While Marlbro' thus does hourly Triumph's raise, / THE QUEEN, (the Center of his Glory,) PRAYS'.[41] In the end, he was forced to remind his readers that Elizabeth, too, had not actually led her troops in battle, which allowed him to point out that British arms had never been so prosperous as under female reigns.[42]

Clergymen, used to the necessity of manipulating Holy Writ to fit any occasion, were often more ingenious. Some reminded their auditors that the Duke's triumphs were accomplished as a result of the Queen's commission; that there would have been no victories – indeed, no Duke of Marlborough – without the royal First Cause.[43] The author of *No Queen: or, No General*, sometimes thought to be Defoe, went farther:

> all that he has now the Honour to be, and all that Glory which dazzles our Eyes from his Extraordinary Performances had been theirs, whosoever Her Majesty had in that Manner Honoured . . . as no Question his Grace will acknowledge at all Times, that all his Honours, all his Greatness, all the Advantages he has gained in the World, are the Effect, are the Natural Produce, of Her Majesties Peculiar Regard to his Person.[44]

Some clergymen argued that such victories, being the fruit of God's blessing, were better attributed to His favour for Anne's well-known piety and religious devotions than to the human agency of a mere military commander: 'It was God who saw the Righteousness and Integrity of all her Enterprises in the Field, who went out before her Armies, who fought her Battles, and who subdued her Enemies under her on every side'.[45] As the reign wore on and the party battle heated up, such disparagement of the Duke's role in favour of the Queen's became increasingly associated with Tory commentators. It was a natural response to the Whig view of Anne as irrelevant to Marlborough's great actions.

These divergent views of the Queen's responsibility for the achievements of her reign became especially pronounced as Anne turned away from the Whigs and the war and towards the Tories and peace in the spring of 1710. The dramatic political events of that year, including the Sacheverell trial, the dismissal of Lord Treasurer Godolphin, the establishment of the Harley ministry, the Tory landslide in the general election and the first tentative moves towards peace with France, intensified party animosities and made a shambles of the Queen's desire to rule above them. Increasingly, she became the darling of Tory commentators who had never been comfortable with the war and the high taxes on land which it required; they saw her desire for peace as consistent with her vaunted concern for her people. As William Hamilton said in one of her funeral sermons: 'Many Kings of England have been great in War . . . But they for the most part were hurried on too far by wild Ambition, and knew not when to stop, and so entaild War and Misery on their Posterity and Subjects.'[46]

But the turn towards the Tories and the peace raised a problem for both sides: if the Queen was right to do so now, was she wrong to have trusted the Whigs and pursued the war up to this point? The view expressed immediately above was that her timing was impeccable. But many contemporary commentators on the reign, especially those writing at her death, refer to previous errors, which they attribute, generally, to the Queen's soft nature and excessive tolerance for those who sought to empower or enrich themselves at her expense. These critics fail to credit the Queen for her timing, her sensitivity to the nation's changing attitudes to war and peace; or her understanding of the strategic shift in the balance of power won by Marlborough's victories and France's declining capacity. Rather, she is accused by Tories of having been duped by the Churchills into prolonging the war; and by Whigs of ending it too soon, either out of a calculating faithlessness possibly born of covert Jacobite sympathies, or because of the influence of a new set of Tory bedchamber attendants (the Masham–Hill group) and backstairs intriguers.[47] On one level, such charges were, of course, a variation on the ancient notion that 'the King can do no wrong'; mistakes committed in his name must have been the work of 'evil councillors'. But in Anne's case this seeming excuse struck home with more point and negativity because she was a woman, because she had no reputation for guile or political savvy, and because she had so long been known to have been advised by Lord Godolphin and the Churchills.

Most often, Anne was portrayed as well-meaning but apt to listen far too much to her attendants and favourites. Thus in the allegorical *Seldom Comes a Better: a Tale of a Lady and Her Servants* she is portrayed as 'a very Good and Wise lady'. Nevertheless, her good fortune owes as much to her 'wise and successful Chief Counsellor' as it does to 'her own Good Conduct'. Moreover 'this Lady is thought to listen a little too much to a Woman that dresses her [i.e. Abigail Masham], and who receives her Instructions from a Kinsman [i.e. Robert Harley]'. Similarly, in *The Second Part of the Impartial Secret History of Arlus* 'the good Lady . . . is persuaded by her bedchamber attendants to change her ministry'.[48] Naturally, this serves to absolve the Queen of wrongdoing: 'she was, and is unblameable, and whatever Blame there is to be found, it lies at the Door of others'.[49] But it also makes her into an innocent puppet, of little intelligence or determination in her own right. By the end of the reign, Anne, herself, was impatient with such absolution: for example, when her physician, Sir David Hamilton, suggested that she was being duped by the Oxford–Masham circle to bring in the Pretender she erupted, uncharacteristically, as follows: 'Oh fye says she, there is no such thing. What, do they think I'm a Child, and to be imposed upon, and that I have only Integrity?'[50] By the end of her reign she had not only integrity, but experience and, in William Speck's words, 'a stomach for the political fight'.[51] But her customary public reserve, poor health and resultant isolation meant that few knew this. Consequently, in life and, later, in death, the only public access to the Queen's character and image, like that to her person, would be provided through the conduit of a bedchamber attendant – in particular, Sarah, Duchess of Marlborough.

The Queen's posthumous image

With Anne's death at 7:45 on the morning of 1 August 1714, her reputation began its posthumous career. According to Abel Boyer, 'few Princes ever died so little regretted and lamented by the Generality of their Subjects'.[52] But as the contours of George I's personality and policies became clear, there arose a certain amount of popular nostalgia for the days of 'Good Queen Anne'. This is indicated by a number of demonstrations by Tory mobs in and around London in honour of her birth, accession and coronation anniversaries during the early years of the Hanoverian regime. However, the generality of the sentiments expressed suggests that these demonstrations had far more to do with current complaints than a real appreciation for the policies and person of the deceased monarch.[53] To the authors of these protests, Anne's primary virtue was that, in her Englishness, her Anglicanism, and her modest decorum, she was not George.

In any case, Anne's posthumous reputation would rest less with the views of plebeian malcontents than with those of her fallen favourite and former friend, Sarah Churchill, Duchess of Marlborough.[54] Unlike Lady Masham, who might have provided a rather different slant on her late mistress, Sarah chose to make her views known to anyone who would listen. She did this, first, in conversation and correspondence with friends during the reign; then in a series of privately circulated manuscripts ghostwritten by a variety of acolytes; and finally via their publication in 1742 as *The Conduct of the Dowager Duchess of Marlborough*.[55] The *Conduct* began as a defence of the Churchills' actions, and so those of Princess Anne, during the dispute with William and Mary. As a result, its early pages present Anne as more sinned against than sinning, a reasonable but rather weak person, utterly reliant on the advice of her beloved Mrs Freeman in her battle with the King and Queen. Even in these early passages, it is clear that Sarah is the brains behind the operation of the Princess of Denmark's court.[56]

When Sarah's various public and private accounts turn to the period of Anne's reign as Queen, the full portrait emerges of a woman who 'wou'd not go to take the air unless somebody advised her to it', who 'loved fawning and adoration and hated plain dealing' and who 'had a soul that nothing could so effectually move as flattery or fear'. The successes of the reign had nothing to do with Anne's foresight or abilities; they were the work of the puppet-masters behind the throne. If Anne was frugal in her household administration, it was because she had the benefit of Sarah's own reforming zeal – 'All that the Queen did when she came first to the crown to prevent selling in the greencloth, & other offices was at my solicitation' – and the wise experience of Lord Treasurer Godolphin who 'conducted the Queen with the care and tenderness of a father or a guardian through a state of helpless ignorance'. Sarah does concede that 'The Queen always meant well, how much soever she might be blinded or misguided' and that 'there was something of majesty in her look', but as the Enlightenment gets under way, this last seems to her (and, no doubt, to many in her audience) a rather negligible quality, one suited to an age of fawners and flatterers of monarchy, something which the Duchess of Marlborough could never be accused of being. As for the Queen's reputation for goodness and concern for her subjects, these are revealed to have been a sham, for the private Anne is perversely self-serving when not being manipulated by courtiers 'practising upon . . . [her] passion and credulity'. Her piety is one part simple-minded delusion, one part Pharisitical hypocrisy. Regarding the Queen's role in Marlborough's victories, it is Anne who is the debtor, the Churchills the creditors. Indeed, if Sarah's campaign against her former mistress has a theme beyond the virtues and sacrifices of the Duchess of Marlborough and her husband, it is the rank ingratitude of the Queen.[57]

The taste of sour grapes on the part of the fallen favourite and former friend is unmistakable and should have caused readers and auditors to view or hear this testimony with critical eyes and ears. A number of Tory responses to the *Conduct* were published, most notably *The Other Side of the Question* by the American James Ralph.[58] But it is a truism that history is one of the spoils of victory. It was Sarah's Whigs who dominated the court, the Parliament and the political and social life of the nation after 1714. Though she eventually retired in high dudgeon to St Albans, Sarah's children, friends, political associates and their descendants would populate Whitehall, Westminster and St James's for the next half-century. It was inevitable, given the forcefulness of the Duchess's personality, the vastness of her acquaintanceship, the length of the Whig ascendancy and the absence of any other extensive and readily available account of court life under Queen Anne, that hers was the picture that would stick.

In fact, the period from 1714 to the mid-twentieth century saw two lines of argument about the Queen, corresponding roughly to the Whig and Tory views of her, but, in the end, both heavily influenced by Sarah's account. The Whig position was entirely hostile. For example, though Macaulay's history did not extend to Anne's reign, her opposition to William and Mary would not have endeared her to the greatest of all Whig historians: 'when in good humour, [Anne] was meekly stupid, and, when in bad humour, was sulkily stupid'. A necessary corollary to this view was that she was the puppet or tool of Sarah Churchill, a situation which necessitated 'a great and wise man', the Duke of Marlborough, to rely on 'one foolish woman, who was often unmanageable, to manage another woman who was more foolish still'.[59] Macaulay's attribution of royal policy to the intrigues of favourites is consistent with the low Whig opinion of Stuart royal government generally. This attitude, along with his associated approval for Marlborough, his detestation of his Duchess and his disdain for the Queen they served often found its way into more popular and less scholarly or reflective works, such as E. Wingfield-Stratford's *History of English Patriotism*:

> The politics of Anne's reign are as sordid as any in our history. . . . It is humiliating to reflect how much Marlborough himself, at his greatest, was dependent on the lowest form of Court intrigue, on whether his termagant Duchess could retain her temper, and her influence over the petty and unqueenly woman who occupied the throne of Elizabeth.[60]

The last gasp of this extreme Whig position among serious scholars may be found in Sir John Plumb's dismissive portrait of the Queen in *The Growth of Political Stability in England*:

> under the pressure of her servants she intervened decisively, some might say disastrously, in politics. But she and her husband were not difficult to manage; yet the waywardness of her emotions, her addiction to intrigue, and the fact that she did choose and dismiss ministers, added rather than subtracted from the political instability of her governments – after all, the crisis of 1710 was partly her doing.[61]

For most of the eighteenth and nineteenth centuries, to the extent that there was a Tory view of the Queen, it differed from Macaulay's primarily in playing up Anne's private virtues and sorrows and in evincing more sympathy for her personal and public difficulties. Its adherents did not, by and large, attempt to prove the Queen up to those difficulties. This view may be traced back to the responses of James Ralph and Samuel Johnson to Sarah's *Conduct*. Ralph's response is amusing in its sheer effrontery as he pulls no punches in making Sarah out to be a rapacious termagant. But this only reduces the Queen to the status of helpless, innocent victim, 'By her Affections bewitched to your Grace . . . in a Manner a Prisoner upon the Throne'. Anne is credited 'with the best Disposition as a Woman, with the noblest Intentions as a Queen' but she is, ultimately, 'impotent in the Midst of Power . . . tho' never blameable, but for being govern'd herself, when alike authoriz'd and qualify'd to govern others'.[62] Johnson, writing, as the *Conduct's* reviewer, in a briefer compass, found in Anne's letters quoted therein 'uncommon clearness of understanding, tenderness of affection and rectitude of intention' but also 'a temper timorous, anxious and impatient of misfortune, a tendency to burst into complaints, helpless dependancy on the affection of others and a weak desire of moving compassion . . . She seems born for friendship, not for Government.'[63]

Subsequent appraisals by Tobias Smollett, Leopold von Ranke, F. W. Wyon and M. O. W. Oliphant would echo these portrayals of a good, well-intentioned woman of limited capacity, beset by favourites and party-men.[64] In some ways the most subtle variation on these Tory themes was that of 'Agnes' – in reality, her sister, Eliza – Strickland. She readily embraced the Whig notion of 'Anne in her youth, as an un-educated and self-indulgent woman' of limited intelligence: 'There are few housemaids at the present day whose progress in the common business of reading and writing is not more respectable'.[65] But Strickland's estimation of Anne, the Queen, is far higher. She notes with approval that Anne was in touch with her people – quite literally in the case of her healing ceremonies for the King's Evil. What to a latitudinarian Whig or a modern sceptic would seem rank superstition is here argued to be evidence of a kind heart and an instinctual knack for endearing herself to her subjects.

> The passionate love that the people bore to 'their good queen Anne,' was partly founded on her condescension in thus suffering the most wretched and pitiable of her subjects to approach her, when she with alms, with benedictions, soothed their miseries for the love of God. . . . One thing is certain, that never was any measure better contrived by the most sagacious statesmen to fix the sovereign in the love of a populace.

Strickland is shrewd enough to realise that Anne's popularity owed less to her being a good woman or a good queen, than it did to her congruence of attitude with the vast majority of her subjects. Indeed, what to a modern observer would be defects were, in contemporary eyes, crowd-pleasing virtues: her 'entirely English' heart may not have beat for her Scottish or Irish subjects, but it certainly appealed to the xenophobia of the largest ethnic group in the three kingdoms. 'Her very limited education' may not have fit her to be the arbiter of Europe but it did, usefully, confine 'her language, tastes, and prejudices entirely to every thing English'. What Strickland calls 'her feminine helplessness of mind' was a constitutional blessing, for it turned out to have

> well fitted her for the limits to which an encroaching oligarchy had confined the functions of a British monarch. If it be a maxim of the constitution 'that the king can do no wrong', who could look on the soft and innocent features of the comfortable matron who filled the British throne, and make her accountable for the wrong-doing of her ministers?

As this implies, even her appearance was an asset, for it 'bore the national characteristics of the middle classes'.[66] Even here, of course, the Queen is celebrated for her qualities, not her achievements; and in particular for her 'negatives' rather than her 'positives'.

The modern reappraisal of Anne's character and political role began with the work of W. T. Morgan in the 1920s. It continued in the 1930s with G. M. Trevelyan's moderately sympathetic portrayal in *England Under Queen Anne* and two biographies by Neville Connell and M. R. Hopkinson, the first scholarly, the latter popular and unreliable.[67] In 1967 appeared G. S. Holmes's authoritative *British Politics in the Age of Anne*. Here, Anne is portrayed as anything but a cipher: no genius perhaps, but very much her own woman whose opinions were to be ignored at the peril of the ministry, party or politician who did so.[68] Finally, Edward Gregg's thoroughly documented study of Anne's reign lays to rest the idea of the weak-minded character of Sarah's memoirs. Rather, the Queen is revealed to have been a woman of great determination who overcame her lack of political instincts and training by careful study and the hard-won benefits of experience. By the time of her change of ministry in 1710, Queen Anne was a political master, able to use the strengths of her position to keep her supporters and opponents sufficiently off-balance as to render her the central player.[69]

The case for and against the Queen

Despite the recent scholarly reappraisal of the last Stuart monarch, it is likely that the old, dismissive view of her abilities and achievements remains the dominant one with the general public, thanks in no small part to textbooks such as that quoted at the beginning of this chapter.[70] The quote is, in fact, a convenient summary of the case against Anne Stuart. Like most sweeping generalisations, it contains more than a grain of truth. It is simply not the whole truth. To begin with the superficial, Anne was indeed the daughter of James II, she did ascend the throne in 1702 and she did suffer from obesity, a ruddy complexion and gout. One might naively ask whether these last facts are relevant to the case, but anyone who lives in the world will know the ancient prejudice that believes that physical form is an outward badge of internal character. The implication in this case is that Anne's well-known appetite for food[71] is indicative of a mind bent on sublunary matters, as well as an absence of self-control. Indeed, in most of the works consulted for this chapter, the author's portrayal of the Queen's physical size and shape – from pleasantly round to grossly obese – is usually a fair index of that author's view of her character and abilities.[72] The significance of her complexion is that it was probably the source of the erroneous rumours that she drank too much, a failing of which even Sarah absolved her.[73] Her gout, a common ailment among the contemporary ruling class, may be attributed to a lack of knowledge about good diet.

In any case, Anne's was not a politically correct age. The Queen's 'shocking' appearance lessened the prestige of the monarchy in the eyes of at least one observer. In an oft-quoted passage, Sir John Clerk of Penecuik, a negotiator for the Union in 1706, recalls finding her at Kensington 'labouring under a fit of the Gout, and in extrem pain and agony', her face 'red and spotted', her dress 'negligent', her gouty foot 'tied up with a pultis and some nasty bandages', her surroundings 'in the same disorder as about the meanest of her subjects'. For Clerk, the notion that this pitiable creature saw herself as the nursing mother of her people was pathetic, ironic and a confirmation of his own views on hierarchy and gender:

> I was much affected at this sight, and the more when she had occasion to mention her people of Scotland. . . . What are you, poor mean like Mortal, thought I, who talks in the style of a Soveraign. Nature seems to be inverted when a poor infirm Woman becomes one of the Rulers of the World.

It is probable that Anne's private appearance had a similar deleterious effect upon the attitudes of other members of the aristocracy and gentry who had close access to the royal person.[74]

But against this must be weighed the effectiveness of the Queen's public appearance. As we have seen, even the Duchess of Marlborough found 'something of majesty in her look' and numerous eyewitness accounts confirm the impressive figure she made on great state occasions.[75] To her regal bearing must be added a mellifluous voice, which seems to have charmed both Houses of Parliament at her first speech from the throne on 11 March 1702. Indeed, on this occasion even her 'flaws' may have proved an advantage: a number of commentators remarked affectionately about her blushing.[76] Nor is it much of a stretch to imagine that the Queen's girth, so unfashionable in our own day, may, along with her tragic obstetrical history, have supported the image she wished to create of being the nursing mother of her people – an image to which her people responded with some enthusiasm.

Perhaps because, as second in line to her sister Mary, she had always had to fight for attention, Queen Anne had a clear understanding of the importance of such public appearances, of regal ceremony and courtly etiquette generally and of her own royal person in particular. Throughout her life she gave or withheld her presence to great political effect: attending the Anglican Chapel Royal under her father, but refusing to assist in the dressing or labour of her stepmother Mary of Modena; removing herself from Whitehall Palace at a crucial stage of the Revolution, but turning up at a drawing room with the Countess of Marlborough in tow after her husband's dismissal under William and Mary; attending public thanksgivings for Marlborough's victories when she was in political sympathy with her Captain General, withdrawing her presence when she was not. When, in December 1711, her ministry bungled the vote on 'No Peace Without Spain', she demonstrated her dissatisfaction by refusing to be escorted out of the House of Lords by government supporters like the Earl of Lindsey or the Duke of Shrewsbury. She chose instead her Whig Master of the Horse, the Duke of Somerset, who had been among the most prominent critics of the Peace.[77] Queen Anne undoubtedly enhanced her popularity, the prestige of the monarchy, and the unity of the nation in the midst of a controversial war by her progresses to Bath, Cambridge, Newmarket and Winchester; by her processions to and attendance at St Paul's on thanksgiving days; and by her encouragement of the national celebration of her accession, coronation and birth days.[78] If, as the authors of the earlier quote seem to argue, appearances matter, then the Queen must be given credit for knowing how to present hers in the best possible light at the most crucial times.

A more damning charge against the Queen is that she was mentally unfit to rule a nation torn by the rage of party at home and threatened by powerful enemies abroad – that she was 'slow-witted, uninformed, obstinate and narrow-minded'. None of Anne's defenders, not even biographer Edward Gregg, argue that she was a genius, political or otherwise. Nor, as Gregg has shown, had her education fit her for a vibrant intellectual or public life. The days when a female member of the royal family acquired an arsenal of languages and philosophical and historical knowledge were long gone by the third quarter of the seventeenth century. Rather, Princess Anne's education consisted largely of training in domestic skills, such as sewing and embroidery, with 'little more than a smattering of history, geography, or constitutional and legal training'.[79] This lack of a more thorough intellectual training may have contributed to her early reserve, apparent lack of confidence and need to be tutored or schooled by men of greater attainments, such as Sidney Godolphin.

A further reason for the perception that the Queen lacked intelligence was that, unlike her uncle or her sister, she was taciturn and a dull conversationalist. In this case, Sarah's verdict that Anne 'never discovered any readiness of parts . . . In matters of ordinary moment her discourse had nothing of brightness or wit; and in weightier matters she never spoke but in a road'[80] is amply confirmed by the testimony of others and even by the record of her actual conversations. In fact, she, herself, admitted 'I am a very ill Speaker.'[81] In her youth, and especially on visits to the notoriously verbal Restoration court, the Princess's lack of such quickness must have caused feelings of self-doubt. But as with a number of Anne's 'defects', she would learn to minimise it by becoming a keen listener and choosing her words carefully. Indeed, the quality of speaking rarely and no 'more than was necessary to answer a question'[82] can be a useful one in a politician, especially a sovereign. Charles II's wit was thought by some, especially the Earl of Halifax, to detract from his royal dignity; there is no question that Mary's loquaciousness detracted from hers.[83] In contrast, Anne's silence was a necessary corollary of her regal dignity and a useful attribute at times when it was necessary to keep her position ambiguous or flexible and her leading politicians off-balance. This was especially the case in 1710.

Moreover, a careful examination of the record of Anne's conversation reveals an occasional turn of phrase which is judicious in its curtness. For example, when the Earl of Godolphin threatened to resign the Treasurership over her favour for Robert Harley in 1708, she responded: 'He should do as he pleas'd, wth all she could find enough glad of that staff'. In 1710 when Richard Hampden used the opportunity of the offer of a position on the Treasury Commission to urge her not to dissolve Parliament, she replied 'that tho' she offer'd him an employment yet she did not ask his advice'.[84] While some have thought her a poor writer,[85] her letters occasionally betray an Elizabethan directness and even regal eloquence. Thus, in the midst of her fight to remain free of the influence of the Junto, she wrote to Godolphin: 'Whoever of the Whigs thinks I am to be hectored or frightened into a compliance, though I am a woman, is mightily mistaken in me. I thank God I have a soul above that, and am too much concerned for my reputation to do anything to forfeit it.'[86]

The judiciousness of these answers reveals something else about Anne: she knew what she was about. Her goals may have been few (to defend the nation, the Church and the prerogative and to remain free of domination by a single party), but they were all pursued with single-mindedness (the 'obstinacy' of the long quotation) and the benefits of her experience. She may not have been a quick study, but she did learn from her mistakes: witness her premature support of Harley, followed by her humiliating capitulation to the parliamentary majority of Marlborough and Godolphin in 1708. In 1710, when she was ready to strike again, she took her time, kept her incumbent ministers off-balance, gauged the state of their parliamentary and popular support and acted effectively, with impeccable timing.[87] The degree to which she had learned not to be dominated by favourites, not to mention her command of clear, unequivocal language when it suited her, is illustrated by the following oft-quoted incident. In the summer of 1713 the office of Treasurer of the Chamber was vacant. Anne had promised the place to an old servant of Prince George's, John West, Lord Delawarr. There is evidence that Lord Treasurer Oxford may have wanted to use the place to reward a more prominent party man. Perhaps because of this desire, perhaps because of his diminishing capacity by this stage, he submitted to the Queen a blank warrant, i.e. one with the name of the officeholder omitted, to be filled in later. Anne's reaction, as conveyed in a letter dated 21 August reveals, in no uncertain terms, that she was not to be trifled with:

> I was very much surprised to find by your letter that, though I had told you the last time you weare hear I entended to give the Treasurer of the Chamber to Lord De Laware, you will bring me a warrant in blank. I desire you would not have soe ill an oppinion of me as to think when I have determined anything in my mind I will alter it. I have told Lord De Laware I will give him this office and he has kissed my hand upon it. Therfore when you com hither bring the warrant with his name.[88]

Obstinacy this may be, but it is also revealing of a woman who had learned to use the language of her birth and the prerogative of her position to get the servants and the results that she wanted.

Nevertheless, as we have seen, contemporaries and historians have often preferred to attribute those results to the influence of those servants rather than to the initiative of their mistress. The theme of Anne's domination by favourites had arisen long before her accession and it was exploited by whichever side was in opposition subsequently. Because the Queen could never be counted on to follow one party's line exclusively, because her gender, poor health and general shyness limited her circle of human contact to ministers and bedchamber attendants,[89] her apparent inconsistency and recalcitrance were most easily explained by partisan commentators as the results of being isolated and swayed by bedchamber attendants of the other side. Prior to 1710 Tory commentators complained that 'Mother Jennings Race/And the Spawn of Her Grace' – a reference to the large number of Churchills and family dependants with places in the bedchamber – 'hold Nanny fast in their clutches'.[90] After 1710 Tory attendants faced the same charges: thus, the Whig physician Sir David Hamilton complained that 'by Management few were admitted to give Her a Contrary Account to what was habitually sounding In Her Ears'.[91] In short, the access to the royal person which bedchamber servants possessed as a right of office and regulated as a duty of it was assumed to imply control of the royal mind and heart as well.

It is certainly true that, from her youth, Anne's isolation from her parents and the main court at Whitehall and her dependance on a small establishment of royal servants at Richmond had led her to embrace wholeheartedly the seventeenth-century usage (both verbal and social) of her personal attendants as 'family'.[92] Throughout her life she would retain an avid interest in the minutest details of household management and she would be renowned for treating her servants almost as equals.[93] As her health declined, she came to be so dependent on them for physical and emotional support as to contribute to the charge of undue influence. But there was never any possibility of Anne being dominated by attendants of one party or the other if only because her bedchamber was always fairly evenly divided into Whigs and Tories.[94] No one side was ever fully excluded, as Hamilton more or less admits: 'If some Persons had been in waiting, however Her Majesty inclin'd to speak to me, yet either the Door must be left Open, or if that shut, I to stay no more than a Minute; whereas if others who had a Personal regard for me, had been then in waiting the door might be Shut, and I stay without her Concern'.[95] Clearly, Anne was, to some extent, the prisoner of her domestic attendants, a corollary of her well-known indulgence of them. But there is also much here that is reminiscent of 'office politics' in any age. This system at least allowed the Queen access to a wide range of opinion and ensured that no one side could presume too much on its position with her or feel, on the other hand, utterly neglected.

Queen Anne's refusal to become the pawn of her attendants or ministers of either party is illustrated by her handling of patronage. For many years, it was assumed that Anne left patronage decisions to her favourites, John and Sarah, Duke and Duchess of Marlborough, and Sidney, Earl Godolphin, up to about 1710; and then to Robert Harley (later Earl of Oxford) and Abigail (later, Lady) Masham thereafter. It is true that superior military appointments were left to the Duke, in keeping with his position as Captain General. But it is equally clear from the Marlborough–Godolphin Correspondence and the Harley Papers preserved in the Portland manuscripts that Anne retained ultimate control of cabinet positions and other civil offices in the royal gift.[96] As a result, for both Lords Treasurers Godolphin and Oxford, the appointment of political supporters was always a matter of delicate negotiation with the Queen, subject to her own personal predilections and sense of what was best for the nation. This is not to say that she frequently failed to accept the advice of her chief ministers; it is simply that they had to take into account her wishes as well as their own political interests. Early in the reign she did accept the appointment of a number of Tory peers with whom she had little personal sympathy, such as Lord Chamberlain Jersey, Secretary of State Nottingham, and, as Lord Lieutenant of Ireland, her more or less estranged uncle, the Earl of Rochester. But when the political winds began to blow Whig in 1704, she dumped all of these individuals quite happily. Thereafter, she sometimes found herself forced to make an appointment against her better judgement, as in the case of Secretary of State Sunderland in 1706 or Lord Admiral Orford in 1709 – but always after a political fight in which she exacted concessions, displaying her characteristic taciturnity and stubbornness to advantage.[97] Thus, in July 1708 John Vanbrugh reports on the attempt to find a position in the cabinet for Lord Somers:

> not all the interests of Lord Treasurer [?] and Lady Marlborough, backed and pressed warmly by every man of the Cabinet, can prevail with the queen to admit my Lord Somers into anything – not so much as to make him Attorney-General. She answers little to them, but stands firm against all they say.[98]

After what has been called 'the Queen's Revenge' of 1710, she grew even less co-operative, as the Duke of Shrewsbury informed one disappointed applicant for a court position: 'those are matters she is grown very nice in, and not willing to admit any who are not perfectly well known to her'.[99] As a result, the Earl of Oxford found himself in an uphill fight to fill his cabinet with individuals who would support the ministry.

Above all, Anne refused to allow the vast field of household patronage to be given over to party fodder. While high-paying near-sinecures such as those at the Board of Greencloth were gradually encroached upon by co-operative party-men (about twenty posts), she never allowed places in what she referred to as her 'family', involving direct access upon her person, nor the vast sea of menial positions at court, to be turned into the spoils of the party battle. Nor were these posts dominated by the machinations of her favourites.[100] While the Duchess of Marlborough did have some patronage rights as Groom of the Stole, and played a crucial advisory role at the Queen's accession, she was thereafter careful to point out to suitors that elsewhere in the household her powers of influence were limited. This is in fact borne out by the record of household appointments.[101] The influence of later favourites such as Abigail Masham and the Duchess of Somerset was even more circumscribed.[102] Indeed, despite the accusations of Sarah and the assumptions of contemporaries on both sides of the political fence, it might be said to have been virtually non-existent.

Among the charges levelled above is that the Queen had 'no interest in art, music, plays, or books'. In fact, it has been among historians of the arts that the most extreme version of the Whig interpretation has found its readiest reception and transmission. Thus Michael Foss in his *Age of Patronage*: 'of patronage in the sense of sympathetic understanding from this fat, dull and persevering lady, there was none'.[103] The author (and former Surveyor) of *The Queen's Pictures* calls her 'the dullest and meanest of the Stuarts', while Nancy Armstrong's *Jewellery* reduces her life to 'one long confusion, never properly resolved . . . her political views were muddled and easily swayed, and the quarrels among her ministers kept her in a perpetual state of worry and unrest'. The end result of Anne's lack of ability was, of course, the most damning one for a specialist in this field: that 'Her twelve year reign had no major effect on the decorative arts'.[104]

In fact, this dismissive view of Anne's record of artistic patronage is simply inaccurate in some instances, and unfair in its disregard of the Queen's circumstances in others. As a young woman, Anne possessed the expected adolescent interest in music, dancing and fashion and she received a good artistic education. She retained a lifelong love of music. Even if we discount eighteenth-century assertions that she played (the harpsichord and guitar) herself, there is plenty of evidence for her patronage of the Chapel Royal and the careers of William Croft, Richard Elford, Henry Purcell, William Turner and, most notably, Georg Frideric Handel. It was for Anne that he wrote his sole birthday ode, *Eternal Source of Light Divine*, and the Utrecht *Jubilate* and *Te Deum*. Her support for the cause of English church music was acknowledged by the dedication of John Blow's *Amphion Anglicus*. She also patronised secular musicians, sponsoring the performance of opera on two royal ceremonial occasions, and, more frequently, that of individual soloists in the more intimate surroundings of her bedchamber.[105]

If Queen Anne was a less distinguished patron of English drama, painting, fashion or architecture, she had, perhaps, good reason. Her uncertain health affected the first three: poor eyesight precluded her from deriving much enjoyment from reading, plays or paintings. While Anne's punctilious nature implied a keen eye for fashion, her decrepit frame prevented her from pursuing it, for, as Sarah explains, 'Her limbs were so weakned with the goute for many years, that she cou'd not endure heavy clothes'. In the case of every one of these art forms there was a price to be paid: writers and artists such as Alexander Pope, Sir Godfrey Kneller, and the London fashion 'industry', discouraged by a relative lack of royal patronage, sought its substitute in the town houses, clubs and coffee houses of the great and less great.[106] If Anne instinctively understood the strategic importance of ceremony, it must be admitted that she was oblivious to the propaganda value of high art.

Perhaps Anne's greatest aesthetic failure as Queen was as a builder. She commissioned no English Versailles to replace Whitehall; what work she did pay for at royal palaces was in the way of continuing Williamite projects (Hampton Court) or renovations made necessary by wear and tear and the fact that the crown was making do with smaller houses (St James's, Kensington) in the absence of a great one. Nor, apart from continuing the work at St Paul's and her only partially fulfilled initiative for fifty new London churches, did Queen Anne do much to enhance her capital city. There were several reasons for this failure. One is that she simply did not have the money. Her civil list was already inadequate to the demands of paying for routine domestic government. From 1704 it was increasingly and notoriously in debt and could never have supported a major building project.[107] Nor could she have asked for extraordinary funds from Parliament: after all, the nation was, for nearly the entire reign, engaged in a great international war for the survival of the Revolution Settlement and the Protestant establishment. That war absorbed what was thought to be an excessive proportion of Britain's landed and commercial wealth; additional taxation to pay for a new house for the Queen was inconsistent with the nation's priorities, not to mention her own.

As this implies, there was, finally, the Queen's temperament. While Anne clearly had a very high regard for the office of sovereign, and expected her subjects to pay their full respects to her as Queen, she does not seem to have hankered after any sort of personal glory or memorial. This may be traceable to her childhood, when she was always second to her elder sister, Mary. She must have realised early on that, in the normal course of things, she would never succeed to a throne. Her dynastic and constitutional position in youth was not unlike that of Princess Margaret in our own time. Moreover, Mary was everything Anne was not: lively, gregarious, fun. It is little wonder that Anne failed to develop a close relationship to her sister; that she embraced and guarded her intimate friendships passionately; or that, in later life, she made so much of royal ceremony and etiquette and took such strong exception to any slight of her royal position. The forms of ceremony were an unchanging manual for human interaction to which she could retreat when uncertain; her royal status provided a claim – perhaps her sole claim – to the friendship and respect of others. These were the only things, apart from the tenets of the Anglican Church, which she could trust as unchanging when, as inevitably happened, personal friendships and relationships failed her. Indeed, it is not insignificant that at her very darkest hour, the death of Prince George in 1708, she seems to have found consolation in losing herself in the detailed arrangement of his funeral.[108] Anne's emphasis on the formality due her rank would sometimes manifest itself in snobbery or excessive punctilio.[109] But it could be argued that her attention to ceremonial did much for the dignity of the royal office after the indignities it had suffered in the seventeenth century. Moreover, as the Stricklands observed above, it helped to form a bond with her people, symbolised by the metaphor of the nursing mother, that never failed her.[110] Thus, it may have been that, never expecting to succeed to the throne, having grown up with little prospect of ever being number one, for all her punctiliousness about the *office* of Queen, there was something about Anne that was hesitant about celebrating her own, *personal* royal status. The Queen was regal; Anne herself was unassuming.

Towards the end of the quote cited above, the authors acknowledge that the actions of this fat, dull, ordinary woman produced a positive effect upon the fortunes of her subjects. In fact, one could go farther. One could begin by arguing that no previous Stuart was so adept at selecting men of ability and delegating royal authority to them. In the Queen's first government her armies were led by the greatest soldier of the day (Marlborough); her administration by an apparent financial genius (Godolphin); and the management of Parliament by its leading political operator (Harley). This government sustained the Grand Alliance, raised colossal sums of money, fielded vast armies and navies and won unprecedented victories against the most powerful state of its time while leading a political nation divided by the rage of party (PLATE 1). It did so without the necessity of terror, tyranny or constitutional chicanery. If Anne's choice of ministers was impeccable, so was her timing. That is, she knew when the military front was yielding diminishing returns (Malplaquet); when her ministers were beginning to presume upon their own power (the abortive address for Masham's removal; Marlborough's demand to be made Captain General for life); and when her people were ready for a change. Her manipulation of the political system in order to engineer such change was, by 1710, subtle and effective. Even if one credits Robert Harley for most of this, one must acknowledge Anne for knowing to whom to listen and when.

The Harley ministry, for all of its problems, secured a peace which effectively eliminated the French threat to the balance of power while tipping that balance firmly (if not yet apparently to all) toward Britain. The acquisition of Gibraltar, additional territory in the West Indies and the Asiento slaving contract would ensure not only that British trade would grow, but that that trade would provide the necessary financial undergirding for future victories. This would, in turn, make possible the triumphs of 1763 and 1815 and the military, naval, commercial and industrial hegemony of the British nineteenth century.

Acknowledging all of this makes Queen Anne neither a saint, nor a genius. Her pursuit of the Asiento is, undeniably, a mark against her humanity, as is her failure to relieve the situation of her poor Irish subjects. Closer to home, her devotion to the Church of England blinded her to the plight of Dissenters, especially at the beginning and end of her reign. In some ways, as the Stricklands observed, her contemporary popularity – left unmentioned by the authors of the quote – may be attributed to her failings of body and sympathy. That is, her Anglocentrism and xenophobia, her staunch Protestantism and anti-Catholicism, her tragic obstetrical and marital history, as well as, more positively, her good husbandry and charitable nature, seem to have played well with her subjects because they appealed to some of their most long-standing and deeply held prejudices. No previous Stuart sovereign had shared them so completely: as F. W. Wyon wrote, perhaps exaggeratedly, over a century ago, 'the most apparent reason of Anne's popularity is that her mind happened to be exactly in harmony with the minds of nineteen-twentieths of the people she governed'.[111] Indeed, the congruence of attitudes between rulers and ruled which characterised Anne's reign is far more reminiscent of the Tudors than her Stuart forebears. In contrast to the views expressed above, Anne was, arguably, the most successful monarch of her line. She prosecuted a successful war, won a favourable (if controversial) peace, defended the Church, maintained (albeit with varying degrees of enthusiasm) the Toleration, respected constitutional proprieties and avoided the fiscal extravagance and political cruelty that had marred earlier reigns (PLATE 2). What Stuart – nay what Tudor – could say so much?

Conclusion: the reason why

We are left with a final question: why, in the face of evidence to the contrary, not to mention the dictates of Ockham's razor, did most professional historians and their readership accept the negative portrayal of

Anne's personality and abilities for so long? Why, despite the existence of first-rate scholarship from the likes of Professors Gregg and Holmes, does the negative view still hold sway in textbooks and, presumably, lecture halls? The answer may lie, in varying degrees, with Anne's ancestry and gender. As a Stuart, she may lay under a subconscious expectation on the part of historians of constitutional ineptitude, domination by favourites and, ultimately, failure. In fact, as has been argued above, Queen Anne broke with many of the most damaging Stuart propensities and peculiarities and proved to be by far the most successful post-1603 sovereign of that line. Indeed, her successes make a mockery of any easy historical verdict on 'the Stuarts'. Perhaps for this reason, historians of the seventeenth century, obsessed with the Civil War and the failures of the Stuart line, have often chosen to omit her and her reign from their analyses. But that omission leaves the Stuart period truncated, for it was during her reign that most of the questions raised by that century and that event – those of Britain's constitutional and religious settlements and its place in the world – were settled.

Perhaps the greatest factor in the acceptance of the negative interpretation of Anne's reign was her gender and, more particularly, her own, apparently ready, acceptance of its contemporary conventions. In this case, a comparison with Elizabeth I is highly instructive. The first Elizabeth is the one female ruler of a British kingdom who has been almost universally praised by professional historians and the general public alike. Her qualities of courage, boldness, steadfastness, duplicity and a witty, even sharp, tongue have all appealed to traditional historians and their readers not least because they are virtues traditionally associated with effective male rulers – and, indeed, effective males generally. William Camden argued that 'by [her] manly cares and counsels, she surpassed her sex', while a more recent biographer asserts that her 'assured self-confidence and assertive will were wholly masculine'.[112] When Elizabeth is criticised, it is for indecisiveness – a traditional attribute of the stereotypical female. She, herself, portrayed the essential quality of her own gender as being 'weak and feeble'. In other words, if Elizabeth is the one universally approved female ruler, it is because she is widely perceived as having 'the heart and stomach of a King', i.e. of being a man inside a woman's body.

In comparison, Anne's considerable virtues were those of the good housewife. She was thrifty, prudent, silent, pious, faithful to her marriage, maternal in her instincts. None of these characteristics is particularly exciting, or calculated to win the unqualified approval of the post-Enlightenment (let alone the post-modern) mind. Nor were they the qualities of the men of action who fought the wars or drafted the legislation which built the modern nation-state. Where Elizabeth hesitated over and finally rejected the matrimonial state, Anne by all appearances submitted to her uncle's wishes meekly, and then gloried in her marriage. Where Elizabeth was the Virgin Queen, wedded to her first love, the people of England (with all of the flirtatious play which that implies), Anne was their nursing mother, a far less titillating image. Where Elizabeth was ostentatiously courageous, Anne was stubbornly tenacious. Where Elizabeth was quick and profligate with words, Anne was slow and parsimonious with them. In the end, both women were exactly what the nation needed at the end of their royal lines and both achieved success unparalleled in the reigns of their respective ancestors. 'Good Queen Bess' has always been so credited. It is now time for 'good Queen Anne' similarly to receive her due.

Notes

1 The author would like to express his heartfelt thanks to Ms Lorna Newman, former Director of Inter-library Loan, Cudahy Library, Loyola University of Chicago, for her heroic efforts to secure for him much of the printed evidence upon which this essay rests; and the editor, Clarissa Campbell Orr, for her generous assistance in helping him to cut it down to a manageable size.

2 J. McCarthy, *The Reign of Queen Anne* (London, Chatto & Windus, 1911), p. 3; B. C. Brown, *Alas, Queen Anne: A Reading of Her Life* (Indianapolis, Bobbs-Merrill, 1929), p. x. See also *Poems on Affairs of State* (hereafter *POAS*) VI, ed. F. H. Ellis (New Haven, Yale University Press, 1970), p. 499; VII, ed. F. H. Ellis (New Haven, Yale University Press, 1975), pp. 6, 603.

3 For example, the recent *Oxford Illustrated History of Tudor and Stuart Britain*, ed. J. Morrill (Oxford, Oxford University Press, 1996), while careful to pay attention to all the non-English residents of the British Isles, is not so scrupulous with regard to just who comprises the Stuarts. The book ends in 1688, some eighteen years before the Act of Union actually created Great Britain as a political entity and twenty-five years before the death of the last Stuart ruler of that nation. The same is true of the recent *Historical Dictionary of Stuart England 1603–1689*, ed. R. H. Fritze and W. B. Robison (Westport CT, Greenwood, 1996) and *The Stuart Court and Europe: Essays in Politics and Political Culture*, ed. R. M. Smuts (Cambridge, Cambridge University Press, 1996).

4 C. Roberts and D. Roberts, *A History of England: Prehistory to 1714*, 2nd edn (Englewood Cliffs NJ, Prentice Hall, 1985), I, p. 404.

5 E. Gregg, *Queen Anne* (London, Routledge, 1980).

6 J. Ralph, *The Other Side of the Question: or, an Attempt to Rescue the Characters of the Two Royal Sisters Q. Mary and Q. Anne Out of the Hands of the D—s D—of——* (London, 1742), p. 44.

7 See *Hymnaeus Cantabrigiensis* (Cambridge, 1683), *passim*.

8 E. E. Morris, *The Age of Anne* (New York, Scribner's, n.d.), p. 25.

9 See R. O. Bucholz, *The Augustan Court: Queen Anne and the Decline of Court Culture* (Stanford, Stanford University Press, 1993), pp. 202, 245. For a discussion of the charge, see *ibid.*, p. 355 n. 191.

10 See H. Keepe, 'Epistle Dedicatory' to *The Genealogies of the High-born Prince and Princess, George and Anne of Denmark, &c* (London, 1684).

11 See *A Pastoral Occasion'd by the Arrival of His Royal Highness Prince George of Denmark* (1683); and poems by H. Crispe, J. Compton, W. Fleetwood, R. Duke and J. Newton, in *Hymnaeus Cantabrigiensis*. The last also praises her wit.

12 J. Adams, untitled, printed in *Hymnaeus Cantabrigiensis*.

13 Gregg, *Anne*, pp. 42–3, 48–51, 65–8, 401; E. Smith, *Sermon Preach'd at Wisbech in the Isle of Ely, 8 August 1714* (London, 1714), p. 3; L. Milbourne, *Great Britain's Loss, in the Death of Our Late Excellent Queen Anne* (London, 1714), pp. 10–11.

14 See A. Maynwaring, 'Tarquin and Tullia' (1689), *POAS* V, ed. W. J. Cameron (New Haven, Yale University Press, 1971), pp. 50–2; 'The Reflection' (1689), *ibid.*, p. 60; 'The Female Parricide' (1689), *ibid.*, p. 157; 'The Duchess of York's Ghost' (1691), *ibid.*, p. 298; see also *ibid.*, p. 148.

15 *POAS* V, pp. 22 n. 16, 50–1, 121.

16 See, for example, 'On the Earl of Dorset, Sir Charles Sedley, etc.' (1692), *POAS* V, pp. 333–8; 'The Universal Health' (?1692), *ibid.*, p. 337 n. 33.

17 J. Sharp, *A Sermon Preach'd at the Coronation of Queen Anne* (London, 1709 edn), esp. pp. 13–16. For other references to Anne defending the liberties of Europe, see H. Sacheverell, *A Defense of Her Majesty's Title to the Crown and a Justification of Her Entring into a war with France and Spain* (London, 1702), p. 24; W. Dawes, *Sermon Preached Before the Queen at St James's-Chappel* (London, 1707), p. 15; M. Prior, *An Ode, Humbly Inscrib'd to the Queen* (London, 1706), p. 16. For references to Anne's Englishness, her devotion to the Church and as nursing mother and new Elizabeth, see below.

18 See F. Atterbury, *Sermon Preached Before the Honourable House of Commons . . . March 8. 1703/4* (London, 1704), pp. 23–5; T. Sherwill, *Sermon Preach'd Before the University of Cambridge March 8 1708/9* (London, 1709), pp. 14–16; W. Dawes, *A Sermon Preach'd Before the . . . House of Lords 8 Mar. 1712* (London, 1712), pp. 6–7; N. Marshall, *The Royal Pattern: or, A Sermon Upon the Death of Her late Most Excellent Majesty Queen Anne . . . August 8th 1714* (London, 1714) pp. 13–15, 18–19; G. Noone, *A Sermon Upon the Death of Queen Anne of Blessed Memory . . . August 15. 1714* (London, 1714), pp. 7–19; Smith, *Sermon Preach'd at Wisbech*, p. 3; J. Smith, *The Duty of the Living to the Memory of the Dead. A Sermon Upon the Death of . . . Queen Anne. Preached . . . Aug. 8. 1714* (London, 1714), pp. 12–13; W. Hamilton, *The Comforts and Advantages Arising from the Belief and Consideration of God's Governing Providence in a Sermon Preached . . . August the 15th. 1714 on the Death of the Late Queen . . .* (Dublin, 1714), pp. 12–14 (also mentioning her support of the gospel in foreign parts); Milbourne, *Great Britain's Loss*, p. 16.

19 Dawes, *Sermon Preach'd Before the . . . House of Lords*, pp. 15–19; W. Atwood, *A Modern Inscription to the Duke of Marlboroughs Fame. Occasioned by an Antique, In Imitation of Spencer* (London, 1706).

20 *The Parliamentary History of England*, ed. W. Cobbett, VI (London, Bagshaw, 1810), p. 25.

21 G. Benson, *A Sermon Preached at Little St Helens, August 2, MDCCXLII* (London, 1742), pp. 24–5. See also J. Adams, *Ahab's Evil: a Funeral Discourse on a Late Occasion* (London, 1714), pp. 30, 33.

22 See T. Hearne *Remarks and Collections of Thomas Hearne*, ed. C. E. Doble (Oxford, Oxford University Press, 1885–1921), I, p. 61; II, pp. 88, 90, 93, 360–1; G. V. Bennett, *The Tory Crisis in Church and State 1688–1730: The Career of Francis Atterbury, Bishop of Rochester* (Oxford, Oxford University Press, 1975), chs 4–9.

23 See Milburne, *Great Britain's Loss*, p. 16.

24 For Sarah's view, see *Memoirs of the Duchess of Marlborough*, ed. W. King (London, Dutton, 1930), pp. 191–2, 232–3. For Dissenting reaction, see *The Letters of Daniel Defoe*, ed. J. H. Healey (Oxford, Oxford University Press, 1955), pp. 50–6.

25 See *Seldom Comes a Better: or, A Tale of a Lady and Her Servants* (London, 1710), p. 11; J. Bates, *Two (United) are Better than One Alone: a Thanksgiving Sermon Upon the Union* (London, 1707), p. 27; Smith, *Duty of the Living*, p. 15; Bucholz, *Augustan Court*, p. 345 n. 43. For Anne as the Mother of the Church, see 'Upon the Vote that Pass'd That the Church was Not in Danger' (1705), *POAS* VII, p. 147; [?A. Maynwaring], 'The Humble Address of the Clergy of London and Westminster, Paraphras'd' (1710), *ibid.*, p. 460; Atterbury, *Sermon Preached Before . . . the House of Commons*, p. 23. For Anne's association with Elizabeth I, see Bucholz, *Augustan Court*, pp. 209, 345 n. 43; Burnet, *Sermon Preach'd Before the Queen*, p. 28; Milbourne, *Great Britain's Loss*, p. 21.

26 See Gregg, *Anne*, p. 150; Bucholz, *Augustan Court*, pp. 209–10, 224–5; Hamiliton, *Comforts and Advantages*, pp. 14–15.

27 See, for example, [?C. Darby], 'The Oxfordshire Nine', *POAS* VII, p. 68.

28 Smith, *Duty of the Living*, pp. 14–15. See also G. Burnet, *A Sermon Preach'd Before the Queen . . . at St Paul's 31st of December 1706* (London, 1707), p. 14; Sherwill, *Sermon Preached Before the University of Cambridge*, p. 13; Marshal, *The Royal Pattern*, pp. 16–17; *Memoirs of the Duchess of Marlborough*, p. 275. Anne's major court pensions list had actually been initiated by her like-minded sister Mary; for its final version see *Calendars of Treasury Books*, ed. W. A. Shaw (1904–62), XXVIII, pp. ccxxi–cclxii.

29 Smith, *Duty of the Living*, p. 14; Bucholz, *Augustan Court*, ch. 2, esp. pp. 48–52, 57–63. For Burnet's assertion see *A History of His Own Time* (Oxford, Oxford University Press, 1833), VI, p. 230.

30 Smith, *The Duty of the Living*, p. 13.

31 D. Green, *Queen Anne* (New York, Scribner's, 1970), p. 178.

32 Atterbury, *Sermon Preached Before the . . . House of Commons*, p. 20. See also *ibid.*, p. 21; *Prologue Spoken before the Queen on Her Majesty's Birthday, 1703/4* (London, 1704); Atwood, *Inscription to the Duke of Marlboroughs Fame*, p. 206; Hamilton, *Comforts and Advantages*, p. 15; Noone, *Sermon Upon the Death of Queen Anne*, p. 16; Smith, *Sermon Preached at Wisbech*, p. 3. For the basis of this reputation see G. M. Trevelyan, *England Under Queen Anne: Blenheim* (London, Longmans, 1930), pp. 169–70.

33 Quoted in G. Holmes, *British Politics in the Age of Anne* (London, Macmillan, 1967), p. 198.

34 Smith, *The Duty of the Living*, pp. 13–14.

35 For a convenient summary of early modern expectations of women, see J. Eales, *Women in Early Modern England 1500–1700* (London, UCL Press, 1998), esp. pp. 3, 23–4, 29. See also M. R. Sommerville, *Sex and Subjection: Attitudes to Women in Early-Modern Society* (London, Arnold, 1995).

36 Milburne, *Great Britain's Loss*, p. 14.

37 Defoe, 'The Mock Mourners', *POAS* VI, p. 397, lines 561–2, 568–71; see also p. 379, lines 108–11; 'An Epistle to Sir Richard Blackmore, Kt., On Occasion of the Late Great Victory in Brabant' (1706), *ibid.* VII, pp. 197–8, lines 17–20.

38 The stereotypical description is from Defoe's 'The Spanish Descent' (1702), *POAS* VI, p. 483, line 345.

39 This is the impression derived from the sheer volume of such works listed in R. D. Horn, comp; *Marlborough: A Survey; Panegyrics, Satires and Biographical Writings, 1688–1788* (New York, Garland, 1975) as compared to the much smaller number dedicated to Anne which have been uncovered in the research for this chapter. Admittedly, the latter has been far more cursory than Professor Horn's thorough survey.

40 Prior, *Ode*, pp. 14–15. Similarly, J. Dennis's *A Poem on the Death of Her Late Majesty Queen Anne, and the Accession of King George, &c.* (London, 1714) spends only two of its thirty-nine pages on 'the great Actions of her wond'rous Reign' before moving on, perhaps understandably, to speculations on the blessings of the new one.

41 D. Defoe, *Hymn for the Thanksgiving* (London, 1706), lines 36–7; nor was the Queen's own laureate any more effective in presenting her as a woman of action: see N. Tate, *The Triumph, or Warriours Welcome: a Poem on the Glorious Successes of the Last Year* (London, 1705).

42 D. Defoe, 'Spanish Descent' (1702), *POAS* VI, p. 484, lines 370–3; 'A Scots Poem: or a New-Years Gift, from a Native of the Universe, to His Fellow-Animals in Albania' (1707), *POAS* VII, pp. 251–2, lines 358–60.

43 Milbourne, *Great Britain's Loss*, p. 15.

44 *No Queen: or, No General. An Argument, Proving the Necessity Her Majesty was in . . . to Displace the D— of M—borough* (London, 1712), pp. 9–10; see also p. 22. For the attribution to Defoe and its refutation, see *Defoe De-Attributions: A Critique of J. R. Moore's Checklist*, ed. P. N. Furbank and W. R. Owens (London, Hambledon, 1994), pp. 53–4. Defoe had made a similar argument in his *Hymn to Victory* (London, 1704) as had Prior in his *Ode*, p. 4.

45 Milbourne, *Great Britain's Loss*, p. 14. See also G. Stanhope, *A Sermon Preach'd Before the Queen at the Cathedral Church of S. Paul, London, The xxviith Day of June MDCCVI* (London, 1706), p. 13.

46 Hamilton, *Comforts and Advantages*, p. 15.

47 See *Memoirs of the Conduct of Her Late Majesty . . . Relating to the Separate Peace With France* (London, 1715), pp. 10–17; 'The British Embassadress's Speech to the French King' (1713), *POAS* VII, p. 593, line 22; *Queen Anne Vindicated From the Base Aspersions of Some Late Pamphlets* (London, ?1714), pp. 4–5, 18–20; Benson, *Sermon Preached at Little St Helens*, p. 24.

48 *Seldom Comes a Better*, pp. 4, 6; *The Second Part of the Impartial Secret History of Arlus* (London, 1710), pp. 30–1; Marshal, *Sermon Upon the Death of Queen Anne*, p. 17. See also Hamilton, *Comforts and Advantages*, p. 16; Milbourne, *Great Britain's Loss*, pp. 13, 19; 'On the Queen's Speech' (1710), *POAS* VII, p. 412 which charges that

by 1710 Anne was 'a mimick Queen' directed by a 'secret Wire and hidden Spring' to say 'Words not her own, in borrow'd Sounds' (lines 2, 7, 10).

49 Smith, *Sermon Preached at Wisbech*, p. 14.

50 *The Diary of Sir David Hamilton 1709–1714*, ed. P. Roberts (Oxford, Oxford University Press, 1975), p. 44.

51 W. A. Speck, *The Birth of Britain: A New Nation 1700–1710* (Oxford, Blackwell, 1994), p. 13.

52 A. Boyer, *The Political State of Great Britain*, VIII (London, 1719), p. 640. For the muted poetic reaction to Anne's death, see *POAS* VII, pp. 604–25. For a much more complimentary assessment of the Queen – 'a princess of as many virtues as ever adorned a private life, and as few frailties as ever blemished a diadem' – from Boyer's pen, see *The History of Queen Anne* (London, 1735), pp. 715–16.

53 N. Rogers, 'Popular Protest in Early Hanoverian London', *Past and Present*, 79 (1978), pp. 71–2, 80.

54 The only other widely disseminated contemporary portrait is by Bishop Burnet. While his *History of His Own Time* exhibits a Whig slant, his portrayal of Queen Anne is more moderate than the Duchess of Marlborough's: 'Queen Anne is easy of access, and hears every thing very gently; but opens herself to so few, and is so cold and general in her answers, that people soon find that the chief application is to be made to her ministers and favourites, who in their turn have an entire credit and full power with her': *History* VI, p. 230.

55 See British Library (BL) Add. MSS 61421–61426 and F. Harris, 'Accounts of the Conduct of Sarah, Duchess of Marlborough, 1704–42', *British Library Journal*, VIII (Spring 1982); Sarah, Duchess of Marlborough, *The Conduct of the Dowager Duchess of Marlborough* (London, 1742) and *The Opinons of Sarah, Dowager Duchess of Marlborough* (London, 1788), both repr. in *Memoirs of the Duchess of Marlborough*.

56 *Memoirs of the Duchess of Marlborough*, pp. 4–85.

57 *Memoirs of the Duchess of Marlborough*, pp. 151, 173, 230, 234–5, 255–6; BL Add. MSS 61422, fo. 156v; 61424, fo. 17v. Most of the quotations derive from manuscript materials upon which the *Conduct* is based; however, they had been circulated among Sarah's Whig friends and thus form an important component of Sarah's posthumous portrait of the Queen. Moreover, while the language of the *Conduct* is more moderate, they nevertheless reflect accurately the picture of Anne which emerges from Sarah's published narrative.

58 Ralph, *Other Side of the Question*. See also *A Review of a Late Treatise entitled An Account of the Conduct of the Dowager D— of M—, &c.* (London, 1742).

59 T. B. Macaulay, *The History of England From the Accession of James the Second* (London, Longman's Popular Edition, 1895), II, pp. 156–7.

60 E. Wingfield-Stratford, *The History of English Patriotism* (London, John Lane, 1913), I, p. 456. In a similar vein, see also Morris, *Age of Anne*; Brown, *Alas, Queen Anne*, pp. x–xi.

61 J. H. Plumb, *The Growth of Political Stability in England 1675–1725* (London, Macmillan, 1967), pp. 105–6. In this context it may be worth noting the obvious pride with which Sir John points out that his copy of *The Works of the Rev. Jonathan Swift*, ed. J. Nichols (1801) was once owned and annotated by Macaulay: see *ibid.*, pp. 151 n. 1, 155, nn. 1, 2.

62 Ralph, *Other Side of the Question*, pp. 220–1, 253, 411.

63 Quoted in D. Green, *Sarah, Duchess of Marlborough* (New York, Scribner's, 1967), p. 300.

64 *The History of England from the text of Hume and Smollett to the Reign of George III*, ed. T. Gaspey (London, London Printing and Publishing Co., n. d.), III, pp. 396–7; F. W. Wyon, *The History of Great Britain During the Reign of Queen Anne* (London, Chapman and Hall, 1876), II, pp. 530–1; L. von Ranke, *A History of England Principally in the Seventeenth Century* (New York, AMS Press, 1966), V, p. 329. M. O. W. Oliphant, *Historical Characters of the Reign of Queen Anne* (New York, Century, 1894), pp. 1–3, 5, 77. See also Philip, Earl Stanhope, *History of England Comprising the Reign of Queen Anne Until the Peace of Utrecht, 1701–1713* (Leipzig, Tauchnitz, 1870), I, pp. 42–3; W. H. Lecky, *A History of England in the Eighteenth Century* (London, Longmans, 1888), I, pp. 31–2; K. Feiling, *A History of the Tory Party 1640–1714* (Oxford, Oxford University Press, 1924), pp. 360–4.

65 A. Strickland, *Lives of the Queen's of England, From the Norman Conquest* (London, Longmans, 1857), VII, p. 10; VIII, 550. See also pp. 4–5, 55; VIII, pp. 213, 220, 523, 526.

66 Strickland, *Queens* VIII, pp. 207, 212–13.

67 W. T. Morgan, *English Political Parties and Leaders in the Reign of Queen Anne 1702–10* (New Haven, Yale University Press, 1920); Trevelyan, *Blenheim*, pp. 165–78; *Peace and the Protestant Succession* (London, Longmans, 1934), pp. 62–3; N. Connell, *Anne, The Last Stuart Monarch* (London, Butterworth, 1937); M. R. Hopkinson, *Anne of England: The Biography of a Great Queen* (New York, Macmillan, 1934). The latter is full of errors, most notably that of misdating Anne's birth to 1664: p. 41.

68 Holmes, *British Politics*, pp. 194–216.

69 Gregg, *Anne*, passim. For other recent, more positive portrayals of the Queen, see Speck, *Birth of Britain*, pp. 13–15, 134–5, 177–8; S. Ross, *The Stewart Dynasty* (Nairn, Thomas and Lochar, 1993), pp. 284–5.

70 In general, textbooks and surveys have tended to be cautious about abandoning the old, dismissive view of Anne: see the lukewarm portraits in J. Black, *The Politics of Britain 1688–1800* (Manchester, Manchester University Press, 1993), p. 27; B. Coward, *The Stuart Age: England 1603–1714* (London, Longman, 2nd edn, 1994), pp. 400–2; *The Lives of the Kings and Queens of England*, ed. A. Fraser (Berkeley, University of California Press, 1998), pp. 253–8; J. Cannon and R. Griffiths, *The Oxford Illustrated History of the British Monarchy* (Oxford, Oxford University Press, 1988), pp. 445–59.

71 For contemporary comment, see Trevelyan, *Blenheim*, p. 169; *The Wentworth Papers, 1705–1739*, ed. J. J. Cartwright (London, Wyman, 1883), p. 301; BL Stowe MSS 226, fo. 176v; 'The Reflection', *POAS* V, p. 61; 'A Letter to the Lady Osborne', *ibid.*, p. 78 and nn. 18, 19; R. Coke, *Detection of the Court and State of England During the Last Four Reigns* (London, 1719), III, pp. 481–2.

72 For Sarah, 'Queen Anne had a person and appearance not at all ungraceful, till she grew exceedingly gross and corpulent' – an exact physical parallel to the trajectory of their celebrated friendship (*Memoirs of the Duchess of Marlborough*, pp. 229–30). Conversely, Strickland, who portrays Anne as 'in her youth, an uneducated and self-indulgent woman' but charts an 'undeniable improvement in her character' as Queen, has her 'round as a ball' as a child, but 'comely' in adulthood (*Queens* VII, p. 5; VIII,

pp. 212, 550–1). Tory adherents of the Queen include Tobias Smollett, who says she was 'of middle size, well proportioned . . . her aspect more comely than majestic' (*History of England* III, p. 396), and Mrs Oliphant, for whom she was 'a fat, placid, middle-aged woman' (*Characters*, p. 2). F. W. Wyon takes this further, writing of her portraits: 'There is a fat, maternal look about them which, although sometimes striking us as vulgar, affords a sufficient warranty that her Majesty was not likely to turn her kingdom into a shambles' (*History* I, p. 44). Neville Connell, whose biography is, in general, an approving portrait, calls her 'moderately tall, and well proportioned' (*Anne*, pp. 110–11). On the other hand, Sarah's most recent biographer, who contrasts her brilliance with Anne's dullness, refers to the latter as 'grotesquely overweight' (F. Harris, *A Passion for Government: The Life of Sarah, Duchess of Marlborough*, Oxford, Oxford University Press, 1991, p. 77). Interestingly, Verrio's 'Tory' portrayal at Hampton Court shows a noticeably thinner woman than that offered in her state portrait by her Whig Principal Painter, Sir Godfrey Kneller. Criticism of Anne' size might also be attributed to gender prejudice, but it should be pointed out that many of the former authors are equally hard on the Prince's girth.

73 For the rumour and its basis in Anne's complexion, see Z. C. Von Uffenbach, *London in 1710: From the Travels of Zacharias Conrad von Uffenbach*, trans. and ed. W. H. Quarrell and M. Mare (London, Faber & Faber, 1934), p. 116; 'The Negative Prophecy Found Under the Ruins of White-hall' (London, 1704), *POAS* VII, p. 619 n. For Sarah's denial, see *Memoirs of the Duchess of Marlborough*, p. 232.

74 Quoted in Bucholz, *Augustan Court*, pp. 220, 246–7, 250.

75 *Memoirs of the Duchess of Marlborough*, p. 273. For the Queen's impressive public appearance, see Bucholz, *Augustan Court*, pp. 205–8, 213, 222, 224; *Flying Post*, no. 1087, 23–25 April 1702.

76 Bucholz, *Augustan Court*, p. 205.

77 *Ibid.*, p. 204.

78 See *ibid.*, ch. 7, esp. pp. 202–28.

79 Gregg, *Anne*, pp. 11–14. Two exceptions to this were her acquisition of the French language while on a sojourn abroad between the ages of three and five; and a thorough grounding in the Anglican faith imparted to her by Bishop Compton.

80 *Memoirs of the Duchess of Marlborough*, pp. 230–1. See also Burnet, *History* VI, p. 230.

81 BL Loan 57/71, fo. 15v: [Anne to Frances, Lady Bathurst], Windsor, 'Fri.', n.d. See also Bucholz, *Augustan Court*, p. 245. For records of dull or stilted conversation see W. Nicolson, *The London Diaries of William Nicolson, Bishop of Carlisle 1702–1708*, ed. C. Jones and G. S. Holmes (Oxford, Oxford University Press, 1985), p. 300; *Hamilton Diary, passim.*

82 *Memoirs of the Duchess of Marlborough*, p. 18.

83 For Halifax's view of Charles II's wit, see D. Ogg, *England in the Reign of Charles II*, 2nd edn (Oxford, Oxford University Press, 1963), p. 750. For Mary, see H. and B van der Zee, *William and Mary* (London, Macmillan, 1973), p. 381; Bucholz, *Augustan Court*, p. 31; Trevelyan, *Blenheim*, p. 169.

84 Quoted in Holmes, *British Politics*, p. 196. For other examples, see *Memoirs of the Duchess of Marlborough*, pp. 24, 170–2, 187.

85 See *Memoirs of the Duchess of Marlborough*, p. 231; Strickland, *Queens* VIII, p. 10.

86 *The Letters and Diplomatic Instructions of Queen Anne*, ed. B. C. Brown (New York, Funk & Wagnalls, 1968), pp. 231–2, Anne to Godolphin, 12 September 1707. See also *ibid.*, pp. 197, 199–201; and Historical Manuscripts Commission (HMC), *Bath MSS* (London, HM Stationery Office, 1904), I, p. 237, quoted below.

87 Gregg, *Anne*, pp. 254–61, 297–329; Holmes, *British Politics*, pp. 206–9.

88 HMC *Bath MSS*, I, p. 237, Anne to Oxford, Windsor, 21 August 1713.

89 Bucholz, *Augustan Court*, pp. 118–19, 123–4, 153–6, 169–72.

90 'A New Ballad Writ by Jacob Tonson and Sung at the Kit Kat Club on the 8th of March 1705' (London, 1705), *POAS* VII, p. 57, lines 7–9. See also 'The Golden Age Revers'd' (1703), *POAS* VI, p. 526, lines 102–3; K. W. Cambell, *Sarah, Duchess of Marlborough* (Boston, Little, Brown, & Co. 1932), p. 166; J. Swift, 'Memoirs Relating to That Change Which Happened in the Queen's Ministry in the Year 1710', *The Prose Works of Jonathan Swift, D. D.*, ed. T. Scott (London, Bell, 1911), V, p. 374.

91 *Hamilton Diary*, pp. 63–4.

92 Gregg, *Anne*, pp. 5–6.

93 Bucholz, *Augustan Court*, pp. 51–2, 58–9, 119.

94 *Ibid.*, pp. 72–4, 92, 154–6.

95 *Hamilton Diary*, p. 35.

96 See the *Marlborough–Godolphin Correspondence*, ed. H. L. Snyder, 3 vols (Oxford, Oxford University Press, 1975); HMC *Portland MSS* IV–X (London, HM Stationery Office, 1893–1931); and BL Loan 29/31–32, 34, 36–38, 64, 311.

97 For the former, see Gregg, *Anne*, pp. 218–30; for the latter, see 'Queen Anne Versus the Junto: The Effort to Place Orford at the Head of the Admiralty in 1709', *Huntington Library Quarterly* XXXV (1972), pp. 323–42.

98 W. D. Montagu, Duke of Manchester, *Court and Society From Elizabeth to Anne* (London, Hurst and Blackett, 1864), II, pp. 378–9; John Vanbrugh to Charles, Earl of Manchester, London, 27 July 1708.

99 BL Eg. MSS 1695, fo. 49, Shrewsbury to Viscountess Longueville, London, 21 November 1711.

100 Bucholz, *Augustan Court*, pp. 90–4.

101 *Ibid.*, pp. 50, 68–84, 92, 95, 103–4, 111, 157, 171–2, 300 n. 85, 307 n. 75.

102 *Ibid.*, pp. 157, 165–8, 299 n. 70, 300 n. 85.

103 M. Foss, *The Age of Patronage: The Arts in England 1660–1750* (Ithaca NY, Cornell University Press, 1976), p. 111.

104 O. Millar, *The Queen's Pictures* (New York, Scribners, 1977), p. 87; N. Armstrong, *Jewellery: An Historical Survey of British Styles and Jewels* (Guildford and London, Lutterworth, 1973), p. 129. For similar verdicts from the worlds of fashion and the theatre, see F. A. Parsons, *The Psychology of Dress* (New York, Doubleday, 1923), p. 240; L. D. Mitchell, 'Command Performances During the Reign of Queen Anne', *Theatre Notebook*, XXIV (1970), p. 112.

105 Bucholz, *Augustan Court*, pp. 229–35; Boyer, *Anne*, pp. 715–16.

106 Bucholz, *Augustan Court*, pp. 237–42.

107 *Ibid.*, pp. 46–8, 53–4, 57, 59–63.

108 BL Add. MSS 61422, fo. 199; *Memoirs of the Duchess of Marlborough*, p. 232.

109 See Bucholz, *Augustan Court*, pp. 203–4.

110 See R. O. Bucholz, '"Nothing but Ceremony": Queen Anne and the Limitations of Royal Ritual', *Journal of British Studies*, XXX (1991), pp. 288–323.
111 Wyon, *Anne* II, p. 552.
112 Quoted in Eales, *Women in Early Modern England*, p. 8; W. MacCaffrey, 'Politics in an Age of Reformation 1485–1585', in *The Oxford Illustrated History of Tudor & Stuart Britain*, p. 322.

4

Queen Caroline of Anspach and the European princely museum tradition

Joanna Marschner

A N EXAMINATION of the artistic and literary patronage of Queen Caroline between 1727 and her death in 1737 reveals a wealth of intriguing material. As Voltaire wrote of her, 'She was born to encourage the whole circle of the arts'. Before her marriage in 1705 to George Augustus, Electoral Prince of Hanover and heir to the throne of Great Britain, she benefited from an upbringing at two important German courts, Dresden and Berlin. Queen Caroline's artistic and literary patronage must be examined first and foremost in the context of the European tradition of princely patronage, which is the author's purpose here. This is the prerequisite for any further exploration of how Caroline's collecting and connoisseurship fit into the context of constructions of British national identity, which, important though they are, is beyond the scope of this chapter.[1]

The sixteenth century saw the opening of a debate in Europe about the definition of the word 'Musaeum'. While to ancient authors 'musaea' were seats of the muses, or places set apart for artistic, literary or scientific occupations, in line with the notion of scientific collecting developed in Renaissance Italy, the term was applied increasingly to buildings accommodating collections of various kinds.

In written description and visual depiction the 'musaeum' assumed an ideal structure with a particular set of furnishings. The space most frequently took the form of a circular classical temple, the domed roof left open to the sky, as may be seen depicted by Raphael in the Camera della Segnatura, and described by Bartolomeo Delbene in 1585, Friederich Sustris in 1594, and Sir Francis Bacon in 1627.[2] The notion of a 'Musaeum Memorial' or pantheon of worthies developed in parallel, encouraged by the writings of Alessandro Allori, and Filarete, and quickly the space was provided with a population.[3]

The ideal museum structure had a further role to accommodate collections. In about 1580 Anton Eisenhoit produced an engraved frontispiece for the catalogue of the natural history collections of Michele Mercati in Rome. The classical building with a barrel vault, through which one looks onto a circular temple, is provided with cupboards, presses and niches, for the storage and display of paintings, sculpture and artefacts.[4]

Since the sixteenth century collections, which were amassed with the purpose of transmitting information by the systematic arrangement of artefacts, have been supported by catalogues. Samuel Quiccheberg (1529–67), employed by Albrecht V at the Bavarian court, is author of possibly the earliest museum tract, which is based on the tenets expounded by Pliny in his *Historia Naturalis*.[5] The ideas provided in *Kunst und Naturalien Kammern* by Johan Damian Major (1636–93), while again grounded in Pliny, develop further ideas from Quiccheberg and were used as organising rationale for the Green Vault collections in Dresden. In Hesse in 1704 and 1714 Michael Bernard Valentini, an experimental scientist employed by the court, produced the publication *Natur-und Materialien Kammern*.

Quiccheberg's encyclopedia of 1565 stresses the importance of classifying artefacts by type, and he includes five categories he deems essential to the well-rounded collection. These include scientific instruments, and naturalia, as well as works of art produced by man from natural products such as ivory and painting and sculpture. Quiccheberg considers it especially important that a painting or sculpture series be included which celebrates the pedigree of the collector. He gives directions about special collections, which he terms 'Kunstkammer' or a repository of artistic objects, and 'Wunderkammer' or repository of extraordinary objects. Both Quiccheberg and Major developed guidelines for the practical organisation of the collections and stressed the importance of catalogues.

There is a parallel category of publications such as the treatise prepared by Gabriel Kaltemarcht for Christian I of Saxony in 1587. As well as providing advice on how a collection should be formed, this stresses the responsibility of a ruler to foster and encourage an appreciation of the arts and sciences and the educational value of collecting.[6] It is evident that all these publications circulated widely, and they were extremely influential in the organisation of many princely collections, especially in Germany.

Queen Caroline spent several years at the Saxon court. She was born Wilhelmina Charlotte Caroline, the younger daughter of John Frederick, Margrave of Brandenburg Anspach by his second wife Eleonore Ermuthe Louise of Saxe Eisenach on 1 March 1683. Following the death of John Frederick in 1686, Eleonore married John George IV of Saxony, and Caroline accompanied her mother to Dresden, remaining there until the death of Eleonore in 1696. Caroline was then taken under the guardianship of Elector Frederick III of Brandenburg and moved to Berlin.

There had been an extensive 'Kunstkammer' in Dresden since about 1560, founded by Augustus I. Tools, scientific instruments and books were richly represented, and they provided a useful resource for the scholars, scientists and craftsman at the forefront of Saxony's industrial expansion. The collection of lathe-turned ivories was especially notable. Caroline seems to have maintained her links with this court into her later years, and Augustus the Strong, her uncle by marriage, sent her a wheelchair as she became more infirm.[7]

It was during her sojourn at the Brandenburg court that Caroline encountered Leibnitz, Voltaire, Handel and other members of the lively intellectual circle cultivated by the Electress Sophie Charlotte, sister of Caroline's future father-in-law. Not only was there an extensive library in Berlin, but another important art collection. Frederick William in the mid-seventeenth century had undertaken a regrouping of the collections lost during the Thirty Years War. They became especially rich in antiquities, retrieved from local excavations and also purchased. Exotic rarities from the Orient and the Americas also had a prominent place. The whole assemblage would be re-housed in spacious new galleries in the Berliner Schloss in 1703, during Caroline's residence.

In 1703, the strong-minded Princess turned down her first very flattering marriage proposal from Archduke Charles of Austria, titular King of Spain, on religious grounds. She accepted the proposal made in 1705 by George Augustus, Electoral Prince of Hanover. Her commitment to Protestantism would later make her very acceptable in British eyes. At the Hanoverian court, overseen by the formidable Electress Sophia, heiress to the British throne, Caroline was again able to pursue her intellectual interests. She enjoyed the company of philosophers, clerics, botanists and historians and continued to research her favourite studies, the pedigrees of noble families. An inventory of the 'Kunst und Wunder Kammer' of the Electress made in 1709 reveals that this collection at Herrenhausen was particularly strong in jewellery and gems.[8]

There can be no doubt that Queen Caroline was influenced by these formative experiences. The inventory of her library reveals she held copies of Pliny's *De Naturalis* together with works by Bacon, and includes an intriguing note of a book concerning temples of muses written by Michel de Merodes.[9] There were catalogues of the collections of medals held by the King of France, and volumes containing the architectural plans for Herrenhausen, as well as Versailles, and other notable princely residences. She would be able to consult Castiglione, Machiavelli and Albergati on princely manners, as well as many other contemporary etiquette manuals.

Caroline's grandmother-in-law Sophia, heiress to the British throne after the 1701 Act of Settlement, almost achieved her ambition to be queen, but died a few weeks before Queen Anne in 1714. The throne of Great Britain passed to Anne's second cousin, George, Elector of Hanover. George Augustus and Caroline, recently created Prince and Princess of Wales, accompanied George I to London. As Christine Gerrard shows in this volume, the couple cultivated their Welsh 'image' as part of their strategy to court popularity. On 11 June 1727, George I died in his carriage on the way to Osnabrück. Archbishop Wake crowned King George II and Queen Caroline on 11 October the same year.

Caroline was now able to utilise her knowledge of princely patronage in her role as Queen consort. She brought these German examples to bear in her creation of an English genealogy of kingship, which would look further back than the recent dynastic changes. Following the idea of a pantheon of worthies, she commissioned her first set of worthies and heroes for a garden pavilion, known as the Hermitage, designed by William Kent for Richmond Park in 1732. The Hermitage project would cost the Queen £1,114.[10]

In its design as a picturesque rural retreat the Hermitage sits at variance to mainstream ideas of the classical pantheon of worthies (FIGURE 7). Approached across a circular lawn, it took the form of a ruin of rough-hewn stones, laid together to form a triple-arched façade, with a central pediment. It jutted out from a hill created by Bridgeman, topped with pine trees in the manner approved by Batty Langley in his publication *New Principles of Gardening* of 1728. The Queen had a copy of this in her library. A central octagon was provided with niches into which were placed busts of Isaac Newton, Samuel Clarke, John Locke and William Wollaston. In a cell behind was an altar, over which sat a bust of Robert Boyle, surrounded by a golden corona. There were small rooms either side of the central space, lit from above through small square lanterns.

Giovanni Guelfi, the Italian sculptor brought to England by Lord Burlington, was paid in instalments for the sculpture series. The main group commissioned in about 1730 cost £48.18.101/2. The bust of Robert Boyle which followed in 1733 cost £8.[11] There is some contemporary comment to suggest that Michael Rysbrack was involved in some way

7 *The Hermitage in the Royal Gardens at Richmond*, 1736

with the project. Public interest in the Hermitage was immense and contemporary comment almost universally favourable. Indeed a poetry competition was organised by the *Gentleman's Magazine* in its celebration.[12] The Queen was particularly applauded for her selection of British worthies. As the *Gentleman's Magazine* pointed out, 'her Leibnitz is not allowed a place here'.

Michael Rysbrack is responsible for the second worthies series to be commissioned by the Queen in 1735. It was to comprise the Kings of England since William the Conqueror and would be placed, the *Gentleman's Magazine* announced, in 'the new building in the gardens at Richmond'.[13] Eleven terracotta models were made, the Queen taking the opportunity to view work in progress at Rysbrack's studio on 10 June.[14] But the series was never completed. Edward I, the Black Prince and Edward VI still survive. Alfred the Great and Henry V were destroyed in 1906, when a shelf on which they were stored collapsed at Windsor Castle.

It is very probable that the 'new building' at Richmond was another of Queen Caroline's rustic retreats, called Merlin's Cave (FIGURE 8). The Cave (though it was built above ground) was built in 1735 to a design of William Kent, to the south side of the Duck Pond. It was a curious structure. Passing though an ogee-shaped gothic door, one entered a

8 *Merlin's Cave in the Royal Gardens at Richmond, 1736*

circular room with a vaulted apse. There were octagonal pavilions placed either side. The whole structure was thatched. It is likely that the busts would have embellished the gothic bookcases placed in the pavilions filled with books selected on the advice of Dr Alured Clarke, and taken there in July 1736.[15] The books were to become the charge of the resident Hermit, the 'Thresher Poet' Stephen Duck. He had been born in the Vale of Pawsey in Wiltshire, the son of an agricultural labourer. After his poetry came to the notice of those in the court circle, Queen Caroline granted him, in 1732, a pension of 30 guineas per annum, and made him Caretaker of the Hermitage. In 1736 he was created 'Cave-keeper'. His wife, Sarah Big, served as a 'Necessary Woman'.

The last series of worthies commissioned by the Queen in about 1737 was intended to embellish her new library in St James's Park. Michael Rysbrack commenced work on busts representing Queens of England. The Queen died before the project had progressed far and Rysbrack was instructed in January 1738 to send the modellos of the faces he was working after back to the King.[16]

One of Mr and Mrs Duck's strangest responsibilities at Merlin's Cave was to explain to visitors the significance of the collection of waxworks, which were housed in the gothic niches in the apse. These represent arguably another form of the worthies and heroes tradition. The waxworks were life-sized, fully dressed and represented Merlin seated with his secretary, Elizabeth of York, Queen Elizabeth, and two further figures. One was possibly Britomart from Spenser's *Faerie Queene*, or else Britannia, Bradamante or Minerva; the other, was either the nurse to Queen Elizabeth, Gaucee who was Britomart's nurse, Melissa the prophetess who accompanied Bradamante, or Mother Shipton. The figures were made by Mrs Salmon, the proprietress of a popular waxworks in the Strand. It was noted that a Page of the Backstairs had posed for the figure of Merlin, a Grenadier Guard for his secretary. Mrs Purcell, Seamstress or Necessary Woman to the Queen, sat for Elizabeth of York, and Miss Paget for Queen Elizabeth.[17]

Even if the Duchess of Marlborough had to admit that the 'puppets are very strange', and the identities of the last figures remain uncertain, it is clear that there are allusions to either Spenser's *Faerie Queene* or Ariosto's *Orlando Furioso*, and that this was a celebration of the antiquity of the British royal pedigree.[18] It would stress the concept of Englishness rather than dwelling on the vagaries of dynastic succession.

The creation of a 'Line of Kings' had its part to play in the princely museum tradition. In 1601, the catalogue of the collection of Frederick II at Ambras Castle includes description of his 125 'viri illustri'. From about 1670 Queen Sophie Amalie of Denmark began her own family portrait gallery as part of the collections at the Amalienburg Palace.

The use of waxworks is interesting but not unusual in an international context. Portraits in wax taken from life and death masks survive from the sixteenth century. Wax portraits were included in Sophie Amalia's portrait gallery in Copenhagen, and Rastrelli's wax portraits of the French royal family were so admired by Peter the Great of Russia that he invited the artist to St Petersburg, and commissioned his own image, which was placed on public exhibition dressed in his own clothes. Augustus II in Dresden had his own icon made up, wearing replicas of the regalia. In London Queen Caroline would have encountered other models which may have been influential. She would have been aware of the series of wax effigies in Westminster Abbey, as in 1732 Baron Wainwright discovered the missing head of Henry VII in France, and this became the talk of the court.[19] This series contains a wax portrait of Queen Elizabeth from 1601. From the 1720s these historical effigies had been assimilated into what became known as the 'Ragged Regiment', with the commissioning by the Abbey authorities of new figures from Mrs Goldsmith to represent recent monarchs. Mrs Salmon's own waxworks in the Strand contained 140 figures.

What is perhaps more intriguing is that the figures are incorporated into tableaux. There is certainly German precedent for this, stemming from the crib traditions in the southern states. Elaborate full-sized plaster tableaux can be found for instance in the 'Holy Mountain' oratories in Piedmont. It is interesting to note that the Huguenot artist Isaac Gossett, from whom Queen Caroline commissioned wax miniatures, and possibly granted a pension, was also responsible for a 'representation of the Court of France, in wax, as big as life' described by Lord Egmont in 1731.[20]

The more conventional exercise in celebration of the British royal pedigree was the creation of the Picture Closet at Kensington Palace. In 1732 the passage room to the west of the State Bedchamber contained just three pictures. Within a few years it was adorned with over two hundred. The basis of the new arrangement was a collection of drawings by Hans Holbein, which had been located by Queen Caroline in 'A Buroe in His Majesty's Great Closet', according to Housekeeper's papers in the British Library.[21] By 1728 they had been removed from Kensington Palace for framing, and they were hung at Richmond where Lord Egmont would inspect them as late as 1735. However, it would seem likely by then that some of the more than one hundred examples noted by Vertue were making their way back to Kensington. They joined the collection of miniatures, sketches, wax profiles and other small pictures, which Vertue described as 'the greatest store of portraits of the English' in the Queen's Closet.[22]

Queen Caroline was well aware of the importance of this collection of pictures. She was coaxed by Lord Egmont and others to allow the set of Holbein drawings to be engraved, but hesitated fearing that they might be damaged by the copy process. Eventually she selected one head, that of the Bishop of Killaloo, which she doubted was by Holbein himself, to be used for a trial.[23] After several tantalising inspections of the little room, Vertue arrived in 1743 with a warrant from the Lord Chamberlain which allowed him to 'copy or draw all those heads'.[24] He was able to categorise them, and to record their history from their acquisition by Charles I from Thomas, Earl of Arundel. The room he noted contained several other paintings which had been part of Charles I's collection. There were other Holbein's such as the portrait of William Restimer and perhaps most curious was the picture of two mice by Raphael.

Queen Caroline had however also made her own purchases. She acquired the splendid portrait by Holbein of Sir Henry Guildford in 1734 from the estate of Lord Stafford, and there was a long set of primitives of the earlier English monarchs 'begged' from Lord Cornwallis.

The Queen's passion for English historical subjects surfaces once more in 1729 when she commissioned from William Kent a series of paintings celebrating the life and exploits of Henry V. The subjects were the Battle of Agincourt, the Marriage of Henry V, and the Meeting between Henry V and the Queen of France. The Queen's accounts for 1730–31 show that Kent was paid £166.5. She also read widely about her English royal predecessors. Her library contains numerous biographies: Francis Bacon on Henry VII, Sir Thomas More on Edward V and Richard II, Camden on Queen Elizabeth.

To complement the collection of pictures, the 'Kunstkammer', there was also a 'Wunderkammer' at Kensington Palace. It was located in the library on the first floor of the north-east pavilion. The first inventory appears to have been made in the 1740s or 1750s by Margaret Purcell, the Queen's Seamstress, for Jane Klein who had succeeded the Lowmans as the Housekeeper at Kensington.[25] It records that in this room, dominated by large portrait of Robert Boyle, were arranged a series of 'very fine curious cabinets', 'glass cases' and a wooden cabinet. It includes practical instructions about how to open the drawers without having all the gems or medals jump out.

The second inventory was made by Horace Walpole and takes the form of a handwritten annotation to his copy of Bathoe's description of the collections at Kensington published in 1758. It is Walpole who adds 'it was fitted up (I believe) by Queen Caroline'.[26] Both of these inventories describe 'flaggons of ivory carved', branches of coral set in gilt mounts, 'a crystal shell and triton set with jewels'. There is a large collection of gems and medals. The group of natural curiosities is smaller, but includes natural minerals, bezours, and 'unicorn horns'. Ethnography is represented by a range of weaponry probably of Middle Eastern origin, including 'a dagger with a crystal handle set with precious stones'.

Horace Walpole notes how once again the Queen had drawn upon the collections made by Charles I. He particularly remarks on a little sculpture of a 'Shock dog'. It is also known that James II acquired rarities, in 1661 sending abroad, Mr Hubbard, a Page of the Presence, on a quest to find 'curiosities of nature'.[27] Perhaps the items described in the first inventory represent some of these too. The list of items recorded in the 'Buroe in the King's Closet' which served as the repository for the Holbein drawings, also includes 'A book with silk Indian pictures', again the legacy of an earlier collector such as Mary II.

However, I believe that there were new additions to the Cabinet of Curiosity made by the Queen herself, either by purchase or being brought from Hanover. There are interesting annotations to the library purchase lists which record information like 'Delive aussy a Mrs. Purcel en presence de Mrs Fany Kemp 10 Janvier 1733 un peau blanche des Indes', and 'Delive aussy a Mrs. Clayton par ordre de la Reine le 5 de mai 1735 un caisse remplie de grandes verres qui sont venue de Hanover' ('Supplied also to Mrs Purcel in the presence of Mrs Fany Kemp 10 January 1733 a white skin from the Indies', and 'Supplied also to Mrs Clayton by order of the Queen 5 May 1735 a chest full of large glasses which has arrived from Hanover').[28]

The collection was to be moved from Kensington Palace to Windsor Castle in 1764. Elements are still identifiable in 1821 recorded in Jephson's receipt book for Carlton House. The daggers are still there, and the 'Shock dog', and 'a small vase made like a horn, mounted in silver gilt with chimera handles, 4 unicorn feet'.

It is very easy to prove the Queen's interest in the exotic. She corresponded with Sir Hans Sloane about plants, and visited his museum in Bloomsbury. She took her younger children to Sir Jeremy Sambrooke's house called Gubbins in Hertfordshire. There they admired his new gardens landscaped by Bridgeman, and its waterworks, but also visited his cabinet of curiosities.[29] Sir Jeremy was an employee of the East India Company. Andrew Fountaine, Vice Chamberlain to the Queen and who served as tutor to the Duke of Cumberland, had a very fine collection of antiquities. The Queen took her children to view the collections made by Sir Robert Walpole and her own library contains books on subjects as diverse as butterflies, cosmography, and traveller's accounts of Buenos Aires and the South Seas.[30] There were books on glass blowing and metal working. There was a book describing the collections of antique sculpture held by the French royal family.

The presence of a library to support a collection was an important part of the European princely museum tradition. The Queen had a new library building designed for her in the 1730s by William Kent. It would be situated on the west side of St James's Palace. It was a single-storey building, 60 feet long by 30 wide. The first plan which survives in Sir John Soane's Museum indicates that the bookshelves were to project from the walls into the main space, each having a niche at the end to accommodate a bust.[31] The eventual plan had the accommodation for the books arranged in arched recesses set in the walls. Between each pair of arches there was a wall bracket to support the busts. Above there was a coved ceiling with a richly carved cornice, and at each end was a chimney piece. Andrews Jelfe, who had worked on the Hermitage and Merlin's Cave, was appointed mason, and the carving was undertaken by James Richards and Richard Lawrence. The library building cost £1618–81/2.[32]

The books in the library were arranged by category. History was divided up into continents, and then by country, with Africa and the Americas being well represented. There were tremendous quantities of books on religion and moral philosophy, but also a very large natural philosophy section which had a substantial subsection on 'physick'. The other categories were philology, poetry, plays, music and miscellaneous. One can find a great many books which relate to the Queen's artistic projects, books of printed heads of the King's and Queen's of England, Sir Thomas Jones's work on the Ancient Britons, William Kent's book on Inigo Jones and about the works at Houghton, Colen Campbell's *Vitruvius Britannicus*, and Batty Langley's books on modern gardening.

There is no doubt that the library was well used. New books arrived regularly from the booksellers Paul Vaillant and Mr Pierre Desnoyer. The annotations to an early list of the books detail how Mrs Purcell and Mr Lowman, from Kensington Palace, and Mrs Clayton were kept busy carrying books back and forth between the palaces.

Queen Caroline was certainly influenced greatly in her forays into the art and literary worlds by William Kent and his patrons Lord Burlington and Sir Robert Walpole and their circle of friends. One can find models for picture cabinets she could have followed in England and there were collections of rarities in Bloomsbury, Oxford, Canterbury and Leeds which contained very high calibre exhibits. However, many of the Queen's projects were very individual and one should also look at the Queen's early experience living at some of the most sophisticated courts in Europe, and should assess how her German princely education would have tempered her decisions.

It was very important to the Queen that she should promote native industries. She purchased English lace, and wore silks made in the British colonies in America. She took a lively interest in overseas exploration and even entertained North American Indian chieftains. Her painting and sculpture commissions and purchases fall into very regular patterns. Alongside her cabinet of rarities she had a printing press installed so that her children could be taught this practical industrial process.[33] Young Prince William, Duke of Cumberland, was taught ivory turning. Each of these initiatives has close parallels in contemporary German princely patronage traditions. As Lord Hervey noted, 'the German and the Queen so rooted in her mind – that the King himself had not more at heart all the trapping and pageantry of sovereignty than she the essential parts of it'.[34]

Notes

1 Joanna Marschner is undertaking research towards a Ph.D. on the artistic and literary patronage of Queen Caroline. The study, while evaluating Caroline's collecting and connoiseurship, learnt in a rich European context, will assess how it was tempered by many competing factors on her elevation to Queen Consort of Great Britain and Ireland. There will be an examination of the Queen's attitude to the responsibilities she perceived devolved on her new status with respect to artistic patronage. It will endeavour to evaluate both her intentions, as well as her skill, in manoeuvring between artistic factions, as well as her terms of reference in embracing or eschewing fashionable trends. Finally, the study will assess the Queen's attitude to new constructs of British national identity. The author would like to thank the staff of the Royal Collections Department, the Royal Botanic Gardens Kew, the Departments of Manuscripts and Rare Books at the British Library and Sir John Soane's Museum for their help with this research.

2 Bartolomeo Delbene, *Civitas Veri* (Paris, 1609). In Marcin Fabianski, 'Iconography of the Architecture of Ideal Musaea', *Journal of the History of Collections*, 2: 2 (1990), pp. 95–134. Sir Francis Bacon, *New Atlantis*, (London, 1627). In A. MacGregor, 'A Magazin of all Manner of Inventions: Museums in the Quest for "Salomon's House" in Seventeenth Century England', *Journal of the History of Collections*, 1: 2 (1989), pp. 207–12.

3 Filarete, *Trattato*, in Fabianski, 'Iconography'.

4 A. M. Kesting, *Anton Eisenhoit* (Munich, 1964), pp. 21 and 56.

5 Samuel Quiccheberg, *Inscriptiones vel Tituli Theatri Amplissimi . . .* (Munich, 1565) in Eva Schutz, 'Notes on the History of Collecting and of Museums', *Journal of the History of Collections*, 2: 2 (1990), pp. 205–18.

6 Gabriel Kaltemarcht, *Bedenken wie eine Kunst-cammer Aufzurichten seyn Möchte* (Dresden, 1587) transcribed and translated in B. Gutfleisch and J. Menzhausen, 'How a Kunstkammer Should be Formed', *Journal of the History of Collections*, 1: 1 (1989), pp. 3–32.

7 Berlin, Dep. XI. 73 Convolut 54, Reichenbach's dispatch, Windsor Oct 15/26, 1728, in R. L. Arkell, *Caroline of Ansbach* (London, 1939), p. 229.

8 Hanover Archives, Dep. 103. XXIV Nr 2487.

9 British Museum (BM) Add. MS 11.511.

10 Public Record Offica (PRO), Works 5/58 March 1731.

11 PRO Works 5/58; PRO AO1/2454/366.

12 *Gentleman's Magazine*, January 1733 p. 41; February 1733, pp. 94–7; April 1733, pp. 207–8; March 1733, p. 167.

13 *Gentleman's Magazine*, March 1735, p. 331.

14 George Vertue, 'Vertue Notebooks, Volume III', *Walpole Society*, 26 (1937–38) p. 75.

15 Mrs Thomson (ed.), *Memoirs of Viscountess Sundon* (London, 1847), I, p. 191.

16 PRO Works 4/7 11 January 1737/38.

17 *Gentleman's Magazine*, August 1735, p. 498.

18 G. S. Thomson (ed.), *Correspondence of Sarah Duchess of Marlborough and Diana Duchess of Bedford* (London, 1954), p. 171.

19 Thomson (ed.), *Memoirs of Viscountess Sundon*, I, p. 106.

20 Historical Manuscripts Commission (HMC), *The Diaries of Viscount Perival, 1st Earl of Egmont 1730–1733* (London, 1920), I, p. 160.

21 BM Add. MS 20.101 fol. 28.

22 Vertue, 'Notebooks, V', p. 23.

23 HMC, *Egmont*, II, p. 297.

24 George Vertue, 'Vertue Notebooks, Volume V', *Walpole Society*, 26 (1937–38), p. 26.

25 BM Add. MS 20.101, fol. 60.

26 W. Bathoe, *Catalogue of the Collection of Pictures etc. belonging to King James the Second, to which is added a Catalogue of the Pictures and Drawings in the Closet of the Late Queen Caroline* (London, 1758), Royal Collection, Surveyor's Office copy.

27 *Calender of State Papers, Domestic*, Charles II 1660–61, I, p. 499.

28 BM C120.h.6.(6).

29 *Gentleman's Magazine*, July 1732, p. 19.

30 W. S. Lewis and J. Riley (eds), *Correspondence of Horace Walpole* (Oxford, 1980), p. 333.

31 Sir John Soane's Museum, Vol. 147/197.

32 PRO Works 5/59; PRO Works 5/105.

33 *Gentleman's Magazine*, February 1731, p. 79.

34 John, Lord Hervey, *Memoirs of the Reign of George II*, ed. J. W. Croker (London, 1884), II, p. 205.

5

Queens-in-waiting: Caroline of Anspach and Augusta of Saxe-Gotha as Princesses of Wales

Christine Gerrard

T HE CROWDS outside Westminster Abbey at George I's coronation on 20 October 1714 witnessed a striking spectacle: three ready-made generations of a royal family, a king, a prince and princess of Wales, and their children.[1] According to the honour traditionally conferred upon the king's eldest son, George Augustus had been created Prince of Wales by Letters Patent the previous month.[2] There was still a rival candidate to the title, the exiled James Francis Stuart, James II's son, considered by Jacobites the 'real' Prince of Wales. But a princess of Wales was a real novelty. Caroline of Anspach, Prince George's wife, was, remarkably, the first Princess of Wales for over two centuries, the last since Catherine of Aragon's brief marriage to Henry VIII's elder brother Arthur in 1502. In fact, princes and princesses of Wales in the role of 'kings and consorts in waiting' are essentially a modern phenomenon dating from the Hanoverian accession – a consequence of Hanoverian fertility, longevity and dynastic stability. But what did it 'mean' to be a princess of Wales in the early eighteenth century? What expectations, public and domestic, shaped the role? Although recent historical scholarship has begun to acknowledge the significance of Caroline of Anspach, and her daughter-in-law Augusta of Saxe-Gotha, wife of Frederick Louis, Prince of Wales, attention in both cases has been focused on the later stages of their lives and careers – on Caroline as powerful Queen Consort and on Augusta as Dowager and influential mother of George III.[3] Caroline's role as the first Hanoverian Princess of Wales, a role whose significance was enhanced by the absence of a queen consort to accompany George I, gave her a degree of freedom to develop a complex, multi-faceted, almost paradoxical public identity – as a popular, patriotic 'British' princess with the common touch, an intellectual and court wit, a devout Protestant within a 'risqué' court circle, a loyal wife and devoted mother (FIGURE 9). Yet as wife, mother and daughter-in-law Caroline was also the victim of Hanoverian court politics. The hostility between the King

9 *Caroline of Brandenburg-Anspach* by Charles Jervas, 1727

and Prince of Wales, which repeated itself in the next generation of Hanoverian royalty, made the role of Princess of Wales fraught with difficulty. The row which broke out between George I and Prince George in November 1717 over the christening of Caroline's second son, George William, led to the King's expulsion of the Prince from St James's and the subsequent establishment of Leicester House. It also entailed his legal 'confiscation' of Caroline's children and the subsequent death of her new-born son. This pattern of intergenerational conflict between Hanoverian father and son was imposed on Augusta of Saxe-Gotha as soon as she arrived in England in 1736 to marry Prince Frederick. Augusta initially had far less room to manouvre than Caroline. Whereas George and Caroline came to Britain as a 31-year-old married couple with children, Augusta, at seventeen little more than a child herself, walked into a political minefield. Over the previous six years, Frederick, adept in the art of self-promotion and public relations, had succeeded in making political capital for himself at his parents' expense. His marriage to Augusta took place just as the Patriot opposition to Walpole's government was rallying round him as figurehead, and he undoubtedly used Augusta, perhaps even exploited her, to enhance his popular appeal. Augusta's rapid initiation into Hanoverian politics forced her to learn, shrewdly, which image to cultivate and project. In both reigns the Prince and Princess of Wales 'played off' against the reigning monarch or monarchs in a bid for popularity.

As Katherine Thomson observed, Caroline's 'acquirements were such as would have distinguished not only any Princess, but any *Prince* of that, or any other period'.[4] Her wide intellectual and cultural interests date, as Joanna Marschner has shown, from the formative teenage years she spent in Berlin under the guardianship of Frederick III of Brandenburg and his wife Sophia Charlotte, clever daughter of the doughty Electress Sophia. Caroline's intellectual attributes are, however, all but invisible in the early British Hanoverian panegyrics, where she appears in essentially two roles – Protestant heroine and fertile mother. In 1704 Caroline had tactfully withdrawn herself from consideration as a possible bride for the Archduke Charles, future Emperor Charles VI, after finding the prerequisite conversion to Catholicism impossible. The episode soon became embroidered in British popular myth as Caroline's staunchly Protestant rejection of a formal marriage proposal to a Holy Roman Emperor: that is, in Gay's much-repeated phrase, she had '*scorn'd an Empire for Religion's sake*'.[5] Poets, among them Addison, who dedicated his famous tragedy *Cato* to Caroline, also emphasise the Princess's role as the bearer of children to secure and strengthen Hanoverian dynastic stability. Unlike Queen Anne, whose symbolic constructions of herself as a 'royal mother' to her people had stood in poignant, ironic contrast to her biological failure (four children, at least thirteen miscarriages, but no surviving heirs), Caroline was manifestly a productive mother.[6] By 1714 she had given birth to four healthy children (a son,

Frederick, and three daughters, Anne, Amelia and Caroline) and over the next fourteen years went on to produce three more surviving children (William, Mary and Louisa). Addison depicts Caroline as a maternal conduit in the chain of paternal inheritance, a vehicle for dynastic stability.

> No longer shall the widow'd Land bemoan
> A broken Lineage, and a doubtful Throne;
> But boast her Royal Progeny's Increase,
> And count the Pledges of her future Peace.

In a series of mirror images, Caroline's individual identity is subsumed into that of her children: 'While you, fair PRINCESS, in your off-spring smile'.[7]

Yet Caroline, highly intelligent and highly ambitious, refused to be defined merely in terms of reproductive usefulness. The fact that there was no first Hanoverian queen with whom to compete gave her considerable latitude. George I's former wife, Sophia Dorothea of Celle, whom he had divorced for adultery in 1694, remained imprisoned in Ahlden castle. His morganatic wife, Melusine von Schulenberg, who accompanied him to Britain in 1714, had no status as consort. Caroline thus took on some of the aspects of a surrogate queen. At the coronation it was she who wore the Hanoverian royal jewels, the so-called Hanover pearls passed down from the King's mother the Electress Sophia.[8] George I's notorious dislike of public appearances, his preference for domestic evenings with Melusine and his close circle, threw some of the social functions of monarchy onto the Prince and Princess. George I did not encourage visitors *en masse* to his private apartments: he did not follow the royal custom of holding morning levées and evening drawing rooms attended by visitors.[9] It was in Princess Caroline's drawing room at St James's, not the King's, that the royal drawing rooms and occasional balls were held. The younger couple channelled their energies into the social and ceremonial side of court life. Arguably, given the limited role permitted the Prince in affairs of state – and in the absence of the round of charitable and civic duties later devised for royals waiting in the wings – there was insufficient 'employment' for a restive Prince and Princess of Wales.[10] Initially the arrangement suited the King. Lord Hervey considered that 'all the pageantry and splendour, badges and trappings of royalty, were as pleasing to the son as they were irksome to the father'.[11] The Prince and Princess of Wales, who took to travelling in style on the royal barge along the Thames from Hampton Court, began to court the public. The image they projected – that of young married royals with small children, invested with a domestic respectability which became the stock-in-trade of later Hanoverian royals – fed off George I's perceived 'foreignness' and 'strangeness'. The King's natural reclusiveness exacerbated the dark rumours which circulated about his private life: the incarceration of his divorced wife, and the murder of her lover Konigsmark, his relations with Sophia von Kielmansegg, his half-sister and possible mistress, and his closeness to his two Turkish 'infidel' Grooms of the Chamber, Mustapha and Mehemet, who controlled access to the King and the privy purse.

The younger royals heightened the contrast by deliberately cultivating a British identity – an initiative, I would argue, driven by Caroline. In Herrenhausen, well before the death of the Electress Sophia placed her husband directly in line to the British throne, Caroline worked hard to establish the 'Anglo-Hanoverian connection' by playing hostess to British envoys on diplomatic missions to the Hanoverian court – Marlborough, James Craggs the younger, Lord Halifax and Lord Dorset, Edward Hyde, Earl of Clarendon, and his secretary John Gay.[12] She cultivated Gay with his knowledge of the London literary scene, on his advice subscribing to Pope's recent translation of Homer's *Iliad*.[13] She also worked hard to master conversational English through daily lessons with a Hanoverian-born English woman, and once in Britain proved ready to converse in the language, as did her husband (albeit with a strong German accent), still a contrast to the 54-year-old German-speaking Hanoverian Elector who never acquired more than a very rudimentary grasp of English. Prince George, both before and after his arrival in Britain, took to boasting of his new national allegiance in much-cited remarks such as 'I have not a drop of blood in my veins that is not English': as Hervey noted, 'everybody imagined this Prince loved England and hated Germany'.[14] George I brought with him from Hanover a large political staff and sixty-three members of his Hanoverian household. Although he gradually dispensed with many members of his 'inner German court', his perceived political and emotional reliance on what Lady Mary Wortley Montagu called his 'German Ministers and playfellows male and female' proved deeply unpopular as well as provoking accusations, not entirely unfounded, that they were draining the Civil List and sucking England dry.[15] By contrast, the Prince and Princess created a distinctively English royal household drawn from the young English aristocracy. The activities of Caroline's circle at this stage – especially those of her high-spirited Maids of Honour, such as Anne Griffith, Mary Lepell and Mary Bellenden – raised some eyebrows ('a vertuous Princesse with a Court so lewd'), but stood in sharp contrast to the perceived stiffness and dullness of the King's court.[16] George and Caroline's activities were not limited to a courtly elite. In 1715 London Welshmen specifically honoured their new Prince and Princess of Wales through the Society of Ancient Britons, a partly patriotic, partly charitable society founded in honour of Caroline's birthday, 1 March, St David's Day, of which the Prince was elected President.[17] At the Society's annual St David's Day celebrations, Welshmen paraded through the streets with leeks in their hats, attended a sermon and a huge dinner followed by Welsh harp recitals and songs descanting on the especial virtues of the Prince and Princess of Wales – songs which imply that the Hanoverians are truly British.[18]

There was, of course, political mileage to be made out of the gambit of appearing 'more patriotic' than the King. This was first in evidence during the long hot summer of 1716. That spring relations between father and son had deteriorated sharply. The Prince had been infuriated by the King's dismissal of Argyll, his Groom of the Stole, and the limited terms set for his regency during the King's first return visit to Hanover. The Prince exploited the unpopularity of the Hanover visit, made in the still unstable atmosphere following the Jacobite rising the previous summer, to win popularity and to form a political opposition to harry the Stanhope–Sunderland administration. The Prince and Princess, who spent the summer at Hampton Court, plunged into a six-month flurry of public relations, holding dinners and fêtes and summer festivities which blended the pastoral and the regal. Caroline had already developed an interest in English rusticity, subsequently reflected in the strangely thatched-cottage style of her Richmond garden building 'Merlin's Cave' and her patronage of the English 'Thresher Poet' Stephen Duck.[19] In 1715 Gay had observed the royal pair dancing 'our English country dances' at a royal ball.[20] At Hampton Court they organised for the local people some 'rural sports' – footraces to win smocks, petticoats and hoods – and the 'numerous Crowds of Country People were delighted with the 'easie Deportment and Affability of the Princess of *Wales*, who would even condescend to talk to a Country-Lass, in a Straw-Hat, with the same gracious Air her Royal Highness entertains Persons of the first Distinction; and yet, at the same Time, lose nothing of her native Grandeur'.[21]

The King responded by cancelling his next planned Hanover visit and taking a newly active interest in court life.[22] In the summer of 1717 at Hampton Court he mingled freely, hosting parties and assemblies so large that they could only be accommodated in a specially converted tennis court. The radical transformation in his behaviour was designed to win back support for the ministry and to outdo his son and daughter-in-law: as Addison noted, 'the king [has] gained many hearts by his affable and condescending way of life'.[23] The physical separation of the King's and Prince's courts following the expulsion of the Prince and Princess from St James's in September increased the rivalry. By April 1718, to improve royal visibility, the King opened the road through St James's Park to coaches. The competition extended to cultural activities. In August 1719 George and Caroline hired the famous actor and manager Penkethman to build a theatre in their Richmond summer house; the King, in response, set up a theatre at the Great Hall at Hampton Court and installed Richard Steele's Drury Lane players for several command performances, as well as more than quadrupling the number of resident musicians.[24]

To the extent that father–son rivalry forced into being the makings of a Hanoverian court culture between 1716 and 1720, there was something to be said for it. One could also argue that the Prince of Wales in opposition functioned as a dynastic safety-valve. Leicester House may have been a magnet for the politically disaffected, but at least it was a Hanoverian rather than a Stuart magnet. Yet the rift between the first two generations of Hanoverian royals caused bad publicity. The inextricable linking of the domestic, or familial, with the political, placed a particular strain on the Princess of Wales. Caroline's solidarity with her husband was notable. In February 1717 she gave short shrift to the King's emissary Stanhope, who lost his temper with her when trying to persuade her to get her husband to return to parliamentary sessions from which he had tactically withdrawn.[25] Yet in the build-up to an all-too-predictable row over the christening of Caroline's second son, George William, born on 20 October that year, she attempted diplomacy to defuse the crisis. The Prince and Princess wanted the child's grand-uncle, Ernst August, Duke of York, as a godfather, but the King insisted on following his ministers' advice that protocol required the appointment of the Lord Chamberlain, the Duke of Newcastle – a man personally disliked by Prince George.[26] Caroline tried to resolve the situation by suggesting that Newcastle act at the ceremony as proxy for Ernst August. When this failed, she tried to buy time by requesting a postponement of the baptism. In the event, immediately after the christening, the Prince was reputed to have threatened Newcastle with 'injurious expressions'. A quarrel rapidly escalated. To some extent the row was politically engineered: the ministry was keen to see the Prince publicly disgraced and isolated, exiled from the royal palaces, so as to end his appeal to the opposition. When the King told him on 2 December to leave St James's he refused to obey until he had received the command in writing. The King also ordered him to leave the royal grandchildren at St James's. He evidently expected Caroline to stay with them, and it is hard to avoid the conclusion that he was exploiting Caroline's maternal emotions to isolate his errant son. But Caroline made the brave decision to follow her husband, leaving her three daughters and new-born son in the care of the Countess zu Schaumburg-Lippe. The royal couple, with their servants and Ladies in Waiting, moved to a rented house in Leicester Square, and subsequently into the house which became known as Leicester House. Contemporary accounts show that the strain placed on Caroline's health was intense.[27] She had already left her first son Frederick behind in Hanover, and had suffered a still-born son the previous November. She undeniably felt guilt: during the negotiations for the 'royal reconciliation' some three years later, Lord and Lady Cowper advised Caroline, then 'in great anguish', to hold out for her children 'for if the *Princess* gives up, she will never have a faithful Friend again, nor be thought a good Mother'.[28] The King permitted Caroline and eventually George clandestine access to the children – but this was not widely known, and many considered his response extreme of a piece with a mode of European absolutism and tyranny alien to Britain. Sympathy for the Prince and Princess was widespread, especially when the three-month-old George William died while in the King's care. Peter Quennell, one of Caroline's twentieth-century biographers, breezily noted that 'luckily Augustan parents were inured to such losses', but it was clearly otherwise.[29] Caroline must have felt profound grief. And the baby's death gave further evidence of George I's perversity in behaving 'unnaturally' to his own kin – imprisoning his ex-wife, throwing out his son and daughter-in-law. The death must have troubled the King sufficiently for him to order an official autopsy to prove that the baby had died from a birth defect, a 'polyps at the heart', and not from neglect or maltreatment. Popular ballads (mostly Jacobite) responded with glee; one or two register a profounder disquiet. The anonymous 'Elegy upon the Young Prince' dwells with pathos on the 'little Bones' buried at 'St Peter's Dome' and on George's perversity, turning his 'Son and Spouse' out of his home. Caroline is figured as a nursing mother bereft of the baby she has suckled: 'Let Baby cry / Or Lit it die / Own Mother's Milk's deny'd, / He no more car'd / How poor thing far'd, / Then for his Lawful Bride'.[30] The Hanoverian Whig poet George Sewell avoids such personal accusations in his *Verses to Her Royal Highness the Princess of Wales, Occasion'd by the Death of the Young Prince*, but still figures the death of the baby, the first '*British-Born*' Hanoverian, as some kind of divine judgement on the political factions exploiting the christening row:

> Thus for our Guilt the *Royal Infant* bleeds;
> The *Royal Mother* weeps for *British* Deeds.
> Unworthy of the Flow'r, as soon as bloom'd,
> Heav'n its own Gift in Anger has resum'd;
> Just shew'd him to the World, then snatch'd him hence,
> To teach us how to prize *Another Prince*.[31]

Although Walpole and Townshend engineered a reconciliation of sorts between King and Prince in April 1720, the royal couple never regained formal control of their children after a majority decision in a court of law in January 1718 had upheld the King's right to legal guardianship. Yet Caroline clearly involved herself in very close detail in her children's tuition. In his 1747 *Essay on the Advantage of a Polite Education*, Stephen Philpot held up Caroline as exemplary parent, relating that she was usually present when her children were under instruction, and if not, ordered the master to supply her with an accurate and objective account of the class.[32] In 1714 Lady Cowper had observed that the 'little *Princesses* are Miracles of their Ages, especially Princess *Anne*, who at five Years old speaks, reads, and writes both German and French to Perfection, knows a great deal of History and Geography, speaks English very prettily, and dances very well'.[33] By the time of her coronation in 1727, in the words of Felicity Nussbaum, 'motherhood as both duty and fashion finds its public representation in Queen Caroline' – the royal icon of a mid-eighteenth-century cult of female domesticity.[34] In 1728 Philip Frowde praised Caroline for her 'Mother's Virtues': 'She shines our Model of domestic Life, / The tender Parent, and endearing Wife'.[35] The public image of Caroline as an ideal mother figure concealed a complex and difficult history of motherhood, including an alienation, perhaps inevitable, from an eldest son from whom she had been required to separate when he was only seven. The fact that Caroline as Queen consort managed to balance a 'domestic' reputation as nurturing mother and submissive wife with an active, even dominant role in royal political decision-making and ecclesiastical and cultural patronage says much about both her shrewdness and flexibility, skills learned as Princess of Wales.

Augusta's initiation into Hanoverian court politics was rather more abrupt. By April 1736, the month of her arrival, the battle-line between Frederick and his parents was well demarcated. Frederick had come to Britain in 1728 under a cloud of parental disapproval for his secret attempts to elope with the Prussian Princess Sophia. He immediately resented the low-key reception arranged for his arrival, harbouring ambitions of something grander. The grudge against his parents was exacerbated by two major factors – their delay in finding him a suitable wife (his younger sister Anne, Princess Royal, had been married in 1734) and his financial dependence on his parents. George II permitted his son less than half the allowance of £10,000 from the Civil List he had himself enjoyed as Prince of Wales.[36] Since Frederick's arrival in Britain, opposition politicians, keen on attaching themselves to the reversionary interest, had competed keenly for his favours. By 1736 he had developed a close relationship with a number of leading opposition or 'Patriot' Whigs such as William Pulteney, George Lyttelton and William Pitt. Unlike the opposition which had cohered briefly a round Prince George between 1717 and 1720 – essentially a platform for the ministerial ambitions of Walpole and Townsend – the opposition to Walpole was a protracted political campaign which had been growing rapidly in strength since the late 1720s, sustained by a vast propaganda machine of newspapers, pamphlets, popular prints, plays and poems.[37] Augusta's marriage to Frederick in May 1736 took place just at the point that he was becoming the focus of new opposition hopes centred on the unifying figure of a 'Patriot King'. The wedding itself was thus shaped from the outset by a political agenda, one which Augusta, almost inevitably, came to serve. Augusta's impeccable Protestant credentials won the approval of most Englishmen: eulogistic pamphlets praised a family lineage committed to the defence of Protestantism, as well as to the maintenance of Britain's political freedom, derived from her original 'Gothic' or Saxon constitution. 'The *Saxon* Virtue is still unextinguished, and that ancient Family which gave so many Heroes to maintain the *Liberties* of *Germany* hath blessed the World with a PRINCESS to protect the *Liberties* of Britain.'[38] Augusta's very innocence and amiability proved the necessary salve to Frederick's somewhat tarnished image. Popular perceptions of the Prince in the first five years after his arrival had not been particularly favourable: satirical squibs and prints had anatomised him unsparingly for his affairs with his mother's Ladies in Waiting and his fathering in 1732 of an illegitimate son FitzFrederick by Anne Vane, also sometime mistress of Lord Hervey.[39] The marriage to Augusta proved genuinely popular, as reflected in some of the poems and plays written in celebration, including the English ballad opera, *The Royal Wedding*, a comic play set in the twenty-four hours before the wedding, culminating in a dramatic representation of the wedding ceremony itself.[40] Yet the nuptial celebrations were inevitably overshadowed by political tensions signalling the growing rift between Frederick and his parents. On 12 May, Covent Gardens staged Handel's spectacular *Atalanta*, written 'In Honour of the Royal Nuptials of their Royal Highnesses the Prince and Princess of Wales', with 'a new Set of Scenes painted in Honour to this Happy Union'. Next day's newspapers reported the production in great detail, including the presence of 'their Majesties, the Duke, and the four Princesses'. But, ironically, no Frederick and Augusta, who had chosen to boycott their 'official' celebrations by attending a production of Addison's politically charged tragedy *Cato*.[41] In the Commons, Lyttelton, Grenville and Pitt, the leading 'Boy Patriots', milked the marriage for political capital in their ironic 'congratulatory' speeches which insinuated that George and Walpole had done everything in their power to delay Frederick's nuptials, which had finally been enforced only by popular pressure.[42]

In the midst of this attritional warfare Augusta sensibly cultivated a policy of appeasement with her in-laws, appearing inoffensive and anxious to please, mirrored in her gesture of prostrating herself at their feet on a first meeting. Augusta, purportedly described by Caroline as 'one whom she would not displease, one who had never offended her or done anything wrong', initially achieved a cipher-like quality of near-invisibility.[43] Poems in praise of Augusta further 'effaced' her individuality by superimposing onto her Caroline's image and turning her into 'a second CAROLINE'. As poets enjoined, 'Be CAROLINE's bright Pattern still in View'; 'O! may thy Steps her Royal Paths pursue, / Still keep the bright Original in view'.[44] Yet, as John Bullion has pointed out, Augusta was more politically astute and adaptable than was widely supposed.[45] Her very active participation in her husband's political campaigning would suggest a conscious choice of role-playing rather than merely passive acquiescence in her husband's schemes. Indeed, if (in the words of one 1736 poet) Frederick and Augusta were to prove 'another GEORGE, another CAROLINE', it was in their calculated effort to win popularity and to appear more British than the King and Queen.[46] The tactics they deployed were essentially a more successful reprise of those used twenty years earlier by the previous Prince and Princess of Wales. During the summer of 1736, just as in the summer of 1716, the younger generation of royals opportunistically exploited the King's absence in Hanover to win popular support. George II's visit to Hanover between June 1736 and January 1737, reputedly motivated by the charms of his German mistress Louise von Walmoden, attracted widespread censure and plunged him to new depths of unpopularity. By contrast, Frederick and Augusta courted the 'mad multitude's caress'.[47] They too took to travelling by barge along the Thames, but Frederick went one better than his parents. In 1732 he had invested £30,000, the best part of his annual income, on a beautiful Kent-designed rococo barge accompanied by boatmen in gold-filigree costumes and followed by an entire floating string ensemble.[48] In a celebrated river trip of June 1736, 'the ships saluted their royal Highnesses all the way they pass'd, and hung out their Streamers and Colours, and the River was cover'd with Boats'. After disembarking, the young couple dined in public, 'the Windows being thrown open, to oblige the Curiosity of the People'.[49] Frederick understood the art of gracious royal appearances better than his two Hanoverian predecessors. Yet he did not merely go in for grandiose display. The royal image he and Augusta cultivated was notably more domestic, more 'in touch' with the lives of ordinary subjects. As a couple, and subsequently as a family, they were far readier to go out on foot, and to mingle with the common crowd. Contemporary accounts record the couple visiting fairground booths, and on one occasion Frederick was rescued from the crush of the crowd by some London leather-workers. The Saddlers' Company subsequently honoured him (much to his parents' derision) with the title of Perpetual Master and altered their audit days to commemorate the birthdays of Frederick and Augusta.[50] Frederick differed most substantially from his father as Prince of Wales in his enthusiastic patronage of trade and commerce. As heir to the throne, Frederick was denied the military role enjoyed by both his father, the last British monarch to lead his troops into battle, and his younger brother William Duke of Cumberland. Yet in both the 1730s and again in the late 1740s, in the aftermath of the bloody reprises against the '45, Hanoverian militarism proved a two-edged sword. Frederick deliberately cultivated a different identity. 'What, tho' the Clarion, sounding from afar, / Calls You not forth, amidst the Din of War', boasted one of his wedding poems, Frederick will reign by 'Goodness' not by 'Pow'r'.[51] During the 1730s and again in the revived Leicester House opposition of 1747–51, he and Augusta assiduously courted the mercantile and trading communities of London, Bristol and Bath. The royal progress which the couple made to Bath and Bristol in 1738 was thus different in character from the tour made alone by George II as Prince of Wales in 1718.[52] Whereas the high points of Prince George's tour were reviews of military and naval parades in Guildford and Portsmouth, Frederick and Augusta attended a civic parade at Bristol in which guildsmen carried the symbolic artefacts of their trade. At the extravagant banquet, Frederick made his customary speeches in support of the advancement of trade and commerce, and Augusta 'talked freely to the Ladies in good *English*, which entirely won their Hearts'.[53] The couple's courtship of the 'cits' yielded political dividends. During the 1730s the Walpole administration managed progressively to alienate Britain's commercial and trading communities through Walpole's deeply unpopular plans for an Excise Bill in 1733–34, and a pacific foreign policy which was widely perceived to damage Britain's mercantile interests. Between 1728 and 1739 the larger mercantile communities of cities such as London, Bath and Liverpool pressed heavily for a trade war with Spain to end the limitations imposed on their trade with Spanish central America. As Kathleen Wilson pointed out, these issues injected opposition patriotism with 'a commercial ethos that made a straightforward appeal to the economic and political concerns of ordinary people [and] tied in the interest of the lowest shopkeeper with the richest overseas merchant'.[54] Frederick's frequent assertions of concern for the welfare of the 'trading' part of the nation (set against the perceived indifference of the Walpole government) thus made him, in a very real sense, 'the people's prince'.

After Walpole's fall in 1742, Frederick, despite his initial insistence that the new Pulteney ministry should include Tory leaders, finally agreed on a reconciliation with his father and the new administration in return for the long-promised raise in his allowance. Yet by 1747 the politically restive prince had begun to formulate plans for a new Leicester House opposition, calculated to win the support of Tories alienated by the self-perpetuating Whig oligarchy and disillusioned by the aftermath of the '45.[55] The reversionary interest was a significant feature of the campaign's appeal: by 1747, George II was sixty-four, and the imminence of Frederick I's rule seemed assured. The Carlton House declaration of 4 June 1747 revived the Patriot promises of the 1730s in the Prince's professed intention of creating a new government above party or faction and of purging political corruption. Bolingbroke, aged seventy, finally published his *Idea of a Patriot King* in 1749 in support of the new campaign – and Frederick actively sought to identify himself with the ideal ruler embodied in that idealising text.[56] He particularly took to heart Bolingbroke's neo-Elizabethan emphasis on trade: 'The wealth and power of all nations depending so much on their trade and commerce the government of a Patriot King will be directed constantly to make the most of every advantage that nature has given, or art can procure, towards the improvement of trade and commerce'.[57] Support for trade once again played a significant role in Frederick and Augusta's publicity exercises. British merchants had protested against the 1748 Peace of Aix-la-Chapelle as unfavourable to the 'Right, Properties, Commerce' and national honour of Britain, and in particular complained bitterly that the Peace had flooded the British market with vast quantities of French goods.[58] The Prince and Princess of Wales thus took every opportunity to sport fashion of English manufacture: they supported a 'Buy British policy' which they stringently enforced on their court. At the impressive celebrations of Augusta's birthday in November 1748, 'his Royal Highness observing some of his lords to wear *French* stuffs, immediately ordered the D. of *Chandos*, his groom of the stole, to acquaint them, and all his servants in general, that after that day he should be greatly displeased to see them appear in any *French* manufactures; the same notice was given to the ladies'.[59] A year later, on the King's birthday, 'the Prince and Princess of Wales were observed, with great pleasure, by the lovers of their country, to be richly dressed in our own manufacture'.[60] In June 1750 Frederick, Augusta and their two eldest children paid a highly publicised visit to the homes of weavers in Spitalfields, previously a hotbed of anti-government sentiment, and 'expressed great satisfaction at their fine and curious manufactures, declaring their resolution of encouraging them', a sentiment reiterated during a royal tour the subsequent month through the south-west which also took in the wool-combers and weavers of Cirencester.[61] Frederick and Augusta were also careful to advertise their support for other forms of 'national treasure': in July 1748 the royal couple visited the Library of Hans Sloane, an opportunity for the Prince to display what was a very genuine interest in art history as well as his cultural patriotism at seeing 'so magnificent a collection in *England*, esteeming it an ornament to the nation'.[62]

By 1748 Augusta had given birth to eight out of her nine children (Caroline Matilda was born posthumously in 1751). A striking feature of the Leicester House publicity machine was the unprecedented visibility of the royal children – accompanying their parents into weavers' cottages and on tours, particularly becoming involved in sporting activities such as the yachting and rowing races sponsored by Frederick and Augusta. Prince George's birthday was the occasion of a yacht race (the prize awarded by the young prince), and the royal children followed their parents 'in a magnificent new built barge, after the *Venetian* manner'.[63] The royal couple also inaugurated Leicester House theatricals – plays staged at Leicester House in which the royal children took the leading roles: perhaps less an initiation of a new tradition than a revival of an older tradition, that of the royal masque.[64] In part this reflected Frederick's own deep love of the theatre, yet the performances, widely reported in the press, also served a political function. One of the first plays thus staged was Addison's *Cato*, that dramatic statement of political liberty which had been harnessed to the Patriot campaign of the late 1730s.[65] Frederick had personally penned a new prologue and epilogue, recited by the eleven-year-old Prince George and printed in the *Gentleman's Magazine*, in which he proclaimed his allegiance to patriotism of a British as well as a classical cast. Looking back to 1688 and the declaration of rights as well as those avatars of British liberty 'whom the great William brought to bless this land', he famously proclaimed himself 'A boy in *England* born – in *England* bred'.[66]

Frederick's sudden death in 1751 put an abrupt end to the Leicester House opposition. Augusta shrewdly distanced herself from opposition politicians, immediately placing herself and her children under her father-in-law's protection, thus ensuring her future control of Prince George's upbringing. The 1750s were to witness a new identity for Augusta as Dowager Princess, perhaps admired and reviled in equal proportion. Shortly after Frederick's death Augusta commissioned a family portrait by George Knapton (PLATE 4).[67] The painting is a carefully staged piece of iconography testifying to the sanctity and permanence of the Hanoverian succession and to the cultural and national interests of the royal family. Augusta is seated, surrounded by her children, with the infant Caroline Matilda in her arms. To her left hangs a large portrait of her dead husband, an absent presence looking down paternally upon his family. To her right stands a statue of Britannia holding a spear and an olive branch, her foot on the globe: below lies a complex relief symbolising the Hanoverian succession and its defence of the Constitution, with a lion crouched over documents inscribed 'Act of Settlement' and 'Magna Carta'. A portfolio on the floor with the inscription 'Survey of Kew House and part of the Gardens' hints at Augusta's considerable role in refashioning Kew gardens. Meanwhile Princess Louisa listens to Princess Elizabeth performing on the lute, while Edward Duke of York, in military uniform, examines with Prince George a 'Plan of the Town and Fortification of Portsmouth' and Prince William, in naval uniform, affixes the royal standard to a model of a royal yacht. The carefully composed scene suggests a Princess with a firm sense of her own, and her progeny's, significance.

Notes

1 George I's two eldest grandchildren, Anne and Amelia, were present at the ceremony. Prince Frederick Louis, seven years old in 1714, was left behind in Hanover to continue his education under the supervision of his great uncle Ernst August.

2 Although James Francis Stuart had been declared Prince of Wales shortly after his birth in June 1688 he spent his 'princehood' in exile. See the Jacobite attack on Prince George, *To a Thing they call Prince of Wales* (1716?), p. 7.

3 See Stephen Taylor, 'Queen Caroline and the Church of England', in *Hanoverian Britain and Empire: Essays in Memory of Philip Lawson*, ed. Stephen Taylor, Richard Connors and Clyve Jones (Woodbridge, Boydell Press, 1998), pp. 82–101; Felicity Nussbaum, *Torrid Zones: Maternity, Sexuality, and Empire in Eighteenth-Century English Narratives* (Baltimore, Johns Hopkins, 1995), pp. 58–61; John Bullion, '"George, Be a King!": The Relationship between Princess Augusta and George III', in *Hanoverian Britain and Empire*, pp. 177–97.

4 Katherine Thomson (ed.), *Memoirs of Viscountess Sundon, Mistress of the Robes to Queen Caroline*, 2 vols (London, 1847), I, pp. 8–9.

5 John Gay, *A Letter to a Lady, Occasion'd by the Arrival of Her Royal Highness the Princess of Wales* (1714), line 4, in Gay, *Poetry and Prose*, ed. V. A. Dearing and C. E. Beckwith, 2 vols (Oxford, Clarendon Press, 1974), I, p. 133.

6 See Toni Bowers, *The Politics of Motherhood: British Writing and Culture, 1680–1780* (Cambridge, Cambridge University Press, 1996), pp. 37–89; Carol Barash, *English Women's Poetry, 1649–1714: Politics, Community, and Linguistic Authority* (Oxford, Clarendon Press, 1996).

7 Joseph Addison, 'To Her Royal Highness the Prince of Wales, with the Tragedy of Cato. Nov. 1714' (published 1716 with 'To Sir Godfrey Kneller, on his Picture of the King'), pp. 1–2. Cf. Gay, *Letter to a Lady*, lines 71–2: 'Observ'd with pleasure ev'ry dawning Grace, / And all the *Mother* op'ning in their Face'.

8 See Ragnhild Hatton, 'The Anglo-Hanoverian Connection, 1714–60', Creighton Trust Lecture, 1982 (London, University of London, 1982), p. 5.

9 See John Beattie, *The English Court in the Reign of George I* (Cambridge, Cambridge University Press, 1967), pp. 261–2.

10 For Prince George's role as Prince of Wales, see Ragnhild Hatton, *George I, Elector and King* (London, Thames and Hudson, 1978), p. 129. For the history of the royal family's involvement in charitable work, see Frank Prochaska, *Royal Bounty: The Making of a Welfare Monarchy* (New Haven CT, Yale University Press, 1995).

11 John, Lord Hervey, *Memoirs of the Reign of King George II*, ed. Romney Sedgwick, 3 vols (London, 1931), I, p. 66.

12 See Lewis Melville [Lewis Benjamin], *Lady Suffolk and her Circle* (London, Hutchinson, 1924), pp. 11–12.

13 See Gay to Charles Ford, 7 August 1714. '[I]f it were not for the Princess and the Countess of Picbourg I should forget my faculty of Speech, for I cannot as yet take the Courage to address a Lady in French, and both these Ladys take a pleasure in speaking English'. Gay, *Letters*, ed. C. F. Burgess (Oxford, 1966), p. 12. The Prince and Princess headed the subscription list to Gay's *Poems on Several Occasions* (1720). Caroline, to whom Gay's play *The Captives* (1724) was dedicated, was also present at its opening night. For details of Gay's relationship with Caroline, see David Nokes, *John Gay: A Profession of Friendship* (Oxford, Oxford University Press, 1995), pp. 172–80.

14 *The Diary of Mary, Countess Cowper, Lady of the Bedchamber to the Princess of Wales*, ed. Spencer Compton (London, 1865), p. 99; Hervey, *Memoirs*, p. 485.

15 Lady Mary Wortley Montagu, 'Account of the Court of George I', in *Essays and Poems and 'Simplicity, A Comedy'*, ed. R. Halsband and I. Grundy (Oxford, Oxford University Press, 1977), p. 84.

16 Lady Mary Wortley Montagu, 'Monday: Roxana, Or the Drawing Room', line 54, *Essays and Poems*, p. 184. See also Pat Rogers, 'Wit, Love and Sin: Pope's *Court Ballad* Reconsidered', in *Eighteenth Century Encounters: Studies in Literature and Society in the Age of Walpole* (Brighton, Harvester, 1985), pp. 53–74.

17 See Sir Thomas Jones, *The Rise and Progress of the Most Honourable and Loyal Society of Antient Britons* (London, 1717). For more recent accounts see Prys Morgan, *The Eighteenth-Century Renaissance: A New History of Wales* (Llandybie, Christopher Davies, 1981), pp. 57–8, and his 'From a Death to a View: The Hunt for the Welsh Past in the Romantic Period', in E. Hobsbawm and T. Ranger (eds), *The Invention of Tradition* (Cambridge, Cambridge University Press, 1983), p. 89. See also Philip Jenkins, *The Making of a Ruling Class: The Glamorgan Gentry, 1640–1790* (Cambridge, Cambridge University Press, 1983), p. 159.

18 See e.g. N. Griffith, *The Leek: A Poem on St David's Day Inscrib'd to the Honourable Society of Antient Britons* (London, 1717). Leibniz, Caroline's favourite philosopher and doyen of the Hanoverian court, researched the dynastic origins of both Britons and Brunswicks.

19 See esp. Judith Colton, 'Merlin's Cave and Queen Caroline: Garden Art as Political Propaganda', *Eighteenth Century Studies*, 10 (1976), pp. 1–120; Michael Wilson, *William Kent: Architect, Designer, Painter, Gardener, 1685–1748I* (London, Routledge and Kegan Paul, 1984), pp. 143–7.

20 Gay, *Letters*, p. 16.

21 See *Saturday's Post*, 29 September 1716, and Abel Boyer, *Political State of Great Britain*, XII (London, 1716), pp. 139–40.

22 For a detailed account, see Beattie, *The English Court in the Reign of George I*, pp. 264–78.

23 J. M. Graham (ed.), *Annals and Correspondence of the Viscount and the First Earl of Stair*, 2 vols (London, 1875), II, p. 28.

24 See H. W. Pedicord, *'By Their Majesties' Command': The House of Hanover at the London Theatres, 1714–1800* (London, Society for Theatre Research, 1991), pp. 6–7.

25 See Hatton, *George I*, p. 200.

26 See Hatton, *George I*, p. 207. The 'custom' of inviting the Lord Chamberlain to be one of the godfathers may have been one invented by George I's ministers for this occasion.

27 See John Van der Kiste, *King George II and Queen Caroline* (Stroud, Sutton Publishing, 1997), pp. 65–6.

28 *Diary of Lady Cowper*, p. 129.

29 Peter Quennell, *Caroline of England: An Augustan Portrait* (London and Glasgow, Collins Clear-Type Press, 1939), p. 72.

30 See Bodleian MS Rawl. poet 207 (153).

31 George Sewell, *Verses to Her Royal Highness the Princess of Wales. Occasion'd by the Death of the Young Prince* (London, 1718), pp. 45–6.

32 See Stephen Philpot, *An Essay on the Advantages of a Polite Education joined with a Learned One* (London, 1747), pp. 26–7.

33 *Diary of Lady Cowper*, p. 38.
34 Nussbaum, *Torrid Zones*, p. 58.
35 Philip Frowde, *Verses on Her Majesty's Birth-Day* (1728), p. 4. This image was much invoked by the essays and elegies on Caroline's death in 1737. See, e.g., Stephen Duck, *The Vision* (1738), p. 3 – 'The tend'rest Mother, most submissive Wife; / Who never yet her Consort disobey'd' – and Alured Clarke, *An Essay Towards the Character of her late Majesty* (2nd edn, 1738), p. 20.
36 For the long-standing controversy over Frederick's allowance, see Hervey, *Memoirs*, pp. 95–6, 196–7, 243–5, 255, 554–5, 661–705.
37 For general studies of the opposition to Walpole, see Isaac Kramnick, *Bolingbroke and His Circle: The Politics of Nostalgia in the Age of Walpole* (Cambridge MA, Harvard University Press, 1968); Bertrand Goldgar, *Walpole and the Wits: The Relation of Politics to Literature, 1722–1742* (Lincoln NE, University of Nebraska Press, 1976); Michael Harris, *London Newspapers in the Age of Walpole: A Study of the Origins of the Modern English Press* (London, Associated University Presses, 1987); Christine Gerrard, *The Patriot Opposition to Walpole: Politics, Poetry, and National Myth, 1725–1742* (Oxford, Oxford University Press, 1994); Alexander Pettit, *Illusory Consensus: Bolingbroke and the Polemical Response to Walpole, 1730–1737* (Delaware NJ, University of Delaware Press, 1997).
38 *The Old Whig: Or, Consistent Protestant*, 6 May 1736. See also *Memoirs of the Ancestors of Her Royal Highness Augusta, Princess of Wales, and of Saxe-Gotha by the Authors of the Abstract of the History of Popery* (1736).
39 See, e.g., *The Christening: A Satirical Poem*; *The Fair Concubine: Or, the Secret History of the beautiful Vanella*; *Love after enjoyment, in two epistles from Alexis to Vanella*; *Vanella; or, the Amours of the Great. An Opera*; *Vanella in the Straw: A Poem, inscrib'd to a certain Lady in St James's-Street, lately delivered of a fine boy* (all London, 1732). Pope also satirised Frederick's affair with Anne Vane in a squib, 'The Six Maidens'. See Norman Ault, *New Light on Pope: With Some Additions to his Poetry Hitherto Unknown* (London, Methuen, 1949), pp. 276–80.
40 See, e.g., William Thompson, *An Epithalamium on the Royal Nuptials* (London, 1736) and Richard Owen Cambridge, *On the Marriage of His Royal Highness, Frederick, Prince of Wales: in Imitation of Spenser* (London, 1736); and the university volume *Gratulatio Academiae Oxoniensis* (Oxford, 1736). See also *The Royal Marriage: A Ballad Opera of Three Acts occasion'd by the ever-memorable Nuptials of their Royal Highnesses the Prince of Wales, and the Princess of Saxe-Gotha* (London, 1736).
41 See Pedicord, 'By Their Majesties' Command', p. 18.
42 Hervey, *Memoirs*, II, p. 553.
43 As recorded by Hervey, *Memoirs*, III, p. 807.
44 See the poems by J. Hardres, William Tatton and Swayne Harben in *Gratulatio Academiae Oxoniensis*, pp. 80, 51, 65.
45 Bullion, ' "*George, Be a King!*" ', p. 181.
46 John Morrison, 'Ode to the Princess of Wales', *Gratulatio Academiae Oxoniensis*, p. 55.
47 Historical Manuscripts Commission Carlisle MSS (HMC 15th Report; Appendix, vi, 1897), p. 158.
48 The barge is now housed in the National Maritime Museum at Greenwich. See Wilson, *William Kent*, pp. 130–3, plates 49, 50, 51.

49 *Gentleman's Magazine*, 6 (1736), p. 231.

50 See J. W. Sherwell, *The History of the Guild of Saddlers* (London, 1937), pp. 93–6.

51 See the poem by Sir Robert Eden Bar, *Gratulatio Academiae Oxoniensis*, pp. 9–10.

52 For a description of Prince George's 1718 tour, see *The Flying Post*, 4–6 October 1716, and *The General Evening Post*, 27–29 September 1716. For Frederick and Augusta's tour taking in Bath and Bristol, see *Gentleman's Magazine*, 8 (1738), pp. 602–4.

53 *Gentleman's Magazine*, 8 (1738), p. 603.

54 Kathleen Wilson, *The Sense of the People: Politics, Culture and Imperialism in England, 1715–1785* (Cambridge, Cambridge University Press, 1995), p. 131.

55 For an account of the Leicester House opposition, see Linda Colley, *In Defiance of Oligarchy: The Tory Party 1714–60* (Cambridge, Cambridge University Press, 1982), pp. 253–60.

56 See J. C. D. Clark, *English Society 1688–1832* (Cambridge, Cambridge University Press, 1985), p. 182, and David Armitage, 'A Patriot for Whom?: The Afterlives of Bolingbroke's *Patriot King*', *Journal of British Studies*, 36 (1997), pp. 397–418.

57 Bolingbroke, *Political Writings*, ed. David Armitage (Cambridge, Cambridge University Press, 1997), p. 275.

58 See *The Pr-t-st of the M-ch-ts of Great Britain, Against the Preliminary Articles for a Peace* (London, 1748), and Wilson, *The Sense of the People*, p. 178.

59 *Gentleman's Magazine*, 18 (1748), p. 521. The edict was also reported in *The Remembrancer*, the publicity organ of the Leicester House opposition, edited by James Ralph, as 'a fresh Instance of the Sense his Royal Highness has of the true Interest of his Country, and of the Regard he has upon all Occasions shewn for it'. See *Remembrancer*, 51 (26 November 1748).

60 *Gentleman's Magazine*, 19 (1749), p. 519.

61 *Gentleman's Magazine*, 20 (1750), p. 329.

62 *Gentleman's Magazine*, 18 (1748), pp. 301–2.

63 *Gentleman's Magazine*, 19 (1749), p. 235.

64 The Prince had already 'revived' the masque form for royal consumption in 1740 by commissioning from James Thomson and David Mallet *The Masque of Alfred*, performed in honour of Augusta's birthday at Leicester House. But the participation of members of the royal family recalled an older tradition.

65 See Hervey, *Memoirs*, III, p. 839 and John Loftis, *The Politics of Drama in Augustan England* (Oxford, Oxford University Press, 1963), p. 122.

66 See *Gentleman's Magazine*, 19 (1749), pp. 37–8 and 40, and Averyl Edwards, *Frederick Louis, Prince of Wales, 1707–1751* (New York and London, Staples Press, 1947), pp. 161–4.

67 See Oliver Millar, *The Tudor, Stuart and Early Georgian Pictures in the Royal Collection*, 2 vols (London, Phaidon Press, 1963). The painting is reproduced in plate 212 and described on p. 189.

6

Anne of Hanover and Orange (1709–59) as patron and practitioner of the arts

Richard G. King

W HEN the young Prince Frederick of Prussia (later Frederick the Great) visited his friend Willem IV, Prince of Orange, and his wife Anne, daughter of George II and Caroline of Anspach, at their summer palace Het Loo in August 1738, he was mightily impressed with both the residence and with Willem's partner. Of one of his conversations with the Princess he wrote, 'J'ai beaucoup parlé de Newton avec la princesse; de Newton nous avons passé à Leibniz, et de Leibniz à la feue reine d'Angleterre' (I spoke at length with the Princess about Newton; from Newton we moved on to Leibnitz and from Leibnitz to the late Queen of England).[1] Frederick and Anne had much more than mathematics and philosophy in common. At one time, a marriage between these two cousins had been a serious possibility.[2] Further, the two shared an uncommon interest in and ability for music, an enthusiasm that was shared in correspondence and gifts of musical manuscripts after Frederick left that summer.

Anne was a remarkable woman of wide-ranging intellectual interests. Although the political and personal aspects of her life have been outlined in Veronica Baker-Smith's recent biography,[3] the many facets of Anne's cultural interests and patronage have yet to receive much attention. This chapter will begin to explore that rich field by examining a variety of topics including her education, her paintings, and music in her life and at her court. I shall also consider Anne as a patron: of art, theatre and music.

Born at Herrenhausen (near Hanover) on 2 November 1709, Anne came to England in 1714, when her grandfather George I assumed the English throne. The earliest known specific reference to Anne comes from the same year, and like most comments from her early years, it suggests that the Princess Royal was a precocious child. In 1714 Mary Cowper noted that Anne, 'at five Years old speaks, reads, and writes both German and French to Perfection, knows a great deal of History and Geography, speaks English very prettily, and dances very well'.[4]

10 *The Princesses Anne, Amelia and Caroline* by Martin Maingaud, *c.* 1721

A defining event of Anne's childhood was the break in 1718 between her father, the Prince of Wales, and her grandfather, George I. The King banished the Prince and his wife from court, took charge of the children, and appointed a governess, Lady Portland, to see to their education. The Prince was forbidden to see the children, and their mother had only limited access. Baker-Smith has suggested that one result of this split between the King and the Prince of Wales was that the three sisters Anne, Amelia and Caroline (FIGURE 10) 'drew together into a close and supportive relationship which was to last all their lives', and that another was that 'Anne's relationship with her parents reflected the detachment from them that had been forced on her by her grandfather'.[5] While the first of these suggestions is debatable,[6] the second is supported by an altogether remarkable anecdote reported by G. J. Schutte. In 1727, while her father was being crowned King, Anne is supposed to have stayed at home in bed reading a novel, and when he queried her about this, she responded: 'Sou een kroonprinses uw kamenier moeten zijn?' (Should a Princess Royal be required to serve as your maid?).[7]

As a young adult, Anne took full advantage of the wide spectrum of musical, theatrical and social events that London had to offer.

Numerous instances can be found when she and other members of her family attended opera, oratorios, plays, masquerades, puppet shows at the fair, and so forth.[8] She danced in the balls at court and played cards with the ladies from a very young age. And she waited, impatiently, for her chance to exercise real power.

That chance finally came in March 1734, when Anne married Willem Karel Hendrik Friso, a Prince of Orange. Apart from a return to England between July and November 1734, she spent the rest of her life in the Netherlands. The political reasons behind the marriage have been ably detailed by Ragnild Hatton and Herbert H. Rowen, and are reviewed in Chapter 7;[9] in brief, the Dutch Republic was an essential ally on the Continent, and George II sought to strengthen the relationship between England and the Netherlands, and to support young Willem's ambition to become Stadtholder of the United Provinces. It was expected in England that the marriage would guarantee him the position, but in fact it only strengthened Dutch opposition, and Willem had to wait until 1747 to be elected Stadtholder.

Willem was no prize: he had neither wealth nor power and he was a hunchback, but then Anne's choices were limited, as she herself apparently recognised. When informed of the match, she is said to have told her father that she would marry the prospective groom 'if it was a baboon'. His response was, 'Well, then, there is baboon enough for you'.[10] The King's reservations notwithstanding, Anne and Willem learned to love each other very deeply. Schutte, one of Anne's most perceptive biographers, notes that their rare absences from each other resulted in frequent, perhaps daily, correspondence,[11] and some of Anne's letters to Willem from the 1730s and 1740s, which survive at the Royal Archive in The Hague, provide very touching reading. For example, when she travelled in 1741 to Herrenhausen to plead Willem's case with George II (Willem had managed to offend the King), she wrote often to her husband, repeatedly noting how dull she found the assembled *haut monde*, the balls, the gardens, and so forth, and how she longed to be with her 'Pip'. One remarkable passage reads: 'Je ne mange ny ne dors, mais n'importe, je conte que la joie de vous embrasser me rendra plus gaye et folle que jamais, après que j'aurés premièrement découvert tout ce qui me mine à celuy qui est le dépositaire de toutes mes pensées, et que j'aime, et adore, bonsoir mon délicieux, et hagel Pépin, je me couche' (Whether I'm sleeping or eating, it doesn't matter what, I depend on the fact that the joy of embracing you will make me more foolishly happy than ever, after I have first explored all that pleases me in the one who is trustee of all my thoughts, and whom I love, and adore, goodnight

11 *William IV and his family* by Pieter Tanjé, *c.* 1750

my delicious and sweet Pépin, I go to sleep).[12] Of their union two children survived: a daughter, Caroline, born 1743, and a son, Willem, later
Willem V, born in 1748 (FIGURE 11).

In the Netherlands Anne generally spent her summers at Het Loo
and other palaces; winters were passed in Leeuwarden until 1747, when
she and her husband moved to The Hague upon his election as
Stadtholder. When Willem died in October 1751, Anne took the reins of
power as Regent (her official title was 'Gouvernante') during the minority of her son. Baker-Smith notes that no English princess has ever
wielded comparable power in a foreign land.[13] In her final years, among
other things, she devoted herself to her children's futures, providing

financial security and a good marriage for Caroline, and most especially securing the Stadtholdership for her son Willem.

The scholarly verdict on Willem and Anne has been less than kind: he is dismissed as a nice fellow but a desperately ineffectual leader; she is often portrayed as a wilful shrew whose accomplishments amounted to little more than securing her son's position and her daughter's marriage. That is not quite fair. Anne certainly was ambitious and proud, and she no doubt had a sharp tongue, as her occasionally derisive comments in the margin of a letter from Willem Bentinck prove.[14] Indeed, there is no shortage of contemporary anecdotes that report her in a less than favourable light. But there are many reports which suggest that as many people were impressed by her as were disappointed. Two of these, written in 1728 and 1737, illustrate the admiration she could inspire:

> Her royal highness goes on prosperously with the water. I think she is the strongest person in this place, if walking every day, modestly speaking, as far as would carry her to Seven Oaks, be a sign of bodily strength. Her highness charms everybody by her affable and courteous behaviour, of which I am not only a witness, but have the honour to be a partaker. I tell her highness she does more good than the waters: for she keeps some ladies in exercise and breath that want it. I have a very great respect for her, and I am only sorry there is no prince in Christendom at present that deserves her.[15]

> To speak truth their Highnesses are adored at Breda by people of all conditions there. I wish the inhabitants of every other town in Holland had the same sentiments for them. I am persuaded they will always deserve them, and I acknowledge to you sincerely it was a solid satisfaction to me to see what good health they enjoy, how happily they live together, and with how much affection and respect they are served by their servants of all degrees. They live magnificently in proportion to their circumstances, receive all people that come with so peculiar a grace that it must needs attach them for ever to their service, and there is not a person of any distinction about them that is not remarkable for a polite and discreet behaviour, so that they cannot fail to increase the goodwill of the people to their Highnesses wherever they go. In a word the Princess and Prince maintain their dignity without pride or affection, and their family is as orderly as that of any private gentleman. Their castle at Breda is a very noble one and finely furnished.[16]

As a political leader, Anne clearly had proven herself before 1751, for it was understood that she would take over when Willem passed away, and when she did, Van Hardenbroek, a member of the States-General,

1660 - 1837

Catherine of Braganza
(wife of Charles II)

Mary Beatrice of Modena
2d wife of James II

Queen Anne.

Queen Caroline of Anspach
wife of George II

Augusta of Saxe-Gotha
wife of Frederick Lewis

Anne of Hanover & Orange
Princess Royal d. 1759 married William IV - Prince of Orange

daughter of
George II
& Caroline

Queen Charlotte
wife of George III

3d child

Queen Adelaide
wife of William IV

1/ Frederick
2/ William
the princes

3/ Anne -
Princess Royal.

Prince of
Wales -
son of George II

George II - Caroline
CHILDREN

1 Frederick Lewis

2 William Augustus

3 Anne - Princess Royal

4 Amelia

5 Caroline

6 Mary

7 Louisa

8

noted that there was 'geen consternatie der werelt; mevrouw de princes aenvaert de regering met veel flegme en fermeteit' (not the slightest upheaval; the Princess took command with calm fortitude and firmness).[17] Moreover, Louis, Duke of Brunswick-Wolfenbüttel, Anne's right-hand man, reported to Maria Theresa that Anne 'was both better informed and also much steadier and harder working than William had been', and to George II, 'the Princess does far more work in a day than the Prince did in fourteen'.[18]

Anne had an extraordinary governess in Jane Martha Temple, Lady Portland, who was responsible for her education from 1718 on, and a still more remarkable example in her own mother, Caroline. Three useful sources of information survive that allow us to reconstruct her studies to some extent. The first is a set of orders written by Lady Portland in 1723 which suggests that Anne's days at this time were filled with reading, praying, walking and music.[19]

The second, and more significant, source is a collection of Anne's own schoolbooks. Extensive manuscript materials relating to her education – six bound volumes of her notes in French, Italian and German – survive in the Royal Archive at The Hague.[20] One of the volumes consists of extracts from history in Anne's hand in French from Herodotus, Plutarch, Thucydides and others. Another is a lengthy transcription in Italian of a history of the Roman Empire, complete with an appendix of thorough lessons in Italian. Others consist of theological extracts in German and a history of the Dutch Republic; the latter may have served as preparation for her marriage to Willem.

The archives at The Hague also show that Anne passed the same broad education on to her own daughter, Caroline. Indeed, there are two identical sets of the *Extraits d'histoire*, one bound and one in loose sheets. The bound volume was only partly written by Anne; the rest of it was completed by Caroline.[21] A further indication of Anne's abilities as educator may be seen in the fact that in 1748 Charles, Margrave of Brandenburg-Anspach, sent his son to be educated by her.[22]

Finally, there is Anne's library. Library catalogues can serve as guides to the education and interests of the books' owners. For this reason, it is revealing to examine the contents of Anne's own library, of which at least three catalogues were made between 1756 and 1760.[23] Her collection was extensive and broad: biography, memoirs, travel and theology are all found in abundance in these catalogues, but the focus of Anne's library was on literature and history (both ancient and modern). She owned the 'Works' of Boileau, Congreve, Dryden, Fénelon, Fontenelle,

Molière, Otway, Racine, St Évremond, and many others; collected editions of *The Guardian*, *The Spectator* and *The Tatler*; and numerous plays by Farquhar, Southern, Steele, Vanbrugh and others. Her historical collection included classic authors like Plutarch as well as modern historical works such as Rollin's two collections, *Histoire Ancienne*, 13 vols (Amsterdam, 1736) and *Histoire Romaine*, 16 vols (Amsterdam, 1739). A discussion of Anne's music library appears below.

Further aspects of Anne's education and accomplishments include languages, dance, painting and music. The Princess Royal appears to have grown up perfectly trilingual (French, German and English; she later added Italian and some Dutch), and at least one commentator noted her ability to converse naturally in the language of whomever she was speaking to. Marie Anne Fiquet du Boccage was introduced along with her travelling companion to Anne and Willem in June 1750, and noted that, 'L'une et l'autre Altesse lui firent l'honneur de lui parler et aux diverses personnes du cercle dans chaque langue de leurs pays aussi facilement que si toutes leur fussent naturelles' (Both of their highnesses did him the honor of speaking to him and to the various persons assembled there in their native languages as fluently as if each was their highnesses' mother tongue).[24] While Ragnild Hatton has shown that such skill in languages at a very young age was not as uncommon as one might think – Anne's sisters and the grandsons of the Gräfin von Schaumburg-Lippe all grew up trilingual[25] – Anne's linguistic abilities certainly enabled her to appreciate a wide range of theatre, literature and music in a variety of languages.

Of course, Anne learned other practical skills, such as dancing. Her lessons with the famous dancer and choreographer Anthony L'Abbé had begun by 1715 at the latest, as evidenced by the composition and dedication of L'Abbé's dance *The Princess Royal*, published that year.[26] Mary Cowper (see above) was not the only one to be impressed by Anne's ability. Two further reports suggest that she must have been a gifted dancer. On 1 March 1715, L'Hermitage, the Dutch representative in London, wrote to the States-General in the Netherlands: 'Il y eut Mercredy a la cour [un] bal et la jeune princesse Anne y dança, qui fut admirée de tous les spectateurs, tant sa dance surpassoit son age, accompagnant de tout d'une grace surprenante' (There was a ball at court on Wednesday and the young Princess Anne danced there. She was admired by all, for her ability surpassed her age [Anne was five] and her dance was performed with surprising grace).[27] A report from 1719, which, once again, comments upon Anne's extraordinary abilities, notes that her dancing was a great source of pleasure to her grandfather

George I, and that she and her sisters were regularly required to demonstrate their skill before the King.[28]

Rather less is known about Anne and the theatre. She often took in plays at London before leaving in 1734 (particularly from 1728 on), and she regularly attended the Comédie française at The Hague in later years. Documents reproduced by Monique de Smet show that the court had a large number of seats reserved and attended the Comédie twice a week in the 1750s.[29] Something of Anne's taste in acting may be suggested by a remark in one of her letters: 'I have seen Ribon as Oreste, he was marvellous and played so naturally that all the others seemed affected'.[30]

Anne's education also included instruction with Philip Mercier in painting, a pastime to which she dedicated considerable resources and energy and in which she distinguished herself. Little is known about her training, but a comment of Mercier's in 1734 preserved by George Vertue suggests that it consisted largely if not exclusively of copying: 'at no time the Princess never drew or painted any peece without his being wittness – nor ever drew from the life at any time tho' she had drawn & Coppyd many several copies in oyl painting done by her – that whilst she lately was in Holland at leisure she first begun to draw, the picture (from the life) one of her waiting maids Mrs . . . in small'.[31]

Financial records of the Dutch court suggest that Anne spent significant sums on painting supplies (see Appendix I, no. 18, p. 185), and house inventories show that her homes, particularly the Huis ten Bosch and Het Loo, were decorated with numerous paintings by the Princess. For example, an inventory of the Huis ten Bosch (a lovely palace just outside The Hague) written in 1757 lists a total of sixty-six paintings by Anne; in the Huys d'Orange, a further thirty-two were listed in 1758 (Appendix I, nos 13–14, p. 185).

References in letters and diaries show that her talent for painting was rather well known, that her work was respected, and that her abilities also extended to works in ivory, amber and embroidery. In December 1733, for example, Lord Egmont called her copies of paintings by Titian, Marat and others, 'as well done as I believe any painter in London could have finished them'.[32] Friends and relatives often wrote to ask Anne to paint for them, or to thank her for gifts of paintings. Among those to whom paintings were sent we may number Frederick the Great; Anne's brother Frederick, Prince of Wales; and Willem's mother, Maria (Appendix I, nos 4, 6, 7, p. 184).

Happily, some of her paintings survive and have recently been identified.[33] Of particular interest is a self-portrait painted perhaps about

1740 now located at the Royal Archive in The Hague (PLATE 3). The painting is a version of an anonymous painting in the Mauritshuis at The Hague;[34] the face is similar to that of Bernardus Accama's 1736 portrait.[35]

The cultural activity to which Anne was probably most attached and for which she was best known and most widely respected was music. Music is also the most thoroughly documented of her many interests, and there is much to say about her training, her talent and her patronage. An appropriate place to begin is Anne's relationship with the composer George Frideric Handel.

Among the women who played a significant role in Handel's life and career, Anne stands out as among his best pupils, as one of his most loyal patrons, and as a friend of very long-standing. She learned well enough from the composer that a knowledgeable contemporary, Jacob Wilhelm Lustig, could observe that she and Frederick the Great were the most accomplished amateur musicians of the century (they were surely the most accomplished *royal* musicians).[36] The details of her patronage of Handel are sketchy, but it is clear that she played an important supporting role in London during the years of the so-called 'Second Academy' (1729–34), and that her patronage continued after she left England in 1734. Her friendship with Handel was such that in 1750 he chose to spend a good part of his final trip to the Continent in her company.

Anne's first documented encounter with the composer occurred on 17 October 1714, when she accompanied her parents to hear him perform at St James's.[37] Her lessons with Handel had begun by June 1723 at the latest, and it is likely they had begun before that, perhaps by 1720.[38] How long the lessons continued is not known.

What did Handel teach her? At the very least, she learned accompaniment from a figured bass and composition. The manuscripts that survive, which have been edited and analysed by Alfred Mann,[39] show an advanced course of study that included the writing of fugue, perhaps the most difficult of all compositional techniques. Handel probably also taught her singing: Lord Hervey called Handel Anne's 'singing master',[40] and this was a talent often mentioned in later years.

The depth of Anne's feeling for Handel can hardly be doubted. A telling comment, spoken upon her final departure from England in November 1734, is preserved by Hervey: 'she had Handel and his operas so much at heart that even in these distressful moments she spoke as much upon his chapter as any other, and begged Lord Hervey to assist him with the utmost attention'.[41] But what about Handel's views on Anne? As usual with this most private of men, that is harder to determine: all the reports we have are second-hand. Jacob Lustig, repeating a converstion he had with Handel in 1734, says that the composer told him that after he left Hamburg (in 1706) 'nothing on earth could induce me to teach music, with one exception – Anne, the flower of Princesses'.[42] Willem IV wrote in one of his letters that Anne was Handel's 'favourite', and he seems to have thought it odd that the composer had not written to her after the death of Anne's mother Caroline in 1737.[43] In the anonymous pamphlet *Harmony in an Uproar*, published on 12 February 1734, the following words were put into Handel's mouth: 'I was prodigiously caress'd at Court . . . particularly [by] the divine Princess *Urania* [Anne], who condescended to be my Scholar [student], and made that Proficiency, as seemed almost miraculous to me her Master; nay to that exquisite Degree, that the Amusement only carried it to as great a Height in her, as in the most Ingenious, who made it their Profession'.[44] *Harmony in an Uproar* was published a month before Anne's marriage, and some scepticism may therefore be permitted: who wrote this and to what purpose?

There are other, perhaps more reliable indications of Handel's esteem for Anne. In July 1734, when the Princess returned to England while Willem was away on military manoeuvres, Handel extended his opera season, adding two performances of *Il Pastor Fido* on 3 and 6 July, past the advertised final performances.[45] Moreover, he began his autumn season early, on 5 October, with *Arianna*, which, it has been suggested, may have been put on because Anne wanted to hear it before leaving.[46] It is impossible to say whether Handel would or could do such things without financial guarantees of some sort.

In the summer and autumn of 1750, Handel travelled to the Continent for the last time, apparently to see his friends, and he spent much of his time with Anne, performing for her on at least three occasions.[47] Financial records in the Royal Archive at The Hague show that Anne continued to purchase Handel's music through his chief copyist J. C. Smith and others while living in Holland.[48] Further support of the composer is seen in Anne's subscriptions to his publications in 1738 and 1740.[49]

Anne had a significant musical relationship with another important eighteenth-century musician, Frederick the Great. Their musical correspondence began no later than 1737. In a letter dated 9 May 1737, Frederick responded to Willem and Anne's attempt to lure him to their court with talk of the quality of Anne's musicians.[50] On 19 October, Frederick offered to send vocal music; his letter is once again a response to an earlier one, which we do not have, in which Anne had raised the subject of Handel's operas, perhaps to discuss them, or, more likely, to ask if he might like copies. Frederick responded with the woefully nearsighted comment, 'Hendel's great days are over, his inspiration is exhausted and his taste behind the fashion'.[51] One can imagine how *that* would have been received in Leeuwarden.

In August 1738, the two great musical amateurs met face to face when Frederick travelled with his father to Het Loo. We do not know whether they played music together, but we do know that Anne performed for Frederick and the rest of the Prussian court. A report published in August 1738 describes an evening concert of voices and instruments in which Anne played the harpsichord.[52]

Anne and Frederick's friendship continued to develop after that. He sent her manuscript music on at least two occasions (in December 1738 and April 1740), including some of his own compositions,[53] and she responded with one of her own paintings, which he praised.[54] No further correspondence is presently known until 1757, when Anne risked Dutch neutrality to warn Frederick of an impending attack from Russia, a dangerous move on her part, which perhaps shows the strength of the bond between them.[55] Upon hearing of her death, Frederick wrote: 'Ik heb eene vriendin verloren, die door hare grootmoedigheid, wijsheid en eene aan hare sekse te boven gaande geestkracht, geheel mijne achting verdiende. Ik zal haar altijd gedenken' (I have lost a friend whose generosity and wisdom were unsurpassed, and whose extraordinary strength of mind – above that normally associated with her sex – merited my utmost respect. I shall always think of her).[56]

Although the records of Anne's public performances are not numerous, those that have surfaced suggest that she was widely respected as a singer and, particularly, as a thoroughbass player (actually, as a singer who could accompany herself from a figured bass part at sight, no mean feat[57]). Certainly, musical performance played an important role in Anne's life. In her letters, music is often mentioned, and when others report her doings, they frequently place her at the keyboard. For example, in November 1733, when her groom Willem arrived in London for the forthcoming wedding, he was met by Lord Hervey, who then went to the palace to report to Caroline and the princesses what he had seen. Anne was not there, which Hervey queried: surely she wanted to hear the news? On the contrary, the Queen told him, '[Anne] was in her own apartment at her harpsichord with some of the opera people', and 'she had been as easy all that afternoon as she had ever seen her in her life'.[58]

Another rich anecdote concerns Anne's accompanying the great singer Farinelli in October 1734. Charles Burney's account of his conversation with the famous castrato some years later reports the event as follows: '[Farinelli] gave me an account of his first performance at court to his late majesty George the IId. in which he was accompanied on the harpsichord by the Princess Royal, afterwards Princess of Orange, who insisted on his singing two of Handel's songs at sight, printed in a different clef, and composed in a different stile from what he had ever been used to'.[59] Farinelli had come to London to sing with the Opera of the Nobility, a rival company set up under the patronage of Anne's brother Frederick against that of her friend Handel. One wonders whether she might have been testing Farinelli, even attempting to embarrass him by insisting on the two songs.

A particularly revealing story, told by Johann Adam Hiller, concerns Anne and Willem's journey to Germany in 1740. The viola da gamba virtuoso Johann Christian Hertel, then in Laubach, heard that Willem IV had come to Dillenburg, and that Willem's wife was 'eine sehr grosse Kennerin der Musik' (a very great master in music).[60] Hertel travelled to Dillenburg and had the honour not only of playing for Anne and Willem, but also, as he put it, the good fortune to hear and be astonished by the Princess's singing and clavier playing. She also gave him a variety of fugue subjects to play extempore on his viol.[61] Burney's Farinelli anecdote and Hertel's story about the fugue subjects together suggest that Anne enjoyed challenging the musicianship of those with whom she played.

Handel's biographer Friedrich Chrysander suggested that Anne's musical abilities made a Kapellmeister (music director) at her court 'superfluous'.[62] He surely had no hard evidence for this, yet it is a curious fact that no such director is known at the Dutch court in her lifetime. Actually, a certain Jean-Baptiste Marchand was hired as director of music in June 1734, while Anne was in England, but he was fired a year later because, as the official document of his dismissal put it, 'there was no more need for him'.[63] We hear no more of a Kapellmeister until 1766, when Christian Ernst Graf was elevated to that position, and it is possible that Anne herself directed the music at her court, at least until 1747 or 1751, when matters of state probably claimed her attention.

What kind of ensemble did Anne direct, or at least have, at her court? When Anne married Willem in 1734 and moved permanently to the Netherlands, she left behind in London what was perhaps the most vibrant musical scene in Europe. One can imagine how bleak her musical prospects must have looked upon arrival in the very provincial northern Dutch town of Leeuwarden, her husband's home. When Willem went away in June, Anne seized the opportunity to return to London, arriving on 2 July, and, after a tiresome journey, going the next night to Handel's *Il Pastor Fido*. She stayed until November (her parents had great difficulty convincing her to leave), and one of the last performances she saw in England was Farinelli's glittering début.[64] When, just a few months before, she had arrived in Leeuwarden, her first state dinner was accompanied by the music of fourteen trumpets, two drums and cannons.[65]

Undaunted, Anne set out to improve music at the court. One of the first things she did was to take one of the local musicians, Jan Frederik Riehman, with her from Leeuwarden to London in July 1734 to study the latest in Italian musical style with one of the Castrucci brothers, who were members of Handel's orchestra; in other words, she set out almost immediately upon her arrival to improve music at the Dutch court in a tangible manner.[66] She then set about establishing a court orchestra.

We do not know exactly when that ensemble was in place; the first record to survive comes from 1739, though the orchestra was surely long established by then. That is suggested by the facts that in 1734 a music director was appointed and that in 1737 she tried to lure Frederick to her court with talk of her musicians (see above). In 1740, the core of the court ensemble consisted of seven or eight musicians, and it appears that at the time Anne was still trying to expand the group.[67] However, the size of her ensemble remained relatively steady as the years passed, even after Anne and Willem moved to The Hague in 1747 and he became Stadtholder: in 1750 there were eight musicians; in 1759 eleven.[68] We should probably add another performer to the lists: Anne herself, on harpsichord, at least until 1747 or 1751. These are modest numbers, but it must be noted that ten musicians are quite enough for much orchestral and even operatic music of the time, and that extra musicians could be (and indeed were) hired to augment the band for special occasions. A later example of this practice occurred on 2 September 1765, when at least twenty-one musicians performed at a ball given in honour of the Hertog van Jork and the Prince and Princess of Brunswick.[69]

It is a testament to her will and to her abilities that Anne succeeded in establishing this ensemble despite the financial crises that she and her husband experienced at this time. A series of plans to reduce court expenses was written during the period 1734–38, when the couple were in severe financial straits,[70] but their troubles do not seem to have affected Anne's musical plans, for it was during this time that she formed her band.

In 1750 the Earl of Chesterfield wrote to Soloman Dayrolles at The Hague on behalf of the child virtuosa Cassandra Frederick, who was about to travel to the Netherlands, noting that, 'The great point is to get the Princess of Orange to hear her, which she thinks will *make her fortune*'.[71] Chesterfield's letter suggests that Anne was known as a patron of music, and her court is certainly notable for the number of famous musicians who performed there. Handel is the most celebrated of these, but many other virtuosos and composers of the first rank also spent time at Anne's court: she showed a talent throughout her reign for retaining performers and composers on their way through Holland to other destinations.

Besides Handel, the most important composers whom she patronised on a regular basis were Jean-Marie Leclair l'aîné, the leading French writer of sonatas and concertos, who worked three months a year at her court sometime between about 1740 and 1743,[72] and Christian Ernst Graf, the most important Dutch composer in the second half of the eighteenth century and a major figure in the early history of the symphony, who was appointed court composer in 1757 or early 1758.[73] Other famous musicians who worked at Anne's court include the singers Anna Strada del Po (1736 and 1738) and Gaetano Guadagni (1754), and the composer Franz Xaver Richter (1758).[74] It is perhaps worth noting that both Graf and Richter were leading musicians in the newer pre-classical style: Anne was no musical reactionary.

From a variety of evidence that I have explored elsewhere,[75] we know that Anne amassed an extraordinary music collection, the most valuable part of which consisted of manuscript and printed copies of Handel's music. Unfortunately, her music library has disappeared almost without a trace, as has the catalogue of the collection, for which her court musician Riehman was paid in 1759.[76]

It is unlikely that either of her children inherited this music. The family's possessions are documented in remarkable detail in the numerous inventories of its houses instigated by Anne herself in the late 1750s,[77] and also in later inventories of what her children owned. Nowhere in this veritable ocean of lists does any mention of the library appear, which suggests that it did not go to a family member. Particularly telling is the fact that none of the music one would expect to have formed part of Anne's library is mentioned in the catalogue of her daughter Caroline's music collection, written in 1760 upon the occasion of her marriage to Charles Christian of Nassau-Weilburg.[78]

Though Anne's music library has not survived (or has not yet surfaced), there are traces of it. A manuscript of lute music that apparently belonged to the Princess is now in the Municipal Museum of The Hague,[79] and the Dutch Royal Archive has a set of eighteenth-century manuscript parts for Handel arias.[80] The Royal Archive manuscripts consist of anonymous arrangements of seven arias by Handel for solo viola da gamba (which takes the voice part) accompanied by recorder and basso continuo. The arias, with the operas from which they were drawn, are as follows:

1 'Il confine della vita' *Muzio Scevola* (1721)
2 'Diedi il core' *Atalanta* (1736)
3 'Nò, non piangete' *Floridante* (1721)
4 'S'è tuo piacer, ch'io mora' *Atalanta* (1736)
5 'O scema mi il diletto' *Radamisto* (1720)
6 'Vedrò più liete e belle' *Lotario* (1729)
7 'Lascia pur amica spene' *Radamisto* (December 1720)

The arrangements are clever, adapting the texture of the original settings to the new chamber music idiom in a convincing manner.

These arias were probably arranged by or for Anne for performance at her court, and they provide an indication of one kind of chamber music played there. The choice of instruments may reflect the abilities of her musicians – the viola da gamba part, for example, might have been intended for Jan Frederick Riehman, a violist da gamba; Anne may have planned to perform the continuo part herself.

Three questions concerning Anne and music remain to be answered. The first involves her musical instruments. From the inventories of her various houses written in the 1750s we know that Anne possessed a significant number of keyboard instruments, mostly harpsichords. Where did these instruments go?

The second question concerns her patronage. As noted above, Anne supported several important composers, but few compositions commissioned by or dedicated to the Princess, aside from Francesco Guerini's op. 2,[81] Leclair's op. 9, and an anonymous composer's twelve sonatas for violin and bass published in 1756,[82] are known. For this, the only explanation I can muster is that the full extent of her music patronage will become clear only when the history of Dutch music in the eighteenth century has been written. However, I offer below some further thoughts on Anne as music patron.

The most intriguing question concerns Anne as composer. To my knowledge, no compositions attributed to Anne, nor even a hint of any, survive. Yet her course of study with Handel surely suggests that she wrote music: composition must have been the intent of her study of such subjects as fugue. Moreover, we know that both her brother Frederick[83] and her daughter Caroline[84] composed – it seems likely that the most musically talented member of the family would too. If she did, then either her music is lost or has not yet surfaced, or, like the roughly contemporary Dutch statesman Unico Wilhelm van Wassenaer,[85] she produced it anonymously or under a pseudonym.

Finally, we consider Anne as patron of art, theatre and music. The topic is complex and much work remains to be done, but it is clear that Anne's patronage was broad and far more significant than has been recognised to date.

The most important aspect of Anne's art patronage was portraiture, and there are many fine images of this famous woman, which have received surprisingly little scholarly attention. It is safe to assume that after 1734, when she came into her own as it were, Anne or Willem paid the artists who painted, drew or sculpted her portrait. A short list of those artists includes Bernardus Accama, Simon Fokke, C. F. Fritzsch, T. P. C. Haag, Philip Mercier, Hendrik Pothoven (FIGURE 12), Rusca, G. Sanders, Jeremias Stagman, Pieter Tanjé, Johann Valentin Tischbein, Heroman Van der Mijn, Phillip Van Dijk and Jan Baptist Xavery.[86] The Swiss artist Jean-Etienne Liotard is not known to have painted Anne's likeness, but she did commission pastel portraits from him of her children and of her ministers Willem Bentinck and the Duke of Brunswick in 1755 and 1756.[87]

Among those artists who are known to have worked for extended periods at the Dutch court, both Van der Mijn and Xavery were patronised by Anne herself in the 1730s. In the Royal Archive at The Hague there is a series of accounts that cover her English income and expenditures for the period 1734–37 (in 1734, in addition to an astounding dowry of £80,000, Anne was granted £5,000 a year in perpetuity to do with as she pleased). From those accounts, we learn that she used some of her English income to support Van der Mijn and Xavery at her court in the Netherlands:[88]

Account 1 (for period 24 April 1734 to end December 1735): 'Expences for painting Vandermine Xavary and several Pictures bought £382.19.00'

Account 2 (for period 5 January to end December 1736): 'Expences of painting Vandermine Xavary and Pictures Bought £285.00.00'

Account 3 (for period 1 January to end November 1737): 'Charges of painting and Pictures bought etc. £537.09.2.' This account also includes a specific reference to £100 'Payd by order to Mr Vandermeins Chill[n] [children]' on 25 January 1737.

12 *Anne, Princess of Orange* by Hendrik Pothoven, engraved Jacobus Houbraken,
1750. Anne's various talents – music, painting, embroidery, and so forth – are
evoked in the bottom half of the image

Anne was also a patron of theatre.[89] As noted above, she regularly attended the Comédie française at The Hague in the 1750s, when she was the company's most significant supporter. The court's support may have begun in 1750, when the French company was paid at least a half-year subscription of 3,000 florins. In 1751 Anne and Willem paid 6,000 florins (approximately £600) for a full year; individuals working in the company also received special gratifications.

Anne continued to support the troupe after Willem's death. A notarial document dated 4 November 1751 shows the company forming a society under her protection and direction, and Monique de Smet suggests that the court was directly involved in the troupe's activities, advising and even choosing the distribution of roles. In 1752 Anne gave a 'gratification extraordinaire' of 2,000 florins to the troupe in addition to her usual subscription. In 1754, when they performed at court, she was still supporting them to the tune of 6,000 florins annually, and in 1755 they were still advertising themselves as 'The French Comedians of her Majesty the Princess of Orange'.[90]

Concerning music, we have already noted Anne's patronage of first-rate composers and musicians such as Leclair, Graf, Guadagni and Strada; many others of the second rank also spent time at her court. A more lasting monument to her music patronage is the organ she commissioned for the Waalse Kerk at Leeuwarden in 1736, which has recently been magnificently restored.[91] The establishment of the Dutch court orchestra, which dates from Anne's reign, is also clearly due to her patronage.

We have observed that Anne and Willem experienced financial troubles in the 1730s, when the court ensemble was formed, and a logical question is: how did they pay for the seeming luxury of an orchestra? Initially, Anne probably used money from her English pension of £5,000. In the accounts at The Hague mentioned above, there are regular payments of substantial sums for musicians, tuning and so forth:[92]

> *Account 1* (24 April 1734 to end December 1735): 'Musical Instruments Books Musicians Tuning etc. £519.08.05'
> *Account 2* (5 January to end December 1736): 'Musical Instruments Books Musicians Singers Tuneing etc. £487.18.06'
> *Account 3* (1 January to end November 1737): 'Musical Instruments Books Musicians Singing Tuning etc. £385.05.6.'

For the period of April 1734 to December 1735 the amount spent on music is the largest sum after 'Charity and Pensions: £676.02.4'.

That these payments applied to her orchestra is suggested by the fact that at the same time she was using the same funds to pay for painting commissions and art supplies in the Netherlands, not to mention such things as Dutch lottery tickets. It would also be difficult to explain why she would support musicians in England while living across the Channel.

The most significant aspect of her music patronage, in my opinion, was her support of Handel from 1728 or 1729 on. Elsewhere, I have noted the influence Anne had with Handel during the Second Academy period (1729–34); drawn attention to the Earl of Shaftesbury's statement that, 'In the Spring 1729 a fresh Subscription was on foot for performing Operas, under the patronage of the Princess Royal'; and suggested that Anne may indeed have played an important financial role in the Second Academy.[93] Carole Taylor addressed this hypothesis, and quite reasonably suggested that Anne's patronage probably consisted more of cachet than of cash, a 'prestige by association' that eased Handel's access to the international aristocracy. Taylor pointed out that Anne was twenty years old at the beginning of the Second Academy in 1729 and unlikely to have the resources to do more than lend her name to the enterprise.[94] At about the same time, Lowell Lindgren published a series of letters from the diplomat Gio. Giacomo Zamboni's correspondence that seemed to support Taylor's thesis, in that they suggested the possibility that Anne may have exerted influence to assist Handel.[95]

The one vital piece of information missing in this is, of course, what kind of financial resources Anne actually had at the time. Unfortunately, that has been impossible to determine, for although we have long had the Treasury Papers which show that the princesses were granted their own household in 1728 and that their annual establishment was no less than £6,671.10s, we have had no idea how that sum was spent.[96]

Happily, we can now say. One of the entries in the published Treasury accounts noted a detailed establishment appending to the King's Warrant Book accounts outlining the princesses' finances, but did not reproduce the document.[97] Dated 19 March 1729, the account is a complete list with salaries of all the members – Ladies of the Bedchamber, Gentlemen Ushers, Pages of Honour and so forth – of the princesses' household.[98] Among those named are the dancing master L'Abbé (£240 per year), the music master Handel (£200), and the Italian master Paolo Rolli (£73.10).[99] According to the document, each of the three Princesses (Anne, Amelia and Caroline) was given £1,200 personal spending money per annum, a sum which Anne could call upon from 1728 or 1729 until 1734, when she married.

Now, £1,200 is a considerable sum (by far the most generous supporter of opera in London at the time was the King at £1,000 per year).

Given the close relationship between Anne and Handel at this time, particularly Anne's involvement in and influence upon Handel's affairs, given the reliable Shaftesbury's statement, and given the fact that Anne had more than enough money to have a very significant financial impact, it is surely not unreasonable to suggest that the Second Academy was in more than a figurative sense 'under the patronage of the Princess Royal'.

The discovery that Anne had such a sum to spend from 1728 or 1729 on has many implications for her patronage. For example, it is possible that Anne herself commissioned some of the portraits painted between 1728 and 1734. These would include many of the finest images of the Princess, by such artists as Jacopo Amigoni, Hans Hysing, Philip Mercier, and Christian Friedrich Zincke. Mercier's image of Anne in riding habit (FIGURE 13), from c. 1731,[100] is a candidate, and if Anne did pay for the painting, it would surely reflect how she herself wished to be portrayed. The choice of riding habit is significant. As Kimerly Rorschach observes, in Anne's time hunting was viewd as much more than an amusing pastime: it was seen as a noble and heroic occupation. The skills of the hunt were regarded as analogous to the skills of war, and these skills were assumed to be useful and necessary accomplishments of princes; thus a sporting picture, like a state portrait, could play a propagandistic role.[101]

Anne of Hanover and Orange was an extraordinary woman of many talents, talents which would have borne greater fruit had she married more fortunately. Indeed, the temptation to speculate is powerful: what if she *had* married Frederick the Great, or, at least, what if Willem had become Stadtholder soon after their marriage in 1734? For it was surely her relative isolation in Leeuwarden and particularly her husband's financial limitations that prevented her from leaving a more formidable legacy.

Nevertheless, her legacy is considerable. According to J. A. van der Veen, Anne and Willem built up the Stadtholder's art collection through a number of important purchases.[102] As this chapter has shown, Anne used her own money to support both art and music at the Dutch court independently of her husband, and further research may reveal to what extent she herself was responsible for the eventual shape of the Dutch collections. It is already clear that Anne deserves credit for the formation of the Dutch court orchestra, which flowered during the reign of her son Willem V. Indeed, as late as 1769, ten years after her death, the band was still referred to as the 'Musiciens de feue Son Altesse Royale'

13 *Anne, Princess Royal*, mezzotint by John Simon after Philip Mercier, *c.* 1731

(musicians of her late Royal Highness);[103] it was understood to be *her* orchestra.

A topic for further research, and one of potentially great significance, is Anne's patronage of the arts before she left England. If I am right, the Princess Royal played a prominent role in keeping the most elite form of art – opera – going in London from 1729 to 1734, and also commissioned works from some of the most important foreign portrait painters working in London. John Brewer has noted that the Hanoverian court was not a patron on the scale or impact of courts elsewhere, this function being taken up by the larger public of London.[104] Nevertheless, the patronage of all George II's children must be considered; only Frederick Prince of Wales is widely acknowledged at present. This book shows the significance of their mother, Caroline, as a patron; further research, taking into account all the royal households (those of the consort and all adult children), may reveal the extent to which not only Anne, but other members of the royal family supported the arts in England. This will lead to a fuller view of Hanoverian royal patronage.

Finally, to what extent did Anne share, or lead Willem's tastes? It would be inaccurate to say that she was the cultured one in the family: Willem's education was similar,[105] he apparently had the same linguistic skills, and so forth. But overall, it does seem fair to suggest that she took charge of culture at the court, probably from the moment she arrived at Leeuwarden in 1734. Anne was a monarch in her own right, more than her husband's equal, and this, combined with the fact that she had her own financial resources, gave her power to exercise patronage in a way she might not normally have been able to do.

Appendix I: notes on Anne's paintings

Anecdotes etc.

1 Lord Egmont's diary, entry dated 19 December 1733: 'I went to court, where the Queen ordered four paintings of the Princess Royal to be brought and shown her levée. They are copies from Vandyke, Titian, and Carlo Marat, and another, and as well done as I believe any painter in London could have finished them. The Princess has many other perfections. She sings fairly and accompanies her voice with the thorough bass on the harpsichord at sight. She works finely at her needle, understands Latin, speaks Italian as well as French and German, is extremely affable, good-natured, disposed to be serious, generous, and charitable' (John, Earl of Egmont, *Manuscripts of the Earl of Egmont*, (London, Historical Manuscripts Commission, 1920–23, I, p. 466).

2 In April 1734 Anne was supposed to have painted Heroman Van der Mijn's portrait, at the insistence of her brother Frederick, but she is also said to have denied it to her teacher Philip Mercier. The story seems to have begun with a newspaper account on 26 April 1734, which reads rather like a puff for both Anne and Van der Mijn. Anne set about the painting and, according to the newspaper report, completed it 'with an affability and ease which charm'd all present, and with so *delicate and masterly execution* (painted in oyle Colours), and so very like, that it strikes all that see it, with admiration' (George Vertue, 'Vertue Note Books, Volume III', *Walpole Society*, 22 (1933–34), p. 69). In August, however, Mercier told Vertue that the Princess Royal had given him a different account, and that she only touched a brush, which had no colour, to the canvas to satisfy Van der Mijn (ibid., p. 72). For the portrait itself, see A. Staring, 'De Van der Mijns in Engeland', *Nederlands Kunsthistorisch Jaarboek*, 17 (1966), p. 229, Afb. 7.

3 An anonymous obituary provides the following observations on Anne's paintings: 'Die Kunstminnendé Vorstin teikende en schilderde zoo in water als olyverven zeer wel, en van dit haer werk is eene groote menigte in het Huis d'Oranjezaal'; we also learn that Anne 'door het onderwys van den Kunstenaer Kramer in het yvoor en amber draeien vry verre gevordert' (Koninklijk Huisarchief, The Hague (hereafter KH), A17/404, f. 49v). For samples of Anne's work in amber and amethyst see Marten Loonstra, *Uit Koninklijk Bezit: Honderd jaar Koninklijk Huisarchief; de verzameling van de Oranjes* (Zwolle, 1996), p. 110.

Letters

4 Letter of Frederick the Great (?), from Berlin, 16 April 1740: 'Madame ma Cousine. Je viens de recevoir avec un extreme plaisir l'honneur de l'obligeant lettre de Votre Altesse Royale qu'Elle a bien voulu faire accompagner d'un excellent tableau fait par ses cheres mains. C'est effectivement un chef d'oeuvre, qui m'a rempli d'admiration et de joye . . . Je le garderai comme un illustre monument de Vos perfections dans les beaux arts' (KH, A17/430).

5 Letter from Anne to Willem, dated 'Cassel de 29 Jan.' [1741?]: 'Je suis bien aise que vous ayes trouvé le Portrait juste que je vous ay fait de Münchhausen' (KH, A17/430).

6 Letter from Frederick, Prince of Wales, to his sister Anne asking for a portrait of his niece (Anne's daughter Caroline), 12 May 1745: 'Je n'ose Vous prier ma chere Soeur de le faire Vous même, mais Je puis Vous assurer qu'il me seroît doublement agréable' (KH, A17/430). Letters described in Veronica P. M. Baker-Smith, *A Life of Anne of Hanover, Princess Royal* (Leiden, 1995), p. 99 show that he received the painting from Anne and that he hung it in his bedroom.

7 A letter from Willem IV to his mother dated 21 March 1750 mentions paintings by Anne of their two children Willem and Caroline: 'La Princesse est actuellement occupé a Les peindre et je lui ai dit que V. A. S. souhaitoit d'avoir le Portrait de Guillaume qu'Elle ne manquera pas de lui envoyer quand il y en aura un bon de fini' (KH, A17/170).

8 With regard to Anne's embroidery, there is a letter dated April 1747 written to Anne by her sister Caroline: 'I make myself a pleasure for the fine imbrodery Meelbaum tells me you are so good as to design for me. I shall be very covetous of it' (KH, A17/430).

The following letters may also refer to paintings by Anne

9 Letter from Maria Louisa to her son Willem IV, dated 17 August 1737: 'mais avant de finir je vous charge de mille excuse a la Princesse des que je ne l'ai pas remercié de son portrait que vous maves fait obtenir, je l'en remercie tres humblement et cela me fait un plaisir Extreme' (KH, A10/2019).

10 Willem's response, dated 21 August 1737: 'J'ai fait selon les ordres de V. A. S. les remercimens a la Princesse du Portrait' (KH, A17/170).

References in letters from Anne to Willem suggest that painting was a regular activity

11   Letter from Anne to Willem, dated 'Leeuwarde Mercredy au matin': 'je languis que ce moment vienne, et ne trouve de Jours ennuyeux que ce que je passe sans vous; même Musique, Peinture, Lecture, et Causilleries, tout me paroît plat sans vous, s'en m'occupant je ne fais que tuer le tems' (KH, A17/430).

12   Letter from Anne to Willem, dated 'Leeuwarde ce 21 Mars': 'Je vais me promener, peindre, tracasser, enfin me dissiper pour passer les Vilains Jours que je suis sans vous' (KH, A17/430).

Inventories

13   S. Drossaers *et al.*, *Inventarissen van de Inboedels in de Verblijven van de Oranjes (1567–1795)*, II (The Hague, 1974), 'Inventaris . . . Huis ten Bosch' (1757), mentions:

28 paintings by Anne herself (32 in 1759) (no. 103, p. 694)
In a different room, another 32 paintings by Anne (37 in 1759) (no. 115, p. 695)
In a further room, 4 more paintings by Anne (no. 151, p. 696)
In the room of Prince Willem, 2 more by Anne (no. 172, p. 697)

14   KH, A17/415, 'Inventaris der Meubelen . . . op 't Huÿs d'Orange . . . op den 28 September 1758': 'In de Roode Damaste Camer: 32 Schilderÿen zoo groot als klein alle in vergulde lysten geschildert door Princes Roÿael'.

15   KH, A17/46^II 10d, 'Inventaris van alle de Meublen en Goederen op beyde de Huyzen te Loo', 25 August 1757, f. 35: 'In de Passage van de Slaap camer nae het Derde Cabinet: agt Stukken door H. kon. Hoogheyd geschildert'.

16   A catalogue of the possessions of Anne's daughter Caroline, made in 1760, lists some of Anne's paintings: '2 Comedie Stukken, 2 Serafÿne Hoofoen, 1 Borststuk, 1 Buitenplaetsje, 1 Heertje en Juffertje' (all in 'vergulde Lÿsten'); and drawings: 'twee Pourtraitten met roode aerde getekent'. KH, A17/516, 'Inventaris van alle de goederen teboorende [*sic*] aen Haere Doorluchtige Hoogheit, Mevrouw de Princesse van Orange en Nassau'.

17   On 28 February 1802 Princess Louise, daughter of Willem V, wrote from Oranienstein to her mother noting that there were some paintings made by her grandmother, Anne, at the castle. An inventory of the contents of Oranienstein describes genre pieces that correspond to copies of works by Nicolas Lancret now attributed to Anne. See Loonstra, *Uit Koninklijk Bezit*, p. 109.

Accounts

18   In Anne's personal accounts written in England by Augustus Schutz covering the period 1734–37 (KH, A17/412), we find references which apparently include purchase of materials for painting as well as salaries for court painters and the acquisition of paintings.

Account for period 24 April 1734 to end December 1735: 'Expences for painting Vandermine Xavary and several Pictures bought £382.19.00'.

Account for period 5 January to end December 1736: 'Expences of painting Vandermine Xavary and Pictures Bought £285.00.00'.

Account for period 1 January to end November 1737: 'Charges of painting and Pictures bought etc. £537.09.2.'

Specific receipts which account for parts of these sums are also to be found in the same volume.

Receipt dated 30 June 1736: 'To Mr Vanderbank for Pictures £105.0.0'.

Receipt [25 January 1737]: 'Payd by order to Mr Vandermeins Chill[n] [children] £100.0.0'.

Appendix II: the court orchestra

Between 1739 and 1759 the number of musicians regularly employed by Anne remained relatively stable. De Smet cites a document from 1 November 1739 that names six musicians – Guerini, Riehman, Baptiste, Mulden, Gundelach and 'le nouveau musicien'[106] – to which we can add the names of two more, Weil and Weis, who travelled to Germany with Anne in 1740;[107] one of these two may be 'le nouveau musicien' named by De Smet. We thus have the names of seven or possibly eight performers who formed the core of Anne's musical establishment as of 1740.

In a document covering wages for the period 7 March to 7 June 1750 we find eight musicians: Riehman, Keller, Weis, Halbsmit, Rholing, Steÿweek and two horn players.[108] In 1752 nine musicians were on the payroll: those named in 1750 plus a performer named Bisschop.[109] By 1759 the total number of musicians in regular employ was eleven. De Smet lists ten (Keller père, Keller fils, Gundelach, Muller, Le Long, Riehman, Weiss, Halbsmid, Röhling and Stechweg),[110] to which we can add the name of Graf, who is listed among a total of eleven musicians in an obituary of Anne written c. 1759.[111]

Appendix III: the royal princesses' daily routine, 1723

Reglee donne a leur house / June le 9me 1723 dimanche au soir/levé a 7 heures jusques a 8 prié dieu / coiffe et dejeuner, depuis 8 jusqu'a 9 salle [saile?] / promener, lire depuis 9 jusqu a 10, et / depuis 10 jusque 11 lire haut avec le / grienault [quenault?] et faire des remarques sur / ce quelle aura lue seule, depuis 11 / jusqu'a midy aprendre; a midi alle au / prieres depuis 1 jusqua 2 etre a diner; / depuis 2 jusqua 3 jouer au volante / ou se promener en parlant des choses / raisonable; de 3 jusqua 4 travailler / pendant que la grienault lit, depuis / 4 jusqua 5 ou jouer du clavesin / ou lire; apres jouer avec Hendel, / a 6 heures et demie ce promener / quant il fait beau.

(Order given at their house / Sunday evening 9 June 1723 / Rise at 7; pray till 8, dress and have breakfast; from 8 till 9 go for a walk; read from 9 till 10; from 10 till 11 read aloud with the *grienault* [Amelia? Caroline?] and discuss what she has read on her own; study from 11 till 12; at noon go to prayers till 1; between 1 and 2 lunch; from 2 till 3 play shuttlecock or walk and discuss rational matters; work from 3 to 4 while the *grienault* reads; from 4 to 5 either practice harpsichord or read; after that, play music with Handel; at 6:30 go for a walk when the weather is nice.)[112]

I imagine that 'grienault' refers to one of Anne's sisters. The hand is similar to that of Anne, and she may well have been required to copy the directions given her by Lady Portland.

Notes

Early versions of this material were read at the Maryland Handel Festival at College Park, MD, in November 1998 and the meeting of the Society for Court Studies at London in September 1999. The research for and writing of this chapter were supported by awards from the Government of the Netherlands as well as the General Research Board and the International Travel Fund of the University of Maryland.

1 Letter to Voltaire from Willem and Anne's palace Het Loo dated 6 August 1738, in *Oeuvres de Frédéric le grand*, ed. J. D. E. Preuss (Berlin, 1846–57), XXI, p. 224.
2 See Ragnhild Hatton, *George I: Elector and King* (London, 1978), pp. 162, 271–2, 280–1.
3 Veronica P. M. Baker-Smith, *A Life of Anne of Hanover, Princess Royal* (Leiden, 1995).
4 *The Diary of Mary Countess Cowper 1714–1720* (London, 1864), p. 38.
5 Baker-Smith, *Anne of Hanover*, pp. 14, 22.
6 It may be objected that the surviving letters become very sporadic after the death of Anne's mother Caroline in 1737. See N. A. Bootsma, 'Prinses Anna van Hannover', in *Voor Rogier* (Hilversum, 1964), p. 138.
7 G. J. Schutte, 'Gouvernante Anna', in *Vrouwen in het Landsbestuur* (The Hague, 1982), p. 148.
8 For a description of the range of entertainments in London during George II's reign, see Peggy Ellen Daub, 'Music at the Court of George II (r. 1727–1760)' (Ph.D. diss., Cornell University, 1985), pp. 10–16. For documentation of Anne's attendance at various events, see *The London Stage 1660–1800*, II, ed. Emmett L. Avery, and III, ed. Arthur H. Scouten (Carbondale IL, 1959, 1961), starting with the *Index to the London Stage 1660–1800*, compiled by Ben Ross Schneider, Jr. (Carbondale IL, 1979), under 'Princesses'.
9 Hatton, *George I*, pp. 156–7, 268; Herbert H. Rowen, *The Princes of Orange* (Cambridge, 1988), pp. 158–9.
10 Horace Walpole, *Memoirs of King George II*, ed. John Brooke (New Haven, 1985), I, p. 139. The baboon anecdote is also found in the Memoirs of Viscountess Sundon, cited in Baker-Smith, *Anne of Hanover*, p. 30. Lady Suffolk even told Walpole that the King 'walked about the room, mimicking the Prince of Orange' (Walpole, *Memoirs*, I, p. 139, n. 5).

11 Schutte, 'Gouvernante Anna', p. 155.

12 P. Geyl, 'Engelsche Correspondentie van Prins Willem IV en Prinses Anna (1734–1743)', *Bijdragen en Mededeelingen van het Historisch Genootschap*, 45 (1924), p. 134. See also pp. 131–2.

13 Baker-Smith, *Anne of Hanover*, p. xi.

14 *Ibid.*, pp. 109–10.

15 Letter dated 4 July 1728 written by Dr John Arbuthnot at Tunbridge Wells to Mrs. Howard, in *Letters To and From Henrietta, Countess of Suffolk, and her second husband, the Hon. George Berkeley; from 1712 to 1767*, I (London, 1824), pp. 295–6.

16 Letter from the diplomat Martin Bladen at Antwerp to Sir Charles Wagner, dated 19 October 1737, describing his visit with the Prince and Princess of Orange, in *Historical Manuscripts Commission, Report on the Laing Manuscripts Preserved in the University of Edinburgh*, II (London, 1925), p. 250.

17 Schutte, 'Gouvernante Anna', p. 162.

18 Baker-Smith, *Anne of Hanover*, p. 143.

19 The full text is reproduced and discussed in Richard G. King, 'On Princess Anne's Lessons with Handel', *Newsletter of the American Handel Society*, 7/2 (August 1992). See Appendix III below.

20 Koninklijk Huisarchief, The Hague (hereafter KH), A17/470, i–iii. These books have also been discussed by Bootsma, 'Prinses Anna van Hannover', pp. 132–3.

21 See KH, A17/323, *Registers en Boeken in de Bibliotheecq van het Kabinet*, quarto section, no. 40. Baker-Smith (*Anne of Hanover*, p. 75) suggests that these translations were done in Leeuwarden after Anne's marriage, but far more likely, I think, is my interpretation of these as schoolbooks, an interpretation which is perhaps supported by the fact that Anne used these same books when she undertook her daughter's education.

22 KH, A17/172, letter dated 19 May 1748.

23 Koninklijk Bibliotheek (Royal Library), The Hague, shelf number 75 E 3, catalogue written by Daniel Langeweg in 1756. A later catalogue of Anne's library at the Hague is found in KH, A17/415, *Catalogus der Boeken door Wyle Haare Koninglyke Hoogheid nagelaten . . . gedaan in s'Hage den 21 January 1760*. A catalogue of her books at Het Loo was also written in June 1759. See KH, A17/46[II], no. 10d.

24 *Receuil des oeuvres de Madame du Boccage*, III: *Lettres sur l'Angleterre, la Holland et l'Italie* (Lyon, 1762), p. 85.

25 Hatton, *George I*, p. 132.

26 *The Princess Royal, a new dance for his Majesty's Birth Day 1715, Compos'd by Mr. L'Abeé*. Other dances composed annually for performance on George I's birthday include *The Princess Anna* (1716) and *The Princess Anne's Chacone* (1719). See Wendy Hilton, *Dance of Court and Theater: The French Noble Style, 1690–1725* (Princeton NJ, 1981), pp. 339, 340.

27 British Library, Additional MS 17,677, I.I.I., fo. 73v. Reference supplied by Daub, 'Music at the Court of George II', p. 96, n. 38.

28 Letter from the Countess of Schaumburg-Lippe to Sophie Catherina v. Münchhausen, dated 13/24 January 1719: 'Die lieben Prinzessen werden alle Tage artiger und sein deß Königes Augapfel, welcher ihnen alle Wochen einen Ball geben lässet, damit er das Vergnügen hat, sie tanzen zu sehen. Sie gehen über dißes 3 mahl die Woche in die Presentz, wo der König alle Leute des Abends siehet, und hält Prinzesin Anna

den Hof so artig, spiehlet Piquet mit den Damens, als ob sie erwachsen wäre, so daß es eine Freude der ganzen Nation is. Wan nur die liebe Frau Mutter und Herr Vater erst wieder dabey wären, so gieng alles gut.' *Briefe der Gräfin Johanne Sophie zu Schaumburg-Lippe an die Familie von Münchhausen zu Remeringhausen 1699–1734,* ed. Friedrich-Wilhelm Schaer (Rinteln, 1968), p. 58.

29 Monique de Smet, *La Musique à la cour de Guillaume V, Prince d'Orange (1748–1806), d'après les archives de la Maison Royale* (Utrecht, 1973), p. 24.

30 Baker-Smith, *Anne of Hanover*, p. 132.

31 George Vertue, 'Vertue Note Books, Volume III', *Walpole Society*, 22 (1933–34), p. 72.

32 Lord Egmont's diary; entry dated 19 December 1733. See Appendix I, no. 1 below.

33 Marten Loonstra, *Uit Koninklijk Bezit: Honderd jaar Koninklijk Huisarchief; de verzameling van de Oranjes* (Zwolle, 1996), pp. 108–10.

34 *Mauritshuis, The Royal Cabinet of Paintings: Illustrated General Catalogue* (The Hague, 1977), no. 504; painting dated *c.* 1750. The date *c.* 1740 for the version at the Royal Archive is suggested by the fact that the painting was originally at Oranienstein, which Anne and Willem visited in 1740 and 1745 (Loonstra, *Uit Koninklijk Bezit,* p. 109).

35 Reproduced as the frontispiece to Baker-Smith, *Anne of Hanover*.

36 Jacob Lustig, *Inleiding tot de Muziekkunde,* 3rd edn (Groningen, 1777), pp. 172–3.

37 Bernd Baselt *et al., Händel-Handbuch, IV: Dokumente zu Leben und Schaffen* (Kassel, 1985), p. 66.

38 See King, 'On Princess Anne's Lessons'.

39 See Alfred Mann, *Aufzeichnungen zur Kompositionslehre (Hallische Händel-Ausgabe),* Supplement, I (Kassel, 1978); idem, *The Great Composer as Teacher and Student: Theory and Practice of Composition* (New York, 1994), pp. 13–39.

40 Lord Hervey, *Some Materials toward Memoirs of the Reign of King George II,* ed. Romney Sedgwick (London, 1931), p. 273.

41 *Ibid.*

42 Otto Erich Deutsch, *Handel: A Documentary Biography* (London, 1955), p. 360. Lustig's statement is not strictly true: Handel had other students after leaving Hamburg.

43 KH, A17/170, letter from Willem to his mother dated 2 April 1738; see Richard King, 'Handel's Travels in The Netherlands in 1750', *Music and Letters,* 72 (1991), p. 378. Willem's letter suggests that Anne and Handel corresponded, although no letters survive.

44 Deutsch, *Handel*, pp. 354–5.

45 See *The London Stage*, III, p. 405; and *Händel-Handbuch*, IV, pp. 242–3.

46 Friedrich Chrysander, *G. F. Händel* (Leipzig, 1858–67; repr. Hildesheim, 1966), II, p. 367.

47 See King, 'Handel's Travels'.

48 *Ibid.,* pp. 378–9.

49 She is named in the subscriber's lists for *Alexander's Feast* and the *Twelve Grand Concertos*. See Deutsch, *Handel*, pp. 453, 498.

50 Leopold von Ranke, *Briefwechsel Friedrich des Grossen mit dem Prinzen Wilhelm IV von Oranien und . . . Anna, geb. Princess Royal von England* (Berlin, 1869), p. 29

51 Deutsch, *Handel*, p. 441.

52 *Europische Mercurius* (August, 1738), p. 136; reference kindly brought to my attention by Dr L. J. van der Klooster.

53 See Frederick's letters of 7, 19 November and 9 December 1738 in Ranke, *Briefwechsel Friedrich des Grossen*, pp. 42, 44. In 1740, Frederick sent music by the composer Lämbre (?) (KH, A17/430, letter dated 30 April 1740).

54 KH, A17/430, letter dated 16 April 1740; see Appendix I, no. 4 below. In both of the 1740 letters Anne is addressed as 'Madame ma Cousine', which suggests that we are dealing here with Frederick and not his father, as is often stated.

55 See Baker-Smith, *Anne of Hanover*, p. 170.

56 *Biographisch Woordenboek der Nederlanden*, ed. A. J. van der Aa (Haarlem, 1852), I, p. 306.

57 See, for example, Lord Egmont's evaluation in Appendix I, no. 1 below. Anne's ability to sight read the most difficult pieces was noted again later: 'In de Musiek was Haere Koninklyke Hoogheit door het onderwys van de vermaerden Hendel zoo verre gevordert, dat Hoogst de zelve, op het eerste gezicht, de zwaerste stukken op het Clavier speelde'. KH, A17/404, 'Levensbericht', fo. 49v.

58 Baker-Smith, *Anne of Hanover*, p. 41.

59 Charles Burney, *The Present State of Music in France and Italy*, 2nd edn, corrected (London, 1773), p. 224.

60 Johann Adam Hiller, *Lebensbeschreibungen berühmter Musikgelehrten und Tonkünstler neurer Zeit*, Erster Theil (Leipzig, 1784; reprint Leipzig, 1975), p. 159.

61 *Ibid.*, pp. 159–60.

62 Chrysander, *G. F. Händel*, II, p. 365.

63 De Smet, *Musique à la cour de Guillaume V*, p. 5.

64 *The London Stage*, III, p. 426.

65 *Het Juichend Friesland ofte Kort Verhaal van de blyde Inkomst van . . . Willem Carel Hendrik Friso . . . en Anna* (Leeuwarden, 1734), p. xx.

66 Richard G. King, 'The Riehman Family of Court Musicians and Composers', *Tijdschrift van de Vereniging voor Nederlandse Muziekgeschiedenis*, 44 (1994), pp. 46–7.

67 Hiller notes that Hertel (see above) could have entered into the service of the Dutch court under favourable conditions, but because he was so well provided for in Eisenach, he turned down the offer.

68 See Appendix II below for documentation concerning the court orchestra.

69 De Smet, *Musique à la cour de Guillaume V*, p. 32.

70 See Anne's 1738 correspondence with Johan Duncan in KH, A17/430; for a wider perspective, see KH, Archief Willem IV, 51, nos 127–31, a series of plans to reduce expenses written during the period 1733–38.

71 Letter dated 14/25 April 1750. Philip Dormer Stanhope, 4th Earl of Chesterfield, *Letters*, ed. B. Dobrée (London, 1932), IV, p. 1524. Cassandra Frederick performed at The Hague in June 1750 ('s *Gravenhaagse Courant*, 1, 3, 15 and 17 June) and Amsterdam in July (King, 'Handel's Travels', p. 373).

72 Although the *New Grove Dictionary of Music and Musicians* (s.v. Leclair) and other modern sources state that Leclair began working at Anne's court in 1738, I think it more likely that he started serving Anne in 1740, when he also assumed the direction of Jacob Lopez de Liz's orchestra at The Hague. The suggestion that his service with Anne began in 1738 is probably based on a mistaken date for Leclair's op. 9 (advertised in 1738 but not actually published until 1743), which was dedicated to the Princess.

73 In the advertisement to Graf's op. 1, from the first half of 1757, there is no mention of the title, but Graf calls himself 'Composer' to Anne in an advertisement for his op. 2 in the *s'Gravenhaagse Courant* of 25 January 1758. I thank Rudolf Rasch for this information.

74 For Strada see Deutsch, *Handel*, pp. 416, 463–4; for Guadagni and Richter, see De Smet, *Musique à la cour de Guillaume V*, pp. 9, 13, 17, 238 n.62.

75 King, 'Handel's Travels'.

76 *Ibid.*, p. 380.

77 According to Baker-Smith, *Anne of Hanover*, pp. 150, 157.

78 KH, A17/516, *Inventaris van alle de goederen toebehoorende aen Haere Doorluchtige Hoogheit, Mevrouw de Princesse van Orange en Nassau*, 18 January 1760, fos. 129–36. A catalogue of Willem V's library, which includes a number of books on music history and theory, similarly contains nothing that we would expect to have belonged to Anne. See KH, A18/40, *Catalogus en lijsten betreffende de Bibliotheek* (written no earlier than 1786).

79 Gemeente Museum, The Hague, MS 4. E. 73. See W. Boetticher, *Handschriftlich Überlieferte Lauten- und Gitarrentabulaturen des 15. bis 18. Jahrhunderts* (*RISM*, vii) (Munich, 1978), pp. 83–4.

80 KH, Library, shelf number K-XIX-1; available on microfiche at the Gemeente Museum of The Hague, MS 3621.

81 Hans Algra, 'Muziek aan het hof van Anna van Hannover en Willem Carel Hendrik Friso', in *Van Leeuwarden naar den Haag: Rond de verplaatsing van het stadhouderlijk hof in 1747*, ed. J. J. Huizinga (Franeker, 1997), pp. 80–1.

82 '12 Sonaten a Violino en Basso dedicate all serenissima Altezza Roale [*sic*] de Oranges a 2 Gld 10 stuyvs' (advertisement in the *'s Gravenhaagse Courant* of 12 May 1756). I thank Aldo Lieffering for kindly supplying this information.

83 An anecdote told by Charles Burney to Margaret Owen *c.* 1777: 'One day the Prince told [Handel] he had compos'd some music & desir'd him to hear it. Handel made a pish at it, but the Prince said he should hear it & had Weideman, Vincent & the band call'd. They began to play' (National Library of Wales, Brogyntyn MS 8499). See Graham Thomas, 'Burney on Handel: A New Source', *Handel Institute Newsletter*, 6/2 (Autumn 1995), p. 2.

84 In a letter written by Caroline to her brother *c.* 1769, she asks, 'souhaitez vous une marche pour les hautbois des arquebusiers? Je vous en composerais une des plus magnifiques, ainsi que son menuet.' De Smet, *Musique à la cour de Guillaume V*, p. 43.

85 See *Unico Wilhelm van Wassenaer 1692–1766: Componist en staatsman*, ed. Rudolf Rasch and Kees Vlaardingerbroek (Zutphen, 1993).

86 To this list we could add the names of at least some of the many artists who engraved the various portraits.

87 See Frans Grijzenhout, *Liotard in Nederland* (Utrecht, 1985), pp. 36, 106–10, 114–17.

88 KH, A17/412. See also Appendix I, no. 18.

89 The following discussion of Anne's theatre patronage is derived from De Smet, *Musique à la cour de Guillaume V*, pp. 6–7, 8, 10, 24, 37 and 48. A substantial study of theatre in The Hague came to my attention too late to be included in this study: Aldo Lieffering, 'De Franse Comedie in Den Haag 1749–1783: Opera, toneel en het stadhouderlijk hof in de Haagse stedelijke cultuur' (Ph.D. dissertation, Utrecht University, 1999).

90 See the *'s Gravenhaagse Courant*, 7 March and 31 October 1755. I thank Aldo Lieffering for these references.

91 See G. P. Karstkarel, 'De Prinsenstallen en het orgel in de Waalse Kerk', *Oranje Nassaue Museum Jaarboek* (1987), pp. 85–91.

92 KH, A17/412.

93 'Handel's Travels'; 'On Princess Anne's Lessons'; 'Two New Letters from Princess Amelia', *Händel-Jahrbuch*, 40/41 (1994/95), pp. 169–71. For the Shaftesbury quote, see Deutsch, *Handel*, p. 845.

94 Carole Taylor, 'Italian Operagoing in London, 1700–1745' (Ph.D. dissertation, Syracuse University, 1991), pp. 155–6, 309ff.

95 Particularly interesting is a letter of 24 September 1732 in which the singer Porporino writes that he cannot get leave from Dresden to sing at Handel's opera in London, but if Anne or her brother Frederick should write, that might make it possible. Lowell Lindgren, 'Musicians and Librettists in the Correspondence of Gio. Giacomo Zamboni', *Research Chronicle of the Royal Musical Association*, 24 (1991), p. 147. See also pp. 144, 146.

96 See, for example, the *Calendar of Treasury Books and Papers, 1729–1730, Preserved in the Public Record Office*, prepared by William A. Shaw (London, 1897), pp. 341, 473.

97 *Ibid.*, p. 341.

98 Public Record Office, Kings Warrant Book, xxx (27 July 1730–20 December 1732), p. 53.

99 Incidentally, this document provides the only proof I know of that Rolli actually taught Anne. The fact that he is not listed in the princesses' household in Chamberlayne's *Magnae Brittaniae Notitia 1728* along with Handel and L'Abbé (see Deutsch, *Handel*, p. 231) suggests that he may have begun teaching the princesses *c.* 1729.

100 See John Ingamells and Robert Raines, 'A Catalogue of the Paintings, Drawings and Etchings of Philip Mercier', *Walpole Society*, 46 (1976–78), p. 15, no. 6.

101 Kimerly Rorschach, 'Frederick, Prince of Wales (1707–1751), as Collector and Patron', *Walpole Society*, 55 (1989/90), p. 11.

102 *The Dictionary of Art*, ed. Jane Turner (London and New York, 1996), XXII, p. 905.

103 De Smet, *Musique à la cour de Guillaume V*, p. 240, n. 83.

104 John Brewer, *The Pleasures of the Imagination: English Culture in the Eighteenth Century* (New York, 1997), pp. xxiv, 18–21.

105 See Marijke Bruggeman's description of Willem's education in *Van Leeuwarden naar den Haag*, pp. 27–9.

106 De Smet, *Musique à la cour de Guillaumev*, p. 5.

107 KH, A17/313, *Stukken betreffende de reis van [Willem IV en Princess Anna] naar Duitsland in 1740*, 'Plan selon lequel on pourroit assigner les apartements du Chateau de Orangestein', fo. 2v. The other musicians taken to Germany were Guerini, Baptiste and Riehman.

108 KH, A17/121, no. 12.

109 De Smet, *Musique à la cour de Guillaume V*, p. 9.

110 *Ibid.*, p. 19.

111 KH, A17/404, fo. 117v.

112 British Library, Egerton 1717, fo. 78.

7

The daughters of George II: marriage and dynastic politics

Veronica Baker-Smith

L ATE in 1733, London society was intrigued by a new addition to the literature of political opposition which poured from the city's printing presses in the form of pamphlets, plays and poems. A small book entitled *A Court Novel: The Secret History of Mama Oello, Princess Royal of Peru*,[1] published at one shilling, tells the story of a princess who is forced to marry the prince of a neighbouring state. Many of these semi-literary texts called for sophisticated decoding, but this particular piece was more forthright: its anonymous author was clearly anti-Whig, close to court circles and hostile to the marriage between Anne, Princess Royal, eldest daughter of George II, and William, Prince of Orange, a distant cousin of the great Stadtholder-King, William III. 'Mama Oello' is subject to the orders of 'the Wicked Minister Curaca Robilda' (Sir Robert Walpole) 'whom all the country hated on Account of his persuading her Royal Grandfather and Father to impose heavy taxes on their subjects'. She bewails the fact that she must go to a country that produces nothing but butter and cheese, and whose inhabitants 'once famed in arts and sciences' now soil their hands in trade and commerce.

Anne was already twenty-five, and with four younger sisters, her marriage was a matter of priority (FIGURE 14). As the eldest she must marry first and better than the others, but the union of England and Hanover in 1714 had created a dynastic problem: the minor German princely families which could have provided the husband for an Elector's daughter were too insignificant for the Princess Royal of England.[2] Yet other options were severely limited, for the royal houses of Spain, Austria, France and Italy could not be considered for fear of compromising the precarious religious basis of that union. The Hanoverian succession had been an extraordinary dynastic phenomenon. When unsavoury rumours about incest with her brother forced a hasty marriage in 1658 on Sophia, granddaughter of James I, the match hardly seemed auspicious.[3] The bride was a twelfth child, the groom Ernest

August, Duke of Celle, the youngest brother of four; yet untimely deaths, dynastic squabbles and, above all, religious attitudes made this match the foundation of the 'Protestant Succession' to the English throne. Ragnild Hatton offers the stunning statistic that fifty-four Catholics held stronger hereditary claims than Sophia: any one of them might have reversed Henry of Navarre's dictum and renounced the Mass for England, or at the very least in the next generation claimed that while Anne of Hanover's two brothers remained unmarried, a Catholic marriage for her invalidated the 1701 Act of Settlement (FIGURE 15).[4]

Twice in the previous century English princesses had married into the House of Orange and a Dutch alliance seemed the only one possible now for Anne, but nevertheless there were disadvantages. The fact that Prince William was a hunchback could be viewed with political equanimity, but, more seriously, his title was no longer synonymous with power. On King William III's death in 1702, most of the Dutch provinces severed their historic connection with his family, repudiating his successor as Stadtholder and proclaiming a Republic. Whether as consequence or coincidence, the date marked the end of the Dutch *Gouden Eeuw*, their golden hundred years when they dominated the cultural life of Europe, and the Maritime Powers of England and Holland formed a triumphant alliance against French ambition and aggression.[5] But nostalgia often plays a part in foreign policy and old attitudes die hard. The basic principle of the alliance had not died with William, though

14 *George II and his children*, attributed to William Aikman, *c.* 1730

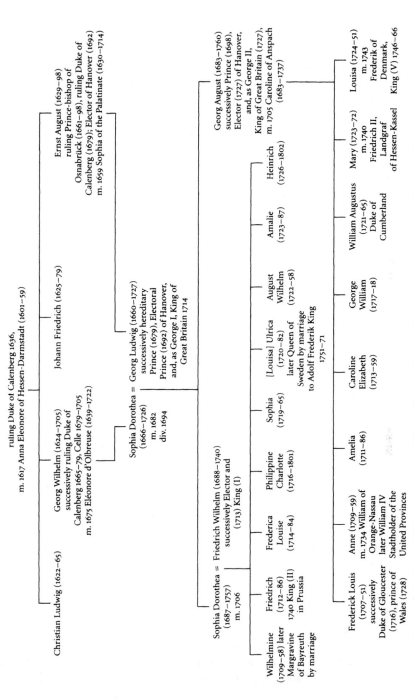

ruling Duke of Calenberg 1636,
m. 1617 Anna Eleonore of Hessen-Darmstadt (1601–59)

Christian Ludwig (1622–65)

Georg Wilhelm (1624–1705)
successively ruling Duke of
Calenberg 1665–79, Celle 1679–1705
m. 1675 Eléonore d'Olbreuse (1639–1722)

Johann Friedrich (1625–79)

Ernst August (1629–98)
ruling Prince-bishop of
Osnabrück (1661–98); Elector of Hanover (1692)
Calenberg (1679); ruling Duke of
m. 1659 Sophia of the Palatinate (1630–1714)

Sophia Dorothea = Georg Ludwig (1660–1727)
(1666–1726)   successively hereditary
m. 1682   Prince (1679), Electoral
div. 1694   Prince (1692) of Hanover,
                   and, as George I, King of
                   Great Britain 1714

Sophia Dorothea = Friedrich Wilhelm (1688–1740)
(1687–1757)   successively Elector and
m. 1706   (1713) King (I)

Wilhelmine   Friedrich   Philippine   Sophia   [Louisa] Ulrica   August   George August (1683–1760)
(1709–58) later   (1712–86)   Charlotte   (1719–65)   (1720–82)   Wilhelm   successively Prince (1698),
Margravine   1740 King (II)   (1716–1801)   later Queen of   (1722–58)   Elector (1727) of Hanover,
of Bayreuth   in Prussia   Sweden by marriage   and, as George II,
by marriage   to Adolf Frederik King   King of Great Britain (1727),
                                                                          1751–71   m. 1705 Caroline of Anspach
                                                                                                                (1683–1737)

Frederick Louis   Anne (1709–59)   Amelia   Caroline   George   Amalie   Heinrich   William Augustus   Mary (1723–72)   Louisa (1724–51)
(1707–51)   m. 1734 William of (1711–86)   Elizabeth   William   (1723–87)   (1726–1802)   (1721–65)   m. 1740   m. 1743
successively   Orange-Nassau   (1713–59)   (1717–18)   Duke of   Friedrich II,   Frederik of
Duke of Gloucester later William IV   Cumberland   Landgraf   Denmark,
(1716), prince of   Stadtholder of the   of Hessen-Kassel   King (V) 1746–66
Wales (1728)   United Provinces

15 Family tree of the House of Hanover, showing children of George II and of his sister Sophia Dorothea, Electress and Queen in Prussia
    (children who died in infancy and daughters of no political importance for this book have generally been omitted)

the Dutch steadfastly refused to commit themselves to the aggressive foreign policy England expected – as her exasperated envoy in The Hague put it, 'the Dutch are dead asleep', and a Dutch historian has continued the image, 'they were sunk in a sweet slumber [enjoying] dreams of durable peace and the clinking of ducats'.[6] The new rulers of the Republic were merchants and feared their enormous personal wealth would be threatened by the interruption to their trade which foreign wars would bring. A prestigious royal marriage would, Walpole considered, remind them of past glories and make the House of Orange a focus once more for national unity with a commitment to English interests.

The King also had his eye on the popularity a traditional alliance could bestow. Parliamentary sessions were becoming ever more stormy despite Walpole's skill, and George's own frequent absences in Hanover were deeply resented as a paper nailed to the gate of St James's showed:

> Lost or strayed out of this house, a man who has left a wife and six children on the parish, whoever will give any tidings of him to the Churchwardens of St James so as he may be got again shall receive four shillings and sixpence reward. N.B. This reward shall not be increased, nobody judging him to be worth a crown.[7]

The formula revived uncomfortable memories of the Englishman's method of dealing with unsatisfactory kings. Though George I had comforted his mistress with the assurance that the king-killers were all on his side, the Hanoverians still sat uneasily on the throne of England. An alliance which clearly fulfilled English interests rather than German ones had much to recommend it. George's announcement of the betrothal of his daughter was greeted with all the enthusiasm he could have wished, but the author of the Mama Oello piece was making a valid point when his heroine bewails her fate: 'why must I who am a Princess Royal of a mighty empire leave my country and friends to be only a co-Partner in a poor Principality?' Anne's dilemma is further elaborated by Lord Hervey in his usual style – should Anne 'wed this piece of deformity in Holland or die an ancient maid immured in her royal convent at St James?'

Times had changed since Joanna, daughter of Henry II, was plucked from a Winchester convent at the age of ten, and despatched across the length of Europe to marry the 23-year-old King of Sicily. Eighteenth-century princesses were usually mature before childhood betrothals were confirmed, and they were often kept informed during negotiations. Anne was certainly consulted by her father and given the option to refuse the Prince of Orange, but maturity also brought awareness of the further stark choice these women faced. Their importance lay in their role as daughter and as marriage prospect – by their late twenties the latter had dwindled, while a King's unmarried sisters lost much of their status. For Anne, who had waged a determined cultural and social rivalry with her brother, Frederick, Prince of Wales, and was barely on speaking terms with him, the prospect of being a spinster at his court was too terrible to contemplate. Hervey commented that her attitude to her brother was one of the few examples of Anne's passions overcoming self-interest – his friendship could have been 'of use to her hereafter and she ought in prudence to have behaved towards him in a manner that would have made [it] less irretrievable'.[8] After all, Frederick's court would have been the most cultured since that of Charles I, and Anne could have continued her musical patronage and maintained a fair degree of independence. But it is a curious fact that George's seven children remained in general aloof from each other; none of them ever made common cause with a sibling politically, and even social relationships were limited. Frederick was cordially disliked by all his sisters, while Cumberland's dry remark at the death of the Prince of Wales – that 'it was a great blow to the country but [he] hoped it would recover' – shows little fraternal feeling either; yet antipathy never led to cabal.[9]

The longevity of George II spared his second and third daughters any loss of status, but both remained unmarried, adopting respectively two of the possible remedies for dealing with their situation: eccentricity and ill-health. Caroline, the third daughter, cherished a hopeless attachment to Lord Hervey, but would have happily settled for anyone. When no suitor was forthcoming she embraced hypochondria instead, spending long periods in Bath or Tunbridge Wells seeking a cure. Anne, in Holland, was once reassured by a correspondent that Caroline was much better, 'though pray don't mention it to her for she only allows of her not being worse'.[10]

While no marriage ever seems to have been proposed for Caroline, George's second daughter, Amelia, featured in three or four years of English negotiation with King Frederick William of Prussia. George I's sister and daughter had married successive rulers of Brandenburg-Prussia, and he was determined to carry the tradition into the third generation. He planned a double wedding of the eldest children in each family – Frederick Prince of Wales to Wilhelmine, and Anne to the future Frederick the Great. Royal enthusiasm for the project was reinforced by his government's perception that the ever-increasing military power of Prussia warranted close attention. The betrothals were to be announced from Hanover in July 1727, but George died that month on his way to the Electorate, and George II was delighted at that stage to frustrate any plan of his father's. However the idea of a Prussian marriage continued to be debated over the next few years with Amelia replacing her sister as the bride for the Crown Prince. Even the day before Frederick's marriage to Elisabeth Christine of Brunswick-Bevern in 1733, the English were offering large sums of money to stop the ceremony. Amelia, like Anne, was kept informed, and the miniature of Frederick which was sent to her then was found in a locket she always wore when she died at the age of seventy-five.[11] In the years between she took refuge in semi-amiable eccentricity. She was reputed to be in love with the Duke of Grafton – described by Jonathan Swift as 'almost a slobberer and without one good quality'. His personal shortcomings were irrelevant – princesses did not marry subjects. Even a century and a half later Edward VII's daughter Princess Victoria could not marry Lord Rosebery, though a curious exception seems to have been made in Victorian times for Scottish aristocrats.

Shrewd and sharp-tongued even in her youth, Amelia set up home in a mansion in Cavendish Square which became a 'whispering gallery', a centre for gossip and scandal where such cronies as Horace Walpole were entertained to lavish suppers and endless card-parties. At Gunnersbury, she created a country retreat and landscaped garden. She had always been a passionate horsewoman – the only one of the family who could keep up with her father in the hunting-field – and she took to attending church in riding costume accompanied by her own hounds and with a smaller dog under each arm, staring down any hapless cleric who dared to protest. Anne, now happily married, tried a little matchmaking for her sisters and received for her pains a veritable tirade in defence of spinsterhood. 'Make no match for Caro or for me', wrote Amelia,

> I sometimes believe you think that unmarried women have no places in heaven for you think nobody can have the least happiness without being tied from morning to night to a creature which may tire one's life out and plague one incessantly with their good advice or commands whilst one is full as wise as they . . . we poor women have great disadvantages without making them still worse and putting oneself in a Jackanapes power.[12]

One former option for women of noble or royal birth wishing to avoid 'a Jackanapes power' was the German institution of the Lutheran convent, with entry limited to women with sufficient aristocratic quarterings. Although they were styled abbesses or canonesses, religion usually played a secondary role to intellectual activity. Two of Sophia's sisters became abbesses: Elizabeth, Abbess of Herford, where later Charlotte of Mecklenberg-Strelitz, George III's wife, was a canoness, and Louise Hollandine, Abbess of Maubuisson, after her controversial conversion to Catholicism. Frederick the Great's remaining unmarried sister, instead of becoming a Danish bride, was Abbess of Quedlingberg. The importance attributed to feminine education by German princesses from Sophia through Caroline of Anspach to her own daughters and on to Queen Charlotte seems to draw upon this tradition, but by this time education had perhaps given women the self-confidence and self-respect to stand alone. Besides, Mary Astell's proposal to found a convent-like institution for gentlewomen in Queen Anne's reign had foundered on the associations it raised with Catholicism.[13] Despite their education, neither Amelia nor Caroline created an individual pathway of conspicuous intellectual self-improvement. But there is no reason to doubt the sincerity of Amelia's polemic, nor her enjoyment of the active rather than the contemplative life she created for herself.

The ten-year gap between Anne, Amelia and Caroline and their younger sisters gave more dynastic choice when the latter reached maturity. Mary, born in 1723, was plain and shy, and since the marriage of a fourth princess into a minor German state would not imply any loss of prestige, she was offered to the ruler of Hesse as a bride for his son – yet another Prince Frederick. Actually Hesse-Kassel had, since the wars against Louis XIV, exerted more influence in Europe than its size warranted. Its ruling Landgraves had always had personal control of the state's financial resources and had used them to build up well-trained military forces on offer to the highest bidder.[14] After the Hanoverian succession in England, wars and the rumours of wars always sent her diplomats with money-bags to Hesse, but to pay for them Walpole had had to impose a land-tax of four shillings in the pound; Parliament's country gentlemen were outraged and there were ominous mutterings about standing armies. A marriage alliance would seem to be the safer and cheaper option.

George II, always tightfisted, was initially delighted to discover that the wedding should take place in the bridegroom's country thus sparing him any expense. At the last moment, however, he decided it was too risky to despatch his daughter without a prior ceremony. A proxy marriage had not been performed in England for two hundred years and the Acts of Succession and Uniformity actually forbade one. The King lost his temper, 'I will hear no more of your church nonsense nor your law nonsense', and after prolonged argument a similar ceremony was held to that of Henry VIII's sister in 1514 to Louis XII of France, after which Mary was sent off to Hesse. Here three weeks of noisy entertainment, elaborate suppers and firework displays till dawn exhausted everybody but they were rumoured to be concealing the fact that Mary's mother-in-law had died and the Landgrave was keeping the body in his room so as not to spoil the party.[15] The bridegroom, too, was behaving oddly – his bad manners, drunkenness and coldness towards his 'nice little wife' caused much comment. The scene was set for a difficult marriage, and Mary was to become one of the very few princesses who escaped from such a situation other than by death.

The five daughters of George II were more or less contemporary with the six daughters of Frederick William of Prussia, so any proposed match found them in competition with each other: Frederick had suggested drowning some of his at birth like kittens. The Hessian negotiations had not involved a Prussian rival. Prussia had its own standing army, and Frederick the Great's attitude to Hessian mercenaries was explicit:

> The institution of the soldier is for the defence of the nation, to rent it out to others to do battle as one might a mastiff [is] a perversion of war and diplomacy. It is said that it is not permitted to sell sacred objects. Well what could be more sacred than the blood of men.[16]

But Prussia and England were poised for rival action in Scandinavia, where two more Crown Princes – of Sweden and Denmark – were the matrimonial prizes. George's youngest daughter, Louisa, born in 1724, was offered to each in turn, and when a Prussian princess won Sweden, a Danish alliance became all the more desirable. In this matter George was acting as Elector rather than King, since England was embroiled in a trade war with Denmark, whereas the Hanoverians had always worked with Denmark, mindful of their common border with the disputed duchy of Holstein. At a critical moment yet another Prussian princess was produced, and the English minister-resident in Copenhagen, Walter Titley, embarked on some creative diplomacy. He obtained a miniature of Louisa – by far the most beautiful of the sisters – and showed it, ostensibly as an example of the artist's work, to Christian VI, who was wondering who to commission for his wife's portrait. The King was intrigued, and on being assured by Titley that Louisa's 'beauty is enlivened by the moving features when she speaks, no picture can express her grace any more than the accent of her voice', he disappeared to show the likeness to the Queen and Prince. An hour later the deal was done.[17] Another double wedding was planned, with Louisa's brother, the Duke of Cumberland, marrying a Danish princess. The Duke's natural inclinations, coupled with the fact that the said princess was deformed, caused him so much alarm that he turned to Robert Walpole for advice. Walpole told him to accept the plan enthusiastically 'on condition of an immediate and most ample establishment . . . believe me, my dear Duke, when I say that the match will not then be pressed'.

Louisa married in 1743 and became Queen of Denmark in 1746. Titley was always shown special favour, but English complacency was shattered when she died at the age of twenty-seven, and Denmark turned again to Prussia. The prospect of a Prussian stepmother for Louisa's three surviving children was anathema, and Titley was instructed from London to warn the King that Frederick the Great's sister was 'disagreeable in her person, ill-natured, proud, and with all these qualities a *coquette*'.[18] The personal warning was perhaps heeded, since the King married a princess of Brunswick, Juliane Christine, but politically the Prussian connection continued, since she was Frederick's sister-in-law.

Louisa had been much loved and respected in Denmark, though she was too young and inexperienced to exert much influence, but marriage brought Anne, and to a lesser extent Mary also, considerable prominence in European affairs. Dynastic pawns they were, but a combination of their own efforts and accidents of history could bring these eighteenth-century princesses to power stretching beyond their role as wife and mother, important as these could be. In Anne's case both these factors played equal parts – the early death of her husband when their son was only three years old gave her greater power in a foreign country than any other English princess before or since when she took over the regency, but it was her own ambition and ability which secured it for her. Her predecessor as Princess Royal, Mary, daughter of Charles I, had fought in vain for the regency during William III's minority, because her querulous and ambivalent attitude to her adopted country had aroused formidable opposition. Anne, on the other hand, had endured tirelessly to identify herself totally with Dutch interests. She had endured fourteen years of personal tragedy (five stillbirths or infant deaths) in a political wilderness, as William struggled to restore princely rule to a country convinced that 'monarchical government was equivalent to a death from which there could be no resurrection'.[19] His death only four years after the restoration of the Stadtholdership left a country already in crisis, and Anne took over at a time of domestic unrest and diplomatic upheaval. But the eight years of her personal rule (and her status was as personal ruler rather than simply regent) represent, in the view of most Dutch historians, a period of relative stability and consolidation in a turbulent century. She had been ambitious from childhood – she once asserted that she 'would die tomorrow to be a queen today' – but the power she always longed for came to her only on the death of a husband to whom she was utterly devoted. In personal terms she was the luckiest of the marrying daughters: Mary's marriage was to end in separation after years of unhappiness, while Louisa's husband proved dissolute and abusive.

The 'accident of history' which propelled Mary involuntarily into a European crisis was the announcement by her husband, the Crown Prince of Hesse, that he had converted to Roman Catholicism. Within five years of the marriage they were living virtually apart: until Louisa's death she spent a great deal of time in Denmark, always taking her two sons with her (they later married their Danish cousins). They were not however allowed to travel to England on her frequent visits there, when she spent much time moping in Bath about the strain of holding formal drawing-room receptions: 'I am so weak and sylly there is no bearing of me'. Rumours abounded that her husband's Catholic lover had ex-acted conversion as the price for her favours (and it was also said that conversion increased his bad temper), but the evidence seems to point to genuine conviction – he had always been fascinated by religion and attracted to elaborate ceremonial. Certainly he must have been well aware of the scandal it would cause and the political and personal price he would have to pay. His father 'although almost overwhelmed by his anger' acted to protect his grandsons from the threat of Rome, although he was unable to disinherit Frederick as he had hoped, since the neces-sary ratification could not be obtained from the Catholic Emperor. Anne, too, feared for her nephews: she had shared her husband's disgust when lightning set fire to a Catholic church while they were visiting Maastricht and the people made no effort to save anything, but merely lit a wax candle and prayed to it: 'this is called devotion ... where blindness and superstition rule'. She ensured recognition by the States-General of the rights of Mary's sons and wrote to a correspondent: 'May God bless the arrangements made for the young princes and for the Protestant religion, and deliver my poor sister from the dangers with which that unworthy Prince Frederick has sought to ensnare her'.[20]

Mary was refused a formal divorce for fear Frederick would marry again and produce a Catholic heir, so she was given an estate in Hanau on the River Main near Frankfurt and granted the governorship of her sons. They did not to return to Cassel for thirty years. On Mary's side, 'release from her tyrant' was said to have renewed her youth, but in 1757 her peace was shattered when the French invaded Hesse and she fled with her family to Hamburg. Here she was at first in such straitened circumstances that Pitt had urgently to convene a session of Parliament to grant her an initial payment of £20,000, and thereafter an annuity on which her two sons continued gratefully to draw until 1821 and 1831 respectively.

The question of subsidy which had been at the heart of the relationship between England and Hesse thus reversed itself; six thousand mercenaries at a reduced price to fight in the War of Austrian Succession the year after the marriage have to be weighed against at least seventy years of pension payments. It leads to consideration of what England gained in political terms from the three royal marriages so carefully planned, and the answer has to be: very little.

Louisa's early death certainly ended hopes of using Denmark as a check to Swedish ambition and French intimidation, but even before that England reaped very little advantage from the match. The Danes flatly refused an appeal for troops in 1745, either to serve in Britain against Prince Charles Edward or on the Continent to protect Hanoverian interests while troops were concentrated across the Channel. France had always cultivated Scandinavia as a useful ballast in the shifting alliances of the time, and Denmark was actually being paid large sums of money by the French to do nothing. The failure of the Jacobite rebellion convinced the Danes they had been right.

English advantage was even less apparent from the most important marriage, and the one from which most had been expected. Even so experienced a diplomat as the Earl of Chesterfield had assumed that the marriage of William and Anne would result in the speedy restoration of the Stadtholdership. In fact the marriage was viewed in Holland as a private affair of the discredited House of Orange – the ruling States-General was never consulted, and responded by virtually ignoring it. Anne suffered years of isolation in her husband's tiny provincial capital of Leeuwarden, in the bleak northern provinces which were the only ones still loyal to the House of Orange. If she and William ventured to The Hague, or even worse, to Amsterdam, they were received by hostile officials and apathetic crowds. The republican equation was simple – Orange power equalled foreign adventure plus commercial decline – and they were having none of it. Finally, in 1747, an uncharacteristic French miscalculation sent twenty thousand of their troops across the frontier of the Dutch Republic. A States-General deputy saw immediately that the threat would drive the country back into the supposedly protective arms of the House of Orange, and he rounded on the French ambassador, 'you're ruining us, you're making a Stadtholder'.[21]

As the Dutch surveyed the ruins of their policy of neutrality, the English moved smoothly in to take advantage of the situation: their ambassador was deeply involved in the consequent collapse of republican power, with English agents whipping up popular revolt and English money pouring into eager hands. As the Prince was accorded powers greater than ever William III had held, the Duke of Newcastle, now Secretary of State in London, looked forward at last to balancing the book opened by the marriage. The Dutch army was summoned to aid Anne's brother, Cumberland, at the Battle of Val against Marshal Saxe. But the troops Newcastle relied upon had shrivelled on the vine of neutrality for forty years and were a sorry bunch. Dutch 'reticence' at the battle was described by Cumberland to Chesterfield: 'I am convinced every Day of the melancholy Consideration, that we must actually reckon upon the Dutch troops as Nothing. It would be very rash in me to answer for anything which must depend upon them.'[22] The Duke of Bedford went further: England, he said, was tying itself to a corpse and calling it an ally. Newcastle still clung obstinately for a few more months to his belief in the old alliance, but when the key Dutch fortress of Bergen-op-Zoom fell to the French and it was discovered that the commander of the garrison was over ninety and senile with it, the scales fell from his eyes too: 'we seem to have been all in a dream, it appears that the Dutch have no army at all or any that they can or will employ'.[23]

English spirits rose briefly when Anne succeeded her husband – the King certainly expected her 'to be guided in all things' by him, but she was far too intelligent to allow him the slightest influence. The patriotic card had been played by the Orangists in 1747, but Anne during her regency accepted that the republicans had been right – only neutrality could ensure European acceptance of the 'free ships, free goods' principle on which commercial prosperity depended. Avoidance of war became her paramount – and skilfully pursued – aim, to the angry frustration of her father and the English government.[24]

To varying degrees, therefore, these three princesses were far more valuable to their adopted countries than to the one which sought to use them for its own purposes, while none of them would have been likely to envy their unmarried sisters despite their own difficulties. Their royal duty was clear and they willingly submitted to it: life as a 'co-partner' on a different stage offered them an independence and influence they could never experience at home, and they seized the opportunity offered. Thanks to their mother's enlightened attitudes all were highly educated, accomplished women, well equipped to create that court culture which could be the key contribution of any consort. Queen Caroline had taken personal responsibility for her daughters' education and was often present during their lessons, her interest in metaphysics, poetry, art and philosophy giving a new dimension to the conventional royal education. It was an example followed by those daughters – Louisa caused astonishment in Denmark by educating her young children herself. She and Anne learned their new and difficult languages, making sure that they were used in preference to English, thus bestowing an important sense of identity. Caroline's example, however, extended further than cultural patronage and intellectual curiosity. The pamphleteer who wrote:

> You may strut, dapper George, but 'twill all be in vain,
> We know 'tis Queen Caroline, not you, that reign.

was exaggerating according to the custom of his kind, but there is no doubt that she exerted a considerable political influence. Walpole used her to help him manage the King but he had great respect for her judgement and valued her advice. It was a tradition carried through to the next generation. There was no opposition in Holland nor Hesse to Anne and Mary assuming sole authority over the heir, and both accepted the challenge with determination and self-confidence. The main aim of every dynastic marriage in every age is, of course, to secure the succession. Louisa's early death left only one surviving son who later died insane, but Anne and Mary were called upon to do much more than give birth to sons – they had to guide them and fight for their political rights in an alien and threatening world, not as princesses of Hanover so much as princesses who had 'gone native'. A dynastic marriage did not make a passive princess.

Notes

1 British Library 1418.d.40.
2 Veronica Baker-Smith, *A Life of Anne of Hanover, Princess Royal* (Leiden, E. J. Brill, 1995), p. 28.
3 Maria Kroll, *Sophia, Electress of Hanover* (London, Gollancz, 1973), p. 69.
4 Ragnhild, Hatton, *George I, Elector and King* (London, Thames and Hudson, 1978), p. 74.
5 Herbert Rowen, *The Princes Of Orange* (Cambridge, Cambridge University Press, 1988), p. 158.
6 J. Huizinga, *Dutch Civilization in the Seventeenth Century and Other Essays*, ed. P. Geyl and F. W. N. Hugenholtz (London, Collins, 1968), p. 33.
7 Charles Chenevix Trench, *George II* (London, Allen Lane, 1973), p. 158.
8 *Some Material towards Memoirs of the Reign of George II by John Lord Hervey*, ed. Romney Sedgwick, 3 vols (London, The King's Printers, [limited edition, privately printed], 1931), I, p. 26.

9 Sir George Young, *Poor Fred* (Oxford, Oxford University Press, 1937), p. 221.
10 Kòninklijk Huis Archief (The Hague), Anna van Hannover, 430.
11 Baker Smith, *Anne, Princess Royal*, p. 29.
12 Koninklijk Huis Archief (The Hague), Anna van Hannover, 430.
13 Ruth Perry, *The Celebrated Mary Astell: An Early English Feminist* (Chicago, University of Chicago Press, 1986).
14 Charles Ingrao, *The Hessian Mercenary State* (Cambridge, Cambridge University Press, 1987).
15 Koninklijk Huis Archief (The Hague), Willem IV, 170, 11.
16 *L'Antimachiavel*, quoted in Giles, MacDonogh, *Frederick the Great* (London, Weidenfeld and Nicolson, 1999), p. 124.
17 J. F. Chance (ed.), *British Diplomatic Instructions 1689–1789, III, Denmark* (London, Royal Historical Society, 1926).
18 *Ibid.*
19 Pieter de la Court, quoted in Pieter Geyl, *The Netherlands in the Seventeenth Century, II, 1648–1715* (London, Ernest Benn, 1964), p. 192.
20 Koninklijk Huis Archief (The Hague), Anna van Hanover, 430.
21 Quoted in Pieter Geyl, *Willem IV en Engeland tot 1748* (The Hague, 1924), p. 213.
22 J. W. Wilkes, *A Whig in Power* (Evanston IL, Northwestern University Press, 1964), p. 122.
23 D. B. Horn, *Great Britain and Europe in the Eighteenth Century* (Oxford, Oxford University Press, 1967), p. 100.
24 Baker-Smith, *Anne, Princess Royal*.

8

'To play what game she pleased without observation': Princess Augusta and the political drama of succession, 1736–56

John L. Bullion

L ONG after her death in 1771, the Earl of Shelburne assessed the part Augusta, Dowager Princess of Wales and mother of King George III, played in the politics of her time (FIGURE 16). He began by observing, 'It seems to have been her fate through life to have been neglected and undervalued'. This did not relegate her to obscurity and unimportance, however. Being overlooked and underestimated were, according to the Earl, the sources of her considerable influence. She was able 'to play what game she pleased without observation'. As a result, 'under cover of that neglect', Augusta 'compassed all her points and gained more power than would have fallen to the lot even of an ambitious person in her situation'.[1]

Why the powerful and ambitious at court paid very little attention to Augusta until too late was not a subject that intrigued Shelburne. The answer was so obvious it did not interest him much. The Princess was skilled at the art of deception, and particularly adroit at convincing others that she was exactly as she appeared before them: a woman without a shrewd intelligence or a strong character, someone who had no grand designs for the future or ulterior motives to conceal. Put another way, she was very good at performing her chosen role. So good, in fact, that her audience at court did not realise she was acting. Shelburne included among the gullible not only those she fooled during the 1750s when she was a widow, but her husband Frederick while he was alive. How did Augusta gain influence over a man who insisted frequently and publicly that he would never be controlled by a woman, as his father George II was? Shelburne concluded that she accomplished this feat 'by flattering [Frederick's] vanity, which was excessive, entering into all his little tricks to gain popularity, and offering herself [as] a ready instrument, in all his plans of falsehood and deception'.[2]

Strip the malice from the Earl's judgements on Augusta, and what remains are statements both instructive and suggestive. They are

16 *Augusta, Princess of Wales* by Jean-Etienne Liotard, 1754

instructive because they supply questions for closer examination. For example, what were Frederick's 'little tricks to gain popularity'? How did his wife assist in them? They are suggestive because they point to the centrality of role-playing at eighteenth-century courts. What roles was Augusta expected to play as royal consort to the heir to the throne, as Dowager Princess of Wales, and as the mother of a future king? Equally important, how did she conceive of her various parts at court, and how did she execute them?[3] To investigate these matters, it is best to begin with Frederick.

Frederick's contemporaries at court knew he loved the theatre. He frequently attended performances at London's playhouses; he often acted in amateur theatricals at his residence; he was in the habit of staging and directing plays with his children and courtiers as actors; and he even co-authored with Lord Hervey a comedy put on by the Covent Garden company. What those in court did not notice, however, was the extent to which the Prince's character itself was theatrical in nature. His attachment to the theatre was encouraged by his affinity with the personalities and *personae* of actors and actresses.

The 1730s saw the beginning of what John Brewer has described as 'the cult of the actor', when men like Colley Cibber and David Garrick, with their dramatic skills and their fascinating lives, 'filled with drinking, impulsiveness, and a casual attitude to the marriage vows', elevated performers over dramatists in the public esteem. It was also a time when women on the stage were 'universally regarded as beautiful, talented, vivacious and impulsive, rather than sober, chaste and discreet'.[4] Impulsiveness was one of the characteristics Frederick shared with these objects of his and the public's affection, as were vivacity and personal charm. Perhaps most important, like the players of his day, the Prince had the ability to switch roles rapidly, depending on the audience and his own moods. The most vivid testimony to his versatility may be found in the diary of Lord Perceval, a man who liked Frederick despite not always approving of him. For instance, on 13 October 1731, Perceval commented, 'The character of the P[rince] is this: he has no reigning passion', other than conversation with small groups of men. Though he was inclined toward generosity, he often spoiled it 'by giving to unworthy objects'. He had several mistresses, including an apothecary's daughter, 'but is not nice in his choice, and talks more of feats this way than he acts'. He was capable of talking 'gravely according to his company, but is sometimes more childish than becomes his age'. Insofar as the practicalities and manoeuvres of politics and government were concerned, 'he thinks he knows business, but attends to none'. Frederick, Perceval judged, 'likes to be flattered'. He was also 'good-natured, and if he meets with a good Ministry [when he is King], may satisfy his people'.[5]

Though Perceval did not note any parallels between the Prince and actors, it is obvious from this account that Frederick, like London's players, enjoyed applause and admiration from his audiences. In effect, Perceval's words describe a series of performances, designed to create illusions and impressions, each intended to appeal to a specific audience. Moreover, these were disciplined performances. Perceval pointed out that Frederick enjoyed spending 'the evening with six or seven others over a glass of wine and hear[ing] them talk of a variety of things, but he does not drink'. This abstinence puzzled the diarist, even though what it reveals is not obscure. The Prince wanted to keep a clear head while he was observing and being observed in a social setting. He was fully aware he was on stage, and he meant to avoid every pitfall and enjoy all the triumphs of acting his part. Perceval noted that Frederick 'loves play, and plays to win'.[6] His observation described more than the Prince's enjoyment of gambling, and his determination to profit from his pastime. Without meaning to, Perceval also described his joyful pleasure at assuming a variety of roles, and his equal determination to achieve his goals by skilfully playing those parts.

Thus Frederick's personality impelled him to believe he was on stage constantly. The environment at court powerfully reinforced that perception. Just as the private lives of actors were public, so were the personal lives of royalty. Popular fascination with all aspects of the lives of those who performed in these two arenas guaranteed this would be the case. Brewer's assessment of actors – 'Players made the stage seductive: their glamour and beauty, the virtuosity of their performances, their private lives, at once the focus of polite society and yet disreputably on its margins, all made the theatre a place of exciting dreams, fantasies, and illusions' – is equally apt when applied to princes and courts.[7] Compare, for instance, Brewer's colourful, trenchant description of the eighteenth-century theatre with Lord Hervey's memorable contemporary description of life at court. To do well at court, suggested Hervey acidly, one had to have sense enough to know the company was black and dirty; honour enough to despise them; goodness enough to hate them; and hypocrisy enough to tell them they were white and clean.[8] Despite these drawbacks, the lure of life at court was irresistible, and to no one more so than the cynical Hervey himself.

Aside from his affinity for actors, and from the similarities between the two milieux, the Prince was keenly aware of the political implications of his taste in drama and comedy. As relations with his parents worsened, Frederick's enthusiastic attendance at performances of Shakespeare became more frequent. George II and Caroline might prefer and patronise foreign music and Italian opera; their son's presence at stagings of the Bard stood as an obvious patriotic counterpoint. When he attended *The Beggar's Opera*, or plays satirising the differences between him and the King and Queen, or productions that disguised George II thinly as the Golden Rump – a scandalous reference to the monarch's agonising haemorrhoids and his notorious flatulence – Frederick drew visible battlelines between himself and those currently in authority. He may even have been inspired in his conception and enacting of the roles of patriot prince and the future people's king by what he saw and heard on stage. Addison's *Cato*, which featured a virtuous leader in a corrupt time, was one of his particular favourites. Of course, he was not blind to the possibility that others would identify him with the true citizen of Rome. During the autumn of 1737, 'the Prince went from Kew to [a performance of *Cato*] in London, and was not only clapped at his coming into the house, which was the absurd compliment paid to any of the Royal Family on these occasions, but was also huzzaed'. When the protagonist proclaimed, '"When vice prevails, and impious men bear sway, the post of honour is a private station," there was another loud huzza, with a great clap, in the latter part of which applause the Prince himself joined in the face of the whole audience'.[9]

Frederick's popularity with Londoners may have even depended to a large extent on his open enjoyment of the theatre and the *demi-monde* Brewer dubbed 'theatreland': the rowdy pit; the mob outside; the whores, pickpockets, cutthroats, and confidence men; the proud display of power, prestige, and position in the boxes.[10] Perhaps this explains why his theatrical disaster did not lower his standing in the eyes of audiences. The play he and Hervey wrote together under the *nom de plume* of Captain Bodin was at best a 'dull comedy'. At its first performance, two men who were specially vocal in their disapproval of Act I were 'hauled out of the gallery by soldiers for showing their disapprobation of the play' and thrown into the street. This example of the perils of criticism produced a relatively peaceful first performance, without affecting the inevitable. When the curtain next went up on the comedy, the audience 'called out for another play', on the grounds 'the highest power on earth should not force the free born subjects of England to approve of nonsense'. Since staging another play 'on the sudden' was impossible, the manager offered to refund the crowd's money. 'The audience were contented, and all trooped home.' Riots over 'nonsense' were not, of course, unusual at London's theatres. Managers regularly had to repair the damage done by the customers to their buildings; players had to face at times real brick bats hurled by their critics. More noteworthy is what happened when the play was staged again. Frederick bravely showed up, and 'the audience out of respect to him made no disturbance'.[11]

After her marriage to Frederick in June 1736, Augusta began attending the theatre with him. Clearly, this was at his command, because her grasp of English was limited at the beginning of her life in Britain. The colloquial language of the street, the contrasting pronunciations of the players, and the highly allusive nature of many of the dramas and comedies, must have made the experience a confusing blur of sound and sensation to her. This did not matter to her husband; what was

important was that Londoners would see her at Covent Garden and
Drury Lane, just as they would become aware that she accompanied
him through the metropolis to enjoy conjurers and consult fortune
tellers. As she presented herself publicly as a quick and enthusiastic
convert to popular amusements in Britain, she would speedily overcome prejudices against her German origins. Compared to her, the King
and Queen would seem more foreign, despite the fact that they had
lived in the country much longer. The outcome of this strategy was
much as Frederick desired. Audiences noticed her presence, and accounts about the royal couple at playhouses began to spread. That they
occasionally had adventures together while attending the theatre helped.
For instance, in January 1737, Londoners could enjoy this story:

> [It] appeared that one Francis Cooke, a gentleman's coachman, who
> had picked up a woman, did in a very impudent, saucy manner as-
> sault the sentry who had the case of His Royal Highness's chair in the
> playhouse passage and would force into the said chair the woman he
> had picked up to make, as he has the impudence to call it, a bawdy
> house of the Prince's chair . . . [This started] so great a disturbance
> and mob that the Captain of the Guard had much ado to quell the
> disturbance and prevent the mob from breaking into the playhouse
> where His Royal Highness, the Prince of Wales and the Princess of
> Wales were.

Thus Augusta was on public display, before the eyes of the crowd in and
out of the theatre, enjoying the excitement and facing the risks of attending a play. Her virtue had its defenders, and they numbered more
than the guards who kept the chair she shared with Frederick from
becoming 'a bawdy house'.[12]

That Londoners could view the Princess going to the theatre
and sitting in the royal box was important to Frederick. It was equally
important to him that she not be seen as part of that world, similar to
actresses or, for that matter, himself. If she were perceived as saucy,
independent, skilled at assuming various roles and playing them believ-
ably, she would not be an appealing, popular consort. He wanted her
to be recognised as a different type of woman. Here Augusta's nature
assisted his plan. Imitating the *savoir faire* and practised, worldly ways
of women who performed on stage would have been extraordinarily
difficult for her, if not absolutely impossible. Such a role would have
compelled her to deny herself completely. Unlike the Prince, her personality was not outgoing and impulsive. Also in contrast to her
husband, her character had been moulded by a deep religious faith. For
her to project his confident, worldly-wise swagger would have been

impossible. Perceval, who witnessed her first meeting with the King and Queen, observed that she 'had a great colour from the heat of the day and the hurry and surprise she was in'. Her obvious nervousness and apprehension worried this veteran observer at court, though he did not comment on what it foretold about her future. Still, he noted 'she has a peculiar affability of behaviour and a very great sweetness of countenance, mixed with innocence, cheerfulness and sense'. To Frederick, all of these characteristics made her an ideal consort. He may have exaggerated a little when he told Queen Caroline that he 'was exceedingly pleased with the Princess, and . . . that if he had been himself to look all Europe over, he should have pitched his choice on her', but not too much. Augusta suited his purposes perfectly, because she had qualities that would enable her to play the parts he had in mind for his wife.[13]

Frederick never described what impressed him about his bride-to-be at their first meeting. Undoubtedly he was moved by considerations similar to those detailed by Lord Hervey when he narrated her presentation to George II and Caroline. Augusta's obvious and – to her unsympathetic observer – flamboyant deference to her royal in-laws, 'joined to the propriety of her whole behaviour' on that occasion, 'gave spectators great prejudices in favour of her understanding'. Why? Hervey went on to explain that 'she was but seventeen . . . , knew not a mortal here, and was suffered to bring nobody but one single man with her'. Moreover, she came 'from the solitude of her mother's country-house in Saxe-Gotha at once into the crowd, intrigues, and pomp of this court'. In such a situation, 'the bare negative good conduct of doing nothing absurd might reasonably prejudice sensible people in her favour'. Sir Robert Walpole went further than that in his assessment of Augusta. He told Hervey that her impressing 'the King last year in one interview enough to make him fond of the match and her behaving at Greenwich to the Prince in such manner as to put him in good humour with it, after all his Royal Highness had uttered against her before he had seen her, were circumstances that spoke strongly in favour of brains that had had but seventeen years to ripen'.[14] By 'brains', Walpole was referring to more than intelligence. Sir Robert discerned in her a precocious maturity and a fixed determination to be the Princess of Wales, and, ultimately, Queen of Great Britain.

Frederick saw these strengths as well, plus something else, something that made them peculiarly attractive to him. Augusta understood that the best way to realise her ambition was to please him and follow his directions. When she and the Prince first met, 'she told him she had one request she should ever make him, which was that he would give leave for her governess to come over'. She had asked the King for this favour so she could have the comforting presence in her new country of a woman who had been with her since childhood. George II had forbidden this, and the two had been separated in Holland when the Princess boarded the ship to Britain. Frederick responded that 'there was nothing she desired but he would do, and accordingly sent an express to bring the governess over'. At that moment, an important bargain was struck. From that point on, Augusta promised to follow his lead. She had also demonstrated she was willing and able to oppose the King's commands in order to get what she and her husband wanted. Not yet man and wife, they had already bonded in a common enterprise.[15]

What roles Frederick wanted Augusta to play are illustrated by this story and its provenance. Perceval heard about her request immediately after the Prince made his decision. That was possible only if Frederick told the story, because the other person privy to the agreement knew no one and spoke so little English that at her wedding the Queen had to translate the vows for her. And, since Perceval did not say the Prince had directly told him this, unquestionably Frederick had made certain it was widely known. It was not a tale intended to be kind to George II, who had, after all, denied to a young woman the presence of even one servant from Saxe-Gotha and thus consigned her to utter isolation at a strange court. Left unsaid, but clearly implied, were the conclusions he was too cheap and mean-spirited to offer her any direct contact with the familiar, while he himself frequently travelled to Hanover to enjoy the favours of a new mistress there. In contrast, her future husband immediately agreed to a reasonable and understandable request and sent for the governess without delay. He was careful, though, to make sure others knew that Augusta had said this would be her first and last request of him. Once more, the morals were unstated but obvious. Unlike his father, whose lust for his mistresses and dependence on his wife left him vulnerable to manipulation and domination by women, the Prince would be literally his own man. And, unlike Caroline, whom Frederick was fond of blaming for any difficulties he had in his relations with his father, Augusta would be properly subservient to her husband.[16]

Augusta's role in the drama Frederick was staging at court, in Parliament, at the theatre, and in London streets was performing as a vivid and more appealing contrast to Caroline. The Queen was sophisticated and cynical; therefore the Princess should be innocent and naive. It cannot have been a difficult role for her. She was, after all, a young woman, in a strange, complex place, surrounded by people she did not know, speaking a language she was still mastering. When servants spied her playing with a doll, and their amused recounting of the scene swiftly spread through the court, that contributed to her persona. Why she had not studied English during the year between the making of the match and her actual wedding – 'her mother said it must be quite unnecessary, for the Hanover family having been above twenty years on the throne, to be sure most people in England spoke German (and especially at court) as often and as well as English' – increased sympathy for her.[17] Thus Augusta's claim in 1737 that she was surprised and dismayed to learn that her husband and her parents were bitter personal and political opponents was perfectly plausible to every one at court, even the King and Queen. If they had thought about this without seeing before them Augusta in her role as wide-eyed innocent, they would have realised how *implausible* such a claim was. Even before they married, Frederick and Augusta were defying the King's commands about her governess. There had been protracted disputes in the House of Commons during the parliamentary sessions of 1736–37 over doubling the Prince's establishment from £50,000 to £100,000 a year, and the financing of their household was the sort of controversy she might be expected to follow. But the court did not make those connections.[18] Occasionally, the Queen would be sufficiently exasperated by her daughter-in-law's apparent ignorance of what was going on around her to lament her 'flat stupidity'. Invariably, she quickly regretted these criticisms, and reminded herself how sorry she felt for that 'poor creature'. 'If she were to spit in my face', Caroline once remarked, 'I should only pity her, for being under a fool's direction, and wipe it off.'[19]

What the Queen did not realise was how Augusta, with the help of Frederick's direction, was creating an image the opposite of her own. Caroline was intensely political and deeply involved in advising the King and his ministers about public issues. The Princess was not political at all; she was a properly submissive and supportive consort. Ironically, the Queen burnished this image with her own words. Her considered judgement of Augusta was that 'there was no sort of harm in her, that she never meant to offend, was very modest and very respectful'.[20] The King and others at court agreed with this verdict. Horace Walpole expressed prevailing opinions about Augusta when he praised 'the quiet inoffensive good sense of the Princess who had never said a foolish thing, or done a disobliging one since her arrival'. This she accomplished, he noted, despite being 'in very difficult situations, young, uninstructed, and besieged by the Queen, Princess Emily, . . . Lady Archibald [Hamilton]'s creatures, and very jarring interests'.[21] Without question, Frederick's strategy succeeded. To their targeted audience,

Augusta was obviously no Caroline: she was not sophisticated, independent, cunning, manipulative, cynical, disloyal to members of her
family or contemptuous of the people of London and their pleasures.
Indeed, her apparently awkward eagerness to maintain friendly relations with the King and Queen had the effect of harming their reputations while enhancing hers. And she did this without arousing any
suspicions in George II or Caroline about the genuineness of the behaviour she showed toward them or the existence of any ulterior motives
on her part.

When the King and Queen dismissed Augusta as totally under
Frederick's control, they were praising her act without meaning to do
so. This was precisely the impression she was trying to make. Moreover,
they were mistaken. Frederick had to persuade Augusta to adopt his strategies; he could not command her to do his bidding. Hervey recorded
an example of how the Prince had to rely on persuasion, without
realising what it revealed about the dynamics of his relationship with
Augusta. When she decided she would only receive Holy Communion at a Lutheran chapel, rather than taking the sacrament according
to the rites of the Anglican church, he could not compel her to set
aside her 'scruples'. As Frederick confessed to the Queen, 'she only wept
and talked of her conscience'. Using arguments similar to those suggested by Sir Robert Walpole, he had explained to her that 'when this
thing came to take air, how ill it would be received not only by the
bishops and clergy, but by the people of England in general; and what
bad consequences it might have, by giving the whole nation prejudices
against' her. This had had no effect. Finally, the Prince added a point
suggested by Hervey to Caroline and passed along from her to him. The
Act of Succession required heirs to the throne 'on no less a penalty than
the forfeiture of the Crown, to receive the Sacrament according to the
manner of the Church of England'. This law might be applied to the
Prince of Wales's wife. Continued refusal to participate in Anglican
communions could lead to the annulment of her marriage and her
return to Saxe-Gotha. Ultimately, as Hervey reported, 'the Princess
was convinced by her husband's reasonings, dried her tears, lulled her
conscience, and went no more to the Lutheran Church'.[22] In time,
she became as devout an Anglican as she had been as a Lutheran.[23]
She immediately agreed to send her governess, the very same governess
whom Frederick had earlier helped her to retain, who according to
Hervey 'was thought to have put this conscientious nonsense into [her]
head' and was 'talking to her too freely also on conjugal points', back
to Germany. Finally, at Frederick's behest, Augusta began regularly

attending Anglican services at the Royal Chapel in Kensington Palace. There she made her entrance as conspicuously as possible, providing undeniable proof of her commitment to the Church of England and the persuasive prowess of her husband.[24]

Alone among those watching her at court, Sir Robert Walpole appreciated Augusta's intelligence and perceived a tendency toward independence on matters important to her. These observations convinced him that the Princess would be capable of exercising considerable influence over Frederick's thoughts and acts. In fact, Walpole foresaw 'no way of keeping the Prince within any tolerable bounds but by the Princess'. He cautioned Caroline, however, not to begin cultivating Augusta too early. That would 'only give the Prince a jealousy, and prevent his ever suffering his wife to have any interest with him or any influence at all over his conduct'. The Queen must be patient. She had to give her daughter-in-law 'time to form an interest in him before she went about to make any use of her Royal Highness to these purposes'.[25] Frederick may have had similar thoughts, and decided to forestall the development of a friendship between the two women by keeping them as much apart as he could manage. Perhaps such a consideration explains the frequent trips he and the Princess took away from Kensington Palace. It may have even contributed to his dangerous decision to move Augusta from Hampton Court to St James's Palace when she went into labour with their first child.

Their dash to London, undertaken in haste, without informing anyone, over rough roads, and to a palace where no one had made preparations for the delivery of a baby or for the witnesses needed to confirm the live birth of an heir to the throne, infuriated the King and Queen. Because they doubted their son was capable of fathering a child, they suspected this might be a plan to palm off some 'chairman's brat he had bought' as his offspring, thereby removing their second son, William, Duke of Cumberland, from the line of succession. Once these fears were relieved – not only by the testimony of some who had hastened to St James's and arrived just in time to see Augusta deliver her namesake, but by the fact the infant was a daughter rather than a son – they were outraged by the Prince's endangering the lives of mother and child.[26] But even this episode eventuated in the improvement of Frederick's popularity. After the King angrily commanded that the Prince and his family leave St James's as soon as the Princess and her baby could safely move, and informed the court that no one who waited on Frederick would be welcome at royal drawing rooms and levees, Augusta suggested in an exchange of notes with the Queen that the blame should lie with the King and Queen. As Hervey aptly pointed out to Caroline, Frederick, by speaking through the Princess, 'has by these means opportunities of saying things to [her] . . . , which he would not dare say to the King himself'. In addition, however she replied to Augusta, she risked losing the battle for the public's opinion. If she softened the criticism she and George II had made of the Prince in a letter to his wife, she would give the impression she was retracting it out of fear. Alternatively, if she kept on painting him 'in his true colours, people will certainly lay hold of that to blame you, and say you were not satisfied with turning him out of the house and blowing up his father against him, but that you endeavoured to set his wife against him too, and to make him uneasy there, by telling her she was married to a knave, a fool, and a liar'. With Hervey's adroit editorial assistance, Caroline tried to slip through the jaws of this trap. She did not wholly succeed. Frederick's popularity in London rose, as did Augusta's, thanks in part to her reference in the published correspondence to the public's pleasure at the birth of their daughter.[27] As they left St James's, 'there was a mob about [the Prince's] coach, who cried, "God bless you!"' Not one to miss a fortuitously timed opportunity, Frederick responded, ' "God bless the King and God bless the poor." '[28] The Queen solaced herself as best she could, perhaps by recalling how she despised all popularity, and especially her son's, which 'makes me vomit'.[29] Had they known about this reaction, doubtless Frederick and Augusta would have been pleased.

The purpose of their acts is evident. Creating an unmistakable contrast to the Queen was vital to Frederick's strategy of succession. Let Augusta portray herself as a loyal, loving wife and consort and as a respectful, dutiful daughter-in-law, and she would become much more popular than Caroline. The Queen was already the target of criticism in London. Subjects in the metropolis tended to blame her for what went wrong in politics and government, while scorning the King as an absentee monarch who placed his beloved Hanover's interests over Britain's.[30] As the reverse of Caroline, Augusta would enjoy public favour for that reason alone. Frederick staged performances of *Henry IV, Part I*; perhaps he realised that, like Prince Hal's, his wife's reputation 'like bright metal on a sullen ground, / . . . Shall show more goodly, and attract more eyes / Than that which hath no foil to set it off'.[31] Such a perception would help insure the popularity of the Prince and Princess before he took the throne, strengthen his political position during the years of waiting, and ease his succession when George II died. By that time, Augusta would no longer be the consort as contrast. She would be far along toward becoming the consort as exemplar.

In fact, Augusta assumed her new role as exemplar sooner than she or the Prince expected. After a brief but painful illness, the Queen died on 20 November 1737. Throughout her final days, she refused to see Frederick, despite his frequent, well-publicised efforts to speak with her. Whether he honestly wished to be reconciled with her is unknowable; mother and son certainly had detested each other for years, and Caroline's hatred for the heir apparent to the throne did not diminish at all as she faced death. Whatever his real feelings, the genuineness of his senti-ments was beside the point as far as the public were concerned. The son was trying to do his filial and Christian duty; the mother was not doing hers. Perceval noted, 'People speak hardly of her for not yielding to the Prince's repeated desire to see her'. This, he thought, was too bad, for 'she was otherwise a tender mother, beloved by all her children; who with watching and sitting up with her have quite worn down, and now are ill'.[32] Frederick hardly needed this response from the public to con-vince him that his consort should try to be viewed as a good mother. That was already part of his plan. Surely, though, it confirmed for him the wisdom of that design. From that time until his own death in 1751, he and Augusta conspicuously spent time with their children, often at the production of amateur theatricals. Even Horace Walpole, who de-spised the Prince, conceded after observing his behaviour and gossiping with others about it that Frederick was 'a better natured man, and a much better father' than George II. The Princess was equally affection-ate in public. To the Prince and Princess, it was important to establish themselves as clearly better parents than the older generation. This they succeeded in doing. The best portraits of Augusta painted during those years show her surrounded by her children, who eventually totalled nine in fourteen years of marriage. The artists duplicated with oil on canvas how she wanted to be perceived in real life by those at court and the public.

Augusta's role as mother underscored another distinction between her husband and his father. On her deathbed, Caroline urged the King to wed again. At this, George II's 'sobs began to rise and his tears to fall with double vehemence' and, 'sobbing between every word, with much ado he got out this answer: "*Non, j'aurai des maîtresses*".'[33] This meant Augusta would be the only royal consort in the realm after Caroline's death. Thus she was noticeably and unmistakably the embodiment of morality at court. Frederick himself was not immune to the charms of other ladies at court; indeed, Horace Walpole claimed 'his chief passion was women', then made a joke of his lust by noting 'like the rest of his race, [for the Prince] beauty was not a necessary ingredient'. 'But', added

Walpole, 'though these mistresses were pretty much declared, he was a good husband', and the Princess 'was likely to have always preserved a chief ascendant over him'.[34] Proof of her ability to win and hold the affection and trust of her husband may be seen in the poem he wrote and then had published about her charms. In it, he celebrated

> ... that gentleness of mind, that love
>   So kindly answering my desire,
> That grace with which you look and speak and move,
>   That thus has set my soul on fire.[35]

There is no reason to question his sincerity in 'The Charms of Sylvia by The Prince of Wales to the Princess'. There is equally no reason to doubt their determination to appear before the public in verse, on canvas, at court, in the royal box at the theatre, and among Londoners in the street as a loving couple, the picture of matrimonial and familial love, as opposed to an ageing keeper of a mistress at public expense.

George II was not merely infamous for his passionate attachment to mistresses. He was also well known – at least according to rumour – for being controlled by the women in his life. Frederick had always vowed women would not dominate him; according to one of his sisters, that was the only belief he had ever held consistently.[36] When Sir George Lyttleton parodied the Prince's verses on his wife, he had Frederick proclaim he loved best

> that all-consenting tongue,
>   That never puts me in the wrong.[37]

Clearly the Prince tried to give the impression that Augusta did not influence his political thoughts and acts. Given his care about this, it is not surprising that there is no documentary record of any effects she possibly had on him.

What is recorded is her knowledge about what he was doing. Augusta was present during part of a confidential discussion Frederick had with his principal man of business in Parliament, the Earl of Egmont, in early 1751 about recruiting new MPs to their faction and establishing the Earl's position as its leader in the House of Commons. Egmont expressed no surprise at this in his notes on the conversation.[38] And, after the Prince's death in 1751, some Tories appealed to the Princess to confirm their version of negotiations with Frederick over parliamentary opposition to the ministry in 1747. So did Bubb Dodington, who wanted Augusta to inform the King that he and she wanted the Prince to follow 'a plan of temper and moderation' in 1749.[39] Unlike the situation in

1737, when she successfully claimed to be ignorant of political issues affecting her, during the 1750s Augusta did not even attempt this role. Nor could she, and retain any reputation for truthfulness. When Dodington returned to the Prince's service in 1749, he took care to inform her about the terms of his agreement with Frederick and 'to beg [her] protection'. That she 'answered me in the most obliging manner' obviously pleased him. As he later recalled, 'knowing her right way of thinking, I ventur'd to communicate it to her, and beg'd her protection in the execution of it'. He presumed that she, too, favoured a muted opposition in Parliament and was willing to consider the possibility of a *rapprochement* with government. His other assumption, that her views would influence Frederick, reveals his conviction that she was an important player in the politics of the Prince of Wales's court.[40] Actually, she, like her husband, did not settle finally on either Dodington's strategy or Egmont's plan for a vigorous parliamentary opposition. They kept their options open. Nor did they want to drive away any current supporters of the Prince or exclude any potential recruits to their cause. So Frederick constantly worked at boosting the morale and flattering the ambitions of both Dodington and Egmont. Augusta played the vital part of sympathetic listener and friendly intercessor for both men in their relations with their leader.

Thus in March 1751 it was Augusta's task to reassure Egmont about her husband's health. The Earl had been concerned about the Prince's illness and his 'low spirits'. After privately sending for him, Augusta talked with Egmont for nearly an hour, 'telling me he was much better [and] only wanted to recover his strength'. She observed Frederick was 'always frightened for himself when he was the least bit out of order but that she laughed him out of it and never would humour him in these fancys'. Then she passed along a message for Egmont from the Prince: 'that he should not die this bout but for the future would take better care of himself, that he might live for the sake of me and the public'.[41] The Earl went home more cheerful about Frederick's life and his own political future, just as she had intended.

Egmont's hopes were soon dashed. The Prince's condition was far more serious than Augusta believed; he died two days after her *tête-à-tête* with the Earl. This should not, however, obscure an important point: how practised she was at manipulating Frederick's moods away from despair and toward optimism. She must have done the same when he fretted about the state of his political health. Certainly she knew about his detailed plans for opposition during the next parliamentary session and for the first days after his accession to the throne. And she knew where to find them: in three chests at Carlton House. When her husband died, she sent immediately for Egmont. The King might seize the chests, she pointed out to him, and 'we might be ruined by these papers'. Pulling 'off the silk covers of the pillow of a couch in the Prince's dressing room to serve as a bag to put them in', she despatched the Earl to retrieve them. When he returned with the chests, she extracted with no hesitation or search 'a book in my own handwriting, containing the Prince's whole disposition' of places he would have to fill early in his reign, and gave it to its author. Because it was in the Earl's distinctive hand, the contents could not be proven to have been Frederick's work. Then 'she opened one of the trunks which I found she knew contained the public papers of our projected settlement – his declaration speeches etc. and list of offices . . . [and] a state of the intended Civil List with reasoning and advice to the Prince upon it'. These she ordered Dr George Lee to burn in the fireplace.[42] Not until the incriminating papers were ashes did she begin thinking about what to do with her husband's body and when to tell her father-in-law. Her disciplined performance revealed more than her intimate knowledge of Frederick's schemes. It showed impressive political acumen and decisiveness. These were both traits she would have to call on again and again during Prince George's minority.

Augusta's first response to Frederick's death speaks volumes about her character. She obviously felt she could not waste time mourning the loss of her husband. Instead, she had to take stock of her political situation and act right away. She could not, she realised instantaneously, risk antagonising George II. To help guard against this, the Prince's political papers had to be destroyed. If the King was angered by anything, it was entirely conceivable he might take George and Edward from her and put them in his household, just as George I had done to him and Caroline. He had disapproved of the Prince's choice of tutors for the boys, but could do nothing about it while Frederick was alive and George was not the next in line to the throne. That they were being taught lessons of factional opposition to the King's ministry had been beyond his control. Now it was not. This was a frightening prospect for the Princess, and not merely because she could no longer exercise any maternal authority over her sons. Once the new Prince of Wales was at St James's, the odds were she would not be the Regent if George II died before his grandson was eighteen. Instead, the Regent would be his uncle, the Duke of Cumberland. This, in Augusta's opinion, would not be just a political defeat for her. She firmly believed Cumberland might take advantage of his position and power as Regent to usurp the throne. In order to preserve her son's birthright and whatever influence she could have on him as his mother, she had to decide swiftly on how best to keep George in her household and to gain the King's support for her as Regent in the event of his death.[43]

Egmont's advice on how to accomplish this was so predictable Augusta did not have to consult with him to know what he would say. The Earl believed it was essential to keep the parliamentary faction loyal to Frederick intact and united. Those forty to sixty votes in the House of Commons, he would argue, would deter George II and his ministers from taking the Prince away and naming his uncle Regent. To the newly widowed Princess such a strategy was a recipe for disaster. Adopting it would serve Egmont's self-interest, because it would demonstrate that his ambitions had not been wholly wrecked by his master's death. But it would guarantee that the Dowager Princess would lose her sons and any possibility of being Regent, because it would arouse George II's and his ministers' enmity while signalling them they had nothing to fear from Egmont or Augusta. Before his death, Frederick and Egmont were having difficulty recruiting more MPs to their cause. Worse, they were having trouble maintaining the numbers of their supporters in Parliament. The message of this was clear to Augusta: '*if the Prince cannot hold them together how shall I*'.[44] She was, after all, a woman, and therefore, according to the wisdom of the day, unsuited for political leadership. Even more important, she was not the heir to the throne, and thus had nothing to promise prospective allies. Under those circumstances, support for her at Westminster would rapidly melt away. Declaring opposition to the King and government while weakening by the moment in the House of Commons was not the way to achieve her goals. She could not coerce the King or his ministers into giving her what she wanted. She would have to persuade them to do that.

Wounded by Augusta's decision, Egmont explained it by saying 'she has been flattered' by his enemies in the moderate faction at Frederick's court 'into a total reliance of the King and has thought it necessary for her own purpose to abandon all the Prince's friends' in Parliament. In fact, she had reached these conclusions herself. It was no accident that Dr George Lee, a leading moderate, was present with the Earl and the Princess at the destruction of Frederick's papers. Augusta summoned him there. This was not for advice about what to do; she could predict his position as easily as she could Egmont's. Lee was there to advise *how* this course of action was to be taken, not *whether* it should be. Nor was it accidental that Egmont, not Lee, was sent to

Carlton House. If this errand became known (and it did), it could be plausibly explained as an effort by Egmont to protect his own interests (as it was).[45] Augusta was not manipulated by others into these decisions. She made them by herself, then *she* manipulated the late Prince's followers. The Earl's explanation of her strategy does not do her justice in another way as well. In her interviews with George II, Augusta did not simply throw herself on his mercy. In an effort to impress and sway the most important gallery of her life, she skilfully reprised a number of roles she had earlier played.

The Princess began the morning after her husband's death. Encouraged by two 'very kind' messages of concern for her sent by the King, she played as the dutiful daughter-in-law and the loving wife and mother to his emissary, the Earl of Lincoln. 'She received him alone; sitting with her eyes fixed; thanked the King much, and said she would write as soon as she was able; [and] in the meantime, recommended her miserable self and children to him.'[46] Soon after Lincoln left, Augusta wrote a letter which reinforced her words and demeanour during that interview.

> The sorrow which overwhelms me does not make me the less sensible of the great goodness of Your Majesty. The only things, Sire, which can console me are the gracious assurances which Your Majesty has given me. I throw myself together with my children at your feet. We commend ourselves, Sire, to your paternal love and royal protection.[47]

Horace Walpole guessed successfully at what was happening here. 'The King and she', he explained in his *Memoirs of George II*, 'both took their parts at once; she, of flinging herself entirely into his hands, and studying nothing but his pleasure, but winding what interest she got with him to the advantage of her own and the Prince's friends.' As for George II, he got the pleasure 'of acting the tender grandfather, which he, who had never acted the tender father, grew so pleased with representing, that he soon became it in earnest'.[48] The only flaws in Walpole's analysis sprang from the persistent tendency to underestimate the Princess that Shelburne called attention to years later. He, like Dodington, Egmont, and most of the men at court, had difficulty giving full credit to Augusta's intelligence, courage, and skill at political performances. In this case, Walpole failed to see that the Princess did not try to move the King to gain advantages for her political friends, but for herself and Prince George. Nor did he discern that she encouraged George II to take up the part of loving grandfather, a role she divined he was prepared to assume.

These were not the only ways in which Augusta improved her position with the King. She had long enjoyed a reputation for prudence and good sense. Her abrupt severing of contact with Egmont, whom she never again admitted into her presence after he brought back the Prince's papers, called attention to those traits. Moreover, she made sure others knew about the Earl's exclusion, by ordering her servants to broadcast it widely and to treat him rudely. For his part, Egmont understood that relying utterly on George II's goodwill and abandoning him and the Prince's other political allies was 'not impolitic in her circumstances'. Still, he faulted her for not 'break[ing this news] decently to those who were so near her husband, and were so much concerned in it as I am, and so faithful to her and her children's interest'.[49] What he did not comprehend was the fact that she could not be courteous to him and still appear to be a prudential, commonsensical woman. Furthermore, seeing him would soon become as widely known as refusing to meet with him was. That would rouse suspicions about her motives and raise questions about the authenticity of her submission to the King and his ministers. It would also keep her from playing convincingly her final role in the crisis created by Frederick's death: that of a woman who was fundamentally uninterested in politics. Augusta was returning to the part she played first as the submissive, uninformed young Princess during 1736–37 and then occasionally thereafter when circumstances demanded it: the dutiful, apolitical consort. She played it as well in 1751 as she had earlier.

By reprising this role, Augusta confirmed opinions the King already held about her. As Earl Waldegrave, who was one of George II's favourites, recalled, 'The Princess of Wales, during the life of the Prince her Husband, had distinguished herself by a most decent & prudent Behavior'. Noticing and approving of this, 'the King, notwithstanding his aversion to his Son, behaved to her not only with great Politeness, but with the appearance of cordiality and Affection'.[50] Augusta had taken a critical step toward winning his affection in February 1742. After Sir Robert Walpole resigned as First Lord of the Treasury and Leader of the House of Commons, some in opposition called for an inquiry into his handling of secret service funds in the hope that grounds could be found for impeaching him for corruption. Determined to spare his long-time minister this indignity, the King took the extraordinary step of meeting privately with Augusta and asking her to persuade Frederick to tell his supporters to vote against any inquiry. Though the Princess respectfully requested to be excused from acting as her father-in-law's advocate, saying her practice was to take no part in politics, she did agree to pass the request along to the Prince.[51] That Frederick ultimately did not do as George II wished did not diminish his pleasure with Augusta's service as liaison between the two men. In 1751, she reaped the reward: '[H]is Majesty gave still stronger Proofs of his Favour and Confidence'.[52] When he went to see the Princess on 31 March 1751, he would not sit in the chair of state prepared for his visit. Instead, he perched next to her on a couch. The two hugged each other, then wept together. When the children arrived, he 'embraced Prince George, said he loved him, bid him to be honest and brave, and mind his mother who was the best of women'. Next, he once more 'embraced the Princess, desired nobody might come between him and her, and that he would do everything for her'. There was, Egmont gathered from the accounts almost instantaneously circulating in London, an 'abundance of speeches and a kind behaviour to her and the children' that so 'captivated Prince George' that he said 'he should not be frighted any more with his grandpapa'.[53] In his memoirs Waldegrave emphasised the political consequences of this meeting. The King 'patronized the Act by which [the Princess] was appointed Regent, in case of a Minority: and, what was of greater Importance, he suffer'd the Heir Apparent to remain under her sole Direction'.[54]

Augusta would have said Waldegrave exaggerated the extent of her victory. If George II died before his grandson's eighteenth birthday on 4 June 1756, she might be Regent, but she would have to share power with a council that would include Cumberland and many of the dead King's ministers. For her son's position to be as secure as she wished, Henry Pelham, currently First Lord of the Treasury, and his brother, the Duke of Newcastle, would have to remain opposed to Cumberland and his man of business, Henry Fox. Probably she was also aware that one reason her sons remained with her was the Pelhams' fear that if they were moved to the King's court at St James's, Cumberland and Fox might gain control of their education. Certainly Augusta knew that although the boys would stay at Leicester House, George II and his ministers would appoint their governors, preceptors and tutors. How and by whom George and Edward were educated would not be decided by her.[55] Against these limitations on her power, the Princess could balance the fact that she still had gained a great deal. To be sure, she could not exercise complete control over George's fate in the years immediately ahead. She did not even feel she could openly protest when she believed either the Pelhams or those they appointed in the Prince's household did not act properly or wisely. Clearly, she would not be able to cross swords with the King, however much it might seem justified to her. But she had positioned herself where she could manoeuvre behind the scenes and play time-tested roles to the best advantage of the future King.

The next years were hard ones for Augusta. She strained to achieve the appearance of what Waldegrave believed was reality before 1755: 'the Princess's Behaviour to the King was wise and dutiful; she consider'd him as her Protector, Benefactor, and Friend; and took no Step, or any consequence without his Approbation'.[56] In fact, she had nothing but contempt for him, scorning in particular to her *confidant* Dodington his inability to say 'no' to his ministers. In her opinion, George II, despite his tantrums and grumblings, was a mere boy in their hands, whom they disciplined when necessary and tolerated at other times.[57] She, on the other hand, had to yield to him. 'There were a hundred good reasons that tied her hands from interfering with the King; those about her children were obvious enough.' 'If she was to stir', she reminded Dodington, 'it would make things worse; she saw no way to extricate herself.'[58] So she continued to play her role, and play it well. Although George II may have come to suspect her dislike for him, her prudential behaviour prevented him from being certain and taking action against her.[59]

Augusta's hatred of Newcastle may have been even greater than her contempt for the King. 'The weakness, meanness, cowardice and base-ness of the Duke of Newcastle – all of which she echoed in the strongest terms' – were frequent subjects of her conversations with Dodington.[60] The Princess did not feel compelled to hide her feelings from Newcastle; during the 1750s, she criticised him to his face for yielding too much to Cumberland and Fox and for excluding Frederick's old supporters from office. Her inability to change his ways depressed Augusta. To her, it was an unmistakable sign of her own weakness that she could not bully the Duke as successfully as others who despised him did.[61] Finally, the performance of Prince George's governors and tutors dissatisfied her. George was not learning very much, and he remained disturbingly im-mature for someone who might be King in the near future. The lion's share of the blame for this she gave to the men appointed by George II and Newcastle.[62] But she knew she 'durst not recommend for fear of offense: while he had governors &c., [and] was under immediate in-spection, all that they did not direct, would be imputed to her'.[63] Once she began complaining, or appeared to be interfering, her enemies would remove 'the Prince into those other hands, at last, by taking him from the people now about him and by degrees, consequently, from her'.[64]

So Augusta accomplished what she could, sometimes by cautious stealth, more often by tightly controlling the contacts George and Edward had with the court and the outside world. Because 'the young people of quality were so ill educated, and so very vicious, that they frighten'd her', she kept them as isolated as she could.[65] The Princess supplemented her close supervision of their social lives with determined efforts to instil her religious piety in them and with constant emphasis on proper and moral behaviour. In particular, she was concerned about the potential that sexual temptations (because 'the behaviour of the women was so indecent, so low, so much against their interest, by making them so cheap') and lust (because they were, after all, the sons and grandsons of men who kept mistresses) had to overturn their moral training and leave them under the domination of self-interested people who would not desire that they serve their nation well.[66] Edward, who evidently once had been her favourite, resisted these lessons and complained about his situation. George was his mother's son, to her relief and delight. Even so, Augusta realised she could not prepare him by herself to be a king. She could not provide the proper education for him, and he desperately needed a better teacher. Nor could she introduce him into the world of politics. The Princess did not believe 'women could . . . inform him' about the realities of power. And, as he came closer to his eighteenth birthday, she 'was highly sensible how necessary it was that the Prince should keep company with men'.[67] Finding the right man to guide the Prince into an understanding of what the world he was entering was like and to teach what the duties of a king were in dealing with and overcoming that world became her principal concern.

Augusta did not have many to choose from. Dodington knew the Prince, and had even discussed public finance with him, but the two had not established any close rapport. Besides, even though the Princess trusted Dodington enough to share her innermost personal thoughts with him, she did not believe he would reinforce her ideals of public and private morality, and she was so wary of his ambitions and motives that she kept him utterly uninformed about her political activities. George would learn to accept things as they were, and to compromise with Newcastle and others on important points, if Dodington taught as he had acted.[68]

The other possible choice was the Earl of Bute, who had been dancing attendance at Leicester House since the mid-1740s. He had impressed her late husband and Egmont enough to be named a Lord of the Bedchamber at the Prince's court and to be slated for election as one of the sixteen Scottish peers in the House of Lords when Frederick became King.[69] That the Prince also 'used frequently to say Bute was a fine Showy Man, who would make an excellent Embassador in a court where there was no Business' did not disqualify him in her eyes.[70] To Augusta, this meant he was not enmeshed in the narrow practicalities of politics and government. Thus his vision of what a patriotic and moral monarch could accomplish was not bounded by what the world was. Moreover, the fact that Bute did not have extensive contacts with politicians was an advantage. By itself, that proved his loyalty to Frederick's heir. Unlike many of the late Prince's supporters, he had not approached the ministry after his master's death in the hope of gaining a pension or an office. This was not due to a lack of connections at court. Bute's uncle, the Duke of Argyll, controlled Scottish patronage. Though his connection with Argyll had frayed over the years, certainly he could have appealed to his relative for aid had he so desired. His decision not to do this proved his commitment to Leicester House. Indeed, that attachment was so strong that he attempted to persuade Argyll to join the opposition to Newcastle's administration.[71] The absence of political connections also meant he would not be influenced in his future dealings with prominent politicians by past negotiations, arrangements, and alliances with them. Most important, the time they had spent together convinced the Princess that Bute shared her morality, her political ideals, and her ambition to make George a good monarch. If he could win her son's confidence, he would be ideal. Augusta did what she could to encourage this bonding. Waldegrave was convinced that 'by the good offices of the Mother, [Bute] also became the avow'd favorite of the Young Prince'.[72] No doubt he exaggerated her role, mostly because he was jealous of his successful rival for George's affections. The establishment of a very close mentor–protégé relationship between the Earl and the Prince was chiefly Bute's doing. Augusta herself was more than happy to give him the credit and to delight in his success.[73]

Whether or not she helped create the foundation for an affectionate relationship between her son and the man who became his 'dearest friend', the Princess did make a crucial contribution to its success. She arranged their meetings, and insured they would be secret even from her personal servants. This she achieved by giving the impression that Bute was visiting her and spending hours in tête-à-têtes. Dodington had no idea what was going on.[74] Inspired by the servants' talk about these meetings, Waldegrave leaped to the conclusion that Bute and Augusta were lovers. This impression was heightened by the behaviour of the two toward each other in public. Bute, who inclined toward grand words and vivid gestures on every occasion, must have become even more theatrical out of gratitude to her. Augusta clearly did not conceal her feelings for her 'best friend' in public.[75] As Horace Walpole later remarked, 'the eagerness of the pages of the backstairs to let her know whenever Lord Bute arrived, a mellowness in her German accent as often as she spoke to him, and that was often and long, and a more than usual swimmingness in her eyes, contributed to dispel the ideas that had been conceived of the rigour of her widowhood'.[76] Did she act and speak this way deliberately, in full awareness she was risking her reputation, in order to prevent anyone from guessing Bute's true role in her household, reporting it, and convincing George II to move his grandson to St James's? There is no way of determining this for sure. But if she did, playing this role was an extraordinary act of maternal love and courage.[77]

During the two decades between her marriage and her son's eighteenth birthday, courts were indeed stages for Augusta. In that time, she played many parts. Some were assigned to her, either by her husband or the realities of her situation. Some she chose. All she executed well. Throughout, her performances were inspired by a determination that her husband or her son would ascend to the throne under the most favourable circumstances possible, popular with his people, independent of the politicians of the old order, and prepared to take up the role of patriot king immediately. What she said about the future George III she had felt about Frederick as well: she 'could have nothing so much at heart as to see him do well, and make the nation happy'.[78] To fulfil that goal, and her other wish, that he be 'great and happy for [his] own sake', Augusta was ready to adopt whatever roles might be required of her, whether they were the dutiful daughter-in-law, the submissive, supportive, and loving wife, the affectionate mother, the prudent, decent, and apolitical woman, perhaps even the lover of Bute.[79] She understood that all of these in turn were necessary to playing well the most crucial parts of her life, as Princess of Wales and as the mother of a king who would make himself and his nation 'great and happy'.

Notes

1 The Earl of Shelburne, 'Autobiography', in Lord Fitzmaurice, *Life of William Earl of Shelburne Afterwards First Marquess of Lansdowne With Extracts from His Papers and Correspondence*, 2 vols, 2nd edn (London, Macmillan, 1912), I, pp. 46, 49.
2 *Ibid.*, I, p. 49.
3 Shelburne commented on role-playing at court and Augusta's aptitude for it: 'Naturally given to dissimulation and intrigue, she had both time and opportunity to improve these important qualifications; she was surrounded by nothing else, and

the perpetual mortifications she submitted to pressed and obliged her to exert both'. He also pointed out that she was very observant, 'had resolution equal to any enterprise, and had a perfect command of temper'. *Ibid.*, I, p. 49.

4 J. Brewer, *The Pleasures of the Imagination: English Culture in the Eighteenth Century* (New York, Farrar, Straus, & Giroux, 1997), pp. 334–48.

5 Viscount Perceval, 'Diary', 13 November 1731, ed. R. A. Roberts, Historical Manuscripts Commission, *Manuscripts of the Earl of Egmont. Diary of Viscount Percival Afterwards First Earl of Egmont*, 3 vols (London, His Majesty's Stationery Office, 1920–23), I, pp. 207–8. In the text, I have spelled 'Perceval' the way most members of the family wrote it, and not 'Percival' as this viscount did.

6 *Ibid.*, 13 November 1731, I, pp. 207–8.

7 Brewer, *Pleasures*, p. 334.

8 Lord Hervey, *Memoirs of the Reign of George the Second From his Accession to the Death of Queen Caroline*, ed. J. W. Croker, 2 vols (London, John Murray, 1848), I, p. 90.

9 *Ibid.*, II, p. 406. For a discussion of the political implications of operas and plays, see Brewer, *Pleasures*, pp. 369–83.

10 Brewer, *Pleasures*, pp. 325–56.

11 Perceval, 'Diary', 11 October 1731 and 16 January 1731/2, I, pp. 205, 216. For another example of Frederick's personal courage in public, see *ibid.*, 1 October 1735, II, pp. 197–8.

12 Quoted in Brewer, *Pleasures*, p. 350. For Augusta's unfamiliarity with English, see Hervey, *Memoirs*, II, p. 115, and Perceval, 'Diary', 27 April 1736, II, p. 264. For another example of how the Prince displayed and proclaimed Augusta's virtues on London's streets, see Perceval, 'Diary', 1 May 1736, II, p. 267.

13 Perceval, 'Diary', 27 April 1736, p. 264. Perceval had become the 1st Earl of Egmont in 1734. I continue to refer to him by his family name to distinguish him from his son, the 2nd Earl of Egmont, who became one of Frederick's principal advisers during the 1740s and who also kept a journal of events that I quote from below in this essay.

14 Hervey, *Memoirs*, II, pp. 114–15.

15 Perceval, 'Diary', 27 April 1736, II, p. 264.

16 *Ibid.*, II, p. 264. For an example of Frederick's penchant for blaming his mother for his difficulties with the King, see Perceval, 'Diary', 21 September 1737, II, p. 435.

17 Hervey, *Memoirs*, II, p. 115. As Hervey sarcastically observed, this was 'a conjecture so well founded that I believe there were not three natives in England that understood one word of it better than in the reign of Queen Anne'.

18 For a contemporary account of this episode, see *ibid.*, II, pp. 407–8. The source for this was Monsieur Dunoyer, a dancing master at court, who, according to Hervey, 'was a sort of licensed spy on both sides', sometimes reporting to the King and Queen about events at the Wales's court, sometimes to the Prince about their Majesties and the courtiers around them. In his account, Augusta accosted him privately, after the Prince had retired, and asked if there was trouble within the family, 'adding with great vehemence, that she would know'. When Dunoyer 'pretended ignorance, she burst into tears, flew into a greater passion than he thought her capable of, and by these means had forced him, half out of fear and half out of pity, to tell her all he

knew'. This has all the marks of a staged scene, one designed to limn further a perception of the Princess's concern about relations with her in-laws while extracting information out of the dancing master.

19 *Ibid.*, II, pp. 132.3.

20 *Ibid.*, II, p. 133.

21 Horace Walpole, *Memoirs of King George II*, ed. J. Brooke, 3 vols (New Haven, Yale University Press, 1985), I, p. 53. Lady Archibald Hamilton was reputed to be the Prince's mistress. He had prevailed upon Augusta to make her one of his Ladies of the Bedchamber, despite the opposition of the Queen. See Hervey, *Memoirs*, II, pp. 119–20, 131–2.

22 Hervey, *Memoirs*, II, pp. 129–30. During the eighteenth century, it was a common practice in the Church of England to take the sacrament of Holy Communion only two or three times a year. Augusta was attending other Anglican services, but she did not feel she could in good conscience take communion according to those rites.

23 For a discussion of her piety as an Anglican, see J. L. Bullion, '"George, Be a King!": The Relationship between Princess Augusta and George III', in S. Taylor, R. Connors and C. Jones (eds), *Hanoverian Britain and Empire: Essays in Memory of Philip Lawson* (London, Boydell Press, 1998), pp. 180–1, 189.

24 Hervey, *Memoirs*, II, pp. 129–31. 'Whether by grandeur or by chance', according to Hervey, Frederick and Augusta 'used generally to come to chapel at Kensington after the service had been some time begun'. This meant the Princess had 'to crowd by the Queen', which irritated Caroline considerably. Hervey believed this was designed by the Prince to provoke a quarrel so he could then describe his mother as unreasonable and difficult to live with. It seems equally probable that a late arrival called attention to Augusta's presence and underscored her commitment to the Church of England. Once this point was established, and it was clear the Queen was not going to rise to the bait, Augusta did not attend this service when she could not be there when it started.

25 *Ibid.*, II, p. 121.

26 *Ibid.*, II, pp. 362–78; the quotation is on p. 372.

27 *Ibid.*, II, pp. 426–41, 457–8.

28 Perceval, 'Diary', 21 September 1737, II, p. 435.

29 Hervey, *Memoirs*, II, p. 210.

30 For examples, see *ibid.*, II, pp. 190–5, 210–11, 223–4.

31 For an example of Frederick's productions of *Henry IV, Part I*, George Bubb Dodington, 'Political Journal', 11 January 1751, in J. Carswell and L. A. Dralle (eds), *The Political Journal of George Bubb Dodington* (Oxford, Clarendon Press, 1965), p. 95. Interestingly George II saw parallels between Shakespeare's creation and his own situation. One morning in late 1735, 'he indulged himself in another sally . . . against his son, by saying, whilst he was talking of the actors he had seen in the play of Harry the Fourth the night before, that there were really some good ones, but for the Prince of Wales, he must own he never saw so awkward a fellow and so mean a scoundrel in his life'. Everyone present, noted Hervey, grasped George II's meaning, 'but all very properly pretended to understand his Majesty literally, joined in the censure, and abused the theatrical Prince of Wales'. Hervey, *Memoirs*, II, pp. 53–4.

32 Perceval, 'Diary', 20 November 1737, II, p. 445. A full account of Caroline's final illness may be found in Hervey, *Memoirs*, II, pp. 490–539.

33 Hervey, *Memoirs*, II, pp. 513–14.

34 Walpole, *Memoirs of George II*, I, p. 53.

35 *Ibid.*, III, p. 145.

36 Hervey, *Memoirs*, II, p. 211.

37 Walpole, *Memoirs of George II*, III, p. 145n.

38 Earl of Egmont, 'Memorandum Book', [12 March 1751], in A. N. Newman (ed.), 'Leicester House Politics, 1750–60, From the Papers of John, Second Earl of Egmont', in *Camden Miscellany Vol. XXIII* (London, Royal Historical Society, Camden Fourth Series Volume 7, 1967), p. 196.

39 Dodington, 'Political Journal', 2 October 1751, 16 July 1752, pp. 135, 165.

40 *Ibid.*, 18 July 1749, p. 7. When Dodington reminded Augusta about their conversation later, she confirmed his understanding of it. 'It was', she said, 'very true, she was a good witness of it, and would always say it, &c.' *Ibid.*, 16 July 1752, p. 165.

41 Egmont, 'Memorandum Book', [18 March 1751], p. 197.

42 *Ibid.*, [20 March 1751], pp. 198–9. Egmont noted that Augusta opened one of the trunks briefly even though 'I knew there was nothing [there] and she too'. This indicates he was well aware she was very familiar with her late husband's most secret records.

43 Augusta's acts can be followed and her motives inferred from *ibid.*, [20 March–13 April 1751], pp. 198–213.

44 *Ibid.*, [26 March 1751], p. 205, italics in original. For the Prince and Egmont's problems in the House of Commons, see the Earl's entry for [12 March 1751], p. 196.

45 *Ibid.*, [28 March 1751], p. 206. Augusta even accused Egmont of spreading the story himself, either personally or by encouraging his servants to do it, in order to inflate his own reputation. He protested his innocence, observing as he did so that by the time he got home after the destruction of the papers his servants already knew he had retrieved them from Carlton House. He also asked her to try to remember if she had told anyone. Augusta did not respond to this thinly veiled accusation.

46 Walpole, *Memoirs of George II*, I, pp. 54–5.

47 Quoted in J. Brooke, *King George III* (New York, McGraw Hill, 1972), p. 26.

48 Walpole, *Memoirs of George II*, I, p. 55.

49 Egmont, 'Memorandum Book', [27 March 1751], p. 205.

50 Earl Waldegrave, 'Memoirs of the Leicester House Years, 1752–1756', in J. C. D. Clark (ed.), *The Memoirs and Speeches of James, 2nd Earl Waldegrave, 1742–1763* (Cambridge, Cambridge University Press, 1988), p. 162.

51 See Morris Marples, *Poor Fred and The Butcher: Sons of George II* (London, Michael Joseph, 1970), p. 97. Soon after George II and Augusta had their conversation in February 1742, the King and Frederick met for the first time in four and a half years. It was a formal occasion at court, intended to signal to the political world that the two were interested in a reconciliation. After the Prince kissed his father's hand, George II broke their long silence by asking, ' "How does the princess do?" ' Then he added, ' "I hope she is well." ' These sentiments not only artfully called attention to the two men's common affection for Augusta, surely one of the few beliefs or feelings they shared. It also hinted at the King's hope she might become the means for

drawing him and the Prince closer together politically and personally. For this exchange, see J. Walters, *The Royal Griffin: Frederick, Prince of Wales, 1707–51* (New York, Stein & Day, 1972), p. 183.

52 Waldegrave, 'Memoirs', p. 162.

53 Walpole, *Memoirs of George II*, I, p. 58; and Egmont, 'Memorandum Book', [31] March 1751, p. 207.

54 Waldegrave, 'Memoirs', p. 162.

55 See Walpole, *Memoirs of George II*, I, pp. 60–105.

56 Waldegrave, 'Memoirs', p. 163.

57 Dodington, 'Political Journal', 8 February 1753, p. 203.

58 *Ibid.*, 27 May 1755, p. 299.

59 According to Walpole, after the passage of the Act of Parliament making Augusta the Regent, George II claimed he had 'assumed to himself the chief direction of the bill'. Then he added in remarks he made to Henry Fox, 'I have a good opinion of the Princess, but I don't quite know her'. Walpole, *Memoirs of George II*, I, p. 103. Walpole also heard that the King told Henry Pelham soon after Frederick's death 'You none of you know this woman, and you none of you will know her till I am dead'. Quoted in Clark, 'Introduction', *Waldegrave*, p. 54.

60 Dodington, 'Political Journal', 27 May 1755, p. 298.

61 *Ibid.*, 8 February 1753, pp. 204–5.

62 Bullion, ' "George, Be a King!" ', pp. 186–8.

63 Dodington, 'Political Journal', 29 May 1754, p. 271.

64 *Ibid.*, 28 December 1752, pp. 192–3.

65 *Ibid.*, 15 October 1752, p. 178; see also the entry for 18 December 1753, p. 244.

66 *Ibid.*, 27 May 1755, p. 300. See also Bullion, ' "George, Be a King!" ', pp. 190–5.

67 Dodington, 'Political Journal', 27 May 1755, p. 300.

68 On 6 August 1755, Dodington talked 'with the Prince, about funding, &c., and other serious things' and he 'seem'd to hear with attention and satisfaction'. 'Political Journal', p. 318. But the Princess's friend emphasised teaching the wisdom of the world, and he often urged Augusta to end George's isolation at court. Although she found it politic to agree with him in principle on these occasions, this was not the sort of advice she welcomed or had any intention of taking. For examples of Dodington's educational philosophy, and the Princess's temporising responses, see 'Political Journal', 15 October 1752, 18 December 1753 and 27 May 1755, pp. 178, 244, 300.

69 Egmont, 'A Plan for the New Parliament', [April 1749], in Newman (ed.), 'Leicester House', p. 171. Frederick made Bute a Lord of the Bedchamber on 16 October 1750. This was not a minor appointment. The Prince reserved these positions for politicians whom he expected could help him in increasing the numbers of his supporters. No doubt he anticipated Bute would assist in the recruitment of Scottish MPs. Such appointments served another purpose as well. Accepting them publicly bound men like Bute to Frederick's cause, and thus improved his reputation and position as leader of the opposition to government. Since the Prince insisted that those accepting posts from him resign places and give up pensions they held from the King, their commitment to him became all the more noticeable. Bute relinquished a pension from the crown. See A. N. Newman, 'Communication: The Political

Patronage of Frederick Lewis, Prince of Wales', *Historical Journal*, 1 : 1 (1958), pp. 73–5.

70 Waldegrave, 'Memoirs', pp. 163–4. Given this description of him as a 'fine Showy Man', it is interesting that Walpole believed what first commended Bute to the Prince was the Earl's skill at acting 'in private companies with a set of his own relations'. Walpole, *Memoirs of George II*, I, pp. 32–3. Shelburne remembered the same story. Shelburne, 'Autobiography', I, p. 51.

71 See A. Murdoch, 'Lord Bute, James Stuart Mackenzie and the Government of Scotland', in K. W. Schweizer (ed.), *Lord Bute: Essays in Re-interpretation* (Leicester, Leicester University Press, 1988), pp. 119–22.

72 Waldegrave, 'Memoirs', p. 176.

73 See J. L. Bullion, 'The Prince's Mentor: A New Perspective on the Friendship between George III and Lord Bute during the 1750s', *Albion*, 21: 1 (1989), pp. 34–55.

74 There is no hint in Dodington's 'Political Journal' that he was aware Bute was tutoring Prince George secretly. Augusta's efforts at deception were successful. 'She may deceive me', mused Dodington, 'but I am persuaded that she has no fix'd digested political plan at all; or regular communication in politics, with anybody, but Mr [James] Cresset', her private secretary. These exchanges illustrate how carefully and skilfully the Princess kept the reality of Bute's significant influence at Leicester House not only from the prying eyes of enemies, but from friends like Dodington as well. Dodington, 'Political Journal', 21 July 1755, 6 August 1755, pp. 310–11, 317.

75 Augusta called Bute her 'best friend' in an undated letter to him reprinted in R. Sedgwick (ed.), *Letters from George III to Lord Bute, 1756–1766* (London, Macmillan, 1939), p. 4. For an account of how they behaved toward each other in public during 1755–56, see J. L. Bullion, 'The Origins and Significance of Gossip about Princess Augusta and Lord Bute, 1755–1756', *Studies in Eighteenth-Century Culture*, 21 : 1 (1991), pp. 357–8.

76 Walpole, *Memoirs of George II*, II, 151. Clark persuasively argues that Waldegrave was Walpole's source for these observations. 'Introduction', *Waldegrave*, p. 78. See also Brooke's notes on this passage in Walpole's *Memoirs of George II*, pp. 251–2n.

77 An account of their relationship during the two years before George's eighteenth birthday, including a discussion of whether Augusta deliberately risked her reputation, may be found in Bullion, 'The Origins and Significance of Gossip', pp. 245–65.

78 Dodington, 'Political Journal', 15 October 1752, p. 180.

79 The quotation describing this wish of Augusta is from Earl of Bute to Prince George, [June 1755], in Sedgwick (ed.), *Letters from George III to Lord Bute, 1756–1766*, p. liii.

9

Queen Charlotte, 'Scientific Queen'

Clarissa Campbell Orr

I N 1781 a poem appeared in the *Ladies Poetical Magazine*, extolling
Queen Charlotte as a model for other women:

> Happy for England, were each female mind,
> To science more, and less to pomp inclin'd;
> If parents, by example, prudence taught,
> And from their QUEEN the flame of virtue caught!
> Skill'd in each art that serves to polish life,
> Behold in HER a scientifick wife![1]

Charlotte, like her mother-in-law Princess Augusta, was extremely interested in botany and zoology. The Rev. Charles Abbott dedicated his
Flora Bedfordiensis to her in 1798, proclaiming her as 'the first female
Botanist in the wide circle of the British Dominions', and saying his
book was 'For the amusement and instruction of "the fair daughters
of Albion"'.[2] This chapter explores some aspects of Queen Charlotte's
character as a 'scientifick wife'. She was associated with both botany,
a science considered eminently suitable for female study, and with geo-
logy, which played an important role in the critique of Deism throughout Charlotte's reign. I will examine the character of royal patronage
and its parallel with aristocratic patronage, and ask whether and in what
sense a queen had a private life.[3] It will be seen that Charlotte's private
inclinations align her with the Bluestockings and a certain kind of aristocratic counter-culture of rational domesticity, which was at variance
with aristocratic libertinism. However these private interests were not
exclusively private, but linked to the more public role of George III and
Queen Charlotte as patrons of a Christian enlightenment, and to public
representations of exemplary life.

Late Hanoverian court culture also displays an interesting paradox:
that one of the iconic figures of late eighteenth-century botany was
Jean-Jacques Rousseau, advocate of a Spartan austerity, scourge of courts,

apostle of rural simplicity, and prophet of an emotional religiosity that was at best Deistic but never specifically Christian. Rousseau's *Letters on the Elements of Botany*, translated by Thomas Martyn in 1785, was one of the most popular introductions to botany, and was specifically slanted to ladies.[4] That George III, staunch upholder of Christian orthodoxy, should have been induced to pension Rousseau is a paradox that seems to me to have been underestimated. Several people in Queen Charlotte's circle were friends or, more accurately, disciples of Rousseau. These include her Reader, Jean-André DeLuc, who saw her as a figurehead to whom critiques of materialism could be addressed which drew on Swiss, German and Dutch scholars, including those in her Electoral domains; her botanical lecturer, the Dissenter James Edward Smith; and above all her close friends in the Portland and Harcourt households. All in their way had strong ties to Rousseau, yet they managed also to accommodate themselves to the court culture of George III and Queen Charlotte.

Charlotte's opportunities to educate herself in the sciences may first be put into the wider context of how elite women acquired education, learning, or connoisseurship. A university education was the prerogative of men, as was membership of the Inns of Court, but the intellectual depths plumbed by these institutions should not be overestimated. For gentlemen wanting to communicate and deepen their cultural knowledge, there were the learned societies such as the Royal Society, the Society of Antiquaries, the Society of Dilettanti and the Linnaean Society, but these were closed to women.[5]

Most women furthered their cultural interests within the family circle, through shared reading and access to libraries, whether private or commercial. There was always anxiety over the choice and extent of women's reading matter. Part of Fanny Burney's role in Queen Charlotte's household was to vet suitable reading for the princesses, as when she read the bluestocking Cornelia Knight's *Dinarbas* to advise the Queen on whether she should accept a dedication.[6] In the general conduct literature of the period, too much frivolous reading for mere entertainment was deplored, as it led to unrealistic ideas about love and marriage. But too much serious reading risked making a girl unmarriagably learned, as even the Bluestocking Hester Chapone warned.[7] However aristocratic women, as distinct from the middling sort, were often the beneficiaries of a certain kind of insouciance, tolerating a woman's immersion in cultivated leisure. A family tradition of intellectuality or literary patronage could foster a woman's pursuit of culture: the

Duchess of Portland, one of the Queen's closest female friends, was the heir to her father's love of learning as well as his fortune.

Conversely, in an age of aristocratic amateurism, men could be the beneficiary of women's approved leisure interests, especially in the study of the natural sciences. Joseph Banks, future President of the Royal Society and friend and adviser to the royal court in scientific matters, first acquired a taste in botany from books he found on his mother's dressing table.[8] Anne Shteir in her study of eighteenth-century botanical culture argues that Queen Charlotte's interest in botany helped give it social approval for leisured ladies.[9]

These family networks linked women to the world of the learned societies. Sophia Banks, Joseph's sister, was a female virtuoso, a collector of coins and medals and a pioneer collector of ephemera, who bequeathed all her collections to the British Museum. She was a beneficiary of the social dimension to his role as President of the Royal Society, and of the way his home acted as an informal club; his friends recognised her connoisseurship. The young Bluestocking Mary Hamilton, niece of Sir William Hamilton, was for a while sub-governess to the princesses. She was familiar with his learned interests and negotiated the sale of the famous vase to the Duchess of Portland.[10] However both women were aware that some of the male sociability forming the context for learned interests was unavailable to them. It was easier, for instance, for Sophia Banks to share in her brother's social world when he married and thereby tempered his contacts with such notorious free-livers as the Earl of Sandwich.[11] Mary Hamilton was familiar with her uncle's liaison with the famous Emma but could not mingle socially with her; indeed, what she liked, precisely, about being part of Bluestocking circles such as Mrs Vesey's was that

> there too one meets with a charming variety of society that suits any mood one happens to be in; viz: the Learned, the witty, – the old & young, the grave, gay, wise & unwise, the fine bred Man & the pert coxcomb; The elegant female, the chaste Matron, the severe prude, & the pert Miss, but be it remembered that you can run no *risque* in Mrs. Vesey's parties of meeting with those who have no claim to respect, as is too often the case in mixed assemblies in London.[12]

The rational domesticity of the Bluestockings and the world of aristocratic libertinism did not take place in completely water-tight compartments, but the women associated with the former could create a mixed social world that excluded the latter as much as possible.

As Addison had said in *The Spectator*, his aim had been to take philosophy 'out of Closets and Libraries, Schools and Colleges, to dwell in Clubs and Assemblies, at Tea-Tables, and in Coffee-Houses'.[13] Lawrence Klein's analysis of the public sphere shows how much, since the beginning of the eighteenth century, women were expected to be a part of the cultural conversation.[14] As Joanna Marschner shows in this collection, Charlotte's predecessor as consort, Caroline of Anspach, had been renowned for her learning, thereby setting a precedent a generation before Charlotte that a queen could devote her leisure to books.[15] Caroline's rival Henrietta Howard, George II's official mistress, did not attempt to usurp the latter's influence over politics, but her exquisite home Marble Hill House was testament to her association with the world of connoisseurship and taste; Pope extolled her as a woman of reason.[16] Following these earlier examples of greater shared participation in cultivated leisure, Charlotte's reign coincides with the heyday of the Bluestockings, and she was linked with many of them. In entering this world mainly via the Queen's botanical interests, it is worth recalling that Benjamin Stillingfleet, who first wore the informal blue wool stockings to the evening parties which gave the name to the learned and high-minded ladies who hosted them, was a botanist.[17]

Irene Brown has argued that the period 1700–60 sees the emergence of a pattern of family life among the elite which she describes as a culture of rational domesticity. She centres her discussion on Mary Granville, later Mary Delany, a friend and beneficiary of George and Charlotte; on Mrs Delany's sisters; and on her friendships with Margaret Cavendish Harley Bentinck, Duchess of Portland, and other like-minded men and women. These friendships supplemented family ties and sustained individuals through widowhood and other bereavements by the sharing of rational interests such as literary and scientific pursuits within a context of Christian piety. Brown argues that in this world-view reason and emotion were not considered opposed, since the passions could be regulated. Women and men's spheres were not rigidly demarcated, but overlapped; this enabled men and women to meet to a large degree as cultural equals.

Brown sees this heterosociality as in marked contrast to Rousseau's separation of sexual roles and advocacy of a submissive kind of domestic femininity.[18] Yet this misses the fact that Rousseau was seen as an advocate of withdrawal from the pressures of fashionable society; he was therefore understood, probably erroneously, to favour the kind of rational domesticity practised by aristocrats not ambitious for public office, who preferred the private pleasures of landed society to the hurly-burly of place-seeking and fashion. Queen Charlotte's Reader, Jean-André DeLuc, explicitly praised George III and Queen Charlotte for appreciating the delights of domesticity and linked this to Rousseau's advocacy of the simple life.[19]

Irene Brown notes that George and Charlotte gave Mrs Delany an honorary position in their domestic circle, but does not pursue the question of how far a queen like Charlotte could reproduce in her own life this kind of rational domesticity she evidently admired in Mrs Delany's circle. Of course the answer must be that the Queen was immensely constrained by virtue of her role; she could not opt out of public life, as could the Duchess of Portland and her husband, who did not pursue public office. A queen could not choose to avoid public obligations, such as holding drawing rooms, to seclude herself with her friends. And indeed forming friendships was itself immensely problematic for a consort in Britain's parliamentary monarchy: she could not afford to become a partisan of factional politics by the unwise extension of her favour. Charlotte's husband George III created immense difficulties for himself at the start of his reign by seeming to be governed by a favourite, Lord Bute, and the story of his first ten years as King usually concentrates on how he managed to make better ministerial choices and distance himself from Bute.[20] Years later Queen Charlotte recalled to her friend Elizabeth, Lady Harcourt, the advice the King had given to her when she was married:

> I am most truly sensible of the dear king's great strictness, at my arrival in England, to prevent my making many acquaintances: for he always used to say, that, in this Country, it was difficult to know how to draw a line, on account of the Politics of the Country; that there never could be kept up a Society without party, which was always dangerous for any woman to take part in, but particularly so for the Royal Family, & with truth do I assure you, that I am not only sensible that He was right, but I feel thankful for it from the bottom of my Heart.

> The party's at the Queen's House have of course been guided by the Ins and Outs of the moment, by the King's orders, but he allowed & encouraged me to be Civil to all . . .[21]

One way the royal couple resolved this dilemma, of being public monarchs in a parliamentary regime, who needed private moments of respite, was to retreat into the family, and value their opportunities for seclusion from public display (whether at St James's, the Queen's House, or the London theatres), by spending time instead at their residences in Kew and later Windsor. Kew and Windsor functioned in some ways as simple country seats, similar to the country residences of the nobility, such as the Portlands' seat at Bulstrode, or the villas along the Thames belonging to Pope or Horace Walpole.

The contrast between *negotium* and *otium* was a well-worn theme in Horatian literature and its neo-classical manifestations.[22] As John Bullion has explored so thoroughly, George's upbringing had made him accustomed to relative isolation from his contemporaries, and he reproduced this in his own family life–to the extent that he was reluctant to see his daughters marry.[23] There can be no doubt that Queen Charlotte shared this taste for domestic retirement and admired those members of the aristocracy who practised it. Writing to Lady Harcourt in 1794, she described the visitors that year to Weymouth, who included Lord and Lady Burlington, whom she admired for their 'very domestic life, their children live on a very agreeable and easy footing with them, and both He and She are adored by their servants. Is it not a pity, when so much real good unites in Private, that in Public it should be the contrary?'[24]

Another glimpse of the private Charlotte is seen in a short note to her brother Charles: 'Je suis entouré des Papiers, Livres, Enfants, Domestique [sic] etc. ce qui m'oblige à finir' (I am surrounded by Papers, Books, Infants, Domestic matters, which means I will have to sign off).[25] But the royal version of this domestic felicity was, paradoxically, also projected semi-publicly at Windsor through the custom of the evening stroll on the terrace, which permitted informal access to the monarchs. During the 1790s, as George became more popular, one source of this popularity was his reputation in private life as a loyal husband and devoted father. George and his consort were identified with family life and the values of the private sphere – notwithstanding the domestic shortcomings of their elder sons. *Private* royal life therefore contributed to the *public* face of monarchy in the revolutionary decades; it did not stay entirely private.[26]

Queen Charlotte's solution to this publicisation of royal privacy was the purchase of Frogmore in 1790 as a truly private retreat (FIGURE 17).[27] Here she could read in her library of over 4,000 volumes, nearly all of which were her own acquisitions (FIGURE 18), oversee her printing press, botanise, and spend time with her daughters and a chosen few. In August 1803 she wrote to her brother Charles, conjuring up a picture of her pastoral idyll, 'J'ai passé les matins en Companie de mes filles à Frogmore, mon petit Paradis Terrestre, en nous amusent avec une bonne lecture, y travaillant autour d'un grande Table dans le jardin sous

17 *Exterior View of Frogmore House* by Charles Wild, 1819

18 *The Queen's Library* by Charles Wild, 1819

l'ombrre des beauy arbres & moyennant quoi la tems s'est passé plus vitesse que nous n'l'avons même souhaite'. (I've been spending the mornings in the company of my daughters at Frogmore, my little Earthly Paradise, amusing ourselves with a good read, working there around a large table in the garden under the shade of some beautiful trees, and marvelling that the time goes by much more quickly than we would have wished) (FIGURE 19).[28]

19   *Queen Charlotte in the Grounds of Frogmore House* by Sir William Beechey, 1796

Although, especially in the early days of her role as consort, the Queen did not choose her own Ladies in Waiting, in time she was able to exercise more freedom of choice as her judgement matured. And women like Lady Harcourt or the Countess Pembroke, who occupied Household positions, also became really intimate friends. The childless Lady Harcourt was like a second mother to the royal princesses and was a great comfort to the unmarried Augusta and Amelia when their mother died. At Frogmore, and in the company of women like Lady Harcourt, the Queen was able to practise her own version of the rational domesticity described by Irene Brown.

What is missing or only implicit in Brown's account of the ethos of this rational domesticity is the extent to which, in addition to ties of friendship, the aristocratic household had at its disposal a range of posts that could assist in women's self-education: chaplains, librarians, tutors and governesses could all be appointed to provide women and their children with a means to a sustained course of self-development, supplementing the stimulus afforded by close friends and family. Their menfolk also benefited from the assistance of such figures, and indeed a young man on coming into his inheritance would often be in a position to reward a previous tutor or bear-leader with preferment in the church or a household position. As the example of the Poet Laureate, William Whitehead, discussed below shows, a person could combine the benefits of aristocratic patronage with royal recognition. Queen Charlotte's household was in some respects only different in degree, not kind, from this pattern of patronage. Like these aristocratic exemplars of rational domesticity, Queen Charlotte's scientific education was fostered within her private circle; the only difference was that she had slightly more powers of appointment than a peeress. In addition to chaplains, librarians or governesses, the Queen was able to appoint salaried Readers– Jean-André DeLuc in French, Elizabeth de la Fite in German–whose reading out loud while she was having her hair dressed, or in the evenings, would enable her to keep mentally occupied. This chapter suggests that this cultural infrastructure reveals close links between aristocratic and royal protégés, both as an intellectual and a social phenomenon: a matter of overlapping interests and intersecting circles of sociability and patronage.

In exploring the cultural interests and patronage of Queen Charlotte, a final point emerges. It is impossible to keep her life and household in a watertight category, separate from the King's. Yet most recent accounts of either the late Hanoverian aristocracy, some of whom were her Ladies in Waiting, Mistress of the Robes, Master of Horse etc., or of the politics of George's reign, are partial insofar as they both underplay or exclude aspects of court life, and also ignore the role of women. Approaching the question of Hanoverian court culture from a perspective centred on the Queen helps explore these neglected dimensions.

For example, recent discussion of the British aristocracy has skimmed over the importance of court office, or looked at it more from the viewpoint of the aristocracy than the monarch. John Cannon comments, 'throughout the century there remained considerable ambiguity about the extent to which the government was royal or ministerial', and shows the high proportion of peers who were crown supporters in George III's reign, approximating 60 per cent. But in his portrayal of the aristocratic century, the King is a passive and silent figure, not a partner in a dynamic and fluid relationship with his peers.[29] Ultimately however, positions at court, in diplomacy, the armed forces, at Westminster and in the Lord Lieutenancies, turn on the King's powers of appointment or advancement. In spite of the fact that the British aristocracy had an institutional basis of their own in the House of Lords and enormous influence over the House of Commons, the King still had to manage his elite in a personal manner.[30]

Conversely, gaining, obtaining or resigning a position in the royal household, such as Lord Chamberlain, or Groom of the Bedchamber, or Governor to royal children, might be a part of an aristocratic family's calculation as to how to manage its resources and position, and maintain careers in public life. The examples of aristocratic lives touched on here show that typically a man could move between, and combine, a household position, a diplomatic post or an office of state; or else reject all these options to lead a 'private' life, largely residing on the country estate, practising philanthropy and following artistic, scientific or antiquarian interests.

Crown–elite relations were therefore personal relations and family relations: how, for example, could a father's relationship with his monarch, for good or ill, bias the opportunities open to his son; and how much loyalty to a father or reaction to his views affected generational choices?[31] Now, in addition to factoring in positions at court to a fuller consideration of the way the aristocracy maximised their advantages, let us factor in the dimension of gender. What difference might it make for an ambitious peer to have a mother or wife in close attendance on the Queen? How would the combined family interests of both sexes be affected by political differences between males – the King and his peers? This question is not easy to answer because of the relative neglect of aristocratic women by historians. Aristocratic women, aside from accounts of a handful of individuals,[32] are so absent from discussions of eighteenth-century aristocratic life, that one might almost think the aristocracy married faceless dolls and reproduced by parthenogenesis.[33] The work of Elaine Chalus in particular is beginning to change this, and the social and familial dimensions to politics are being better comprehended.[34] This process needs I believe to be completed by a fuller understanding of how entire families participated in court life as well as Westminster politics. How does the picture change if we consider what position a mother, wife, sister or daughter of a leading aristocrat might hold? Are there tensions between partners or generations? And might common cultural interests override or mitigate political differences? Finally, how does the 'cultural infrastructure' of an aristocratic household–its librarians, chaplains, tutors – mesh in with the cultural interests of the court? The example of the Portland and Harcourt connections illustrates these questions, and underlines, I believe, the usefulness of taking a cross-section across an entire family, to include male and female members in successive generations, instead of concentrating mainly on men in office, in order to understand court culture as a whole.

Although it was not until a full thirty years after her marriage that the Queen was able to purchase Frogmore, she had always been the beneficiary of her mother-in-law's work at Kew. After her widowhood, Augusta had continued to develop the gardens, with the assistance of Bute. Bute's interests in natural history, especially botany, were deep-rooted. He had studied in Leyden and had been both critic and advocate of the Linnaean system of classification since the 1740s.[35] After Bute's retirement from politics, one of his main occupations was the cultivation of his various scientific interests. He was widely respected among the informally organised circle of botanical experts in mid-eighteenth-century Britain. He laboured for years over his own botanical tables and in 1784 was given permission to dedicate them to Queen Charlotte, noting that the work was composed 'solely for the Amusement of the Fair Sex under the Protection of your Royal name'.[36] He acted as a patron to several botanical artists and writers, and it would only be natural for him to pass on recommendations to others, and for Queen Charlotte to consult Bute when she felt the need to have someone in her household to further her interests in natural science. In 1774 she appointed Jean-André DeLuc as her Reader, probably on Bute's recomendation. After ending his association with Kew, Bute concentrated more on his fossil and mineral collection, and here DeLuc would have been of great assistance, since he was primarily a geologist.[37] Alternatively, DeLuc's appointment as Reader may have come about through meeting the former diplomat Lord Holdernesse, who became governor to the Prince of Wales and the Duke of York in 1771. Holdernesse was an opera enthusiast, a member of the Dilettante Society, and ecclesiastical patron of the Rev. William Mason, whose influence at Frogmore we shall explore below.[38]

Jean-André DeLuc (1727–1817) was a native of Geneva. He came from the middling orders of Genevan society, of a family of watchmakers and instrument makers, who also had full citizenship within Geneva's complex republican constitution. His father, Jacques-François, and his brother, Guillaume-Antoine DeLuc, were both prosperous enough to be active in politics and to pursue philosophical and scientific interests in addition to their skilled trade. The family represented far better than did Jean-Jacques Rousseau's own rather bohemian father the kind of well-read artisan-citizen idealised by Rousseau in his *Confessions*. They were central figures in the welcome given by the middling sort in Geneva to Rousseau when he resumed his citizenship, and their party, the Répresentants, were his political advocates when the ruling elite in Geneva orchestrated the banning of Rousseau's *Emile* and *Social Contract*.[39] Rousseau was their cultural hero because he had taken issue with the francophile tastes of the elite and publicly disagreed with D'Alembert when his *Encyclopédie* article on Geneva suggested the city drop its ban on the theatre.[40] The defeat of the Représentant party by the ruling oligarchy in 1765 after some initial success against their control seems to have played a part in DeLuc's decision to leave Geneva, and he was evidently able to accommodate himself comfortably to a court culture linked to a parliamentary monarchy.[41]

Jean-André DeLuc was representative of Geneva's unique position in the European Enlightenment, as a francophone society that rejected the Deism of the Paris Enlightenment, although devoted to rational philosophy.[42] One has to feel sympathetic to the position of the Genevan elite and clerical intelligentsia when not one intellectual giant and literary celebrity, but two, chose to come there: Voltaire settled there permanently in 1754, first at Les Délices, then at Ferney, and Rousseau visited and reclaimed his citizenship in the same year. This must have been a little like having two nuclear reactors, neither of which could be accounted entirely safe, located nearby. While the oligarchical elite flocked delightedly to Voltaire's private theatricals, the middling sort followed the line taken by Rousseau.[43] The DeLucs went on boating expeditions around Lake Geneva, inadvertently inspiring their friend to set *La Nouvelle Eloise* in these surroundings, and thus fostered Rousseau's growing interests in botany. After all the cordiality of Rousseau's visit to his birthplace and resumption of citizenship, which they had so actively promoted after Rousseau had again been received into the Reformed Church, they were appalled six years later by the heterodox religious views expressed by Rousseau's mouthpiece in *Emile*, the Savoyard priest, and only felt able to resume contact with their hero when he was received as a communicant in nearby Motiers.[44]

Jean-André DeLuc was meanwhile studying the physical geography of the Alps with a view to understanding how the earth's surface had developed. When he came to England he wrote the first sketch of his theory of earth's development and dedicated it to Queen Charlotte: *Lettres Physiques et Morales sur les Montagnes, et sur l'Histoire de la Terre, Adressées à la Reine de la Grande Bretagne.*[45] Much of it consisted of topographical descriptions which provided his geological evidence— but this gave him the opportunity of writing letters to his queen about her electoral lands in Hanover, which she had never seen, and describing its social customs, mineral wealth, and university at Göttingen. Additionally, there were hundreds of pages of discourses on his philosophy of science and his metaphysics, as well as a critical appraisal of all existing geological theories, and the explanation of his own, and of how it accorded with the scriptural account. A central feature of this additional philosophical discussion was his refutation of the materialism professed in France by Helvétius and in Britain by Hartley and Priestley.

In this critique, the insights provided by Rousseau were indispensable. DeLuc was able to make use of Rousseau's annotations of Helvétius' controversial text, *De L'Esprit*, published after Rousseau's death by Victor Louis Dutens, a protégé of Bute's brother, James Stuart Mackenzie.[46] DeLuc's letters to Queen Charlotte reflect the dilemma visited on many of Rousseau's admirers by his paradoxical religious views. On the one hand he seemed to provide them with a religiosity, a spiritual conviction determinedly opposed to the materialist view that man was just a mechanistic bundle of sensations. In the contemplation of natural beauty in the Swiss mountains, amidst people with simple customs and manners, both DeLuc and Rousseau were convinced that man's soul was a palpable entity. DeLuc rhapsodised over this simplicity of living in the Swiss valleys, believing it held the key to happiness, and wrote to Charlotte that she was well placed, even in her elevated rank, to appreciate the blessings of domestic contentment.[47] On the other hand, it could not be denied that Rousseau fell short in his Christian convictions, even though he had set himself against the atheism of his Parisian associates with the *Encyclopédie*. However, DeLuc wrote to Charlotte, Rousseau really did respect Christianity from the bottom of his heart. What had gone wrong was that Rousseau had wanted to weaken the freethinkers' objections to Christianity by showing that some of what they objected to, especially a tendency to literalism, was not essential doctrine: and in the process Rousseau had become contaminated by their own doubts.[48] Hence the unorthodox aspects of *Emile*, which DeLuc believed had been adequately answered by another Genevan now in Britain, Antoine Roustan, who had left controversy behind him when his critical appraisal of Rousseau had been burnt by the Genevan authorities and he was appointed Swiss pastor in London.[49] This suggests that, as for so many, before he was made into a cult figure by French republicans, Rousseau represented an ally against the worst tendencies of the French Enlightenment, even if his religious orthodoxy was a problem.

DeLuc's concern to provide a modern yet Christian account of earth history also suggests that a generation before the French Revolution and the anti-Jacobin attack on the *philosophes*, George III's court saw itself as a centre of Protestant Enlightenment, with contacts to like-minded writers and scholars in Germany, including the electoral university in Hanover, who were on guard against the tendency toward Deism or materialism.[50] The outbreak of the French Revolution only confirmed long-standing concerns about the trends undermining established religion. Certainly the Queen was in no doubt when she wrote to her brother in December 1789 that 'la manque de Principe et l'oubli de tout devoir vis à vis de Dieu et de l'Homme et la manque de la Religion est regardé comme bon cause des Malheurs de nos voisins'. (lack of principle, forgetting all duties to God and Man, and lack of Religion, is seen as the main reason for the distresses amongst our neighbours).[51] We would probably be more aware of this aspect of Hanoverian court culture had the King's planned chapel dedicated to revealed religion been completed. This religious and intellectual stance would then have had its architectural and visual embodiment, with an ambitious cycle of paintings by Benjamin West. As it turned out, George III was already falling out of sympathy with the *Sturm und Drang* character of West's mature style when his permanent collapse in health halted the scheme altogether. The site for the planned chapel was incorporated by the Prince of Wales into the Waterloo chamber, a testament to the military rather than the metaphysical triumphs of the crown.[52]

Although it lacked tangible embodiment in bricks and mortar, the association of Charlotte's entourage with the defence of Christian philosophy against Deism and atheism was a significant element of the court's intellectual outlook.

When Rousseau had actually visited England, he had made personal contact with two people who were to be great friends of Queen Charlotte: the Duchess of Portland, and George Simon, Earl Harcourt. While he was in Derbyshire Rousseau occupied himself with botanical walks, and some of the best-known botanical amateurs of the day visited him. Among them was the Duchess of Portland, who was staying with Rousseau's neighbour Bernard Granville.[53] His sister was Mrs Delany, the cultivated widow and amateur botanical artist who shared the Duchess's home. The Duchess and Rousseau corresponded about plant specimens and botanical systems. He told her how botany kept him from thinking of his woes, and signed his letters to her and to Bernard Granville 'L'Herboriste de Mme la Duchesse de Portland'. Despite his resistance to patronage, Rousseau always got on well with grand aristocratic women, either side of the Channel. The correspondence continued after his return to France, with his sending her specimens and the Duchess sending him William Mason's poem *The English Garden*, which will be further discussed further below.[54]

The Duchess of Portland (1715–85) was the leading female connoisseur and scientific amateur of her day. At her death when her collections were auctioned they amounted to over 4,000 lots, in categories including collections of minerals, fossils, shells, insects, birds, and their nests and eggs.[55] Traditions of aristocratic learning were well-established in her family, for her father was the bibliophile and collector Edward Harley, Earl of Oxford, son of Queen Anne's Lord Treasurer. Unlike his father, Queen Anne's Lord Treasurer, the second Lord Harley kept out of politics and pursued a life of cultivated leisure instead. His daughter educated herself, like so many women of her rank, largely through her own reading and through social contact with her parents' friends. Her husband William Bentinck, 2nd Duke of Portland, followed this pattern of eschewing political office in favour of a cultured private life enriched by a select circle of friends. Although the marriage of the Duke and Duchess began as an arranged one, it soon developed into an exemplary companionate marriage. The whole household was the matrix in which Elizabeth Montagu, the Queen of the Bluestockings, developed her own literary leanings and learnt how a household could become a centre for female intellectuality.[56]

The Duchess's household included several people who helped her develop her scholarly and scientific interests. Among them was the Anglo-Saxon scholar Elizabeth Elstob, who had been discovered living under straitened means as a dame-school teacher.[57] The Duchess made her governess to her daughters, and evidently hoped that she would enjoy conversations with Elstob on their antiquarian interests, but evidently Elstob became too absorbed in caring for the young girls for this.[58] One of them, Elizabeth, who became Viscountess Weymouth and later Marchioness of Bath on her marriage, spent a lifetime as a courtier, first as one of Queen Charlotte's first Ladies of the Bedchamber, and subsequently as her Mistress of the Robes.[59]

Another protégé of the Portlands was the clergyman naturalist John Lightfoot (1735–88), who was appointed domestic chaplain to the now widowed Duchess in 1767, just when the Duchess was corresponding with Rousseau. Lightfoot, who became a founder member of the Linnaean Society, was principally involved with arranging and cataloguing her natural history collections. The steward and the gardener were also made part of this study, and were invited to the drawing room discussions alongside guests of higher rank but with the same interests. Mrs Delany described the breakfast room at Bulstrode, the country seat, as so littered with botanical specimens and paraphernalia that it was impossible to sit down. The Duchess welcomed specimens from far afield and was eager to hear of the results of the first expedition of Captain Cook, which included her friends Joseph Banks and Daniel Solander. Lightfoot's botanical tours were nearer home, to Scotland, to Wales, where he accompanied Banks, and to the West Country, where the Bluestocking Frances Boscawen, wife to the Admiral, helped make arrangements for him.[60]

Lightfoot was directly introduced to the Queen by Frances Burney, although Charlotte must have been familiar with his work for the Duchess from her many visits to Bulstrode, which was within easy enough reach for the King and Queen to visit on very easy, informal terms. Mrs Delany describes for instance the occasion when George III strolled unnoticed into the long gallery where she and the Duchess were busy to tell them of the birth of Princess Amelia.[61] When Lightfoot died, George III bought his herbarium for the Queen and it was installed in its twenty-four mahogany cabinets at Frogmore. A few years later another Portland protégé, Bishop Goodenough, who ran the school at Ealing attended by the Duchess's grandsons and who had co-founded the Linnaean Society, was consulting the herbarium. He advised Queen Charlotte that it needed repair.[62] The task was given to the botanist J. E. Smith, a co-founder of the Linnaean Society, and author of the 36-volume *English Botany*.[63] Women were not formal members of the society, but instead their botanical interests could be nourished by the lectures Smith gave at his house in Chelsea, which the Duchess of Portland among others attended.

Instead of attending this kind of informal, semi-public seminar, once Smith was working at Frogmore the Queen asked him to provide some private sessions for her and the princesses. His account of these occasions sheds light on the methodical attention Charlotte gave to her botanical studies: the repair of the herbarium, he explained,

> led to his frequent invitation as a visitor at Frogmore, and to a regular course of conversations, rather than lectures, on botany and zoology, which her majesty, and the Princesses Augusta and Elizabeth honoured with their diligent attention; the queen regularly taking notes of every lecture which she read over aloud at its conclusion, to prevent mistake.[64]

However Smith also gives us a clear instance of how the connection of botany to Rousseau could be productive of tension, especially during the 1790s, when even liberal and enlightened England became wary of French influences. Smith was a Unitarian dissenter from Norwich, a city which included many sympathisers to the French Revolution among its citizens. He was a great disciple of Rousseau; when he visited France in 1786 he paid a call on Thérèse, his hero's widow. When he wrote up his account of these travels in 1793, he said how delighted he was to find that Rousseau had become a hero to the Genevan republic which had rejected him, with his portrait in every window and his songs sung in the streets. 'I respect him', he wrote,

> as a writer eminently favourable on the whole to the interests of humanity, reason, and religion. Wherever he goes counter to any of these, I as freely dissent from him; but do not on that account throw all his works into the fire . . . Nor can any defects or inconsistencies in the private character of Rousseau, depreciate the refined moral and religious principles with which his works abound . . .[65]

According to his wife, these sentiments, and his description of Marie Antoinette as a Messalina, gave offence to the royal family, and relations rapidly cooled. The second edition of the travel account supposedly removed the remarks. In fact, Marie Antoinette is not described as a Messalina in either edition, and Smith speaks as much about the profligate court of Louis XV as the hedonism of Marie Antoinette's. The comments on Rousseau are identical in both editions, but his stout avowal that the Revolution was really a noble spectacle, when the people burst their chains in the name of God and nature, must have been what he was later told was 'injurious in these times to crowned heads'. His wife believed that 'Her Majesty's mind was prejudiced against him by one who had been a mutual friend, but whose personal contests with

Rousseau had warped his judgement': almost certainly, I suggest, this was DeLuc, now ever more persuaded that the French Revolution had come about as a result of a hideous conspiracy between Freemasons and *philosophes* to destroy throne and altar.[66]

If King George purchased the Lightfoot herbal for the Queen, so continuing the link with the Portlands, it is also well known how he and the Queen provided a home at Windsor for Mrs Delany, the Duchess's great friend, after her death in 1785, until Mrs Delany herself died. Opie's portrait of her hung in Queen Charlotte's bedroom at her London house, and she began a herbal in imitation of the exquisite paper cutouts Mrs Delany had invented.[67] DeLuc assisted her with arranging plants on a black background. Later he helped with her botanical painting, and together they wrote to Prince Charles of Mecklenburg-Strelitz, specifying the exact kind of artist's colours they required which were obtainable in Nuremburg.[68]

Queen Charlotte and King George therefore had close ties of friendship with the Portland women, mother and daughter, and their protégés. Yet the Duchess's son and Lady Weymouth's brother, William, 3rd Duke of Portland, illustrates a different aspect of court culture. The Duke was the King's Lord Chamberlain in 1765, and an associate of the Rockingham Whigs. He married Lady Dorothy Cavendish, only daughter of the 4th Duke of Devonshire, and thereby became closely associated with the Whig opposition to Lords Grafton and North. By 1783 he was the head of the notorious Fox–North coalition ministry which the King felt had been forced upon him, and which he managed to dismiss quickly in favour of one headed by William Pitt. Portland remained nominally head of the Rockingham Whigs, but mainly devoted himself to his musical interests. Fox and Burke were the tacticians and chief personalities of the group. By 1794, Portland's disenchantment with the French Revolution led him to a rapprochement with Pitt, and he took office as Home Secretary. This brief account of Portland as a Westminster politician suggests a man in opposition to his monarch for nearly thirty years. Yet this political opposition must have been tempered by the friendship of the King and the Queen with his mother and sister, by the common interests they all had in music, and by shared patronage to Charles Burney, who regularly spent his summers at Bulstrode with the Duke.

The other example I want to explore of shared scientific and literary interests between the Queen and the aristocracy is the Harcourt family, who over several generations moved between on the one hand political and cultural opposition to the monarch, and on the other, service in the Hanoverian court coupled with confidential friendship. The letters between Charlotte and the Harcourts give us one of the best glimpses, too, of the Queen in her private moments.

The Harcourt family had Anglo-Norman roots and continued to have contact with the French branch of the family, whom they helped when they emigrated after the French Revolution. Simon, Earl Harcourt (1714–77), succeeded his grandfather, Lord Chancellor, as Viscount in 1727. He was Lord of the Bedchamber in 1735 to George II, was at his side at the Battle of Dettingen, and briefly became governor to George III when Prince of Wales.[69] At the start of the new reign he was the Ambassador Extraordinary to Mecklenburg to arrange Charlotte's marriage, marrying her by proxy. When the coronation took place, his daughter Lady Elizabeth was one of the Queen's trainbearers. Harcourt's role was rewarded by appointments as Master of the Horse to the Queen (1761) and Lord Chamberlain (1763). He then served as French Ambassador, and as Lord Lieutenant of Ireland. However, his son George Simon, 2nd Earl Harcourt, (1736–1809), felt his father's distinguished service had been insufficiently recognised, and he did not immediately follow the traditions of courtiership and public office. As a young MP he had already supported the radical hero Wilkes, much to his father's embarrassment; he did not have his father's or brother's robust health, suited to a military career; and already on his Grand Tour, which had included various German courts with a view to impressing George II, he had evinced a distaste for the petty formality of German court life, and perhaps also a reaction against court life in general. Rousseau's indictment of artifice in modern life must therefore have appealed deeply to him. He chose to pursue his private interests as a connoisseur and well-regarded amateur artist. His father was one of the founder-members of the Society of Dilettanti, and had moved the family seat from the old manor at Stanton Harcourt to a new home at Nuneham Courtenay.[70]

The 2nd Earl continued to beautify the house and garden, assisted by his cultured cousin and wife Elizabeth Vernon. Where his father had benefited from 'Athenian' Stuart's advice in the interiors, the son relied on Paul Sandby, who designed a mantelpiece for the house, and taught etching to his patron. Together with his brother Thomas, and their cousins George and William, the Sandbys were extremely successful in obtaining patronage from the royal family, but not from George and Charlotte so much as from George III's brothers, the Dukes of Cumberland and Gloucester, although both Paul and Thomas were founder members of George's Royal Academy.[71] Paul Sandby's introduction to George Simon Harcourt was probably through William

Whitehead, the poet, who had been at Winchester School with Paul's cousin George.[72]

Whitehead was made Poet Laureate in 1757 but was as much the house poet of the Harcourt and Villiers families as he was part of royal literary culture.[73] His position illustrates the parallel between aristocratic and royal entourages and the interconnections between royal and aristocratic patronage. His appointment, together with the sinecures of secretary and registrar of the Order of the Bath, was effected by two aristocratic women: Lady Jersey, wife of the 3rd Earl Villiers, and her relative, the Duchess of Newcastle. The latter's husband was then Lord Chamberlain, whose office controlled appointments to the Laureate-ship. Lady Jersey wanted to reward Whitehead, who had tutored her son George Bussy Villiers, the 4th Earl, at Cambridge, and had then acted as bear-leader to him and to the young George Simon Harcourt on their Grand Tour (1754–56). The Harcourts and Villiers were neighbouring Oxfordshire families.[74] Although Whitehead wrote his quota of occasional poetry to celebrate royal occasions, he spent most of his time in residence in his patrons' London or Oxfordshire houses. He composed various odes to be inscribed on urns in the flower garden at Nuneham Courtenay, commemorating the Harcourts' friends. The entrance to the garden was inscribed with Rousseau's saying 'Si l'auteur de la nature est grand dans les grandes choses, il est très grand dans les petites', and there was also a bust of Rousseau with an admiring inscription by Brooke Boothby, friend and fellow-admirer of Rousseau.[75]

Horace Walpole considered this garden of sensibility to be most beautiful garden in England; his friend William Mason, clergyman, aesthete, and garden theorist, was Harcourt's principal adviser in devising it. His curate Christopher Alderson was then Queen Charlotte's main adviser at Frogmore, and followed Mason's principles.[76] However it would be false to infer an uninterrupted connection between the Harcourts and the royal family through common interests in gardening. At the beginning of the reign, just as Harcourt was politically at odds with the crown, so Mason and Walpole were at odds with Sir William Chambers, the creator of the buildings at Kew. Mason's 'An Heroic Epistle' was a critique of Chambers's *Dissertation on Oriental Gardening*, suggesting that Chambers was unEnglish, bent on ruining Queen Caroline's garden, and fostering 'Asiatic' or despotic tendencies in George III.[77]

While Earl Harcourt was keeping his distance from court circles, in the 1770s, he was not simply indulging in aesthetic pursuits: he was also discovering the pleasures and obligations of philanthropy. This awakening of social conscience he ascribed not to Christian precepts, to the dismay of Whitehead, but to Rousseau.[78] As he wrote to Frances Poole, Viscountess Palmerston, a close confidante:

> The Nuneham Life is too public and too bustling for me, and nothing but the attention I give the poor villagers could have kept me here until now, for that is the only amusement I have; they have reason to bless Jean Jacques, for to him alone, not to me have they any obligation, as but for his writings I might have still left them in the misery and sickness they have for so many years been a prey to; nearer observation, and all the scenes I am dayly [sic] witness to, have entirely cured me of vanity, and whenever I return from their cottages, I feel ashamed and hurt at silver dishes, and gilt ceilings.[79]

Harcourt and his wife instituted a Rousseauesque spinning festival at Nuneham, which combined prizes for craftmanship with annual merit awards to virtuous villagers. Their names were then inscribed in church, and their cottages adorned with a letter M for merit. William Combe, gentleman turned literary hack, who attended this festival in 1794, thought that it meant 'there is a moral charm attached to Nuneham, which more than rivals all its natural beauties'.[80] A few years later Hannah More, who would have been horrified at the Rousseauesque rather than the Christian inspiration for the Harcourts' village philanthropy, extolled the Harcourts in her *Strictures on Female Education* (1799) as just the kind of responsible aristocracy – residing on their estates and taking notice of their parishioners – who should be a model for young women in their conduct and choice of husband.[81]

Lord Harcourt maintained an admiration for Rousseau throughout his life. He was one of the first to call on him when he took refuge in England in 1766. When Rousseau decided to leave the country, it was Harcourt who helped with the purchase of his collection of prints, just as Dutens had bought the books.[82] One of the prints which Rousseau kept, however, was an engraving of a Ramsay portrait of George III. Harcourt retained some contact with Rousseau after he returned to France, and kept prints at Nuneham Courtenay of Rousseau's house at Motiers, and of his tomb at Ermenonville. A replica of his death-mask was in his study, and Thérèse sent him Rousseau's own copy of Tasso as a momento.

It is of course tantalising to wonder what Queen Charlotte knew and thought of the Harcourts' admiration for Rousseau. Her brother Charles, the ruling Duke of Mecklenburg-Strelitz after 1794, may have predisposed her in his favour. Charles had studied at Geneva in 1758 and had become acquainted with Rousseau's ideas then. He was interested in landscape garden, and admired his sister's splendid domain at Kew; he hired an English landscape gardener, Thompson, to design the park at his country estate of Hohenzieritz. As late as 1796, Duke Charles instigated a Rousseauesque festival for the local population by a consecrated forest altar in this garden.[83]

After Rousseau's death in 1778, George III continued to pay Rousseau's pension to his widow, Thérèse, but according to Fanny Burney in 1785 he considered Rousseau to be full of 'savage pride and insolent gratitude'.[84] Just at this time the Queen and George III made their first visit to Nuneham Courtenay,[85] so they would have seen the tributes to him in the flower garden and the mementoes in the house. All we do know is that once the Harcourts were reconciled to the court, after about six years absence, they became extremely confidential friends.[86] Lord Harcourt became Master of the Horse to the Queen, and his brother, General Harcourt, was a Groom of the Bedchamber to George III at the very sensitive time when the King was ill in 1788, and was therefore able to control access to and information about the king.[87] Lady Harcourt was not only a Lady of the Bedchamber,[88] but a personal friend in whom Charlotte could truly confide. Lady Harcourt recalled:

> Her confidence she imparted to few, from a strong fear lest she should be suspected of favouritism. She judged characters quickly and truly, and her warm heart was truly attached to those who she felt loved the individual as much as they respected the Queen. I remember once my saying to her, 'I should like to tell *you* something, but pray promise never to let the *Queen* know it.' She laughed, and said, 'Oh no, *she* can have no business with what passes between us in our private, unreserved conversation'.[89]

Lady Harcourt's words indicate the constant restraint and self-possession required of a consort who constantly, by virtue of her role, had to think carefully of what she said and to whom she was speaking. Perhaps this explains Charlotte's attraction to a couple who by contrast had opted out of the proprieties and formalities of court life for a while, and in Rousseau's style made a cult of friendship and effusive tenderness.

The Queen admired the way that Lady Harcourt had created 'your little Paradise, Nuneham',[90] and this outstanding example of a country retreat whose owners devoted themselves to cultivated leisure and philanthropy must have been an inspiration to Charlotte in acquiring Frogmore and making it her own version of a terrestrial paradise.[91] Once it was hers, as we have seen, she lost no time in gaining advice from a Harcourt protégé in designing the garden. The Queen also admired Lady Harcourt's literary gifts. She used to write verses to hang on busts in the garden to greet her friends, like Mrs Montagu. The Queen asked Lady Harcourt to compose a little tableau for the royal children to perform to celebrate their father's accession day in 1785. Fifteen years later she contributed a song, at Princess Elizabeth's request, for the fête held at Frogmore to celebrate the King's escape from a shot fired at the theatre. And was there a trace of wistfulness in the Queen's request that Lady Harcourt send her the collection of verses she and friends had composed one day with the requirement that each poem had to include the six words 'marvellous', 'when', 'robin' 'modest', 'friend' and 'abstruse'? Did Charlotte wish for the kind of opportunity to play these literary games at a private house party?[92]

Unfortunately, because the private papers in royal hands were almost entirely destroyed after her death, there are only hints and scraps such as these which give us the opportunity to try to gauge the nature of the Queen's private life, and to trace the nature of her literary and scientific interests. The physical evidence of her retreats such as the cottage at Kew or the altered and restored Frogmore also give us some idea of the setting in which these tastes were pursued (Plate 5). But of her library of over 4,000 volumes, nearly all of which were purchased by herself,[93] only the catalogue remains. From this we can see that she possessed most of the key works of Rousseau: the *Lettre à Mr. D'Alembert*, which discussed his ideas about the theatre; the *Discourse on Inequality amongst Mankind*; the educational treatise *Emile*; his *Letter to the Archbishop of Paris*, in which he answered the strictures against *Emile*; a German edition of *La Nouvelle Eloise; The Social Contract*; and two English translations of his *Letters on the Elements of Botany*.[94] But what did she *really* think of them? That we shall never know. But perhaps it is fitting that a queen, who by virtue of her position had restricted opportunities for privacy, should retain some secrets from the historian.

Notes

Quotations from material from the Royal Archives are with gracious permission of Her Majesty the Queen. I also wish to thank Lady Sheila de Bellaigue and her staff for their help in providing material. I am indebted to the Hon. Mrs C. Gascoigne for kindly letting me use the Harcourt Mss at Stanton Harcourt. I am grateful to James Raven, Felicia Gordon, Robert Wokler and Nigel Aston for helpful comments on various drafts of this chapter.

1 Cited in Anne Shteir, *Cultivating Women, Cultivating Science: Flora's Daughters and Botany in England 1760–1860*, Baltimore, Johns Hopkins University Press, 1996, p. 36, and discussion pp. 36–7. I am grateful to Anne Shteir for sharing this reference with me in advance of her book's publication.

2 Cited in Olwen Hedley, *Queen Charlotte*, London, John Murray, 1975, p. 309, and Shteir, *Cultivating Women*, p. 21.

3 These leisure interests are also related to the educational programmes she had for her children, especially her daughters, which I can only touch on briefly here. See especially note 64 below.

4 Shteir, *Cultivating Women*, pp. 18–21.

5 George III's new Royal Academy was not closed to women; both Mary Moser and Angelica Kaufman, the two female founder members, were beneficiaries of the Queen's patronage.

6 'From the time that the Queen condescended to desire to place me in immediate attendance upon her own person, I had always secretly concluded she meant me for her English Reader', Fanny Burney wrote in her diary, Wednesday 17 August 1786. *Diary and Letters of Madame D'Arblay, as edited by her niece Charlotte Barrett*, preface and notes by Austin Dobson, 6 vols, London, 1904, III, p. 5.

7 See Hester Chapone, *Letters on the Improvement of the Mind, addressed to a Young Lady*, 1773, cited in Vivien Jones, ed., *Women in the Eighteenth Century*, London, Routledge, 1990, pp. 104–6.

8 John Gascoigne, *Joseph Banks and the English Enlightenment*, Cambridge, Cambridge University Press, 1998.

9 Shteir, *Cultivating Women*, pp. 35–7; see also pp. 50–7.

10 Elizabeth and Florence Anson, *Mary Hamilton . . . From Letters and Diaries*, London, John Murray, 1925, pp. 132–3; Ruth Hayden, *Mrs Delany: Her Life and Her Flowers*, London, British Museum Publications, 1988, pp. 127–9.

11 Gascoigne, *Joseph Banks*, ch. 3; also idem, forthcoming entry on Sophia Banks in *New Dictionary of National Biography*. My thanks to John Gascoigne for showing this to me in advance of publication.

12 Anson, *Mary Hamilton*, p. 132.

13 Cited from *The Spectator*, no. 10, by Lawrence Klein, 'Gender, Conversation and the Public Sphere in Early Eighteenth-Century England', in Judith Still and Michael Worton, eds, *Textuality and Sexuality: Reading Theories and Practices*, Manchester, Manchester University Press, 1993, pp. 100–15.

14 Klein, 'Gender, Conversation and the Public Sphere'.

15 Stephen Taylor, 'Queen Caroline and the Church of England', in S. Taylor, R. Connors and C. Jones, eds, *Hanoverian Britain and Empire*, Woodbridge, Boydell Press, 1998, is the most recent discussion of the Queen's leaning and theological interests.

16 Julius Bryant, *Mrs Howard: A Woman of Reason*, London, English Heritage, 1988.

17 See *DNB* and Shteir, *Cultivating Women*, p. 18.

18 Irene Q. Brown, 'Domesticity, Feminism, and Friendship: Female Aristocratic Culture and Marriage in England, 1660–1760', *Journal of Family History*, 7 : 4 (1982), pp. 406–24.

19 See note 47 below.

20 Richard Pares, *George III and the Politicians*, Oxford, Oxford University Press, 1953, reprinted 1988, being the *locus classicus*.

21 Edward William Harcourt, *The Harcourt Papers*, 14 vols, privately printed, Oxford, 1880–1905, VI, pp. 109–10.

22 Maren-Softe Røstvig, *The Happy Man, Vol. II, 1700–1760*, 2nd edn, Oslo, Universitetsforlaget, 1971. The invocation of rural retreat was also the prerogative of the

happy woman, as the example of the Duchess of Portland attests; when her son inherited, she arranged with him to keep Bulstrode for herself. Elizabeth Montagu, the future Queen of the Blues, saw Bulstrode as the embodiment of the Horatian ideal; even if women read the classics only in translation, they could still interpret their experience through the classical idiom. Sylvia Harcstark Myers, *The Bluestocking Circle*, Oxford, Clarendon Press, 1990, ch. 1.

23 John Bullion, ' "George, Be a King!" The Relationship between Princess Augusta and George III', in Taylor, Connors and Jones, eds, *Hanoverian Britain and Empire*.

24 *Harcourt Papers*, VI, pp. 43–4.

25 Royal Archives (RA), Georgian Add. MSS 21/121, Undated letter from Queen Charlotte to Prince Charles of Mecklenburg-Strelitz.

26 Marilyn Morris, *The British Monarchy and the French Revolution*, New Haven, Yale University Press, 1998.

27 Hedley, *Charlotte*, pp. 179–90.

28 RA, Add. MSS 21/121, Letter from Queen Charlotte to Prince Charles of Mecklenburg-Strelitz, 3 August 1803.

29 John Cannon, *Aristocratic Century*, Cambridge, Cambridge University Press, 1984, p. 103. Michael Bush, *The English Aristocracy*, Manchester, Manchester University Press, 1984, makes no mention of the eighteenth-century court, believing the conflict with royal absolutism in the seventeenth century to have settled the matter of crown/aristocratic relations. On p. 125 he talks of the 'stable relationship between government and aristocracy, sustained by royal patronage' but does not explore the dynamics of this patronage.

30 The British position may therefore resemble that of the Habsburgs, where the social relationship between the ruler and the grandees in the component parts of the Austrian monarchy is paramount, more than is usually assumed. See R. J. W. Evans, *The Making of the Habsburg Monarchy 1550–1700: An Interpretation*, Oxford, Clarendon Press, 1979.

31 L. G. Mitchell, *Charles James Fox*, Harmondsworth, Penguin Books, 1997, explores the importance of family tradition in shaping Fox's career and relationship to George III.

32 Notably Frances Harris, *The Life of Sarah, Duchess of Marlborough*, Oxford, Oxford University Press, 1991; also Amanda Foreman, *Georgiana, Duchess of Devonshire*, London, Harper Collins, 1998.

33 Cannon, *Aristocratic Century*, frequently notes that aristocratic connections are often provided by women, but never explores this from the women's point of view, only from the men's. Marriage is discussed only from the aspect of men's options; women's education is never mentioned (not even to say how little formal education women received). Judith Schneid Lewis, *In the Family Way: Childbearing in the British Aristocracy 1760–1860*, New Brunswick, Rutgers University Press, 1986, demonstrates that the aristocracy did indeed reproduce normally.

34 Elaine Chalus, ' "That Epidemical Madness": Women and Electoral Politics in the Late Eighteenth Century', in Hannah Barker and Elaine Chalus, eds, *Gender in Eighteenth-Century England*, London, Addison Wesley Longman, 1997; idem, ' "My Minerva at my Elbow": The Political Roles of Women in Eighteenth-Century England', in Taylor, Connor and Jones, eds, *Hanoverian Britain*. K. D. Reynolds,

Aristocratic Women and Political Society in Victorian Britain, Oxford, Clarendon Press, 1998, provides a nuanced portrait of the many facets of the Victorian female aristocrat.

35 By this time the King felt it politic to distance himself in every way from Bute and Banks succeeded him as Director of the Gardens.

36 Cited by Hedley, *Charlotte*, p. 138. I am grateful to the Librarian of the Royal Library, Windsor, for permission to inspect the set of tables, which are still in their original case.

37 For a recent assessment of Bute's scientific interests see David P. Miller, '"My Favourite Studdys": Lord Bute as a Naturalist', in Karl W. Schweizer, ed., *Lord Bute: Essays in Re-interpretation*, Leicester, Leicester University Press, 1988.

38 The position of Reader was no sinecure, as Mme de Genlis describes it: 'the Queen of England really loved reading, and at Windsor, where that princess lived in complete privacy, M. DeLuc was daily summoned to read for three or four hours; he always found the queen alone in her cabinet, and read while she embroidered or worked tapestry . . . M De Luc assured me that he always read to the queen without being allowed a seat; he was constantly on his legs in one spot, reading for three or four hours.' Mme de Genlis, *Memoirs*, 12 vols, London, 1825, III, p. 285, note.

39 The Représentants believed this to be an abuse of power on behalf of the governing Small Council, and as their name suggests they stood for more active representation within the republic's oligarchic politics.

40 This was the theme of Rousseau's *Lettre à M. D'Alembert sur les spectacles*, 1758.

41 Maurice Cranston, *Jean-Jacques: The Early Life and Work of Jean-Jacques Rousseau, 1712–1754*, London, Allen Lane, 1983, esp. ch. 17, passim; idem, *The Noble Savage: Jean Jacques Rousseau 1754–1762*, London, Allen Lane, 1991; and idem, *The Solitary Self: Jean-Jacques Rousseau in Exile and Adversity*, London, Allen Lane, 1997, give a useful account of Rousseau's relationship with the DeLuc family, which can be supplemented by studying their correspondence with him in R. A. Leigh, *Corréspondence complète de Jean-Jacques Rousseau*, 51 vols, Geneva, Banbury and Oxford, 1965–95. Also: Helena Rosenblatt, *Rousseau and Geneva: From the First Discourse to the Social Contract, 1749–1762*, Cambridge, Cambridge University Press, 1997; J. S. Spink, *Jean-Jacques Rousseau et Génève*, Paris, Boivin et Cie, 1934; Gaspard Vallette, *Jean-Jacques Rousseau, Génévois*, Geneva, A. Jullien, 1911.

42 For Geneva's relationship to the Enlightenment and the pre-Romanticism inaugurated by Rousseau, in addition to the three-volume biography of Rousseau by Cranston, see S. S. B. Taylor, 'The Enlightenment in Switzerland', in Roy Porter and Mikulás Teich, eds, *The Enlightenment in National Context*, Cambridge, Cambridge University Press, 1981; and Clarissa Campbell Orr, 'Romanticism in Switzerland', in Roy Porter and Mikulás Teich, eds, *Romanticism in National Context*, Cambridge, Cambridge University Press, 1988.

43 For Voltaire and Geneva, see Peter Gay, *Voltaire's Politics, The Poet as Realist*, 2nd edn, New Haven, Yale Unversity Press, 1988. Pastor Jacob Vernet warned Voltaire not to mistake Genebva's liberal Protestantism for heterodoxy: letter of 8 February 1755, Letter D6146 in Voltaire, *Correspondance and Related Documents*, ed. Theodore Besterman, Geneva, Institut et Musée Voltaire, XV, 1971.

44 Cranston, *The Solitary Self*, pp. 42–3. Jacques-François DeLuc even thought that Rousseau's views would not have been so wayward had he read his *Observations sur les savants incrédules*.

45 The Hague, 1778. His views were amplified in a six-volume version a year later, *Lettres Physiques et Morales sur l'Histoire de la Terre et de l'Homme, Adressées à la Reine de la Grande Bretagne*, The Hague and Paris.

46 For Dutens' contacts with Rousseau, which seem to have begun with his forwarding a parcel to Rousseau from his literary admirer Henri Laliaud, and the purchase of the library, see Leigh, ed., *Correspondance* esp. Letters 5671, 5672, 5704, 5724, 5729, 5734, 5746, 5761, 5765, 5766, 5783, 5795, 5802. Further information on Dutens can be found in the *DNB* and in R. A. Leigh, 'New Light on the Genesis of the *Lettres de la Montagne*: Rousseau's Marginalia on Tronchin', in *Studies on Volatire and the Eighteenth Century*, 94, Banbury, 1972, pp. 89–119.

47 'Qui mieux que VOTRE MAJESTÉ sait que au rang le plus élevé, les biens de la vie domestique sont au premier rang encore! Qui mieux que Votre Auguste Epoux, sait que les peines de la vie y trouvent un de leurs plus grands soulagemens.' *Lettres physiques et morales sur les Montagnes et sur l'Histoire de la terre, addressées à la Reine de la Grande Bretagne*, The Hague, 1778, p. 131. See also Letter XI, pp. 155–72, on the delights of the simple life. The 1779 edition enlarges on this in Discourse IV.

48 *Lettres sur l'histoire physique de la Terre, adressées à M. Le professeur Blumenbach, renfermant de nouvelles Preuves géologiques et historiques de la Mission divine de Moyse*, Paris, 1798, p. cxi.

49 Antoine Jacques Roustan, *Offrande aux autels et à la patrie*, Geneva, 1764; see Cranston, *The Solitary Self*, p. 80. The Queen had Roustan's *Sur l'état présent du Christianisme*, 1768, in her library.

50 DeLuc's other mentors in refuting materialism included the Dutch Platonist François Hemsterhuis, and the great Jewish scholar in Berlin, Moses Mendelssohn.

51 RA Georgian Add. MSS 21/121, Letter of Queen Charlotte to Prince Charles of Mecklenburg-Strelitz, 23 December 1789.

52 John Dillenberger, *Benjamin West: The Context of His Life's Work, with Particular Attention to the Paintings with Religious Subject Matter*, San Antonio, Trinity University Press, 1977; Robert C. Alberts, *Benjamin West: A Biography*, Boston, Houghton Mifflin, 1978.

53 Rousseau told Granville in November 1766 that the only sweet moments of his life were when he was near his home: Leigh, ed., *Corréspondence*, Letter 5591.

54 *Ibid.*, Letters 5482, 5633, 5725, 5741, 5752, 5772, 5971, 6063, 6088, 6220, 6372, 6606, 6643, 6658bis, 6925, 6934, 6940, 6940, 6955, 6996, 7015, 7093.

55 Queen Charlotte's library included the catalogue for this collection, sold at her death. See also Shteir, *Cultivating Women*, pp. 47–50, on aristocratic patronesses of botany.

56 Myers, *The Bluestocking Circle*.

57 Elizabeth Elstob had compiled an *Anglo-Saxon Grammar*, translated the *Homily of St Gregory*, and planned other translations, when her clergyman brother's death plunged her into poverty and cut off her access to the world of scholarship via him and his friends. She was tracked down to Gloucestershire by the journalist George Ballard who was compiling *Memoirs of Several Ladies of Great Britain* (1752), a history of learned women. Queen Charlotte had a copy of this book in her library. Elstob obtained subscriptions for it from five Portlands (the Duchess, her three daughters, and William, the future 3rd duke), and others from Mrs Delany and her sister. Janet

Todd, *Dictionary of British Women Writers*, London, Routledge, 1989, entry by Maureen Mulvihill.

58 Myers, *The Bluestocking Circle*, p. 129. I think there are parallels here to the Queen's appointment of Fanny Burney. The Diaries show that the Queen wanted to have literary conversations with Burney, but the only place at her disposal for her, which was also suitable to her middling social rank, was as Second Keeper of the Robes, which entailed various and constant tasks, unlike the courtier positions given to women of higher rank such as Lady of the Bedchamber. See note 6 above.

59 Hedley, *Charlotte*, pp. 64, 290.

60 Jean K. Bowden, *John Lightfoot: His Work and Travels*, The Bentham-Moxon Trust, Royal Botanic Gardens, Kew, and Hunt Institute for Botanical Documentation, Carnegie Mellon University, Kew and Pittsburgh, 1989, pp. 16, 26, 95, 98.

61 Several of these visits are cited from Mrs Delany's diary by Hayden, *Mrs Delany* e.g. pp. 146–51, a visit of 12 August 1778; pp. 155–7, describing the Queen's gift of a pocket case to assist her in her work in 1781; p. 135, describing the announcement of Amelia in 1783.

62 Bowden, *Lightfoot*, pp. 125–6

63 *English Botany*, 1790–1814, 36 vols, illustrated by James Sowerby.

64 Abraham Rees, with the assistance of eminent professional gentlemen, ed., *New Cyclopaedia or Universal Dictionary of Arts and Sciences . . . Biography, Geography and History*, 45 vols, London, 1802–20, XXI, 1819, entry on John Lightfoot by J. E. Smith. The entry continues 'The plan of this exemplary mother, on which she has often been heard to decant, was, in the education of her royal offspring, to open as many resources to them as possible, in a variety of studies and pursuits; out of which they might subsequently make their own choice, and thus be independent of circumstances for occupation and amusement.'

65 James Edward Smith, *A Sketch of a Tour on the Continent*, 3 vols, London, 1793, 2nd edn, 1807, I, p. 118.

66 Pleasance Smith, *Memoir and Correspondence of the late Sir James Edward Smith*, 2 vols, London, 1832, I, pp. 291–2, 297. Smith's exonerations of Rousseau are in his *Sketch*, I, pp. 117–18.

67 Hayden, *Mrs Delany*; see also Shteir, *Cultivating Women*, pp. 39–46, on leisured ladies and botanical painting.

68 RA Georgian Add. MSS 21/121, Letter of Queen Charlotte and accompanying note of Jean-André DeLuc to Prince Charles of Mecklenburg-Strelitz, 23 February 1790. DeLuc expalined 'La Reine s'amuse à peindre des Fleurs, ou plutot des Plantes, d'aupres Nature'. See also Hedley, *Charlotte*, pp. 179 and 139.

69 See Bullion, '"George, Be a King!"'.

70 The redesign of the village into classical elegance is generally thought to be the catalyst for Goldsmith's poem 'The Deserted Village', though in fact the Harcourts did not make any of the villagers homeless; one stayed on in the newly landscaped garden in her old cottage, regarded as a picturesque, unlettered shepherdess.

71 The Harcourts were in any case friends of the Duke and Duchess of Gloucester, the latter of whom was related to Horace Walpole, who catalogued the Harcourt pictures. The connection of Paul Sandby to Nuneham Courtenay was therefore very natural, as he was known to an interconnected circle of patrons and connoisseurs.

72 Johnson Ball, *Paul and Thomas Sandby, Royal Academicians: An Anglo-Danish Saga of Art, Love and War in Georgian England*, Cheddar, Somerset, Charles Shilton Ltd., 1985.

73 His *Plays and Poems*, 2 vols, 1774, contain only eight odes written for George III's birthday and the New Year, and the same number of poems dedicated to the Villiers or Harcourt families or written for inscriptions for the gardens of Nuneham Courtenay or Middleton Park (the Oxfordshire seat of the Villiers). See *Harcourt Papers*, VII for Whitehead and the Harcourt family.

74 George Villiers, 4th Earl of Jersey (1735–1805) was dubbed the Prince of Macaronies by the Queen of the Bluestockings, Mrs Montagu, for his courtly manners. He was the *mari complaisant* to the notoriously unfaithful Frances, née Twysden, whose conquests included the young George Prince of Wales. The Queen wrote a sympathetic letter to George Simon Harcourt on the occasion of his old friend's death in 1805, saying she knew he was indulgent to a 'bewitching wife' but remarking tactfully that no one can judge another's domestic affairs. Harcourt mss, Letter to Lord Harcourt from Queen Charlotte, 27 August 1805, printed in *Harcourt Papers*, VI, p. 80

75 'Say, is thy honest heart to virtue won / can genius animate thy feeling breast! / Approach, behold this venerable form / Tis Rousseau, let they Bosom speak the rest.' Cited in Jacques Vosine, *Jean-Jacques Rousseau en Angleterre à l'epoque romantique*, Paris, Didier, 1956, see pp. 31–5.

76 Alderson was recommended to the Queen by the Dowager Countess of Holdernesse, a Lady of the Bedchamber. Alderson's father-in-law was steward to the Holdernesse estates in Yorkshire at Aston, and George Mason's patron. The 4th Earl of Holdernesse's mother was Frederica, daughter of the 3rd Duke of Schomberg, whose mother in turn was Caroline Elizabeth, a daughter of Sophia of Hanover's brother, Charles Louis of the Palatine, through his morganatic marriage. Holdernesse therefore had a distant link, albeit through marriage and through morganatic descent, to the House of Hanoner. Holdernesse was governor to George Prince of Wales and his brother the Duke of York in 1771 and may have introduced DeLuc to the King.

77 For George Mason, see *DNB*: *Harcourt Papers*, VIII; J. W. Draper, *William Mason*, New York, University Press, 1924; J. Harris, ed., William Chamber's *Dissertation on Oriental Gardening*, 1772, and George Mason, *An Heroic Epistle*, 1772, and *An Heroic Postscript*, 8th edn, 1774, London, Gregg International Publishers Ltd, 1972.

78 Leigh, ed., *Corréspondence*, XXXV. Whitehead and Goerge Villiers both thought Harcourt's admiration for Rousseau misguided, and tried to point out how self-absorbed he was. E.g. Letters 6017, 6078 and 6086: William Whitehead to George Simon Harcourt, 30 September 1767: 'But is it Rousseau who has taught you to feed the hungry and cloath the naked? I fancy you might have found a greater guide.'

79 Leigh, ed., *Corréspondence*, Letter 5182; see also, Letter 2963. Frances, née Poole (1733–69), had a tender friendship with Harcourt but married Henry Temple, 2nd Viscount Palmerston, in 1767. Her early death was commemorated at Nuneham Courtenay by an urn inscribed with a poem by Whitehead. See *Corréspondence*, XVIII, pp. 28–9.

80 [William Combe], *An History of the River Thames*, 2 vols, Boydell Press, 1794, 1796, I, p. 200. Combe (1741–1823) was a friend of Lyttelton, Charles James Fox and

Beckford at Eton, but by the age of thirty had squandered his fortune. He then spent most of his time as a superior kind of Grub St hack, writing eighty-six books in all, the best known of which was *Dr Syntax in Search of the Picturesque* (1812), the text to Rowlandson's drawings. It was possibly through his Harcourt connection that Combe came to write six poems illustrating etchings by Princess Elizabeth, published in 1810. In his correspondence with George Simon Harcourt, Combe described the spinning feast as the Harcourts' version of the *Rosière de Salency* village festival (Harcourt mss, letters to George Simon Lord Harcourt, 25 June 1793). This was a village tradition from Picardy, supposedly dating from the sixth century, in which villagers nominated the most virtuous girl in the village, who was then honoured by the priest and seigneur and given a dowry. This custom was popularised by Mme de Genlis, educational writer and governess to the House of Orléans, and prompted various French aristocrats to invent their own versions in an attempt to appropriate rustic virtue to justify aristocratic rank. Sara Maza points out that Mme de Genlis's original description was probably coloured by Rousseau's account of peasant festivals in the *Lettre à D'Alembert sur les spectacles*. See Maza, *Private Lives and Public Affairs: The Causes Célèbres of Pre-Revolutionary France*, Berkeley, University of California Press, 1993. When Mme de Genlis was visiting England in 1785, Mrs Montagu, the Bluestocking, wrote to Lord Harcourt, 'A spirit of national vanity makes me hope Mme de Genlis had the honour of seeing Lady Harcourt before she left England', *Harcourt Papers*, VIII, p. 127.

81 Hannah More, *Strictures on Female Education*, London, 1799, p. 148, note: 'It would be a pleasant summer amusement for our young ladies of fortune, if they were to preside at such spinning feasts as are instituted at Nuneham for the promotion of virtue and industry in their own sex. Pleasurable anniversaries of this kind would serve to combine in the minds of the poor two ideas which ought never to be separated, but which *they* are not very forward to unite, – that the great wish to make them *happy* as well as good. Occasional approximations of the rich and poor, for the purposes of relief and instruction, and annual meetings for the purpose of innocent pleasure, would do much towards wearing away discontent, and contribute to reconcile the lower class to that state in which it has pleased God to place them.'

82 Harcourt and Dutens were both involved with advising Rousseau on the sale of the books until the solution of Dutens' purchase emerged. Richard Davenport, owner of Wootton Hall in Derbyshire where Rousseau stayed, wrote to him saying 'Lord Newnham desires to have the pleasure of looking into your L'Esprit, will take care it passes into no other hands, but his own'. Leigh, ed., *Corréspondence*, Letter 5765 Harcourt was Viscount Nuneham (here spelt by Davenport as Newnham) before succeeding to the title. Also: 'there are many difficulty's occur in relation to the books Mr. Du Tems [*sic*] & Lord Newnham [*sic*] are both ready to give any Assistance in their power. If I possibly can will prevent any of them falling into the Hands of a Bookseller especially those upon whose margins you have wrote, and will take strict care of L'Esprit.'

83 I am grateful to Dr Marcus Köhler of the Fachhochschule of Neubrandenburg for making available information on Duke Charles on Hohenzieritz; and to Eva Bjerregaard for assistance with German translation.

84 R. A. Leigh, 'Rousseau's English Pension', in J. H. Fox, M. H. Waddior and D. A. Watts, eds, *Studies in Eighteenth Century French Literature presented to Robert Niklaus*, Exeter, University of Exeter Press, 1975; *Diary and Letters of Madame D'Arblay, as edited by her niece Charlotte Barrett*, preface and notes by Austin Dobson, 6 vols, London, 1904, II, p. 342. Fanny Burney also told the King that her father had visited Rousseau in Paris and seen the print of George III he had saved from the sale on the wall.

85 They made visits in 1785, 1786 and 1788.

86 *Harcourt Papers*, III, pp. 169–74, letters between Lady Elizabeth Harcourt and Horace Walpole, show how Lady Harcourt used her influence with Horace Walpole to effect the offer of a court position.

87 In 1761 he had accompanied his father to Mecklenburg and was an equerry to the Queen. During the War of American Independence he captured General Lee. In 1782 he bought St Leonard's Hill near Windsor from the King's brother, the Duke of Gloucester, and became Deputy Ranger of Windsor Great Park. In 1793 he served in the Low Countries under the Duke of York and was commanding officer when York returned to Britain. His wife Mary's journal and letters recording her accompanying her husband throughout this campaign and then being appointed to attend Caroline of Brunswick on her journey to England, published as vol. V of the *Harcourt Papers*, make compelling reading. Information complied from *DNB*, Hedley, *Charlotte*, and *Harcourt Papers*.

88 Appointed 1784. Hedley, *Charlotte*, p. 141 notes that by this time the Queen was able to make her own appointments, while twenty years earlier she had had to submit to other's judgements.

89 *Harcourt Papers*, IV, p. 79.

90 *Harcourt MSS*, volume of letters of Queen Charlotte, p. 29, Letter from Queen Charlotte to Elizabeth Lady Harcourt, 13 September 1786.

91 Hedley, *Charlotte*, pp. 179–205, esp. p. 187.

92 *Harcourt MSS*, verses by Elizabeth, Countess of Harcourt, 1750–1804, booklets 7, 16, 21.

93 It is thought that some volumes may have been in Queen Caroline's collection.

94 She also had an unauthorised collection of extracts compiled by J. de la Porte and published in 1763, the *Pensées de Jean-Jacques Rousseau*, which went through many editions.

IO

Queen Adelaide: malign influence or consort maligned?

A. W. Purdue

Q UEEN ADELAIDE was not a romantic figure. The word most commonly used to describe her was amiable, as with 'this amiable princess' or 'a most amiable woman', while alternatives were 'dutiful' and 'virtuous'. Portraits of her almost certainly did her more than justice, disguising the poor complexion that candid contemporaries remarked upon (FIGURE 20). Her husband's reign was brief and she failed to produce an heir to the throne. In her widowhood she was much respected, having, as the *Dictionary of National Biography* entry puts it, 'won universal esteem by her blameless life and royal munificence in charity'.[1] However, despite bequeathing her name to an Australian city, miles of Adelaide terraces, crescents and squares, numerous public houses and some islands, she was soon forgotten. Her first biographer described her as this 'homely Duchess'[2] and there have been few subsequent studies of her.[3]

Historians have granted her a limited importance in helping to make the monarchy more acceptable to an age which increasingly demanded at least the outward appearance of domestic propriety and sobriety from its public figures. She has been seen as assisting by her influence upon William IV a transition of the monarchy from what has been conventionally seen as its nadir under George IV to its serene security under Queen Victoria. Recent work has, conversely, emphasised continuity, seeing her rather dowdy respectability, her charitable impulses and earnest Christian outlook as having done much to return the monarchy to the image created by George III and Queen Charlotte and endear it to the middle orders of society.[4]

Paradoxically, however, Adelaide's other claim to fame lies in her opposition to the political reforms that those very middle orders favoured. She has been seen as responsible for stiffening William's resistance to parliamentary reform and as behind his decision to dismiss the Whig ministry in 1834, the last time a British monarch dismissed a

20 *Queen Adelaide* by Sir Martin Archer Shee, 1837

ministry. We have thus two images of Queen Adelaide: the dominant image of 'Good Queen Adelaide', a kindly and charitable princess,
duchess, queen and then dowager; and that which interrupted this worthy,
if unexciting, reputation during the during the years 1831–34, when she
was portrayed as a scheming hide-bound reactionary and was hissed by
the London mob on her every public appearance. There is, however, no
contradiction between these images and, if both philanthropy and a
cautious conservatism were not unusual in a British context, Adelaide's
attitudes had their origins in her upbringing in a small German state.

Saxe-Meiningen, the small duchy of which Adelaide's father, Duke
George, was the ruler, is situated to the north of Bavaria and Coburg.
The duchy covered some 423 square miles and much of it was thickly
forested. Adelaide, the eldest of three children, was born in 1792. Her
sister, Ida, was born in 1795 and there were great celebrations at the
birth of her brother, Bernhard, in 1800. The state was a paternal auto-
cracy and Duke George has been described as 'boring and benevolent'.[5]
Saxe-Meiningen enjoyed a cosy existence under his worthy rule and he
was much mourned by the inhabitants on his death in 1803. As Bernhard
was only three, Adelaide's mother, Louisa Eleanora, had to act as Regent in difficult times when tiny Saxe-Meiningen was caught up in great
events as Napoleon's armies crossed and recrossed Germany, occupying
the dukedom on several occasions. The Duchess acquitted herself well
and her timely decision to join the allies in 1813 secured the future of the
duchy.

Adelaide's experiences during her youth did much to shape her
character and social and political attitudes. She was brought up to have
a strong sense of Christian mission and in the Protestant states of Germany Lutheranism had long demanded that such a mission gave royalty
a responsibility to care for the poor and distressed. The young Adelaide
had spent much of her time overseeing the relief of poverty and super-
vising schools for the poor. These early years also did much to shape
her political attitudes. No radical political currents had stirred Saxe-
Meiningen, a state content enough with its rulers until its tranquillity
was rudely disturbed by the Napoleonic Wars. Like most European
royalty, Adelaide had been instilled with a horror and fear of revolution
and had witnessed something of the disruption unleashed by events
in France. Well educated, thanks to her father's progressive views on
female education, and kindly and sympathetic to the poor and unfortunate, she yet viewed radicalism with horror and considered that any
conciliation of it would be likely to lead to greater extremes and revolution. Both her social and political attitudes were shaped, therefore, not

by England, but by the context of a small German duchy, where intimacy with all sectors of society did not preclude sharp awareness of rank and where paternalist duty towards the lower orders did not conflict with a conviction that political democracy was dangerous.

That a German princess should necessarily be in need of a husband of royal birth was axiomatic. Marriage was not only Adelaide's *métier*, it was her earnest wish, not merely to please her mother or to fulfil her role, but because she had strong maternal instincts and dearly wished to have children. Plain and with no great dowry, her main qualification for the marriage market was her impeccably royal lineage, yet by 1818 at the age of twenty-six she was still unmarried. She had one other qualification, which was to prove of crucial importance. As well as being royal, she was a Protestant. This was to lead to a proposal of marriage from Prince William, Duke of Clarence.

The death of Charlotte, Princess of Wales, in November 1817 led to a rush to the altar by the ageing bachelor sons of George III, the Dukes of Clarence, Kent and Cambridge. All three had been on the outlook for brides for some time, but a new urgency was brought to their search by the possibility of producing an heir to the throne, while so far as Clarence and Kent were concerned, there was the added inducement that Parliament might pay off their debts in return for suitable marriages. Thus it was that, largely at the instigation of Queen Charlotte, negotiations were begun for Adelaide's marriage to Clarence and on 19 April 1818 the betrothal was announced at Meiningen.

Marriage to a prince who might well become King of the United Kingdom was a glittering prize but Clarence himself must have appeared far from a desirable bridegroom. He was fifty-two and had lived for twenty years in apparent domestic bliss with the actress Mrs Jordan, by whom he had fathered ten children, before parting with her for combined financial and dynastic reasons. A bluff sailor, for he had been sent to sea at the age of fourteen, he drank a lot, his manners were unpolished and his speech rough, while, like most of his brothers, he had accumulated considerable debts. Largely because of these debts, he had made several attempts to marry but these had been frustrated, as one biographer has put it, 'either by the Regent, who considered the ladies concerned impossible, or by the ladies themselves, who considered William Henry impossible'.[6] Nor can the prospective bride have been impressed by her suitor's ardour for, after Parliament had reduced the grants proposed to pay off the debts of the dukes on their marriages, George Canning assured the House of Commons: 'It would never have been in the contemplation of his Royal Highness to contract the alliance under discussion, if it had not been pressed upon him as an act of public duty'.[7]

To ask why it was considered necessary for the Dukes of Clarence, Kent and Cambridge to marry German princesses may seem a jejune question. One had to go back to Henry VIII to find an heir to the throne marrying a subject, while George III had instigated the Royal Marriages Act expressly to prevent such marriages. Of course royal marriages had for long been a tool of diplomacy and intended to promote alliances between kingdoms, but there was little gain to Britain in close relations with Saxe-Meiningen. Indeed there had been no great advantage to Britain in even the earlier marriages of the Hanoverian dynasty, though they had been of some advantage to Hanover, a case, perhaps, of the Hanoverian tail wagging the British dog. Essentially, however, the royal marriages of 1818 can be seen as reflecting a desire to distinguish between royalty and aristocracy and emphasise royalty as a peculiar caste. As with virtually all legitimate Hanoverian marriages,[8] they were endogamic within the circle of Protestant German royalty. They thus had the effect of constantly recharging the German nature of the royal family. We thus have the curious repetitive scenario of Hanoverian princes and kings, anglicised and even emphasising their Britishness, but, as with Frederick, Prince of Wales and George III, marrying German princesses.

Few members of the royal family were as emphatically British as Clarence, who joined the Royal Navy at the age of fourteen, but circumstances dictated that he follow the family tradition. That these German marriages were an institutional requirement that did not always accord with the instincts of the male suitors can of course be seen from the secret and illegal marriage of George IV to Mrs Fitzherbert and the Duke of Sussex's marriage to Lady Augusta Murray.

As with much else about Clarence, there was something eccentric and bizarre about his marriage. Adelaide and her mother had to come to England for the wedding and, on arrival, were lodged in Grillons Hotel. There was no one there to meet them and they had to await the arrival of a bridegroom they had never met. At 10 p.m. an unexpected visitor arrived, the Prince Regent, affable and expansive, followed half an hour later by Clarence. It was considered more convenient and, no doubt, cheaper to have a double wedding at Kew Palace, with the Duke of Kent and his bride, the widowed Maria Louisa Victoria of Saxe-Coburg, being married at the same time, and the ceremony took place on 11 July.[9] The Duke of Clarence and his bride, along with his mother-in-law, then repaired to his bachelor apartment at St James's Palace.

Within a few weeks Clarence's precarious financial situation made a move to Hanover necessary.

It was an inauspicious beginning to what was to be a very successful marriage. William was odd, impulsive and rough-mannered but he was well-meaning, jovial and kind-hearted and became devoted to his wife. The word most frequently applied to Adelaide was, as we have seen, amiable, which seems mild praise unless we interpret it, as many contemporaries did, as loveable. Their hopes of producing an heir to the throne were confounded. Adelaide became pregnant four times but there were two miscarriages, one daughter lived for only a few hours, while the infant Princess Elizabeth died at the age of three months. This was a severe blow to this most maternal woman, but Adelaide and William settled into a cosy domesticity at Bushy Park and, from 1824, Clarence House. She was a kind stepmother to the FitzClarences, William's children by Mrs Jordan, and affectionate to their children, while she was a fond aunt to her nieces and nephews.

A recurring theme of court history is the struggle for influence between the consort and royal mistresses. In Adelaide's case the rivalry of the mistress, if ethereal, was ever present in the shape of her husband's numerous and demanding children, while the image of the elfin actress Mrs Jordan was everywhere at Bushy Park. One of the first acts of William IV on his accession was to commission a work of sculpture, not of his wife, but of his deceased mistress, Mrs Jordan.[10] Such a rival was difficult to compete with.

If she failed in the central queenly purpose, the production of an heir, Adelaide's great achievement was to make her husband fit for the throne. William's good nature and common sense were offset by his impulsiveness, excitability and lack of dignity. He tended to get particularly excited in the spring. It may well be the case that the reign of William IV would have been impossible without her, for it seems that William's fits of feverish and eccentric behaviour bore a strong resemblance to those which affected his father during his periods of 'madness' and were probably, similarly, caused by the hereditary disease of porphyria. Adelaide's ability to calm and soothe him may have prevented his being declared insane when, in 1827, his euphoria on becoming heir to the throne on the death of the Duke of York precipitated one of these fits.

Appointed to the revived position of Lord High Admiral, William overestimated the power that this largely honorific post gave him and, after a bizarre episode, when he took the fleet to sea on his own initiative, he was effectively dismissed. Clearly, Adelaide's restraint on his impulsiveness only went so far. She was able to be a moderating influence so far as his personal habits were concerned, cutting down his heavy drinking and his smoking, persuading him to cultivate a more dignified manner and curtail, if not abandon, his quarter-deck language. Did she wish, and, if she did, was she able, to influence him when it came to policies and the substance rather than the style of his public role? This question became more important when, on the death of George IV, William became King.

If a consort's formal position, duties and powers are prescribed by constitution or custom, the actual influence he or she exerts depends on the dynamics of a marital relationship. A consort's influence is exerted on the sovereign, through the sovereign, over the sovereign or even in default of the sovereign. That Queen Adelaide exerted considerable influence over King William IV cannot be doubted. Whether she exercised influence through him is the important question. Certainly, she had little independent power.

Without her guidance, William's reign might have been strange indeed. In the first weeks after his ascent to the throne he had to be persuaded to give up his habit of strolling round London like an ordinary citizen as it attracted a mob of unruly followers, while his generous tendency to ask casual and often not very suitable acquaintances back to dinner had to be similarly discouraged. Charles Greville commented: 'I tremble for him; at present he is only a mountebank, but he bids fair to be a maniac'.[11] That Adelaide helped bring some dignity to his demeanour is certain but how much the style of the monarchy during William's reign owed to her is debatable. She and her husband shared a taste for a low-key royal ethos. In some ways this was a pity for in lavish and spectacular ceremony lay much of the appeal of kingship, especially to the lower orders. George IV had fully appreciated this and, of course, display coincided with his own tastes. His age and health when he became King had meant, however, that, after his grand coronation and his successful visits to Dublin and Edinburgh, he had increasingly withdrawn into a laudanum-imbued twilight with his mistress, Lady Conyngham. William's frugal 'half-crownation' with Adelaide's crown created with her own jewels was unpopular with the London crowd. Despite his ability to get into debt, William had never shared his brother's taste for the theatrical and the extravagant. It was not until the late nineteenth century that royal display and ceremony were once more mounted on a grand scale and William's reign can be seen as inaugurating a long period in which ceremony was in eclipse and the theatre of monarchy was all but closed. It has been argued that this was in accordance with the taste of contemporaries:

The early and mid-Victorians saw themselves as the leaders of progress and pioneers of civilization, and prided themselves on the limited nature of their government, their lack of interest in formal empire, their hatred of show, extravagance, ceremonial and ostentation.[12]

Such a view concentrates more on the tastes of the middle classes than on those of workers and artisans and, as the influence of the mass of subjects increased, it was to be found necessary to refurbish the theatre of monarchy. The dull everyday nature of the monarchy, which resembled closely the style of a minor German state, was, nevertheless, in accordance with the tastes of many solid subjects.

Adelaide clearly influenced the pace and tone of the life of the court, unpalatable as her influence was to many of those who had to attend it. The court of William and Adelaide was, indeed, an odd mixture. A bibulous, friendly and informal man, set in an environment dedicated to formality and dignity, was held in check by a queen whose strict morality was modified by her good nature. In his latter years George IV's court had scarcely been lively but many found the court of the new reign dull in comparison.[13] 'The Queen is a prude', complained Greville, 'and will not let the ladies come *decolletées* to her parties. George IV, who liked ample expanses of that sort, would not let them be covered.'[14]

Lady Grey, after a brief visit to Windsor, said:

> . . . all the boring she had ever endured before was literally nothing compared with her misery of the two previous nights. She hoped she never should see a mahogany table again, she was so tired with the one that the Queen and the King, the Duchess of Gloucester, Princess Augusta, Madame Lieven and herself had sat round for *hours* – the Queen knitting or netting a purse – the King sleeping and occasionally waking for the purpose of saying: – 'Exactly so, ma'am!' and then sleeping again.[15]

Several groups were at the heart of the regular court circle: the wider royal family, including the King's brothers and sisters and their wives and husbands, with one virtually permanent absentee, the Duchess of Kent, and others, the Cumberlands and Sussex, sometimes estranged; a large German contingent, including Count and Countess Munster, Count and Countess von Bulow, and Prince and Princess Esterhazy; Prince Lieven, the Russian Ambassador and his scheming wife; a sprinkling of the British aristocracy who made up the King's and Queen's households; and finally numerous demanding FitzClarences. It was scarcely representative of upper-class British society; no wonder Whig grandees found it dull.

What was very strange was the contrast between the Queen's strict morality and the ubiquity of the FitzClarences. There was a certain piquancy in a situation where the Queen's strong sense of propriety led her to refuse to recognise Lady Ferrers because she had lived with her husband before their marriage or to receive the Duchess of St Albans because she had a reputation, yet she mixed on intimate terms with the results of her husband's fecund relationship with his mistress. The D'Este offspring of the Duke of Sussex posed another problem but, as with the FitzClarences, Adelaide's kindness triumphed over her propriety and she became a close friend of Mademoiselle Augusta D'Este.[16] Despite this physical testimony to the less than orderly lives of the sons of George III, Adelaide's influence was to make the court Victorian before Victoria and more Victorian than it was under the young Victoria. She brought to it that combination, typical of many German courts, of formality and *gemütlichkeit*. It was dull and dowdy but comfortable and good-natured.

The reign of a king and consort without an heir of their union is permeated by a special transience. William and Adelaide could have been forgiven for resenting the alternative court that grew up around the young Princess Victoria and it says much for both that they had little but goodwill towards the Princess. There was ill-feeling but it was entirely directed, and with reason, against the Duchess of Kent and her Court Comptroller, Sir John Conroy. That Victoria's affection for her uncle and his wife remained firm says much for her youthful judgement and for Adelaide's boundless love for children. When Victoria became Queen and was able to shake off the influences of the Duchess and her dishonest adviser, she was able to express her fondness for the Queen Dowager.

An important difference between William and his wife was that he was not only British but emphatically so, while she was not only German but never really understood the country of which she became Queen. This was of course characteristic of the consorts of Hanoverian sovereigns. George III might have gloried in the name of Briton and been seen as 'Farmer George' but cartoonists and lampoonists fastened upon Queen Charlotte's German accent and habits. Queen Caroline, George IV's estranged consort, might have been the temporary heroine of the London mob, while Adelaide was for a while its hate figure, but neither really understood the mob and its relationship to the establishment. Probably none of these consorts comprehended the essential stability of English society underpinned by the middle orders and the gentry in provincial towns and countryside. Certainly they found the aristocracy difficult to understand for no German state had such wealthy and arrogant subjects.

England must have seemed a peculiar and rather frightening place to Adelaide. She had married a man who was at first two and then one heartbeat away from the throne of Britain and yet compared to many an English aristocrat he was comparatively poor, indeed considerably in debt, and was looked down upon by fashionable society. Even when she was Queen, she must have been aware of the contrast between high society's respect for the monarchy and its social condescension to the actual monarch and his consort. When the press referred to this 'German frow', its spelling might have been awry but the description was substantially correct.

The Queen's essentially German outlook was, however, no handicap when it came to her image and influence amongst important elements in British society: the middle orders, nonconformists and especially the women of these sectors. Just as George III's and Queen Charlotte's quiet and frugal domesticity and patronage of worthy and charitable causes and institutions had appealed to the middle of society, so did the rather dull but respectable court of William and Adelaide and their extension of such patronage. It has been suggested that the German influence upon British philanthropy was significant[17] and the monarchy can be seen as a transmission belt. Perhaps this should be seen as part of a wider German influence acting upon British society's changing tastes in art and furniture and attitudes to nature and scenery, and tangible in such diverse forms as uniforms and Christmas trees.[18] It is significant that nineteenth-century commentators were apt to refer to Britain's 'Teutonic' roots.

The respectability and formal domesticity of the court and the royal couple's dedication to good works projected to the nation at large a positive image of monarchy, which reinforced that established under George III. The long struggle against revolutionary and Napoleonic France had revealed the strength of the monarchy as of the social order of which it was the acknowledged head. What was most impressive was the monarchy's appeal to the solid middle of society, to voluntary and civic organisations in industrial and provincial towns as well as to gentry society in rural Britain. If recent work has reassessed George IV and pointed to his many admirable qualities,[19] it cannot be denied that his reign saw both the continued decline of the crown's political power and a hiatus in the compensatory development of its social influence. That the monarchy during William's reign came to be seen as respectable, despite the very tangible reminders of the King's life before marriage in the shape of the numerous FitzClarences, owed much to Adelaide.

She was exactly the right figure to consolidate support for the monarchy in an increasingly earnest and serious age. Unselfconsciously religious in her outlook and dedicated to good works, while she was both prudish and a guardian of propriety, few members of the royal family were so finely tuned to the pieties of the day. As Frank Prochaska has argued persuasively, a central role of the modern monarchy has been its support for charitable causes, which has enabled it to place itself at the head of civil society as its effective political role as governor of the state has diminished.[20] Although the tradition of the royal patronage of charities and worthy causes was well established by William IV's reign, Adelaide did much to expand it. If her particular fondness for orphanages and charities involved with maternity care reflected her love of children and her own failure to produce a family, she was the patron and supporter of a wide range of charities. Naval officers' widows, Protestant clergymen in Ireland, infirmaries, schools and lunatic asylums were all beholden to her. All in all the royal couple extended their patronage to at least 125 institutions.

There thus emerges a portrait of a queen who seems to have been superbly equipped to gain support for the monarchy and to help project it beyond the aristocracy and gentry to a wider Britain in which not only were the middle ranks of society more important, but the needs and problems of the lower orders were seen as pressing. She can be seen as epitomising the spirit of an age which was increasingly earnest, sober, religious and philanthropic in outlook. A queen who did much to make the court respectable and who could link the monarchy to worthy causes and to nonconformist and provincial society can be seen as significant in a reinterpretation of monarchy commensurate with a diminished political role in a rapidly changing society.

In apparent contrast to this role as midwife to the 'welfare monarchy', we have Adelaide's political views and supposed political influence. She was implacably opposed to any reduction of royal power or interference with the established political order. A queen whose political instincts and opinions ran counter to the democratic tide of her time was seen as cajoling and nagging her husband to thwart the cause of parliamentary reform and intrigue against his Whig ministries. As *The Times* put it when William dismissed the Melbourne government in 1834, 'The Queen has done it all'.[21]

The charge against Adelaide is not, of course, that she interfered, but that she was on the 'wrong' side. The almost universal consensus of posterity that both the Great Reform Act and the withdrawal of the monarchy from the direct exercise of political power were necessary and 'progressive' developments is what has made the Queen's supposed influence contentious. Had she appeared to influence her husband in a contrary direction, radical and Whig contemporaries would have approved and most historians applauded.

There is, thus, more than a whiff of partisanship and of hindsight about criticisms of the Queen's supposed political influence. There was, at the time, a respectable case against and a serious, if minority, body of opinion opposed to the Great Reform Act. In the event, not only was the new electoral system quickly accepted, the aristocracy and landed interest were able to work skilfully within it, retaining enormous power and influence until late in the century. Opponents of the reform have therefore found few defenders. To liberal and socialist historians they were simply wrong and to conservative historians they were wrong in opposing what was an inevitable and moderate measure, rather than a revolutionary step. Their opposition threatened, it is argued, to bring about a crisis which could have resulted in far more radical changes. It is worth noting, however, the comment, after the event, of that moderate Whig reformer, Lord Melbourne: 'What all the wise men promised has not happened; and what all the damn fools said would happen has come to pass'. Jonathan Clark has recently challenged what may be termed the evolutionary view of the Reform Act, seeing it, along with the Repeal of the Test and Corporations Act and Catholic Emancipation, as marking the end of the old order and of the power of aristocracy, church and crown.[22] Certainly the ability of the sovereign to choose and sustain a ministry was fatally weakened, as the failure of William's dismissal of Melbourne's government soon demonstrated.

We need to consider, therefore, whether the Queen did indeed use her influence and, if she did, her reasons for doing so and whether such influence was effective. One view would suggest that both she and her husband totally accepted the notion of the separation of the domestic and public spheres and that in the one female influence was legitimate and in the latter unacceptable, while in any case the Queen's own monarchical convictions would have made her look with horror at any suggestion of influence on public policy once William was King. Another view would be that any woman able to wield such influence over her husband's personal habits would be able, if she so wished, to influence him in matters of policy, and that, if she held strong opinions on public matters, she would find it difficult to resist exerting such influence. A further question is whether she had much need to influence him as opposed to supporting him. Was there really much difference between William's and Adelaide's approach to politics and particularly their views on parliamentary reform?

The popularity the King enjoyed because of his supposed support for reform was always based on a misreading of him. William's lack of grandeur and his affability to all and sundry gave him a democratic, almost a citizen king, air, which was far from his view of the monarch's role. He was never a reformer but nor was he a reactionary. He was rather a conservative. In his view he should choose a government which could command the support of Parliament and he should be loyal to it until it had demonstrably lost support. There was never any doubt in his mind, however, that it was his right to choose a government and that the government in return owed him support. His perfectly accurate constitutional understanding was that the Commons was by no means master of the Lords and that the monarch had a right to a government to his liking.

Britain remained very much a monarchical state in the later Hanoverian period and the gradual decline of the King's power owed much to circumstance, including the ill-health of monarchs, the decline of crown patronage and the lack of ability of particular monarchs. When it became clear that Grey's government was unwilling to head off the wilder Whigs and introduce only a modest measure of parliamentary reform, William was appalled and faced with a choice between conflicting principles: support for his government; respect for the Lords; and dislike of his government's reform bill. The old sailor manoeuvred with some skill but he was handicapped by the combination of division and inflexibility in the Tory ranks and by feeling in the country which temporarily removed the normal capacity for compromise and accommodation from political life. He found himself forced in the end to accept a constitutional change of which he disapproved.

The sequence of events is well known. The King gained great popularity by acceding to Grey's request for a dissolution of Parliament in April 1831. After the Whig success at the subsequent general election, he reluctantly agreed to create sufficient pro-reform peers if the need arose and put pressure on the Lords to allow a reform bill to pass its second reading in April 1832. When, however, the cabinet called upon him to agree to the creation of fifty peers as a sign of his support, he accepted the government's resignation and called upon Wellington to form an administration. Wellington abandoned the attempt after a week and the King was left to turn to Grey once more and promise to create the peers required. Faced with this prospect, the Tory majority in the Lords gave way and on 7 June 1832 the Great Reform Act became law.

But what was the Queen's role in all this? J. R. M. Butler has summed up the attitudes of the royal couple towards the reform question at the beginning of 1831 as follows:

> Fear of the Radicals was in fact William's dominant motive at this time . . . His sentiments were heartily shared by Queen Adelaide . . . She made no secret of her personal preference for the Tories, and, sweet-tempered as she usually was, seems to have shown little civility to Lady Grey at Windsor. The King's secretary, however, Sir Herbert Taylor, denied that she made any attempt to influence the King, or indeed discussed politics with him. The false rumours on this head, which did so much afterwards to disturb her peace of mind, were not yet rife, but it as well to understand at the outset that such conduct was most uncharacteristic of her and was believed by no one who had any means of knowing.[23]

Contemporaries and historians alike have concurred as to the Queen's opinions but have disagreed as to whether she exerted her influence and whether, if she did, she had any effect on the King's conduct. Greville considered that: 'The Queen and the Royal Family are extremely unhappy at all these things, but the former has no influence whatever with the King'.[24] Princess Augusta said: 'The Queen is like my good mother – never interferes or even gives an opinion. We *may* think, we *must* think, we *do* think, but we need not speak.'[25] E. J. Littleton, however, recorded in his diary Lord Wellesley's opinion of the Queen: 'She had been educated in the very worst principles of passive obedience and Divine Right, had continually thwarted the King, and that at length the Ministry and the state of affairs was a topic on which neither spoke, either between themselves or to others'.[26]

Certainly Queen Adelaide was discreet in public. On the one occasion she is supposed to have aired her views at the dinner table it is said that her husband responded with a firm 'Women should not mix in politics', but as one authority has argued: 'who can be sure that she was equally reticent when in bed with her husband rather than at dinner with the King? The persistent drip of her prejudices was to erode William's frail loyalty to the cause of liberalism.'[27]

Adelaide was not alone, among the court circle, in her strong antipathy to reform. The daughters of George III, Elizabeth, Princess of Hesse-Homberg, and Mary, Duchess of Gloucester, were both hot against the reform bill, as was the latter's husband. Sir Herbert Taylor, however, reassured Grey that:

> Politics are never the subject at dinner or at evening parties; indeed, his Majesty professes not to allow it and he never touches on the

subject with the Queen, who indeed does not seem at all disposed to break through a rule so essential in such a society, and whose superior judgement and good sense would induce her to feel its importance, and to discourage any departure from it in others.

Grey, however, remained suspicious and wrote to Taylor about 'the known opinion of persons composing her Majesty's household, and the declared hostility of the Princesses'.[28]

Grey's remark about persons composing Her Majesty's household was primarily directed at Lord Howe, the Queen's Chamberlain. Lord Howe and the Queen did not just share similar attitudes towards reform, they were extremely close to a degree which enabled ill-disposed contemporaries to suggest they were lovers. 'Oh Lord *Howe* wonderful are thy ways', Lord Alderney remarked, when it was rumoured that Adelaide was pregnant. Allegations that a queen and a member of her household were lovers are as easy to make as they are difficult, in the end impossible, to disprove.[29] Contemporaries close to the court found the rumours ridiculous, though Princess Lieven, a notorious gossip, claimed that Lady Grey attempted to persuade her of the truth of the rumours. Nor have historians lent credence to an affair between Adelaide and Howe. He certainly doted on her and she was fond of and relied upon him. Greville maliciously wrote of Howe as 'like a boy in love with this frightful spotted Majesty',[30] but even he admitted that 'She admits his attentions and acquiesces in his devotion; at the same time there is not the smallest evidence that She treats him as a lover'.[31] There was perhaps a romantic but platonic element in their relationship.[32] She needed an admiring confidante and sprung to his defence when the Whigs demanded his dismissal.

Howe went out of his way to flaunt his Tory views and played a prominent part in the opposition to reform. He signed addresses against the reform bill, probably wrote a letter attacking the government, which appeared in the *Standard*, and voted in the Lords against the bill. Members of the King's household who had voted against reform had had to resign their positions[33] but Adelaide was infuriated by the pressure from Grey that led to Howe's enforced resignation, and took the dismissal of her Chamberlain as an insult. Even her normally good relations with her husband were affected:

> I would not believe it, for I had trusted in, and built firmly on the king's love to me. But unfortunately he has not been able to resist the representations of his ministers, and yielded, and I fear it will be the beginning of much evil. May God support us and protect and shield the country and save the king from ruin. I had a hard struggle before

I appeared at table after the blow, which I felt deeply as an insult, which filled me with 'Indignation'. I felt myself deeply wounded both as a wife and a queen, and I cannot conquer the feeling. It was for me a distressing evening which I shall never forget.[34]

For a week or so she did not dine with the King or the rest of the family at Brighton. She refused to appoint another Chamberlain and Howe continued to perform the duties of that office. Lyttleton remarked that 'She is too obstinate and self-willed to see that she herself was behaving ill to her husband in causing his sincerity to be questioned by retaining opponents of his Ministers in his Queen's Household'.[35]

For the Queen, Wellington was the only hope, though she had little reason to love the Duke, whom she blamed for the peremptory dismissal of William from his post of Lord High Admiral and whom she did not thank for the decision that, in the event of the Princess Victoria succeeding to the throne as a minor, the Duchess of Kent and not Adelaide should be Regent. She thought, however, that he was the only hope of the anti-reform cause as a letter to Lord Howe in January 1832 demonstrates:

> His [the King's] eyes are open to see the great difficulties in which he is placed; he sees everything in the right light, but I am afraid has the fixed idea that no other administration could be formed at present among your friends, and he thinks they are aware of it themselves. How far he is right or not I cannot pretend to say, for I do not understand these important things, but I should like to know what the Duke of Wellington thinks, for he must be a good judge of this question.[36]

Howe, as she obviously expected, passed her letter on to the Duke, thus exposing the Queen to the charge of plotting with the opponents of the King's government. Wellington's reply revealed his icy fatalism: 'I have never doubted that if public affairs go on as they are, this country will be lost . . . I can do no more in Parliament. I can do nothing out of Parliament.'[37] Indeed, when Wellington failed in May, he demonstrated the truth of his own words and Adelaide's misplaced faith in him. If Adelaide's influence was indeed behind the attempt to form a Wellington government, she did the anti-reform cause no favour, for the best hope would have been for the King to be awkward and hope to reveal divisions amongst the Whig cabinet.

Clearly the Queen was indiscreet. She was also badly frightened but, despite this, defiant. Both the King and Queen were opposed to the bill but there were significant differences in their attitudes. William viewed reform with alarm but he saw it in a British context. He foresaw that it would weaken royal and aristocratic power. The Queen saw the crisis in continental terms and feared that giving in to the reformers would be the first step towards revolution and exile or worse. Charles X was in exile after the 1830 revolution in France and Adelaide had recently comforted his sister, the Duchess of Angoulême. Belgium had won its independence from Holland and the Queen's sympathies were with the dispossessed House of Orange. She had been badly frightened on a number of occsions by the hostility of the mob and recent revolutions awakened memories of the fates of Louis XVI and his Queen. Adelaide feared that she might be called upon to play the part of Marie Antoinette, whose end she was reminded of by the reformers of Newcastle. It was rumoured that she wanted to play that part all too faithfully by persuading the King into a sort of 'flight to Varennes', or rather to Hanover, though it is difficult to imagine William countenancing such a scheme.

The Queen's influence may well have been exaggerated by those reformers who, having lauded the King as the champion of reform in April 1831, preferred to see him as weak rather than a villain in 1832 and as having been led astray by the Queen, his sisters or the Duke of Cumberland. The Queen was the usual suspect and became enormously unpopular in radical quarters. 'The Queen and the Princesses have in fact never ceased tormenting his Majesty with all manner of sinister reports and forebodings as to the evils which will result from reform. It is proper that the nation should know without disguise or reserve, that the Queen has done more injury to the cause of reform than any person living', thundered the *Morning Chronicle*.[38]

Does Adelaide's unpopularity need to be seen in the context of contemporary debates over the role and position of women? The prominence of women in a number of patriotic and moral causes had led to disquiet as to women's proper role.[39] For the most part Adelaide fitted perfectly into the 'separate spheres' model, making the court decorous, supporting her husband and devoting herself to charitable causes, but here she was trespassing into male territory. If Queen Caroline had been 'the woman wronged', was Adelaide the interfering shrew? She was both supporting an unpopular cause and entering the public sphere in a way that was inappropriate for a woman in the light of the emergent view of what were male and female roles. No doubt fears of 'petticoat government' aided and gave a bite to polemicists' pens, while 'foreign consort government' was unpopular whatever the sex of the consort, as is shown by the unpopularity of Prince Albert in the early 1850s for his supposed interference and German bias. An additional candidate for the role of hated royal reactionary was in any case on hand in the figure of the Duke of Cumberland.

If the events of 1834–35 were to demonstrate how correct the King's fears were, they again ignited the Queen's nightmares. William, out of sympathy with his Whig administration, dismissed Melbourne, occasioning *The Times*'s comment, 'The Queen has done it all'. The failure of Peel's government to win the subsequent general election underlined the decline of the sovereign's political power; a comparison between Pitt's fortunes in 1785 and Peel's in 1835 is instructive. The Queen's impression was, according to Creevey, 'that an English revolution is rapidly approaching, and that her own fate is to be that of Marie Antoinette, and she trusts she will be able to act her part with courage'.[40] If such fears seem ridiculous, we have to remember the virulent political language of 1831 and 1832, the riots at Bristol and the burning down of the Duke of Newcastle's residence at Nottingham Castle. But the revolution was not to be and, in truth, Adelaide would have been an inadequate Marie Antoinette.

The return of Melbourne to office marked the consolidation of a new phase of constitutional monarchy and the Queen devoted the last years of her husband's reign to both protecting and restraining the King. As Queen Dowager for more than a decade after William's death, she was a respected figure, continuing her charitable activities both in Britain and the resorts overseas, which she favoured in her attempts to improve her poor health (FIGURE 21). She established a close and warm relationship with Queen Victoria and carried on a regular correspondence with her. That she maintained her strong Tory sympathies is demonstrated by the only cloud that temporarily darkened that relationship, an 'ill-judged' letter congratulating Victoria on the appointment of the Conservative ministry in August 1841:

> I hope that the selection of your government is to your own satisfaction, altho' the change must have been very trying to you, I trust that you will have perfect confidence in the able men who form your Council. Our beloved late king's anxious wishes – to see Wellington and Peel again at the head of the Administration – is now fulfilled.[41]

Queen Victoria was not amused and wrote to her half-sister, Princess Feodora: 'The poor, good Queen Dow[age]r wrote me a really tho' well meant the foolishest and most ill-judged letter upon the political events I ever saw'.[42]

Adelaide had brought to her role as Queen Consort a kindly nature and the values she had imbibed during her youth in Saxe-Meiningen.

21 *Queen Adelaide* by Franz Xavier Winterhalter, 1849

These included her serious religiosity, proclivity for good works, and respect for monarchy and the established order. Never really understanding British society, her outlook remained that of a member of a minor German dynasty and a staunch Metternichian conservative. She did play a minor role in stiffening William IV's resistance to the demands of his Whig ministers, but by the time of her death in 1849, she had outlived her temporary unpopularity with reformers and had become 'Good Queen Adelaide', celebrated for her charitable activities and unassuming demeanour.

Notes

1 Miss E. M. Clerke, *Dictionary of National Biography*.

2 Dr Doran, *Memoire of Queen Adelaide* (1861), p. 22.

3 Mary F. Sandars, *Queen Adelaide* (London, Stanley Paul, 1915); Mary Hopkirk, *Queen Adelaide* (London, John Murray, 1946).

4 Frank Prochaska, *Royal Bounty: The Making of a Welfare Monarchy* (New Haven and London, Yale University Press, 1995), pp. 54–60.

5 Hopkirk, *Queen Adelaide*, p. 12.

6 *Ibid.*, p. 5.

7 Sandars, *Queen Adelaide*, p. 42.

8 The marriage of William Henry, Duke of Gloucester (1743–1845), to Maria, widow of the 2nd Earl of Waldgrave, and that of Prince Ernest Augustus, Duke of Cumberland, to Anne Horton were exceptions and were valid but it was George III's determination to avoid such marriages in the future which led to the Royal Marriages Act of 1772.

9 There is some confusion over the date of these marriages, some authorities giving 11 July and some 13 July. Queen Adelaide celebrated her wedding anniversay on 11 July. *Queen Adelaide's Diary, 1830–31*, translated from the German by Mrs Clotilda Marson, Royal Archives (hereafter RA) GEO/Add. 21/7/A.

10 Claire Tomalin, *Mrs Jordan's Profession* (London, Viking, 1994), p. 1.

11 *The Greville Memoirs 1814–1860*, II, ed. Lytton Strachey and Roger Fulford (London, Macmillan, 1938), p. 18.

12 David Cannadine, 'The British Monarchy, *c.* 1820–1977', in *The Invention of Tradition*, eds. Eric Hobsbawm and Terence Ranger (Cambridge, Cambridge, 1983), p. 112.

13 It was to be rather similar in the next century when George V and Queen Mary followed another elderly roué, Edward VII. See Max Beerbohm's *Ballade Tragique a Double Refrain* in which the respective degrees of dullness of the King and Queen are discussed.

14 *The Greville Memoirs*, II, 19 January 1831, p. 107.

15 *The Creevey Papers*, II, ed. Sir Herbert Maxwell (London, John Murray, 1903), 5 September 1833, p. 262.

16 The son and daughter of Sussex and Lady Augusta Murray were known as d'Este.

17 Prochaska, *Royal Bounty*, p. 56.

18 The court had a considerable influence on the development of the Victorian Christmas. Queen Charlotte and Queen Adelaide both made much of Christmas and celebrated it with Christmas trees and the exchange of presents, though it was when an illustration of Victoria and Albert and their children around a Christmas tree appeared in the *Illustrated London News* that Christmas trees became popular in Britain. See J. M. Golby and A. W. Purdue, *The Making of the Modern Christmas* (London, Batsford, 1986 and Stroud, Sutton, 2000).

19 E. A. Smith, *George IV* (New Haven and London, Yale, 1999).

20 Prochaska, *Royal Bounty*.

21 *The Times*, 15 November 1834.

22 J. C. D. Clark, *English Society 1688–1832* (Cambridge, Cambridge University Press, 1985).

23 J. R. M. Butler, *The Passing of the Great Reform Act* (London, 1915), p. 185.

24 *The Greville Memoirs*, II, 14 April 1831, p. 140.

25 Sandars, *Queen Adelaide*, p. 153.

26 *Three Early Nineteenth Century Diaries*, ed. A. Aspinall (London, Williams and Norgate, 1952). Littleton's entry for 20 November 1831, p. 156.

27 Philip Ziegler, *King William IV* (London, Collins, 1971), p. 175.

28 Sandars, *Queen Adelaide*, pp. 154–5.

29 It is certainly the case that female members of the royal family have a limited choice of possible lovers and have found them often within the royal household. Examples range from the daughters of George III, who became involved with equerries, to Princess Margaret's romance with another equerry, Group Captain Peter Townsend, a century and a half later.

30 *The Greville Memoirs*, II, 14 December 1832, p. 333.

31 *Ibid.*, 31 December 1932, p. 337.

32 Sir Dighton Probyn's platonic passion for Queen Alexandra is perhaps a parallel, though he was a bachelor and Lord Howe was married to a woman esteemed as a beauty.

33 Horace Seymour and Captain Meynell were dismissed from the royal household for voting against the government in the Common's division of 22 March.

34 Queen Adelaide's diary, 8 October 1831, RA GEO/Add. 21/7/A.

35 Littleton's Diary, 20 November 1831, *Three Early Nineteenth Century Diaries*, p. 156.

36 Cited in Sandars, *Queen Adelaide*, p. 192.

37 *Ibid.*, p. 193.

38 *Morning Chronicle*, 9 May 1832.

39 See Linda Colley, *Britons: Forging the Nation 1707–1837* (New Haven and London, Yale University Press, 1992) and Amanda Vickery 'Golden Age to Separate Spheres? A Review of the Categories and Chronology of English Women's History', *Historical Journal*, 36: 2 (June 1993).

40 *The Creevey Papers*, II, November 1834, p. 300.

41 Queen Adelaide to Queen Victoria, 8 September 1841, RA VIC/C 27/54, Letters of Queen Adelaide 1821–1842 Vol. Y 1.

42 Queen Victoria to Feodora, Princess of Hohenlohe-Langenburgh, RA VIC add U/171/147.

Index

Note: page references in *italics* are to illustrations.

Lightning Source UK Ltd.
Milton Keynes UK
UKOW030754140413

209196UK00006B/73/P